Professional Service Firms and Politics in a Global Era

Chris Hurl · Anne Vogelpohl
Editors

Professional Service Firms and Politics in a Global Era

Public Policy, Private Expertise

palgrave
macmillan

Editors
Chris Hurl
Department of Sociology and Anthropology
Concordia University
Montreal, QC, Canada

Anne Vogelpohl
Department of Social Work
Hamburg University of Applied Sciences
Hamburg, Germany

ISBN 978-3-030-72127-5 ISBN 978-3-030-72128-2 (eBook)
https://doi.org/10.1007/978-3-030-72128-2

This Palgrave Macmillan imprint is published by the registered company Springer Nature Switzerland AG
The registered company address is: Gewerbestrasse 11, 6330 Cham, Switzerland

Contents

Notes on Contributors

Shriya Anand is a faculty member at the Indian Institute for Human Settlements, teaching on topics related to urban economic development and quantitative research methods. She anchors the Urban Informatics Lab at IIHS, which analyzes, communicates and disseminates data and information related to India's urbanization. Her research at IIHS is primarily centered on the Indian urban economy and economic geography, with a particular focus on the role of employment in urban development and poverty reduction. She holds a Master's in Public Affairs from Princeton University, and a Master's in Mathematics from Cambridge University, UK.

Nicholas Hildyard works with The Corner House, a UK solidarity and mutual learning group. He is the author of *Licensed Larceny: Infrastructure, Financial Extraction and the Global South* (Manchester University Press, 2016), "Extreme Infrastructure: Infrastructure Corridors in Context" (*Counterbalance*, 2017) and *More than Bricks and Mortar: Infrastructure-as-asset-class—Financing development or developing finance?* (Corner House Research, 2012).

Chris Hurl is an Assistant Professor in the Department of Sociology and Anthropology at Concordia University in Montréal, Quebec, Canada. His research, exploring urban governance, state formation, and the politics of the public sector in Canada, has appeared in *Environment and Planning A*, *Studies in Political Economy*, *International Journal of Urban* *and Regional Research*, *Labour/Le Travail*, and the *Journal of Canadian Studies*. He is the co-editor of *Corporatizing Canada* (Between the Lines, 2018).

Svenja Keele is a human geographer researching the ways in which government, business and expertise interact to govern complex environmental problems, with a particular interest in the political economies and the spatial effects of these interactions. Her work on climate adaptation has examined the outsourcing of policy decisions and the influence of corporate expertise. Her current work investigates the commercialization of climate intelligence services, the creation of new markets for urban resilience and the drivers of urban growth that produce maladaptive land use change. Dr. Keele has also worked professionally in consulting and government in Australia and the UK.

Matthias Kipping is a Professor of Policy and Richard E. Waugh Chair in Business History at the Schulich School of Business, York University in Toronto, Canada. He has published widely on the consulting industry, its evolution and role, including co-editing (with T. Clark) *The Oxford Handbook of Management Consulting* (Oxford University Press, 2012) and co-authoring (with L. Engwall and B. Üsdiken) *Defining Management: Business Schools, Consultants, Media* (Routledge, 2016). He is currently researching the expansion of consulting to and from India and working on a monograph that tries to summarize the overall history of the industry.

Orly Linovski is an Assistant Professor in the Department of City Planning at the University of Manitoba. Her research and teaching are motivated by a concern with equity in planning and design, through the lens of professional practice. Her current research focuses on two main areas: the changing nature of professional practice in the private sector, and the integration of transportation equity in planning processes. Previously, she worked as a planner at the municipal and provincial levels.

Lise Mahieus is pursuing a Master's degree in Geography at Simon Fraser University, Vancouver, Canada. Her research interests are focused on publics and their negotiations of public space in gentrifying neighborhoods.

Eugene McCann is a Professor of Geography at Simon Fraser University, Vancouver, Canada. An urban political geographer, he researches policy mobilities, harm reduction, public space, development, governance, and planning. He is co-editor, with Kevin Ward, of *Mobile Urbanism* (Minnesota, 2011) and of *Cities & Social Change*, with Ronan Paddison (Sage, 2014). He is co-author, with Andy Jonas and Mary Thomas, of *Urban Geography: A Critical Introduction* (Wiley, 2015). He has published in numerous journals and is managing editor of *EPC: Politics & Space*, a journal of critical research on the relations between the political and the spatial.

Sebastian Möller has been a member of the research group "Transnational political ordering in global finance" and program coordinator in Political Science at the University of Bremen and now works at Cusanus Hochschule für Gesellschaftsgestaltung. He conducted research stays at Manchester Business School and the Institute for Comprehensive Analysis of the Economy in Linz. Sebastian holds a B.A. in Political Science and History from the University of Wuppertal and a M.A. in Political Science from Goethe University Frankfurt. In his Ph.D. project "Finance and the City," he analyzes the financialization of European municipal debt management.

Uttara Purandare is a Ph.D. researcher at the IITB-Monash Research Academy, a joint Ph.D. program offered by the Indian Institute of Technology (Bombay), Mumbai and Monash University, Melbourne. Her area of research is safety and surveillance in the smart city, focusing specifically on how surveillance infrastructures are constructed under the garb keeping vulnerable groups, like women, safe. She is interested in understanding the role of the private sector in building these smart cities in India and what this means for urban democracy.

Mike Raco is a Professor of Urban Governance and Development in the Bartlett School of Planning, University College London. He has published widely on the topics of urban governance and regeneration, urban sustainability, social diversity, and the politics of urban and regional economic development. He is currently leading a team working on an ORA-ESRC funded project on investment flows and residential development in London, Paris and Amsterdam named WHIG: What is Governed in Cities. Recent works include: *State-led Privatisation and the Demise of the Democratic State: Welfare Reform and Localism in an Era of Regulatory Capitalism* (Routledge, London).

Janet Roitman is a University Professor at The New School. She is the author of *Fiscal Disobedience: An Anthropology of Economic Regulation in Central Africa* (Princeton University Press), an analysis of emergent forms of economic regulation in the Chad Basin, and *Anti-Crisis* (Duke University Press), an inquiry into the concept of crisis as an object of knowledge in the social sciences. She is co-founder of The Platform Economies Research Group at The New School. Her current research, "High Finance in Africa," is supported by a National Science Foundation Grant and focuses on emergent FinTech and middle-class politics in Africa.

Neha Sami studies infrastructure and environmental planning and governance in post-liberalization urban India. She is currently faculty at the Indian Institute for Human Settlements in Bangalore, India where she teaches on questions of governance and sustainability and anchors the Research Programme. She is a corresponding editor for the International Journal of Urban and Regional Research, and has served on the Editorial Collective of Urbanization. She holds a Ph.D. in Urban Planning from the University of Michigan, a Master's degree in Environmental Management from the Yale School of the Environment and a B.A. in Economics from the University of Mumbai.

Jean Shaoul an economist, is an Emerita Professor of public accountability at the University of Manchester. Her work, focusing not on shareholders but the broader social distributional consequences of public decision-making, provides financial evidence of the degree to which public policy—including privatization and the use of private finance in public infrastructure under the UK government's Private Finance Initiative and Public–Private Partnerships—has enabled a massive transfer of wealth from the broad mass of the population to the financial elite. Providing an important critique of international public policy, her work is very accessible to a broad audience.

Andrew Sturdy is a Professor of Management and Organisation at the University of Bristol and a Visiting Professor at VU Amsterdam. Previously, he held posts at Imperial College London and the Universities of Bath, Melbourne and Warwick. His research lies mostly in the field of organizational innovation and the role of management consultancy. His work includes co-authored books such as *Management as Consultancy* (2017, Cambridge University Press) and the co-edited *Oxford Handbook* *of Management Ideas* (2019, Oxford University Press). He has worked with diverse organizations in research projects on the use of consulting and adoption of new management ideas. His latest work explores consultancy in national and transnational public sector contexts, including the NHS in the UK.

Laura Valentukeviciute holds a B.A. in Social Work from Vilnius University and an M.A. in Social Sciences from Osnabrück University. Since 2007, she has been working on privatization and public–private partnerships, since 2010 as board member and spokesperson of the non-profit association Gemeingut in BürgerInnenhand (GiB, Common Goods in Citizens' Hands). Before joining GiB, she worked for the development of policy spokesperson of Alliance 90/The Greens in the German Parliament. Valentukeviciute is a speaker and writer on privatization and has been invited as an expert to parliamentary hearings in the German Federal Parliament.

Anne Vogelpohl is an urban and economic geographer focusing on expertise and urban policies, precarious labor, and housing policies. She is co-chair of the geographical Working Group "Feminist Geographies" in the German-speaking countries. Anne Vogelpohl currently is a temporary professor for social policy at the Department of Social Work at Hamburg University of Applied Sciences.

Daria Volkova is an assistant researcher at the Laboratory of Urban Sociology at HSE University in Russia and a Ph.D. student at Bauhaus-University Weimar in Germany. She conducts research on urban policy and housing in Russia, including studies about discourses on new large housing estates, and residential mobility. In her current Ph.D. project, she focuses on urban heritage of mass housing in Russia and Germany.

List of Figures

List of Tables

Introduction: The Rise of Professional Service Firms as Public Policy Actors

Chris Hurl and Anne Vogelpohl

"How the German state surrenders itself to global advisory firms" (Becker et al., 2019).[1] "Government spends almost £100 m on Brexit consultants" (Murphy, 2019). "India's public sector increasingly turning to management consultants".[2]—Headlines like these indicate a stark, and sometimes unreasonable, growth of professional service firms in advising governments. Increasingly management consultancies, law firms, accountancies, and engineering service providers are selling knowledge-intensive services to public sector clients (Empson et al., 2015), extending their influence over a range of areas—from auditing the books and assessing

[1] German original quotes are translated by the authors in this chapter.

[2] https://www.consultancy.in/news/2344/indias-public-sector-increasingly-turning-to-management-consultants, accessed 15.08.2019.

C. Hurl (✉)
Concordia University, Montreal, QC, Canada
e-mail: chris.hurl@concordia.ca

A. Vogelpohl
Hamburg University of Applied Sciences, Hamburg, Germany
e-mail: anne.vogelpohl@haw-hamburg.de

C. Hurl and A. Vogelpohl (eds.), *Professional Service Firms and Politics in a Global Era*, https://doi.org/10.1007/978-3-030-72128-2_1

public services to advising on digital governance, smart cities, trash collection, taxation policies and public health, for example.[3] However, while proponents argue that these sorts of professional intermediaries play a vital role in providing governments with requisite expertise and advice in an increasingly complex world, critics argue that these agencies have hollowed out the state, undermining democratic decision-making and reducing the space for public deliberation through their cookie-cutter solutions. How are we to understand the role of professional service firms in public policymaking today?

While there is a large body of literature on think tanks and consultants, research focusing on the role of professional service firms (PSFs) as transnational *policy*-actors in their own right has been limited. PSFs are quite diverse in terms of their scale and scope; however, Empson et al. (2015, 3) note that these enterprises share a common focus in providing "intangible experiential services in the form of knowledge-rich, time-sensitive advice that is tailored to a specific client's needs." Over the past three decades, firms offering specialized knowledge have exploded, becoming some of the largest corporations around the world. These firms have become central actors in packaging and circulating specialized knowledge and advice across jurisdictions. However, they remain underexamined in the interdisciplinary critical policy studies literature.

The focus of this volume is on the influence of these firms in state restructuring and public policymaking. Our authors document the growing involvement of PSFs in advising governments and critically investigate this trend with regard to their influence in brokering access to the policymaking process, developing metrics guiding decision-making, and shaping policy outcomes. For these purposes, we have invited scholars from across disciplines (including business, political science, sociology, geography, and urban planning) and from different regions (including Russia, India, the UK, and Australia). The book addresses a range of

[3] Indeed, the government spending on professional services firms (PSFs) has grown significantly over the past few years: in Germany by 6.6% between 2010 and 2019 to more than 3 billion € per year (https://www.bdu.de/berateraffaere/, accessed 15.08.2019); in Canada from $56 million in 1984 to $689 million in 2017 (https://www.accountingtoday.com/news/big-four-firms-grow-consulting-unit-revenue-in-canada); in the Asia Pacific Region by 9% between 2015 and 2017 (https://www.consultancy.asia/news/1411/asia-pacific-management-consulting-industry-breaks-50-billion-barrier, accessed 15.08.2019 and https://www.consultancy.com.au/news/10/australian-government-underestimated-consulting-spend-by-billions).

issues, including the historical emergence of professional service firms as a distinctive mode of organization, their role in advising governments at different levels and jurisdictions, and their influence on key policy debates such as privatization, remunicipalization, smart cities, infrastructure procurement, and financialization.

In framing the field of research, our introduction outlines three lines of inquiry for the investigation of professional service firms that are taken up in different ways by each of our authors. First, we identify questions of power and agency between PSFs and public agencies. How are these firms positioned in relation to the state? Who drives and shapes the agenda between public and private actors? And with what implications? Second, we explore the professional rationalities and technologies guiding the work of PSFs: How do firms (re)imagine the policymaking process through professional discourses? What kinds of performance metrics, diagnostic instruments, and information technologies do they draw from in making sense of policy? And how have these rationalities and technologies changed the policymaking process? Third, we look at the work of firms in circulating policy knowledges with a focus on their role in the translation of policy ideas across different contexts. To what extent do these firms contribute to the convergence of governance practices and policy decisions across jurisdictions? And how might they transform the tempo of policymaking processes through their time-sensitive mobilization of policy ideas? For each topic, we introduce key concepts applied in different disciplines and discuss the kinds of research questions being addressed in the literature. We conclude by discussing the contributions of each of our chapters.

Power/Agency: Understanding the Drivers of the Private–Public Nexus

Over the past three decades, public agencies around the world have increasingly commissioned private experts to assess services and provide advice on a range of issues. In 2018 alone, the revenue generated by management consultants in advising governments was estimated at over 85 billion dollars globally (IBIS World, 2019). Moreover, the growing influence of these firms is not just reflected in growing expenditures on professional service firms, but also in frequency of use, and areas of service. As large firms diversify their services, Saint Martin (2013) notes, they often maintain ongoing connections with public agencies through a variety of different service lines. In this context, how is the relationship between private firms and public agencies changing? Has the power and authority of PSFs been enhanced in setting the political agenda? Or are they rather contractors delivering made-to-order services for their respective clients?

In the literature, we can find both arguments. On the one hand, it is argued that these firms serve public officials as "intellectual mercenaries," "foot soldiers," or "hired guns" acting on their client's interests (Leys, 1999; Hodge and Bowman, 2006; Dollery and Drew, 2017; McKenna, 2006). By outsourcing advice to these firms, governments are able to lend a veneer of credibility to their policy decisions by appealing to outside professional authority. A more state-centered research agenda has consequently focused on cases in which these firms have worked to justify the decisions of the political elite (Beveridge, 2012). From this perspective, the dominant actors are politicians and public officials who use PSFs in order to advance their own agenda. The allegiance of these firms ultimately lies with the public officials who hired them and upon whom they are dependent for future contracts. As Leys (1999, 448) found in his early study of the NHS in the UK, consultants are "dependent on getting consultancy business." Consequently, they "can rarely afford to give unwelcome advice or refuse a brief even if its real aim is, frequently, to secure legitimation for a policy to which the client is already committed." Along these lines, many commentators have questioned the degree of value added by consultants, who tell governments things that they already know. As the old saying goes, consultants will borrow your watch in order to tell you the time (O'Mahoney and Markham, 2013, 329).

On the other hand, another set of scholars has argued that PSFs themselves are the dominant actors who have increasingly captured the policymaking process from the outside. From this perspective, there is a sense that consultants have come to form an elite that shapes the agendas of governments from behind the scenes. Guttman and Willner (1976) set the tone when they argued that consultants had effectively formed a "shadow government" in the United States. This alludes to the opacity of their advice, which is often difficult to track and evaluate, but also speaks to "how their internal business strategy is focused on particular areas of public services that they target for product development and delivery in ways that become monopolies" (Gunter and Mills, 2017, 108). In this context, it has been argued that these firms and their personnel make up a sort of "consultocracy" that has come to stand in for the civil service (Jupe and Funnell, 2015; Ylönen and Kuusela, 2019; McCann, 2011b). In appraising the influx of consultants into the UK public sector, Hood and Jackson (1991, 23–24) have argued that this has contributed to "social forgetting" in public administration, which "makes us slaves to the meretricities of the administrative fashion trade of consultocracy and pop management". From this perspective, PSFs have contributed to the hollowing out of the state—or what Merrifield (2014, 419) refers to as the "outsourcing of democracy"—reducing state capacities while interjecting their own forms of knowledge and decision-making.

Empirically, a linear track running either from the private firm to the public agency, or vice versa, is hard to find. Most studies situate the power of private expertise between these two poles, recognizing the complex and contradictory relationships that often arise through the process of delivering professional services. They try to unravel the different roles that experts may play within a policy process and trace how the ambitions of private firms and public officials are interwoven (Owens, 2015; Sturdy et al., 2010; Vogelpohl, 2018). Professional services can meet different needs for different actors, including creating new knowledge and framing emergent issues, facilitating reform and restructuring, absorbing criticism, and integrating policies across jurisdictions (Saint Martin, 2012; Kagi, 1969; Gellner, 1994). Moreover, the growing public sector demand for professional services can also foster the development of new markets for private firms, opening up new areas for commodification as existing markets become saturated. Along these lines, the literature has pointed to the variable role played by consultants and consulting firms in both legitimizing government reforms and building markets for advisory services (Akers, 2013; Mitchell, 2009; Saint Martin, 2012; Vogelpohl, 2018). In the end, the relationships are nuanced, demanding research strategies that focus on the interconnections between private firms and public agencies at different levels:

Understanding elite networks. A first line of analysis involves examining the interconnections between PSFs and public agencies through the circulation of personnel. Indeed, a research agenda has emerged from the 1970s onward tracing the embeddedness of consultants in elite networks (Guttman and Willner, 1976; Heinz et al., 1990; Peck, 2010; Wedel, 2017). A central contention arising from this research is that the impartiality of consultants is compromised to the extent that they circulate in revolving door relationships, moving between the private and public sectors, generating potential conflicts of interest and raising questions of their allegiances (Eyal and Buchholz, 2010). Who are they speaking for? For instance, in their research the Private Finance Initiative in the UK, Shaoul et al. (2007, 15) have noted that "[t]he constant flow of personnel between the higher echelons of the public sector and the private sector" has created a sort of beltway for the advancement of self-serving economic policies (see also Shaoul in this volume). However, while a number of high-profile scandals have emerged that expose the conflicts of interest between these firms and the political and economic elites[4] that they advise, the links connecting these firms and their personnel with public officials are often anecdotal and remain to be systematically documented through in-depth research. Moreover, the nature of these relationships remains uncertain in the absence of qualitative research documenting how officials use their connectivity in order to advance particular agendas, as Volkova (this volume) demonstrates in her discussion of Russian planning consultants who rely on personal networks with political elites in order to get business.

Understanding structural ties. In advancing the view that public agencies have been recently co-opted by a private consultocracy, the literature on elite networks can, at times, lead to assumptions that the state was somehow less open to private sector influences in the past. However, private consultants have long played a role in advising governments, with actors frequently moving between the private and public sectors (see Kipping in this volume for an historical overview). Beyond focusing on elite networks, a growing literature has explored the changing structures mediating the relationship between public agencies and private firms. From this perspective, it is not so much a matter of understanding "who is pulling the strings," as it is about "'the ties that bind' these actors together" (O'Reilly, 2010, 196). While consultants were previously enlisted by public officials through more ad hoc relationships, a number of studies have noted a shift over the past three decades to more continuous and diversified relationships. "Over time," Saint Martin (2013, 173–174) notes, "as they developed more intimate links with governments, large consulting firms mutated into somewhat less 'private' and more 'public' entities," framing themselves as "co-pilots in the steering of government organizations." O'Reilly (2010) has described this as a process

[4] A recent scandal in Germany is the extensive and nontransparent use of management consultancies, namely Accenture, by the Federal Ministry of Defense which was facilitated through close personal networks between public officials and consultants.

of "state-corporate symbiosis," in which public agencies and PSFs are increasingly integrated at the structural level. For instance, in their study of urban planning in India, Sami and Anand (this volume) highlight how professional service firms have been increasingly integrated in core planning functions that were previously administered by state bureaucracies. From this perspective, it is necessary to explore the changing governance structures through which PSFs are incorporated into the policymaking process.

Understanding procurement practices. In understanding the changing relationship between public agencies and PSFs, a number of studies have explored the regulatory frameworks through which these relationships are governed. As Sturdy (this volume) notes, the regulation of these relationships is fraught, given consultancy's ambiguity, commercial form, growth and power imbalances. This has, in part, been exacerbated by the emergence of new arrangements for the procurement of public services and infrastructure. For instance, Raco (this volume) speaks to the centrality of PSFs in what he describes as the emergence of the "parastate" forms of governance, in which governments come to both enter into complex contractual arrangements with private firms in outsourcing services, and increasingly rely on private experts in order to assess and advise on these contracts. As infrastructure development is increasingly rolled out through complicated financial arrangements bringing together public agencies and an array of private actors, Hildyard (this volume) notes, the largest professional service firms—the so-called "Big Four" (Deloitte, PwC, EY and KPMG)—have developed instruments that have rendered infrastructure governable through novel conceptions of risk and risk sharing. In some countries, they have become institutionally embedded in infrastructure procurement agencies such as the Canadian Infrastructure Bank, PartnershipsUK, or the German Infrastructure Agency (see Hurl and Vogelpohl, 2021).

Understanding markets for services. While many studies have focused on the changing demand for professional services on the part of public agencies, recent studies have noted that the supply of professional services is also changing (Beaverstock et al., 2015). Historically, due to low capital requirements and the knowledge-intensive focus, the field of professional services has tended to be made up of small, geographically specific operators, often specializing in a distinctive niche (IBIS World, 2019). However, over the past thirty years, large transnational firms have increasingly consolidated their power in a number of professional domains (Brooks, 2018). Revenues are increasingly concentrated through scale advantages, changing procurement practices, and industry consolidation through mergers and acquisitions. Indeed, while the Big Four firms initially divested from management consulting in response to the conflicts of interest exposed during the Enron scandal in 2001, they have reversed course since 2005, acquiring dozens of smaller consulting firms working with public sector agencies across the globe. Moreover, large firms often outsource components of their services to smaller boutique firms, with expertise in a specific area. This has enabled these firms to diversify the range of services that they offer, developing more continuous relationships with public agencies. However, it has also led to complex ecologies for professional advice, as the structure of firms is becoming more complex, variegated, and intermingled, as we discuss in the next section.

Rationalities/Technologies: Understanding the Logics of Professional Service Firms

A second set of research questions has arisen from Science and Technology Studies (STS), critical management studies and the governmentality literature, exploring how the work of professional service firms is assembled and how these firms draw from professional discourses and technologies in generating new objects of expertise. The focus here is, on the one hand, on the role of firms in rolling out new governmental programs—new "ways of *thinking*" that underpin governance practices, including "the ideas and concepts which shape the mission of the practice and attach the practice to broader policy objectives in the political sphere" (Power, 1997, 6). On the other hand, these firms have played an influential role in developing new *technologies* of government, which include the "mechanisms through which programs of government are articulated and made operable" (Miller, 2001, 379). The focus here is on the models, metrics, and instruments that firms draw from in rendering problems legible and governable. In exploring the influence of professional discourses and technologies in policymaking, this literature traces the ways in which PSFs generate credibility through appealing to different forms of expertise.

Understanding professional discourses. In formulating new programs for governance, public officials have often appealed to the credibility of outside experts. Drawing from the work of Michel Foucault (1991), a central focus of the governmentality literature has been on the unspoken rules and assumptions—the historically constructed "regimes of truth"—guiding the work of doctors, engineers, accountants, lawyers, and economists and how they have changed over time (see Miller and Rose, 2008; Lemke, 2002; Walters, 2012; Rose et al., 2006). Rather than focusing on the individual aptitudes of these professionals, there is a focus on the historically variable rules of thumb and know-how that they apply in making sense of the issues on which they work. As Said (2000, 196) notes, "what enables a doctor to practice medicine or a historian to write history is not mainly a set of individual gifts, but an ability to follow rules that are taken for granted as an unconscious a priori by all professionals." From this perspective, we can ask what rules guide the work of PSFs and how have they changed over time.

Along these lines, studies have explored the know-how that has been applied by PSFs in advising corporations and governments. Over the years, these firms have appealed to a range of different professional discourses—such as law, engineering, and managerial science—in framing their work (McKenna, 2006). As Roitman (this volume) notes, the orientation of PSFs has evolved from a focus on cost accounting and scientific management, to strategy consulting and business re-engineering, to cultivating corporate cultures and reputations, and most recently, to new forms of finance-based expertise. Many studies have highlighted the influence of professional discourses in reshaping how the corporation was imagined and governed, from the rise of Taylorism onward (McKenna, 2006; Kiechel, 2010; Kipping and Kirkpatrick, 2013). Moreover, building from Saint Martin's (2000) groundbreaking work, a growing literature has looked at the role of professional consultants and advisors in shaping discourses of public sector reform. Indeed, government restructuring through the 1990s was driven by management consultants, most prominently David Osborne and Ted Gaebler, the chief architects of New Public Management, who advocated for a shift from "bureaucratic systems" to "entrepreneurial" forms of governance in their canonical text, *Reinventing Government* (1992), spurring a whole industry dedicated to retooling government (Saint Martin, 2000, 587).

In the battle for credibility, a few professional discourses have achieved prominence. In the advancement of neoliberal government programs, many studies have pointed to the growing role and influence of auditing discourses in reframing government objectives (Power, 1997; Strathern, 2000; Shore and Wright, 2015). As Shore and Wright (1999, 559) note, this has entailed the introduction of a new cluster of terms that have provided the "epistemological foundation for the rise of new institutions." Through the introduction of concepts like "performance," "quality assurance," "transparency," "efficiency," "effectiveness," "benchmarks," "best practices," and "value for money," professional service firms have actively transformed the way in which public policymaking is imagined and public services are governed. Möller (this volume) explains the long-term effects of these reforms in the realm of municipal finances.

More recently, there is a growing focus on IT consultancies, who are threatening to supplant accountancy and strategy firms as the chief advisors to government through their championing of discourses of "smartness." For instance, through its smart city strategy, Söderstrom et al. (2014, 313) argue, IBM consultants have drawn from systems engineering discourses in reimagining urban environments: "The city is made to speak the language of IBM." Such discourses generate a surface of equivalence in which very different urban phenomena can be rendered commensurable, translated into a "unitary language" (also McNeill, 2015).

Understanding technologies and metrics. Beyond focusing on the governmental programs advanced by these firms, recent studies inspired by STS have also explored the technologies that firms draw from in rendering problems legible and governable (McNeill, 2015; Bruno, 2009; Kitchin et al., 2015). This means attending to how these firms have assembled information through new metrics, databases, and technologies of commensuration. For instance, Hurl (this volume) explores the role and influence of PSFs in developing enterprise architecture mapping programs through the 1990s that enabled public services to be compared in new ways, drawing previously distant jurisdictions into proximity under a regime of competition by which they were encouraged to adhere to "normal" service levels. Through circulating these kinds of artifacts, PSFs have been able to generate a degree of consensus around municipal service delivery without requiring an in-depth knowledge of its inner workings.

Through the application of calculative metrics, critics argue that these firms have framed political issues as domains of professional knowledge outside of the purview of public deliberation and thus contributed to a process of depoliticization (Christensen and Skaerbaek 2010; Beveridge 2012; Kitchin et al., 2015; Shore, 2008). In contrast to think tanks or policy gurus who explicitly advocate a particular policy position, PSFs and their personnel often present themselves as mere rapporteurs simply communicating the facts (Davies, 2017). Following accounting logics, much of the literature has highlighted an easy slip between the "descriptive" and the "normative" as these firms mask their advocacy functions through appealing to a logic of "best practices" (Kornberger and Carter, 2010). By reframing public issues as technical problems, it is argued that they have diminished the space for public deliberation in the policymaking process, restricting participation to a community of experts. For instance, Purandare (this volume) shows how such a reliance on seemingly "neutral" experts has contributed to the depoliticization of India's smart city policy.

However, the degree of depoliticization can sometimes be overstated. As we will see in the next section, it is important to recognize that the institutional networks through which firms operate can be tenuous and open to contestation. The work of bridging different epistemic communities, standing as intermediaries between different jurisdictions, is never fully accomplished (Johns, 2011). Rather, it entails ongoing work of translation.

Understanding professional domains. The governmentality literature has provided insights on how different forms of professional knowledge are taken up and applied in the governance process. However, not as much research has been done on how this work is organized and negotiated within firms and what influence this has on professional identities. The study of PSFs poses a challenge from this perspective to the extent that large firms often brand themselves as jacks-of-all-trades offering services and advice in areas ranging from smart cities and IT infrastructure to legal services and taxation policy. While expertise in some firms is shaped more by professional credentials, in others credentials are not required (McKenna, 2006; IBISWorld, 2019). In the absence of a clear identity, how are these firms able to assume the position of professionals?

There is some literature in critical management studies and the sociology of professions interrogating the professional standpoint of these firms (McKenna, 2006; Suddaby and Greenwood, 2001). For instance, McKenna (2006) notes that consultancy firms have tended to avoid professionalizing as a process while at the same time espousing professionalism as an ideology. Through adopting a discourse of professionalism, and building the firm's reputation, generating experience with a steady stream of high-end clients, they are able to sell themselves as credible actors, even without credentialed staff. This is augmented through processes of codification and commodification, through which knowledge is standardized and packaged in ways that remove professional discretion from the assessment process.

Moreover, the boundaries between professional domains are shifting. Scholars in the sociology of professions and critical management studies have noted a tendency to "knowledge colonization" as these firms have worked "to expand the scale and scope of their managerial knowledge products" (Suddaby and Greenwood, 2001, 935). Indeed, the "Big Four" all got their start in auditing and accounting and have only recently extended their work to other areas, including information technology, law, and education. Big Four firms have consequently shifted their business model and professional orientation from auditing, based on assessing existing accounts, to become increasingly focused on forecasting and speculation with the aim of advising governments on future trends and opportunities. In the wake of the global pandemic, these firms are being taken up by governments in advising on restructuring and recovery efforts. For instance, Deloitte (2020) has recently developed a COVID-19 "economic recovery dashboard" which sets out to monitor "health, community/social activity, financial and economic indicators that will signal when the rebound stage has arrived."

Future research could explore the changing orientation of these firms, illuminating the increasingly blurry line between the assessment of existing accounts and speculating on future prospects, anticipating risks, and developing strategies for their mitigation. This has, at times, provoked controversy, as the blurry lines provoke claims of conflict of interest. Indeed, the Enron scandal, which led the Big Four firms to briefly divest from consulting in the early 2000s, was fueled by Arthur Andersen's conflict in both assessing and advising, with the firm maintaining a vested interest in making the books look good as a means of bringing in more lucrative business in advisory services. This example raises the question: How are boundaries between different professional domains maintained, and to what extent are they blurred together, changing conceptions of professional identity and purpose in advising the public sector?

Convergence/Translation: Understanding Global Effects of Private Influence on Public Policy

Finally, a third area of research has emerged in human geography and political science, exploring the role of PSFs in circulating policy ideas around the world. From this perspective, a range of studies have argued that these firms have contributed to the convergence of policy ideas across jurisdictions (Stone, 2004; Kipping and Wright, 2012; Boussebaa and Faulconbridge, 2018). Describing this as a process of "institutional isomorphism," DiMaggio and Powell (1983, 152) have likened these actors to "Johnny Appleseeds" that "spread a few organizational models throughout the land." Along these lines, critics have challenged these firms for offering cookie-cutter solutions to complex problems, though the more recent literature on "policy mobilities" has questioned the degree of homogeneity generated, as firms must actively ***translate*** their advice to different contexts and institutional settings (McCann, 2011b; Robinson, 2011). From this perspective, PSFs do not necessarily contribute to policy "convergence" but may adapt and tailor ideas in ways that contribute to policy "mutation" (Peck, 2011). In order to understand the degree of political influence wielded by PSFs, we thus identify their role in mobilizing policy ideas, between the poles of convergence and mutation, as a final area of research.

Understanding policy mobilities. Certainly, a case could be made that transnational professional service firms have contributed to institutional isomorphism. By 2019, the Big Four firms employed over 1,090,000 people (Statista, 2020) in 150 countries (Brooks, 2018). They audit most of the world's large publicly traded companies and have played a central role in auditing many of the world's governments (Brooks, 2018). Moreover, they are actively advising many governments around the world. Through operating at such a scale, they command a significant degree of power, and are capable of mobilizing knowledge personnel across jurisdictions. Existing research indicates that the global activity of PSFs has contributed to standardizing a certain style of policymaking (Kipping and Wright, 2012), focussing on top-down approaches. This has resulted in a certain kind of "economic globalization" (Boussebaa and Faulconbridge, 2018), shaped by a global hegemony of market-oriented political economy with a strong focus on competition (Kipping and Wright, 2012).

Cook and Ward (2012, 142) argue that these kinds of policy actors generate "policy pipelines," "assembling [...] elements of different geographical reach into interlocking sets of relations that connect geographically discrete locations." The formation of policy pipelines has been facilitated by the codification and commodification of knowledge by these firms, enabling its circulation across jurisdictions. For instance, McCann and Mahieus (this volume) note how Gehl architects have codified a distinctive, standardized and apolitical approach to the study of place-making that they have marketed to cities around the world as a means to help them improve their public spaces.

However, the argument for policy convergence can downplay the degree to which firms must change and adapt policy advice to different institutional settings. Often the same firm will be offering different, and even divergent, policy advice across contexts—which also shapes the "professions and the expertise created therein" (Kuus, 2020). For instance, in our research, we have found that, while Big Four firms are advocating for public–private partnerships (PPPs) in Canada, they are also advising remunicipalization, effectively bringing municipal services back under public ownership, in Germany (Hurl and Vogelpohl, 2021). How can we explain the variation in policy advice? The more recent literature has been critical of overly linear understandings of "transfer" in which "policy innovations travel unidirectionally across a practically inert landscape." (Peck, 2011, 789). Against this view, Peck argues that a more relational approach is necessary: As he notes, "policy 'objects' that pass through these networks are not only transformed on the journey, they are transform*ing* of both network and its nodes." The key question inspired by the policy mobilities approach is not merely how private experts transfer policies over space, but how do they actively transform them during their journeys. As Peck (2011, 793) argues: "The policy transfer process, for all its trappings of 'disembedded' policy development, must itself be understood as an institutionally produced and embedded phenomena." Along these lines, Keele (this volume) takes up a more nuanced approach in her study of climate policy advice in Australia, exploring how consultants operate in a number of different spatial registers—within territories, across networks, and through relational proximities—in order to generate influence.

Understanding policy assemblages. The work of translating policy ideas across contexts has also been explored in the recent literature on policy assemblages (Prince, 2010; McCann, 2011a; Savage, 2019). According to Prince (2010, 173), policy transfer is the result of an "assemblage of texts, actors, agencies, institutions, and networks that ... come together at particular policy-making locales." The emphasis here is on how agency is materially distributed, made possible through an array of different tools and technologies. From this perspective, PSFs should not be understood as singular actors, setting policy priorities from on high. It is important to consider the diverse and multifaceted institutional arrangements within the firms themselves. For example, the few studies that have emerged on Big Four firms have noted their dispersed style of organization. As Shore and Wright (2018, 310) observe, "the Big 4 have helped to pioneer a new form of business entity that is neither a multinational corporation, a global partnership, nor a single firm. Their role, instead, is to act as coordinating entities for their network of global affiliates, who are to be unified around 'brand,' 'risk,' 'quality', 'values' and 'ethics' by adhering to a common code of conduct." Even then, there are tensions in drawing firms together under a common code. As Linovski (this volume) observes, codes of conduct governing PSFs are contradictory and often unfeasible in regulating the complex relationships both between public and private actors, and within private firms themselves.

In this context, it is difficult to assert that these firms simply generate ideas from a head office and seek to circulate them in different contexts. In fact, the translation of policy ideas across the firm itself is often fraught. In his study of transnational service firms, Jones (2002, 346) notes that "strategic control is spread through the organization in a way which does not necessitate the 'centre' being heavily involved in individual business decisions." Financial power is negotiated and wielded by senior management from a centralized perspective; yet global corporate strategy remains negotiated and fluid, mediated through information and knowledge of line managers. This complex prompts the question of how centrality, diffusion, and particularities are negotiated by professionals in organizing their advisory service market.

Understanding temporalities. The literature has tended to focus on the spatial dimensions of policy diffusion, looking at how firms circulate knowledge ideas across space. However, there is also an emerging literature exploring their role in compressing the policymaking process across time (Vogelpohl, 2017; Peck and Theodore, 2015; Stubbs, 2018). How have professional service firms transformed the temporalities of policymaking? In the recent literature it is argued that these firms have accelerated the flow of policy knowledge *across* jurisdictions—facilitating what Jamie Peck and Nik Theodore (2015, 223) describe as "fast policy," or a policymaking condition that is characterized by "the intensified and instantaneous connectivity of sites, channels, arenas, and nodes of policy development, evolution, and reproduction." From this perspective, private experts have contributed to accelerating the circulation of policy ideas, leading to swifter policy transformations over time.

However, expert-led policymaking also facilitates the intensified flow of policymaking *within* jurisdictions (Kuus, 2015), with attendant limitations concerning participation or the acknowledgment of ambivalences and differences. In this sense, Stubbs (2018) notes that consultants do not just craft new scales of policymaking but are also engaged in what he calls "timecraft": "Temporalities, in the form of dates, times and durations of meetings, deadlines for submitting proposals, timelines for taking action on decisions, amongst many others are, of course, always central in these interactions" (Stubbs, 2018, 30). Moreover, recent studies have linked the work of PSFs to the abbreviated temporalities of disaster capitalism, as consultants are commissioned in the aftermath of a crisis to advise on restructuring (Klein, 2008; Peck and Whiteside, 2016; O'Reilly, 2011). This has come to light, for example, during the COVID-19 pandemic, as firms such as McKinsey and Deloitte have been widely taken up in coordinating government responses (see Kipping in this volume). In order to understand the influence of PSFs within the policy process, future research could address the temporalities shaping professional services for public policy. How does these temporalities influence the formulation of problems and resulting programs? How sustainable are they?

Understanding the embeddedness of advice in local contexts. Beyond accounting for the circulation of policy advice across jurisdictions, it is also important to consider how it is adapted to different contexts and institutional settings. Policymaking is a complex process, with policy actors variably embedded in diverse polity structures and processes, and communities of interest (Dolowitz and Marsh, 2000). It is important, in this context, to recognize the various ways in which consulting work *takes place* and its longer-term impacts on policymaking in specific locales.

A number of studies have noted how consultants face the challenge of embedding themselves in local communities, connecting to processes and practices, and in relation to actors of varying affiliation (Sturdy et al., 2010; Armbrüster, 2006; Jones, 2002). For instance, Bathelt et al. (2004: 38) highlight the importance of local "buzz" in fostering an environment conducive to policy translation, speaking to an "information and communication ecology created by face-to-face contacts, co-presence and co-location of people and firms within the same industry and place or region." Along these lines, the capacity for consultants to generate influence is shaped by the ecology into which they enter, as well as the physical sites and event spaces through which they can encounter and influence policymakers.

Expert advice will often leave impacts on a specific milieu long after advisors have moved on to other projects. However, research has largely focused on the time in which consultants are commissioned to examine a specific issue. There is also a need to follow up to examine the impacts of consultants after they have left. Furthermore, the specific advice offered to governments can often remain unimplemented or, as Dolowitz and Marsh (2000, 6) note, result in policy failure.

Understanding limits and resistance. The use of consultants in different contexts is also actively challenged. Social activists and community groups often contest the suitability of policy advice to specific contexts. For instance, Valentukeviciute (this volume) shows how a German NGO exposed and confronted the opaque networks between PSFs and public agencies in public–private partnerships. Whereas the critiques are diverse, two aspects should be highlighted: (1) the potential threat to democratic decision-making through opaque back-room politics; and (2) the economization of all fields of policy through the introduction of efficiency and competition logics. However, there is very little research on how professional service firms have been challenged, and the critical engagement with PSFs is often confined to local struggles. Along these lines, we see a need to communicate research on how the role of PSFs in policymaking has been criticized and confronted in a way that facilitates knowledge-sharing across different contexts.

Structure of the Book

With our book we start to answer some of the above-mentioned questions, framing an agenda for research on the role and influence of private experts in public policymaking.

Part I focuses on the strategies and practices that have enabled the rise of Professional Service Firms in public policy-making from a historical and geographic perspective. Matthias Kipping looks at historical dimensions of this, tracing the emergence of PSFs in the United States in the early twentieth century and their spread, catalyzed by commissions of inquiry and wartime mobilizations (Chapter 2). Undertaking a case study of Australia's climate adaption policies, Svenja Keele explores the geographical dimensions of this, looking at the spatial strategies of private consultants, which are configured through different territorial, networked, and topological arrangements (Chapter 3).

Part II looks at the role of PSFs in advising on urban policies. With the proliferation of new infrastructures, place-making campaigns, and redevelopment initiatives, cities have become a central site for commissioning advisory services. A central growth area for these firms has been the promotion of smart cities. Looking at the role of consultants in India's Smart Cities Mission, which aims to transform 100 cities into smart cities, Uttara Purandare notes that transnational consulting firms have become increasingly embedded in the governance process (Chapter 4). Consultants have also been taken up in advising on public spaces, with the aim of enriching the quality of urban life. Exploring the role of Gehl Architects in developing and disseminating best practices on the design of public space, Eugene McCann and Lise Mahieus look at how transnational firms have generated influence, in part, through the stories that they tell (Chapter 5). However, while firms like Gehl have generated a global market for their services, in some places local consultancies have carved out a place for themselves. Daria Volkova discusses how a homegrown market for urban consultancy has emerged in Russia, where local consultants have been able to draw from their personal networks in sustaining boutique operations (Chapter 6).

Part III addresses the role of private experts in financializing governments. Recent studies have highlighted the growing prominence of financial actors, financial markets, and financial motives in society. Professional Service Firms have played an important role in fostering the development of financial imaginaries and financial markets in policymaking. Janet Roitman investigates the role of PSFs in fostering new markets in Africa through the packaging of remittances in securities that can be traded on financial markets and used by governments as an economic development strategy (Chapter 7). Chris Hurl explores the role of PSFs in exporting enterprise architecture models to local government which has enabled new forms of auditing municipal budgets (Chapter 8). Sebastian Möller looks at the role of these firms in popularizing municipal debt management policies in the UK and Germany, showing how the use of interest rate derivatives facilitates state financialization (Chapter 9).

Part IV discusses the role of PSFs in privatization and public–private partnerships (PPPs), which have transformed the orientation of the state to public infrastructures. Nicholas Hildyard explores the role of the Big Four firms and the World Bank in advocating for privatized forms of infrastructure procurement over the past three decades (Chapter 10). Exploring the influence of financial consultants in the Private Finance Initiative (PFI), one of the earliest PPP schemes, developed in the UK, Jean Shaoul looks at how conflicts of interest were generated that compromised the objectivity of consultants in appraising the value of infrastructure development (Chapter 11). Laura Valentukeviciute explores how this has played out in the context of school construction in Berlin, showing how PwC played a key role in legitimizing the process through "camouflaging" the nature and extent of private sector involvement (Chapter 12).

However, PSFs have gone much further than simply providing advice. Part Five demonstrates the institutional entrenchment of these firms in public service delivery. Mike Raco looks at how this has played out in local government in the UK, as five PSFs have come to dominate the market in service delivery. This has culminated in the emergence of a distinctive "parastate" sector which has rendered the boundaries between state agencies and private experts increasingly fluid (Chapter 13). Neha Sami and Shriya Anand look at how this has played out in India's urban and regional planning policies. As they show, core planning functions have increasingly been outsourced to these firms, which have become entrenched in the policymaking through the formation of powerful hybrid agencies, integrating public and private authority (Chapter 14).

The final section looks at challenges in regulating relationships between private experts and governments in the policymaking process. As state planning functions are increasingly outsourced to PSFs, Orly Linovski notes the limits of professional codes of conduct as professionals are increasingly beholden to the imperatives of shareholder maximization in the financialized firm. Andrew Sturdy concludes the volume by exploring problems and potential practices of regulating management consultancy. He suggests options to de-marketize, internalize, diversify, monitor, and/or regulate forms of external consultancy use (Chapter 16).

While we provide a more comprehensive understanding of how private expertise operates in the policymaking process in different parts of the world, further research is required in order to better understand these relationships. For starters, many of our studies are focused on local government. The few papers that address global, regional, or national policies indicate that much more research on these scales is needed.

Moreover, most of our studies explore how PSFs take root in particular contexts. Further research is required to understand the transnational and intersectional footprint of these firms across contexts, especially in reformatting knowledge production between the Global North and the Global South. Along these lines, we see our collection as just a starting place for a much broader international research agenda.

References

Akers, J.M. (2013) 'Making markets—Think tank legislation and private property in Detroit', *Urban Geography,* 34(8): 1070–1095.

Armbrüster, T. (2006) *The Economics and Sociology of Management Consulting*, Cambridge University Press.

Bathelt, H., Malmberg, A. and Maskell, P. (2004) 'Clusters and knowledge: Local buzz, global pipelines and the process of knowledge creation', *Progress in Human Geography* 28(1): 31–56.

Beaverstock, J., Faulconbridge, J.R. and Hall, S. (2015) *The Globalization of Executive Search. Professional Services Strategy and Dynamics in the Contemporary World,* London: Routledge.

Becker, S. et al. (2019) *McKinsey, Roland Berger und Co.: Wie sich der deutsche Staat globalen Beraterfirmen* ausliefert, 25 January, https://www.spiegel.de/plus/deutschland-wie-sich-der-staat-globalen-beraterfirmen-ausliefert-a-00000000-0002-0001-0000-000162036086, accessed 29 January 2019.

Beveridge, R. (2012) 'Consultants, depoliticization and arena-shifting in the policy process: Privatizing water in Berlin', *Policy Sciences* 45(1): 47–68.

Boussebaa, M. and Faulconbridge, J.R. (2018) 'Professional service firms as agents of economic globalization: A political perspective', *Journal of Professions and Organization* 6(1): 72–90.

Brooks, R. (2018) *Bean Counters: The Triumph of the Accountants and How They Broke Capitalism,* London: Atlantic Books.

Bruno, I. (2009) 'The "indefinite discipline" of competitiveness benchmarking as a neoliberal technology of government', *Minerva* 47(3): 261.

Christensen, M. and Skaerbaek, P. (2010) 'Consultancy outputs and the purification of accounting technologies', *Accounting, Organizations and Society* 35: 524–545.

Cook, I. and Ward, K. (2012) 'Conferences, informational infrastructures and mobile policies: The process of getting Sweden 'BID ready,'' *European Urban and Regional Studies* 19(2): 137–152.

Davies, W. (2017) 'Elite power under advanced neoliberalism', *Theory, Culture and Society* 34(5–6): 227–250.

Deloitte (2020) *Predicting the post-pandemic rebound: A Live Look at Canada's Economy to Prepare Businesses for Recovery*, https://www2.deloitte.com/ca/en/pages/about-deloitte/articles/covid-dashboard.html, accessed 23 November 2020.

DiMaggio, P.J. and Powell, W. (1983) 'The iron cage revisited: Institutional isomorphism and collective rationality in organizational fields', *American Sociological Review* 48(2): 147–160.

Dollery, B. and Drew, J. (2017) 'Hired guns: Local government mergers in New South Wales and the KPMG modelling report', *Australian Accounting Review* 27(3): 263–272.

Dolowitz, D.P. and Marsh, D. (2000) 'Learning from abroad: The role of policy transfer in contemporary policy-making', *Governance* 13(1): 5–23.

Empson, L., Muzio, D., Broschak, J. P. and Hinings, B. (2015) 'Researching professional service firms: An introduction and overview', in L. Empson, D. Muzio, J.P. Broschak, and B. Hinings (eds). *Oxford Handbook of Professional Service Firms*, Oxford: Oxford University Press, pp. 1–23.

Eyal, G., and Buchholz, L. (2010) 'From the sociology of intellectuals to the sociology of interventions', *Annual Review of Sociology* 36: 117–137.

Foucault, M. (1991) 'Governmentality', in G. Burchell, C. Gordon, and P. Miller (eds). *The Foucault Effect*, Chicago: University of Chicago Press.

Gellner, W. (1994) 'Politikberatung durch nichtstaatliche Akteure – Typen, Funktionen, Strategien', in Murswieck, A. (ed.) *Regieren und Politikberatung*. Opladen: Leske + Budrich, pp. 175–192.

Gunter, H. and Mills, C. (2017) *Consultants and consultancy: The case of education*, Switzerland: Springer International Publishing.

Guttman, D. and Willner, B. (1976) *The Shadow Government*, New York: Pantheon Books.

Heinz, J.P., Laumann, E.O., Salisbury, R.H. and Nelson, R.L. (1990) 'Inner circles or hollow cores? Elite networks in national policy systems', *Journal of Politics* 52(2): 356–390.

Hodge, G. and Bowman, D. (2006) 'The 'consultocracy': The business of reforming government', in Graeme Hodge (ed.), *Privatization and Market Development*, Northamton, MA: Edward Elgar.

Hood, C. and Jackson, M.W. (1991) *Administrative Argument*. Aldershot: Dartmouth.

Hurl, C. and Vogelpohl, A. (2021) 'Transnational professional service firms and the corporatization of infrastructure procurement', in S. Aguiton, M. Deplaude, N. Jas, E. Henry and V. Thomas (eds). *Pervasive Powers: The Politics of Corporate Authority*, London: Routledge, pp. 149–169.

IBIS World (2019) *Global Management Consultants Industry Report*.

Johns, F. (2011) 'Financing as governance', *Oxford Journal of Legal Studies* 31(2): 391–415.

Jones, A. (2002) 'The global city' misconceived: the myth of global management in transnational service firms', *Geoforum* 33(3): 335–350.

Jupe, R. and Funnell, W. (2015) 'Neoliberalism, consultants and the privatisation of public policy formulation: The case of Britain's rail industry', *Critical Perspectives on Accounting* 29: 65–85.

Kagi, H. M. (1969) 'The roles of private consultants in urban governing', *Urban Affairs Review* 5(1): 145–158.

Kiechel, W. (2010) *Lords of strategy: The secret intellectual history of the new corporate world*. Harvard Business Press.

Kipping, M. and Kirkpatrick, I. (2013) 'Alternative pathways of change in professional services firms: The case of management consulting', *Journal of Management Studies* 50(5): 777–807.

Kipping, M. and Wright, C. (2012) 'Consultants in context: Global dominance, societal effect, and the capitalist system', in M. Kipping and T. Clark (eds). *The Oxford Handbook of Management Consulting*, Oxford, New York: Oxford University Press, pp. 165–185.

Kitchin, R., Lauriault, T.P. and McArdle, G. (2015) 'Knowing and governing cities through urban indicators, city benchmarking and real-time dashboards', *Regional Studies, Regional Science* 2(1): 6–28.

Klein, N. (2008) *The Shock Doctrine: The Rise of Disaster Capitalism,* Toronto: Vintage.

Kornberger, M. and Carter, C. (2010) 'Manufacturing competition: How accounting practices shape strategy making in cities', *Accounting, Auditing & Accountability Journal*, 23(3): 325–249.

Kuus, M. (2015) 'For slow research', *International Journal of Urban and Regional Research* 39(4): 838–840.

Kuus, M. (2020) 'Professions and their expertise: Charting the spaces of 'elite' occupations', *Progress in Human Geography*, https://doi.org/10.1177/0309132520950466.

Lemke, T. (2002) 'Foucault, governmentality, and critique', *Rethinking Marxism* 14(3): 49–64.

Leys, C. (1999) 'Intellectual mercenaries and the public interest: Management consultants and the NHS', *Policy & Politics* 27(4): 447–465.

McCann, E. (2011a) 'Veritable inventions: Cities, policies and assemblage', *Area* 43(2): 143–147.

McCann, E. (2011b) 'Urban Policy mobilities and global circuits of knowledge: Toward a research agenda', *Annals of the Association of American Geographers* 101(1): 107–130.

McKenna, C. (2006) *The World's Newest Profession: Management Consulting in the Twentieth Century*, Cambridge University Press.

McNeill, D. (2015) 'Global firms and smart technologies: IBM and the reduction of cities', *Transactions of the Institute of British Geographers* 40: 562–574.

Merrifield, A. (2014) 'Against accountancy governance: Notes towards a new urban collective consumption', *City* 18(4–5): 416–426.

Miller, P. (2001) 'Governing by numbers: Why calculative practices matter', *Social Research* 68(2): 379–396.

Miller, P. and Rose, N. (2008) *Governing the Present,* Cambridge, UK: Polity Press.

Mitchell, T. (2009) 'How neoliberalism makes its world—The urban property rights project in Peru', in P. Mirowski and D. Plehwe (eds). *The Road from Mont Pèlerin—The Making of the Neoliberal Thought Collective*, Cambridge, MA: Harvard University Press, pp. 386–416.

Murphy, S. (2019) 'Government spends almost £100m on Brexit consultants',*The Guardian*, 29 May.

O'Mahoney, J. and Markham, C. (2013) *Management Consultancy*, Second Edition. Oxford: Oxford University Press.

O'Reilly, C. (2010) 'The transnational security consultancy industry: A case of state-corporate symbiosis', *Theoretical Criminology* 14(2): 183–210.

O'Reilly, C. (2011) '"From Kidnaps to Contagious Diseases": Elite rescue and the strategic expansion of the transnational security consultancy industry', *International Political Sociology* 5(2): 178–197.

Osborne, D. and Gaebler, T. (1992) *Reinventing government: How the entrepreneurial spirit is transforming the public sector*, Reading, MA: Addison Wesley.

Owens, S. (2015) *Knowledge, policy, and expertise: The UK Royal Commission on environmental pollution 1970–2011,* Oxford: Oxford University Press.

Peck, J. (2011) 'Geographies of policy: From transfer-diffusion to mobility-mutation', *Progress in Human Geography* 35(6): 773–797.

Peck, J. (2010) *Constructions of Neoliberal Reason,* Oxford, New York: Oxford University Press.

Peck, J. and Theodore, N. (2015) *Fast policy—Experimental Statecraft at the Thresholds of Neoliberalism,* Minneapolis, London: University of Minnesota Press.

Peck, J., and Whiteside, H. (2016) 'Financializing Detroit', *Economic Geography* 92(3): 235–268.

Power, M. (1997) *The Audit Society: Rituals of Verification*, Oxford: Oxford University Press.

Prince, R. (2010) 'Policy transfer as policy assemblage: Making policy for the creative industries in New Zealand', *Environment and Planning A* 42(1): 169–186.

Robinson, J. (2011) 'The spaces of circulating knowledge: City strategies and global urban governmentality', in E. McCann and K. Ward (eds). *Mobile Urbanism—Cities and Policymaking in the Global Age*, Minneapolis: University of Minnesota Press, pp. 15–40.

Rose, N., O'Malley and Valverde, M. (2006) 'Governmentality', *Annual Review of Law and Social Science* 2: 83–104.

Said, E. (2000). "Michel Foucault, 1927–1984," in *Reflections on Exile and Other Essays*, Cambridge, MA: Harvard University Press, pp. 187–197.

Saint Martin, D. (2013) 'Making government more 'Business-Like': Management consultants as agents of isomorphism in modern political economies', in John Mikler (ed.) *The Handbook of Global Companies*. West Sussex: Wiley-Blackwell, pp. 173–192.

Saint Martin, D. (2012) 'Governments and management consultants: Supply, demand, and effectiveness', in M. Kipping and T. Clark (eds). *The Oxford Handbook of Management Consulting*. Oxford, New York: Oxford University Press, pp. 447–464.

Saint Martin, D. (2000) *Building the New Managerialist State: Consultants and the Politics of Bureaucratic Reform in Britain, Canada, and France*, Oxford University Press.

Savage, G. (2019) 'What is policy assemblage?', *Territory, Politics, Governance*: 1–17.

Shaoul, J., Stafford, A. and Stapleton, P. (2007) 'Partnerships and the role of financial advisors: private control over public policy?', *Policy and Politics* 35(3): 479–495.

Shore, C. (2008) 'Audit culture and illiberal governance', *Anthropological Theory* 8: 278–289.

Shore, C. and Wright, S. (1999) 'Audit culture and anthropology: Neo-liberalism in British higher education', *Journal of the Royal Anthropological Institute* 5(4): 557–575.

Shore, C. and Wright, S. (2015) 'Audit culture revisited: Rankings, ratings, and the reassembling of society', *Current Anthropology* 56(3): 431–432.

Shore, C. and Wright, S. (2018) 'How the Big 4 got big: Audit culture and the metamorphosis of international accountancy firms', *Critique of Anthropology* 38(3): 303–324.

Söderstrom, O., Paasche, T. and Klauser, F. (2014) 'Smart cities as corporate storytelling', *City* 18(3): 307-320.

Statista (2020) *Number of employees of the Big Four accounting / audit firms worldwide in 2019*, https://www.statista.com/statistics/250503/big-four-accounting-firms-number-of-employees/, accessed 26 November 2020.

Stone, D. (2004) 'Transfer agents and global networks in the 'Transnationalisation' of Policy', *Journal of European Public Policy* 11(3): 545–566.

Sturdy, A., Handley, K., Clark, T. and Fincham, R. (2010) *Management Consultancy. Boundaries and Knowledge in Action*, Oxford: Oxford University Press.

Strathern, M. (2000) 'Introduction: new accountabilities', in M. Strathern (ed). *Audit Cultures*. London: Routledge.

Stubbs, P. (2018) 'Slow, slow, quick, quick, slow: Power, expertise and the hegemonic temporalities of austerity', *Innovation: The European Journal of Social Science Research* 31(1): 25–39.
Suddaby, R. and Greenwood, R. (2001) 'Colonizing knowledge: Commodification as a dynamic of jurisdiction expansion in professional service firms', *Human Relations* 54(7): 933–953.
Vogelpohl, A. (2017) 'Consulting completed: Temporal aspects of expertise in urban development during times of fast policies', *Geographica Helvetica (Special Edition Social Geography)* 72(1): 65–76.
Vogelpohl, A. (2018) 'Consulting as a threat to local democracy? Flexible management consultants, pacified citizens, and political tactics of strategic development in German cities', *Urban Geography* 39(9): 1345–1365.
Walters, W. (2012) *Governmentality: Critical Encounters*, London: Routledge.
Wedel, J.R. (2017) 'From power elites to influence elites: Resetting elite studies for the 21st century', *Theory, Culture & Society* 34(5–6): 153-178.
Ylönen, Matti, and Kuusela, Hanna. (2019) 'Consultocracy and its discontents: A critical typology and a call for a research agenda', *Governance* 32(2): 241–258.

Strategies and Practices of Professional Service Firms

America First: How Consultants Got into the Public Sector

Matthias Kipping

Introduction

In a recent article for ProPublica—a New York-based non-profit producing "investigative journalism in the public interest"—MacDougall (2020) detailed how, from March 2020 onward, McKinsey convinced various city, state, and federal agencies in the US, including the Department of Veteran Affairs, to use their services in dealing with the Covid-19 pandemic—without proper bidding processes, given the expediency. An email from the Managing Partner of McKinsey's Miami Office to a Miami Dade County official, reproduced by the investigators, shows how such work was obtained through little more than very generic promises of providing "COVID analytics" and "sharing best practices." It also contains a list of discounted "Covid pricing," where the rate for an "EM [=Engagement Manager] and 4 Associates or Business Analysts" was a whopping $178,000 per week. According to the author, by mid-July 2020, the consulting firm had collected around $100 million from the various agencies, without it being "clear what the government has gotten in return." McKinsey is no stranger to the US government, as I

M. Kipping (✉)
Schulich School of Business, York University, Toronto, ON, Canada
e-mail: mkipping@schulich.yorku.ca

C. Hurl and A. Vogelpohl (eds.), *Professional Service Firms and Politics in a Global Era*, https://doi.org/10.1007/978-3-030-72128-2_2

will show below. One of the recent—and most controversial—engagements concerned their role in an "organizational transformation" of Immigration and Customs Enforcement (ICE) initiated under President Obama and intensified as part of President Trump's crackdown on illegal immigrants, where McKinsey apparently helped ramp up hiring of ICE personnel, obtained "reductions in time to remove a detainee" and identified "detention savings opportunities" (MacDougall, 2019a).

McKinsey also worked with governments or state-owned enterprises elsewhere. The firm was hired by the European Union to create a "streamlined end-to-end asylum process" on Greek Islands in 2016 and 2017 (Stavinoha and Fotiadis, 2020) after conducting similar work in Germany since 2015 for tens of millions of Euros together with Ernst & Young and German consultant Roland Berger (Stanley-Becker, 2017). In South Africa McKinsey became entangled in a complex web of corruption, when it signed a contract with the state-owned power company Eskom, which could have potentially netted the firm $700 million (Bogdanich and Forsythe, 2018a). The scandal surrounding Eskom was so vast that it prompted a major inquiry by the country's Public Protector (2016) and eventually forced President Zuma to resign. McKinsey admitted an error in judgment and even repaid fees received—though without admitting any wrongdoing. State-owned enterprises also helped the firm gain a major presence in China though the kind of advice as well as its relationship with the Chinese government and Communist Party remain largely obscure (Bogdanich and Forsythe, 2018b). The same is true for its role in Saudi Arabia, where little will happen without the involvement or approval of the government. Carrying out close to 600 projects in the country between 2011 and 2016 (ibid.), the consulting firm was apparently sarcastically referred to by some Saudi bureaucrats as the "Ministry of McKinsey" (Saif, 2016).

It should be noted that controversies surrounding McKinsey's work are far from limited to the public sector. Some might recall its implication in the 2001 Enron scandal (McDonald, 2013). A more recent example is charges of advising "Purdue Pharma how to 'turbocharge' opioid sales" (Forsythe and Bogdanich, 2019). And, while McKinsey receives most attention—not surprising, given its status as "the world's best-known corporate management consultants" (MacDougall, 2020)—other consulting firms have their fair share of government work and related controversies. Thus, KPMG was also involved in the Eskom scandal, for which it issued a formal apology and returned or donated related fees

(Cropley and Brock, 2017). And the most famous whistle-blower of all, Edward Snowden, not only revealed that government agencies in the US spy on people around the world, but also gave a glimpse into the extent to which these agencies relied on external consultants—in his case Booz Allen Hamilton, a firm that was also embroiled in other controversies at the time (Chatterjee, 2013).

The most important thing to note—and the key to this chapter—is that none of this is new: neither the involvement of consultants in the public sector, nor the scrutiny it prompts or the scandals it occasionally causes. To give but one quite telling example from the beginning of the twentieth century—when McKinsey had yet to be founded—in 1913, the US Congress held hearings about the Taylor System of work study, prompted by the strike of workers against its implementation at the government arsenal in Watertown, Massachusetts two years earlier (Aitken, 1960). These public hearings increased the notoriety of Frederick W. Taylor—one of many proponents of such systems to measure and reward worker effort. These systems had already received a major boost from the future supreme court judge Louis Brandeis, who had argued at a hearing before the Interstate Commerce Commission in 1910 that the Eastern railroads did not need to increase their freight rates for its business clients, if only they applied the "scientific efficiency methods" developed by Taylor and others, many of whom he called upon to testify. Brandeis' claims of million-dollar daily savings caught the attention of the press (Kraines, 1960) and his terminology was used by Taylor in *The Principles of Scientific Management* published the following year, which became a national and international bestseller—all contributing to his current characterization as the "grandfather of consulting" (Engwall et al., 2016, 60 and 66).

This contribution complements the other chapters in this volume, which look in-depth at the more recent involvement of consultants in the public sector, by stressing that this involvement has a long history. And it provides an overview of that history in broad—rather than detailed—strokes, pointing to additional readings for those wanting to know more. It starts by sketching the growth of the consulting industry from modest and contested origins in the late nineteenth century to ubiquity and taken-for-grantedness today—all the while highlighting elements of continuity and change. The first substantive section demonstrates the early interactions between consultants and governments in the US and their subsequent expansion in scale, scope, and geography. The second examines the importance of the military as a site for consulting activity and of wars as a major catalyst for their expansion both at home and further afield. The third and final section looks beyond consulting projects, which marked the interaction between consultants and government in general and the military in particular, showing how they more permanently inserted themselves into the policymaking process via think tank-like activities and via their "alumni" entering politics and government. A brief outlook explains why they are there to stay.

It Comes in Waves: The Evolving Nature and Faces of the Consulting Industry

While some have gone back to look for the origins of management and of consulting in the bible or the oracles of ancient Greece, it is perhaps more pertinent to look to their rise alongside the growth of larger and more complex organizations during the first and second industrial revolutions, commencing, respectively, in the late eighteenth and nineteenth centuries (Engwall et al., 2016, 10–12). It was during the second that consulting became more commonplace, concentrating on the control over labor as well as the flows of raw material, production, and distribution—though the creation of accounting systems and the systematization of office work also played a role. That these developments started in the US is one of the reasons for the country becoming the cradle of management consulting activities and the birthplace of many of the firms providing them (see below for several other reasons). What needs to be stressed here is that the current term "management consulting" is of more recent origin being used first in the 1930s and more widely only after World War II. Earlier consultants tended to highlight their links to the extant professions, framing their activity as (cost) accountants or efficiency engineers or, if they did not have these credentials, as efficiency "experts." The interwar period saw the emergence of "management engineer" as the main term, combining the old with the new, while the leading management consultants after 1945 mimicked law firms in their partnership structure, the up-or-out promotion system, and even the dress code (McKenna, 2006). If these claims weren't hollow from the beginning—driven largely by legitimacy concerns—they have become increasingly so, with today's images of professionalism often relying on associations with elite competitive sport—see Accenture's (in)famous "Go on. Be a Tiger" advertising campaign with Tiger Woods as a recent example (Kipping, 2011).

Not only reference to extant professions or images of professionalism—and the related quests for legitimacy and visibility—changed over time, so did the dominant consulting firms, the background of their consultants, and the technologies (in the broadest sense of the term) they used to generate and present their advice. Regarding the evolution of these service providers Kipping (2002) has used the notions of "waves" and "generations" to highlight that they overlapped, often during prolonged periods, rather than neatly following each other in succession. The first wave started in the late nineteenth century and was marked mainly by engineers, often operating as individual practitioners, with the already mentioned Frederick W. Taylor (1856–1915) probably the most well-known among them. The leading early firms also employed at most a few hundred consultants—the organization created by the French immigrant Charles E. Bedaux in the US being the most visible and globally active during the interwar period. Among their main services were the introduction of efficiency enhancing systems on shop floors or in offices. These became increasingly sophisticated and were used well into the 1970s, when the firm founded by H.B. Maynard in 1934 based on the Methods-Time-Management (MTM) system was the largest US service provider in Western Europe according to the number of offices and consultants (Kipping, 1999). But it subsequently declined, and its small remaining operations were acquired, in 2007, by Accenture, which marked the end of the first wave—though many consulting firms continue to offer efficiency improvements today (Wright and Kipping, 2012).

The second wave originated during the interwar period but saw its greatest successes during the three decades of post-WWII growth. Among its protagonists, McKinsey is widely perceived—and projects itself—as the epitome of "modern" or "professional" management consulting (e.g., David et al., 2013; McKenna, 2006). Founded by University of Chicago accounting professor James O. McKinsey (1889–1937) in 1926, it employed experienced businessmen to conduct business surveys. McKinsey himself left in 1935 to become CEO at one of his clients, the Chicago department store Marshall Fields, but died two years later. The firm was transformed after World War II by the partners in its New York office, first and foremost Marvin Bower who held degrees from the Harvard Law and Business Schools. It was the innovations introduced in the 1950s, such as the hiring of MBA graduates from top business schools and the mimicry of law firms, including the up-or-out system that made it an exemplar of the second wave (see above). This eventually led to management consulting becoming a highly coveted destination for graduates of top universities and business schools (Rivera, 2015; Ruef, 2002). And McKinsey became a model for others—a model that also spread globally as the firm opened offices abroad from later that decade (Kipping, 1999; McDonald, 2013). During the 1960s and 1970s other firms, with a focus on strategy, joined this wave, namely the Boston Consulting Group (BCG) and Bain—the latter a spin-off from the former. The founder of what was to become Germany's most well-known consulting firm, Roland Berger, had also worked for BCG in Italy and the US before establishing his own organization in 1967 (Engwall et al., 2016, 183–184, 248–250).

The mainstay of the third wave, which started in the 1950s and surged since the 1990s, was large-scale organizational transformations involving information technology. Firms in this wave came from different backgrounds, including IT service providers, such as Electronic Data Services (EDS), that had emerged in the post-WWII period, hardware producers, like IBM, that gradually developed service activities (Engwall et al., 2016; Yost, 2017). But the firms that eventually dominated this wave were the large globally active accounting and audit firms, which represent an enduring undercurrent of the consulting industry since the nineteenth century, yet only came to the fore since the mid-twentieth century after a consolidation process. Initially, their consulting activities were limited, often related to bankruptcies. They set up separate management advisory departments after World War II and began offering IT-related services since the 1970s based on their own experiences with data processing (see Hurl in this volume). The fast growth of these consulting arms prompted internal tensions and, together with regulatory pressures, led to spin-offs, notably Accenture from Arthur Andersen (McDougald and Greenwood, 2012). But all firms rebuilt these lucrative activities and, as can be seen in Table 1, led the consulting industry in the 2010s in revenue and employment terms (Engwall et al., 2016, Chapter 14).

Such "expert" rankings have to be taken with a mountain of salt for a whole host of reasons. They are largely based on estimates, since some consulting firms don't share any revenue data and others don't provide an accurate breakdown for their different activities—hence the big gaps between most of the entries. Another reason might be the difficulty in distinguishing "true" management consulting from "pure" outsourcing,

Table 1 Rankings of the largest consulting firms in 2013 by two industry experts

	Gartner			*Kennedy*		
	Firm	*Revenue (billion US dollars)*	*Growth (%)*	*Firm*	*Revenue (billion US dollars)*	*Growth (%)*
1	Deloitte	14.7	6.0	Deloitte	18.3	7.0
2	PwC	12.7	10.0	PwC	16.1	10.5
3	EY	12.1	12.7	EY	13.7	10.1
4	KPMG	10.7	5.2	KPMG	11.3	6.5
5	Accenture	4.1	4.4	Accenture	7.3	−2.5
6	IBM	4.0	2.1	IBM	4.0	−0.4
7	McKinsey	2.3	5.5	McKinsey	5.9	4.5
8	Booz Allen Hamilton	2.1	−2.9	BCG	3.6	7.0
9	CGI	1.5	3.4	Booz Allen Hamilton	3.4	−5.5
10	CSC	1.4	−3.6	Mercer	3.3	1.6

Source Engwall et al. (2016, 241) (reproduced with permission)

which is also characteristic of these firms. The latter is often transformative, not just for the lives of those whose jobs are moved offshore, but also for the boundaries of the organization and its ongoing relationships with the now externalized activities. Most importantly, the largest and most well-known consulting firms only represent the tip of the iceberg of an industry that ranges from large global firms to a multitude of single practitioners, some of which set out to translate—literally and figuratively—the latest ideas peddled by the former for small and localized client organizations (see, e.g., Crucini and Kipping, 2001; Volkova in this volume). Moreover, it is an industry that changes constantly. Thus, if one had to redo the above table at the time of writing, possible additions might be (a) the large IT consultants originating in India, i.e., Tata Consultancy Services (TCS), Infosys, and Wipro—even if all of them have been struggling to move beyond outsourcing, and (b) the global advertising agencies like Publicis—though for them consulting is still a somewhat marginal, albeit growing activity (Engwall et al., 2016, 245; Kipping, 2019).

The public sector has played a crucial part in the development of consulting activities. First, and this is probably not stressed enough in the extant literature, by largely refraining from regulating the industry, allowing consultants to run wild, so to speak (for an overview, see Sturdy in this volume). Second, the public sector, in all of its manifold manifestations, has both been shaped by but also shaped management consulting from the outset—first and foremost, as the next section will suggest, in the US.

And There It Began: Consultants and the Making of Government in America

There are many reasons why management consulting as we know it originated in the US and why the country is still the home of many well-known consulting firms as well as being by far the largest consumer of these services. These reasons include the country's head start in the second industrial revolution with its large, increasingly unwieldy firms (see above) as well as the—related—early recourse to hired managers, which, in combination with the power of financial institutions and outside shareholders, created a need for the former to justify their decisions. This quest for legitimacy increased since the 1980s with financialization and pressure to manage in the interests of increasing "shareholder value"—thanks to Milton Friedman and Michael Jensen (see also Linovski in this volume). Also related is the early adoption of anti-trust legislation, starting with the Sherman Act of 1890, which made the sharing of ideas and practices among companies more complicated. And there was the pervasive merchant culture in the US, which saw knowledge as a tradable commodity rather than a common good (d'Iribarne, 1989).

Another—often overlooked but equally important—factor is the role of government. Historically, and culturally, the US has always been suspicious of government—a government that has been less professionalized and bureaucratized than in most other nation states—with a federal civil service only established in 1883. From the outset, the US government has therefore been more open to external influences, visible in the extraordinary number of lobbyists and the numerous high-level positions filled by so-called "in-and-outers," "individuals for whom government service is neither a profession nor a career" (Mackenzie, 1987, xiii; see also Heclo, 1988). Over time, the US government did become more structured and more involved, through laws and regulations, in individual, societal and economic activities. This happened in particular during the Progressive Era around the turn of the twentieth century, Roosevelt's New Deal in the 1930s, World War II and Lyndon B. Johnson's Great Society in the 1960s (Grisinger, 2012). It is important to note that in this system of "government without bureaucracy" (Rourke, 1992) consultants gained a significant and growing influence from the outset, and not only since the Reagan era and the triumph of "neoliberalism" in the 1980s. At the same time, these consultants came to increasingly rely on the federal, state, and municipal governments as well as numerous public agencies for their own revenue. The long-lasting and ongoing relationship between consultants and government in the US can therefore be characterized as co-evolutionary and mutually constitutive. A good illustration for the origins and development of this unique relationship is the consultants' role in three successive efforts to reorganize the federal government.

The first of these was the Dockery-Cockrell Commission (1893–1895), established by both chambers of Congress in 1893 to address the discrepancy between stagnant revenues and vastly increased expenditures of a federal government that had seen its number of employees triple since the early nineteenth century (see, for this and the following, Kraines, 1954). Its main remit was "to secure greater efficiency and economy" through "a reduction in the number or compensation of the persons authorized to be employed" though "without injury to the public service" (quoted ibid., 418). What is important to stress here, is that these efforts occurred contemporaneously with debates at the recently founded American Society of Mechanical Engineers (ASME), which aimed at improving efficiency in private industry, marked by increasingly large companies and growing tensions between managers, usually trained as engineers, and workers (Engwall et al., 2016, 64–65). It was here where Taylor, in 1895, first presented his ideas for a "piece rate-system" as "a partial step toward the solution of the labor problem," which he would further elaborate in *Shop Management* (1903) and *The Principles of Scientific Management* (1911) and which, as noted above, for many came to signify the starting point of the consulting industry.

However, already two years earlier the Dockery-Cockerill Commission relied on three "private professional business experts [...] in a general investigation of administration" (Kraines, 1954, 420). All three of them had significant experiences in the railway industry and expertise in designing accounting systems. And—demonstrating how the US government contributed to the development of consulting activities—after submitting their recommendations to the commission, two of them,

Charles W. Haskins (1852–1903) and Elijah W. Sells (1858–1924), established a firm with "the announced purpose of offering their services to corporations, trustees, assignees, receivers, committees, courts, municipalities, etc." (Haskin & Sells, 1935, 11). In 1972 it merged with the firm founded in 1845 in London, England by William Welch Deloitte into Deloitte Haskins & Sells, which after several additional combinations resulted in today's market leader (see Table 1).

The second example is the "President's Committee on Administrative Management" put in place by President Roosevelt in 1936 (see, e.g., Fesler, 1987; Arnold, 2007). When presented with the report in 1937, Roosevelt himself, succinctly summarized its ultimate objective: "The purpose of making Federal administrative management modern and businesslike is to make American democracy efficient."[1] The committee consisted of Louis Brownlow (1879–1963) as Chair, Charles Edward Merriam Jr. (1874–1953), and Luther Halsey Gulick III (1892–1993). All three belong to an era where boundary spanning individuals moved quite seamlessly between investigation—Brownlow used to be a journalist—or research—Merriam and Gulick were political science professors, respectively, at Chicago and Columbia Universities—practice—all of them held positions in public administration at some point in their careers—and consulting.

Among them, Gulick was probably the most visible and influential boundary spanner (Blumberg, 1981; Fitch, 1990). For his Ph.D. from Columbia University, he conducted a project on budgetary reform in Massachusetts. Subsequently, in 1921, he became director of the New York-based Institute for Public Administration (IPA), an early think tank (Smith, 1991)—a position he held for almost 40 years, followed by another two decades as chairman. In 1931, he was also appointed Eaton Professor of Municipal Science and Administration at Columbia. Among his most well-known publications are the *Papers on the Science of Administration* (Gulick and Urwick, 1937), which he originally compiled for the Brownlow Committee. Gulick left Columbia in 1942 to advise the US government during the war and post-war reconstruction efforts in Europe and Asia. Upon his return to New York, he directed a major reorganization of the municipal government in the early 1950s and was the first to occupy the newly created post of City Administrator in 1954

[1] https://www.presidency.ucsb.edu/documents/summary-the-report-the-committee-administrative-management.

though left it, in some frustration, two years later. During the late 1950s and early 1960s Gulick carried out consulting projects in Iran, India, and Egypt, funded among others by the Ford Foundation and the World Bank. Thereafter, he gradually withdrew from public life until his death, aged 100, in 1993.

While many of the consulting pioneers had similar boundary-spanning careers (see, for Taylor and McKinsey above; and C. B. Thompson below), since the 1930s public sector consulting gradually started to become the purview of the larger consulting firms, which had gained in prominence and size during the aftermath of the Great Depression. To no surprise therefore, the "Commission on Organization of the Executive Branch of the Government" in 1947 drew on firms rather than individuals for advice (McKenna, 2006, Chapter 4). Also known as the first Hoover Commission, since it was chaired by the former President Herbert C. Hoover, it continued the "managerialization" of the federal government (e.g., Arnold, 1976; Moe, 1982). For the firms involved in three of the approximately 20 task forces and for management consulting as a whole it provided visibility and legitimacy: (i) Trundle Engineering conducted a survey of Veterans Affairs; (ii) Robert Heller & Associates were asked to cut costs at the US Post Office; and (iii) Cresap, McCormick & Paget examined personnel management in the executive branch.

These projects—and the contacts made with the businesspeople heading many of the Commission's task forces—led to follow-up engagements both for those involved and others among the better-known firms, with Heller, for instance, asked to organize the newly created Department of Defense (DOD) and McKinsey working for the Atomic Energy Commission (AEC) in the early 1950s and the newly established National Aeronautics and Space Administration (NASA) in the late 1950s (McDonald, 2013). The involvement of a larger number of consulting firms in the second Hoover Commission from 1953 to 1955 confirmed the advance to what McKenna (2006) has called the "contractor state" and which Guttman and Willner (1976), more critically, referred to as "shadow government" by "private management consultants, 'experts,' and think tanks." As the examples cited in the Introduction suggest, this reliance of the US government and its agencies on consultants and the resulting reliance of consultants on public sector projects have not abated since—probably the opposite.

But while this kind of mutually constitutive relationship between management consultants and governments was and, probably, remains unique to the US, the former also made inroads into the public sector in other countries—generally later and more tentatively though usually earlier than is widely known. Thus, in the 1930s, Charles Bedaux, whose firm was the largest and most international at the time (see above), advised the government of Greece, which was facing a debt crisis at the time, and also visited the Soviet Union (Christy, 1984, 131–134; 192–193). The US consultant Wallace Clark worked with state monopolies in Poland, Romania, and Turkey (Wren, 2015). In France, the local consulting firm Paul Planus conducted studies for the national railways and the postal service in the 1930s (Moutet, 1997, 216; also, for public sector projects by other consultants)—more than a decade before Heller did the same for the US Postal Service—and reorganized the Budget department in the Finance Ministry in the early 1950s (Descamps, 2009). And in post-WWII Germany, as ongoing research by Marktanner (2021) shows, medium-sized German consulting firms conducted a variety of projects for regional and local administrations. It is only since the 1980s that the US- and UK-based global firms came to dominate public sector consulting elsewhere—albeit with some persistent national differences (see, for an overview, Saint-Martin, 2012; and numerous other contributions to this volume).

Military Connections: Accelerating Consulting Growth by Preparing for War

While the US federal government and its agencies were instrumental in the initial and subsequent growth of management consulting, it was the military and wars that accelerated its expansion. Armed conflicts, and preparation for such conflicts, played a catalytic role by widely spreading ideas and practices—within the military and, subsequently, into the private sector. And in the process, they fomented the growth and institutionalization of those who spread them, the consultants. To wit, in the UK during World War II, consultants were exempt from military service (Kipping, 1999). And once again, the relationship was mutually constitutive, if not dependent. Thus, in many cases the military relied on consultants for novel ideas, while developing or applying these ideas in the military gave consultants a launchpad for their more widespread dissemination. And, once again, this relationship between the military and consulting was there from the outset, in particular through efforts to make armaments production more efficient. The already mentioned strike of workers at the US government arsenal in Watertown against the introduction of the Taylor system in 1911 is probably the earliest known example. As noted, the strike and, even more so, the subsequent congressional hearings contributed to Taylor's notoriety at the time.

World War I played an important catalytic role, also in terms of projecting consultants and their ideas globally, as can be seen from two illustrative cases. One is the Gantt chart, a graphic planning and control tool—an example of what Hoof (2020) calls "visual management" (see esp. Chapter 2). Still in use today, it was developed during World War I by Henry L. Gantt (1861–1919), who had worked closely with Taylor before becoming an independent consultant in 1901. During the war, he developed the chart to schedule and coordinate munitions production at the US Army's Frankford Arsenal and then employed it successfully at the Emergency Fleet Corporation to coordinate the construction and launching of over 1200 vessels from close to 350 shipyards. After Gantt's death in 1919, two of his collaborators continued to promote the chart around the world: Wallace Clark in Western and Central Europe (Wren, 2015) and Walter Polakov, the "Red Taylorist," in Soviet Russia, where it was used in the first five-year plan (Kelly, 2020). Another example for how war accelerated the expansion of consulting is C. B. Thompson (1882–1969) (Wren et al., 2015). Holding degrees in law from the University of California as well as economics and sociology from Harvard University, Thompson became an early researcher—and critic—of Taylor and Taylorism. He lectured at the new Graduate School of Business Administration at Harvard since 1910 but, in 1916, turned down a professorship, moved to France to advise the Ministry of Armaments on efficient munitions production, and remained after the war, spreading not only his own efficiency system, but also the very idea of consulting. Among his collaborators was the abovementioned Paul Planus who, in 1929, established his own firm which conducted many projects in the public sector until the 1960s (see also Moutet, 1997).

An example spanning both world wars is the firm originally founded by the industrial psychologist Edwin G. Booz (1887–1951) in Evanston in 1914 (see for this and the following Kleiner, 2004; McKenna, 2006; Engwall et al., 2016). His first—temporary—association with the military occurred during World War I, when he joined his former mentor at Northwestern University, psychology professor Walter Dill Scott, to develop a system for the US Army that selected, placed, and promoted personnel, including officers, based on the required abilities for a given position. During the interwar period the firm mainly conducted business surveys for a wide range of private sector clients. But in 1940, Booz and his partners James L. Allen and Carl L. Hamilton took on a major project readying the US Navy for operations on two oceans, which, in hindsight, was "pivotal" for a "new, more expansive role as a partner to government" (Kleiner, 2004, 23).

After 1945, Booz, Allen & Hamilton continued to draw on its growing expertise in computing technology and operations research to work for various US government agencies, in particular the Department of Defense (DOD). Since 1955, much of this work was carried out by a Washington-based subsidiary, Booz Allen Applied Research, Inc. (BAARINC), which accounted for close to 40% of the firm's revenue. Among the ideas that also found application in the private sector was the Program Evaluation and Review Technique (PERT), originally developed for the US Navy's nuclear submarine program Polaris. BAARINC's contribution helped propel Booz Allen into the top three consulting firms in the US during the first post-WWII decades but also made it vulnerable to reductions in government funding. And while the firm suffered after the Vietnam War and the oil crises of the 1970s—compounded by some ill-timed, unrelated acquisitions—it thrived since the 1980s drawing on strong government relationships and technological know-how. In 2008 Booz Allen Hamilton spun off commercial operations as Booz & Co.—later acquired by PwC and renamed Strategy&—in order to focus on large-scale projects for defense and intelligence agencies. In 2013 its hitherto largely obscure role in (cyber)security and surveillance came into public view because of Edward Snowden (see above), with two journalists calling it "the world's most profitable spy organization" (Bennett and Riley, 2013; see, earlier, Shorrock, 2008).

Booz Allen had already worked with governments outside the US since the 1950s, often based on funding from the US Agency for International Development (AID), including projects in the Philippines, Egypt, Iran, and several Latin American countries. And among its earliest clients in Europe were companies belonging to the Italian state holding IRI (Kleiner, 2004). Not surprisingly, just like in the US, its more recent projects abroad have focused on cybersecurity, intelligence gathering, and the military, with those in the Middle East attracting particular attention. They include the creation of a National Security Agency (NSA) in the United Arab Emirates (Sanger and Perlroth, 2013) and, more recently, the training of cybersecurity experts and the Royal Navy in

Saudi Arabia (Forsythe et al., 2018). Here, as elsewhere, Booz Allen is not alone. The Boston Consulting Group (BCG) and McKinsey are also heavily invested in the Kingdom, with the combined fees of all three apparently reaching into the hundreds of million dollars (ibid.). While historically McKinsey was much less involved with the military proper (see above), it now seems to have discovered this lucrative market. Recently, it touted the introduction of "agility" in the British Army (Chinn et al., 2019), suggesting—though not explicitly confirming—that the firm was involved in this transformation. We do know for certain that McKinsey—alongside, among others, Accenture—was responsible for projects costing several hundred million Euros in the German Defense Ministry since the mid-2010s (see below).

What all these detailed examples show is how wars and the military acted as a catalyst or, using a recent expression, superspreader for consultants and their ideas in the US and elsewhere. They accelerated the dissemination of available management tools, such as the Gantt chart, or those developed in a military context, such as PERT, to the private sector. And while assisting armaments production might have been motivated by a sense of duty in some early cases, like C. B. Thompson, the armed forces and intelligence communities became increasingly important and lucrative clients, discovered early by the likes of Booz Allen and somewhat later by others like McKinsey. And similar to government-related work in general, military projects were also subject to the vagaries of public budgets. But, as the next section will discuss, consultants found ways to make their influence felt and their business grow more permanently.

Permanent Presence: Shaping Public Policy from the Outside and the Inside

The major challenge for any consultant and consulting firm is the temporary, project-based nature of their business. This is probably an even more pressing problem in the public sector, where budgets can be cut easily—except in war times—and are subject to considerable scrutiny—at least in democracies, which might explain some of their recently documented predilection for working in and with authoritarian regimes (Bogdanich and Forsythe, 2018b). Over time, consultants did find ways to make their influence and presence more stable and permanent. One of them, their involvement in think tanks, has a natural—hence, early—connection to the public sector. The other resulted from the combination of their increasing reputation with the up-or-out system of promotion, which put an increasing number of their more and more coveted alumni into leading positions, first in business but, more recently, also in the public sector.

Kipping (2021) has provided an overview of when, how, and why consultants became involved in the think tank realm. A number of the early consultants were not only connected to academia and practice but also involved in think tanks and their activities, which usually centered on generic rather than specific advice to policymakers (see, among others, Smith, 1991). That connection is most obvious in the case of Luther Gulick, who directed such an early think tank, the Institute for Public Administration (IPA). But others, including C.B. Thompson, were also loosely linked to think tanks—in his case the Twentieth Century Fund (TCF). During the post-WWII period, some consulting firms, notably the Stanford Research Institute (SRI) emulated think tanks in providing more general recommendations but it was mainly aimed at decision-makers in business, not government. A major change occurred in the late twentieth century when most of the top consulting firms established their own think tanks or research institutes—nominally separate from their commercial operations. McKinsey was the first in 1990 with its McKinsey Global Institute (MGI), but others followed suit and now include BCG's Henderson Institute (named after its founder), the IBM Institute for Business Value, and the Accenture Institute for High Performance, the latter tellingly describing itself as an "think and act tank" which "conducts breakthrough original research that helps businesses and governments achieve and sustain high performance."[2] And while their reports are mainly intended to inform—or rather, worry—business leaders about future trends, some of their topics, such as the "future of work" or "smart cities" are also of indirect or direct relevance for policymakers (see, for more details, Kipping, 2021).

Another way in which consulting firms have achieved some more permanence in their business was through the subsequent careers of their former consultants. While not automatically guaranteeing new projects, alumni networks helped by establishing more permanent relationships between the firm and its actual and potential client organizations. This depended on the decision-making level these alumni could aspire to, which in turn was dependent on the reputation of the consulting firm.

[2] https://newsroom.accenture.com/subjects/accenture-institute-for-high-performance/.

While journalists (esp. Byrnes, 1993) had already earlier identified some former McKinsey consultants in CEO positions, Mintzberg (1996, 66) characterized it as a systematic, post-MBA career path, pointing to "a new and more insidious track to the executive suite" through "work as a consultant with some prestigious firm for a time." He referred in particular to Louis V. Gerstner, who, after a Harvard MBA had started his career at McKinsey, then joined Amex before becoming CEO at RJR Nabisco and, ultimately, IBM. But while there have yet to be systematic and comprehensive studies (cf. Rivera, 2015), the growing number of known cases, which currently include Sundar Pichai, CEO of Google and its parent company Alphabet and Facebook COO Sheryl Sandberg (Engwall et al., 2016, 251), suggests that consulting alumni becoming CEOs has turned into a widespread phenomenon—and is no longer confined, if it ever was, to the private sector.

And in the public sector, it does not only include the leaders of state-owned companies—with *Deutsche Post* CEO Frank Appel, a former McKinsey consultant as a current example—it also reaches into the heart of government and the policymaking process. In the US, the abovementioned "in-and-outer" system seems to have facilitated the movement of people from consulting into the government. Kipping (2021) gives the example of Diana Farrell, who joined McKinsey after a Harvard MBA, rose through the ranks and became the Director of MGI, the firm's "think tank" (see above), before entering the Obama White House in 2009 as Deputy Director of the National Economic Council and Deputy Assistant to the President on Economic Policy, dealing in particular with the fallout from the 2008 financial crisis. She exited in 2011, rejoined McKinsey, co-founding and directing its "Center for Government." Then, and until recently, Farrell was President and Chief Executive Officer of the JPMorgan Chase Institute, which she founded in 2014 as a "think tank dedicated to delivering data-rich analyses and expert insights for the public good." Her trajectory, in many ways, resembles the boundary-spanning activities of Luther Gulick, discussed above, though with the crucial difference that these kinds of individuals are now part of an extensive—and actively maintained, if not managed—global alumni network. How deep this network has penetrated into the upper echelons of government and politics can be seen from President Biden considering Michèle Flournoy as possible Secretary of Defense. A veteran of the Clinton and Obama administration, Flournoy subsequently joined BCG as an advisor, helping them grow their defense-related business, and now sits on the

Board of Booz Allen Hamilton (see, for details and other examples, Guyer, 2020).

And neither are these cases limited to the US. Thus, the former British Foreign Secretary and Conservative Party Leader, William Hague, had also been a McKinsey consultant. And so was the current Greek Prime Minister, Kyriakos Mitsotakis, after, you guessed it, obtaining a Harvard MBA. Probably the most telling—and concerning—evidence comes from the role of consultants in the German Defense Ministry under the leadership of the current EU Commission President Ursula von der Leyen between 2013 and 2019. This received significant press coverage, spiraled into the so-called *Berateraffäre* or consultants' scandal, and was investigated by a parliamentary committee, which issued its 745-page report on September 16, 2020 (Deutscher Bundestag, 2020). The central person in this scandal was Katrin Suder. After a doctorate in physics at a German university, she joined McKinsey in 2000, became head of the firm's Berlin office in 2007 and responsible for its German public sector practice in 2009, directing projects for the Federal Employment Agency and the state of Berlin, among others. In 2014, von der Leyen asked her to join the ministry as the vice minister (*Staatssekretärin*) in charge of procurement. Suder was accused in the press and questioned by the investigative committee about allocating many costly projects to her own former firm and to consultants she knew at other firms—one project leader from Accenture, which conducted work on cybersecurity, recalled their friendship and joint family trip (Anon., 2020). During the hearings, Suder denied these allegations, while often claiming not to have any recollection. Both she and von der Leyen were exonerated from any wrongdoing with the votes of the governing coalition. Suder had left the ministry in April 2018 and a few months later accepted an invitation from the German government to chair the newly established Digitalization Council.

What all these examples show is how much it has not only become commonplace but also widely acceptable to find former consultants in high-level permanent positions in government and the public sector, even in Europe. Nevertheless, indications of them having favored their old buddies still caused a significant public uproar, at least in Germany. The time might nevertheless be near, when the in-and-outer trajectories between government and consulting practices in the US by the likes of Diana Farrell or Michèle Flournoy, will be equally frequent elsewhere. Thus, Katrin Suder brought one of her colleagues to the Ministry, who returned to McKinsey after a couple of years and now conducts projects in the aerospace and security industry (Anon., 2020).

No End in Sight: Summarizing and Looking Ahead

Many would suggest that the role of consultants in public policy and the public sector originated with—and can be explained by—neo-liberalism. This chapter has shown that the connection between consultants and governments goes back much further in time and was basically there from the outset of the consulting industry. It constitutes one of the reasons why the US became its cradle but also explains why the US government relied consistently and increasingly on outside advice. The chapter has also pointed to the key role played by the military and by wars in accelerating the expansion of consultants and consulting firms and the widespread dissemination of certain ideas. Last not least, it has shown how consultants went beyond project-based work and influenced public policy in the US—and increasingly elsewhere—through think tanks as well as the in-and-outer system, with the latter still somewhat less common in countries with more stable and established bureaucracies, where consultants often took more permanent positions.

While historians deal with the past, one cannot help but ask whether there is any chance of slowing down, stopping—let alone reversing—the momentum the consultants have created and accelerated over the past century and a half. Investigative journalists have done an admirable job in exposing some of the most shocking (wrong)doings by the consultants—though are largely ignored by the broader public and decision-makers, and consequently by the consulting firms. Rare was the statement issued by McKinsey (2019) in reaction to the investigations of its role in ICE—quickly rebutted by MacDougall (2019b). Academics have shown limited interest in a deeper examination of the consultants and their increasing influence on our economies and societies, this book being one of the rare exceptions. The reasons are manifold: lack of access, with most consulting work shrouded in secrecy; the difficulty of generalizing from such a complex phenomenon—with theory, rather than practice, having become the one-and-all for academic success; and, for some of those in the business schools, the hope of starting their own consulting business or at least increasing their chance of publishing in the *Harvard Business Review* with a consultant as a co-author.

Students will continue to flock in droves to these ever larger and ever more prestigious consulting firms—though the actual work is usually much less glamorous than expected. Already at the turn of the twenty-first century Accenture apparently attracted three million applicants per annum. And the consulting firms have done their utmost to maintain this flow of the "best and the brightest" (Rivera, 2015), especially with respect to the supposedly more conscious millennial generation by enrobing themselves with social and environmental responsibility, all the while continuing their highly lucrative work for the fossil fuel industry or for authoritarian governments. Most importantly, a stint in consulting has become increasingly helpful in gaining a more permanent position in other organizations. And these organizations now include the body politic and government, which before might have acted as a corrective for the excesses of the private sector but have increasingly given themselves up to the ideas (business knows best!) and the personnel from the consulting firms both as temporary advisors and, increasingly, as more or less permanent decision-makers. So far, nobody has contemplated a circuit breaker to stop the infection (former consultants should refrain from applying!) and an effective vaccine seems a long way off—and, as we know, consultants have been a long-standing advisor to big pharma anyway.

References

Aitken, H. (1960) *Taylorism at Watertown Arsenal: Scientific Management in Action, 1908–1915*, Cambridge, MA: Harvard University Press.

Anon (2020) 'McKinsey's Client Projects', *GERMAN-FOREIGN-POLICY.com*, 30 January.

Arnold, P.E. (1976) 'The First Hoover Commission and the Managerial Presidency', *Journal of Politics* 38(1): 46–70.

Arnold, P.E. (2007) 'The Brownlow Committee, Regulation, and the Presidency: Seventy Years Later', *Public Administration Review* 67(6): 1030–1040.

Bennett, D. and Riley, M. (2013) 'Booz Allen, The World's Most Profitable Spy Organization', *Bloomberg Businessweek*, 21 June.

Blumberg, S.K. (1981) 'Seven Decades of Public Administration: A Tribute to Luther Gulick', *Public Administration Review* 41(2): 245–248.

Bogdanich, W. and Forsythe, M. (2018a) 'How McKinsey Lost Its Way in South Africa', *New York Times*, 26 June.

Bogdanich, W. and Forsythe, M. (2018b) 'How McKinsey has Helped Raise the Stature of Authoritarian Governments', *New York Times*, 15 December.

Byrne, J. A. (1993) 'The McKinsey Mystique', *Businessweek*, 19 September.

Chatterjee, P. (2013) 'Investigate Booz Allen Hamilton, Not Edward Snowden', *Guardian*, 14 June.

Chinn, D. et al. (2019) 'Building Agility in the British Army's Headquarters', https://www.mckinsey.com/business-functions/organization/our-insights/building-agility-in-the-british-armys-headquarters, accessed 25 November 2020.

Christy, J. (1984) *The Price of Power: A Biography of Charles Eugène Bedaux*, Toronto: Doubleday.

Cropley, E. and Brock, J. (2017) 'KPMG's South Africa Bosses Purged Over Gupta Scandal', https://www.reuters.com/article/us-kpmg-safrica-idUSKCN1BQ16P, accessed 25 November 2020.

Crucini, C. and Kipping, M. (2001) 'Management Consultancies as Global Change Agents? Evidence from Italy', *Journal of Organizational Change Management* 14(6): 570–589.

David, R.J., Sine, W.D. and Haveman, H.A. (2013) 'Seizing Opportunity in Emerging Fields: How Institutional Entrepreneurs Legitimated the Professional form of Management Consulting', *Organization Science* 24(2): 356–377.

Descamps, F. (2009) 'Quand La Direction Du Budget Faisait Appel À Un Cabinet De Conseil Privé Pour Sa Propre Réorganisation.1950-1952', *Revue Française D'administration Publique* 131: 513–525.

d'Iribarne, P. (1989) *La Logique De L'honneur: Gestion Des Entreprises Et Traditions Nationales*, Paris: Seuil.

Deutscher Bundestag (2020) *Drucksache 19/22400: Beschlussempfehlung und Bericht des Verteidigungsausschusses als 1. Untersuchungsausschuss*, 16 November; https://dip21.bundestag.de/dip21/btd/19/224/1922400.pdf, accessed 27 November 2020.

Engwall, L., Kipping, M. and Üsdiken, B. (2016) *Defining Management: Business Schools, Consultants, Media*, New York: Routledge.

Fesler, J.W. (1987) 'The Brownlow Committee Fifty Years Later', *Public Administration Review* 47(4): 291–296.

Fitch, L.C. (1990) 'Luther Gulick', *Public Administration Review* 50(6): 604–608.

Forsythe, M. and Bogdanich, W. (2019) 'McKinsey Advised Purdue Pharma How to "Turbocharge" Opioid Sales, Lawsuit Says', *New York Times*, 1 February.

Forsythe, M., Mazzetti, M., Hubbard, B. and Bogdanich, W. (2018) 'Consulting Firms Keep Lucrative Saudi Alliance, Shaping Crown Prince's Vision', *New York Times*, 4 November.

Grisinger, J. (2012) *The Unwieldy American State: Administrative Politics Since the New Deal*, New York: Cambridge University Press.

Gulick, L.H. and Urwick, L. (1937) (eds). *Papers on the Science of Administration*, New York: Columbia University.

Guttman, D. and Willner, B. (1976) *The Shadow Government: The Government's Multi-Billion-Dollar Giveaway of Its Decision-Making Powers to Private Management Consultants, 'Experts,' and Think Tanks*, New York: Pantheon Books.

Guyer, J. (2020) 'How Biden's Foreign-Policy Team Got Rich: Strategic Consultants Will Define Biden's Relationship to the World', *American Prospect*, 6 July.

Haskins & Sells (1935) *Haskins & Sells, Certified Public Accountants. A History of the Origin and Growth of the Firm, 1895–1935*, New York: Haskins & Sells; https://egrove.olemiss.edu/dl_hs/1703, accessed 25 November 2020.

Heclo, H. (1988) 'The In-And-Outer System: A Critical Assessment', *Political Science Quarterly* 103(1): 37–56.

Hoof, F. (2020) *Angels of Efficiency: A Media History of Consulting*, Oxford: Oxford University Press.

Kelly, D. (2020) *The Red Taylorist: The Life and Times of Walter Nicholas Polakov*, Bingley, UK: Emerald.

Kipping, M. (1999) 'American Management Consulting Companies in Western Europe, 1920 to 1990: Products, Reputation and Relationships', *Business History Review* 73(2): 190–220.

Kipping, M. (2002) 'Trapped in their Wave: The Evolution of Management Consultancies', in T. Clark and R. Fincham (eds). *Critical Consulting: New Perspectives on the Management Advice Industry*, Oxford: Blackwell, pp. 28–49

Kipping, M. (2011) 'Hollow from the Start? Image Professionalism in Management Consulting', *Current Sociology* 59(4): 530–50.

Kipping, M. (2019) 'Masters of Global: Consultants and Internationalization', in T. Silva, C. Lubinski and H. Tworek (eds). *The Routledge Companion to Makers of Global Business*, London: Routledge, pp. 138–155.

Kipping, M. (2021) 'From Private Avice to Public Policy? The Evolution of Consultancy Think Tanks', in J. Landry (ed). *Critical Perspectives on Think Tanks: Power, Politics, Knowledge*, Aldershot: Edward Elgar.

Kleiner, A. (2004) *Booz Allen Hamilton: Helping Clients Envision the Future*, Old Saybrook, CT: Greenwich Publishing.

Kraines, O. (1954) 'The Dockery-Cockrell Commission, 1893–1895', *Western Political Quarterly* 7(3): 417–462.

Kraines, O. (1960) 'Brandeis' Philosophy of Scientific Management', *Western Political Quarterly* 13(1): 191–201.

Mackenzie, G.C. (1987) (ed). *The In-and-Outers: Presidential Appointees and Transient Government in Washington*, Baltimore, MD: Johns Hopkins University Press.

MacDougall, I. (2020) 'How McKinsey is Making $100 Million (and Counting) Advising on the Government's Bumbling Coronavirus Response', *ProPublica*, 15 July.

MacDougall, I. (2019a) 'How McKinsey Helped the Trump Administration Carry Out its Immigration Policies', *New York Times*, 3 December.

MacDougall, I. (2019b) 'McKinsey Called Our Story About its ICE Contract False. It's Not,' *ProPublica*, 16 December.

Marktanner, A. (2021) *Engineering Political Discourse: Business Consultants in the German Public Sector, 1950s to 1990s*. Paper presented at the Business History Conference online meeting, 11–13 March.

McDonald, D. (2013) *The Firm: The Story of McKinsey and Its Secret Influence on American Business*, New York: Simon & Schuster.

McDougald, M.S. and Greenwood, R. (2012) 'Cuckoo in the Nest? The Rise of Management Consulting in Large Accounting Firms', in M. Kipping and T. Clark (eds). *The Oxford Handbook of Management Consulting*, Oxford: Oxford University Press, pp. 93–116.

McKenna, C.D. (2006) *The World's Newest Profession: Management Consulting in the Twentieth Century*, New York: Cambridge University Press.

McKinsey (2019) 'McKinsey Statement on New York Times and ProPublica Article Regarding ICE and CBP', https://www.mckinsey.com/about-us/media/mckinsey-statement-on-new-york-times-and-propublica-article-regarding-ice-and-cbp, accessed 25 November 2020.

Mintzberg, H. (1996) 'Musings on Management', *Harvard Business Review* 74(4): 61–67.

Moe, R. C. (1982) *The Hoover Commissions Revisited*, Boulder, CO: Westview Press.

Moutet, A. (1997) *Les Logiques De L'entreprise: La Rationalisation Dans L'industrie Française De L'entre-deux-guerres*, Paris: Éditions de l'EHESS.

Public Protector (2016) *"State of Capture". A Report of the Public Protector, South Africa*, https://www.sahistory.org.za/archive/state-capture-report-public-protector-14-october-2016, accessed 25 November 2020.

Rivera, L. A. (2015) *Pedigree: How Elite Students Get Elite Jobs*, Princeton, NJ: Princeton University Press.

Ruef, M. (2002) 'At the Interstices of Organizations: The Expansion of the Management Consulting Profession, 1933–97', in K. Sahlin-Andersson and L. Engwall (eds). *The Expansion of Management Knowledge: Carriers, Flows, and Sources*, Stanford, CA: Stanford University Press, pp. 74–95.

Rourke, F.E. (1992) 'American Exceptionalism: Government Without Bureaucracy', in L.B. Hill (ed). *The State of Public Bureaucracy*, Armonk, NY: M.E. Sharpe, pp. 223–229.

Saif, S. (2016) 'When Consultants Reign', *Jacobin*, 9 May.

Saint-Martin, D. (2012) 'Governments and Management Consultants: Supply, Demand, and Effectiveness', in M. Kipping and T. Clark (eds). *The Oxford Handbook of Management Consulting*, Oxford: Oxford University Press, pp. 447–464.

Sanger, D.E. and Perlroth, N. (2013) 'After Profits, Defense Contractor Faces the Pitfalls of Cybersecurity', *New York Times*, 15 June.

Shorrock, T. (2008) *Spies for Hire: The Secret World of Intelligence Outsourcing*, New York: Simon & Schuster.

Smith, J. A. (1991) *Idea Brokers: Think Tanks and the Rise of the New Policy Elite*, New York: The Free Press.

Stanley-Becker, I. (2017) 'How McKinsey Quietly Shaped Europe's Response to the Refugee Crisis', *Washington Post*, 24 July.

Stavinoha, L. and Fotiadis, A. (2020) 'Asylum Outsourced: McKinsey's Secret Role in Europe's Refugee Crisis', *BalkanInsight*, 22 June.

Wren, D.A. (2015) 'Implementing the Gantt Chart in Europe and Britain: The Contributions of Wallace Clark', *Journal of Management History* 21(3): 309–327.

Wren, D.A., Greenwood, R.A., Teahen, J. and Bedeian, A.G. (2015) 'C. Bertrand Thompson and Management Consulting in Europe, 1917–1934', *Journal of Management History* 21(1): 15–39.

Wright, C. and Kipping, M. (2012) 'The Engineering Origins of Management Consulting—And Their Long Shadow', in M. Kipping and T. Clark (eds). *The Oxford Handbook of Management Consulting*, Oxford: Oxford University Press, pp. 29–49.

Yost, J. R. (2017) *Making IT Work: A History of the Computer Services Industry*, Cambridge, MA: MIT Press.

Taming Uncertainty: Climate Policymaking and the Spatial Politics of Privatized Advice

Svenja Keele

Introduction

This chapter makes two distinct but interrelated claims about public policymaking and private expertise in a global era. The first is that issues arising from rapid and globalized environmental change, including climate change, pose enormous and quite distinct policy challenges that are stimulating new advisory industries. The hyper-complexity of these problems—multi-scalar, multi-sector, cross-border, intergenerational, non-linear, and uncertain—genuinely confounds many long-standing policymaking practices. This complexity has driven demands from policymakers for new kinds of credible, contextualized, and actionable advice that, across many parts of the world, is being sourced (voluntarily or otherwise) from the private sector. Yet the industries that have emerged to provide a plethora of products and services to decision-makers remain largely unstudied (see e.g. Bouteligier, 2011; Lovell and Ghaleigh, 2013; Bock, 2014; Scott and Carter, 2019 for exceptions). Professional service firms—taken here to encompass firms selling management, legal, auditing, design and consulting services—have been quick

S. Keele (✉)
Monash University, 20 Chancellors Walk, Clayton, VIC, Australia
e-mail: Svenja.Keele@monash.edu

C. Hurl and A. Vogelpohl (eds.), *Professional Service Firms and Politics in a Global Era*, https://doi.org/10.1007/978-3-030-72128-2_3

to reconfigure existing networks, reputations, and techniques to assist governments assemble new policy domains and render these wicked problems governable.

The second claim is that a geographical perspective on the work of private sector experts provides crucial insights into the ways in which particular policy prescriptions are formulated, circulated, and legitimized. This perspective takes a situated approach to the practices and worlds of policymaking, interrogating the constitutive role of spatiality in the way we govern. Policy advisory work makes places as it assesses socio-environmental risk and prepares responses (Prince, 2014a); it forms relationships across space (McCann, 2008); and it itself is shaped by the spaces and mobilities of precarious commercialized professional work (Larner and Laurie, 2010) as much as by the multi-scalar and uncertain characteristics of unruly environmental policy issues. Geographical approaches attentive to spatial processes—spatial imaginaries, knowledge, relationships, and mobilities—offer powerful conceptual frameworks and methodological tools to study the practices and influence of private expertise in public policymaking more broadly, and contemporary global environmental change policy more specifically.

This chapter illustrates these arguments using a case study of climate adaptation consulting to the public sector in Australia, a country that is already experiencing the effects of unprecedented climatic conditions consistent with global heating projections and is also heavily reliant on the private sector to contribute to public policymaking. The chapter begins with a brief overview of the emergence of climate policy consulting from diverse origins in pre-existing consulting fields (Sect. 2). It then sketches a conceptual approach drawn from geographies of policy and power that makes visible both the topographical and topological spatial relations that policy consulting enacts (Sect. 3). The chapter illustrates this approach through a case study in Australia (Sect. 4). The following section (Sect. 5) highlights three ways in which public policymaking and professional service firms derive mutual benefit from the privatization of advice. First, consultants and bureaucrats have exploited the spatial politics of climate change to diversify and expand their influence whilst helping to accomplish multi-level climate policy. Second, consultants circulating best practice models of adaptation through practitioner networks have simultaneously entrenched public–private partnerships. Third, the work of consultancies in establishing global league tables of adaptation action has positioned them as locales of authority while enrolling places and communities in new forms of comparison and competition. The chapter concludes with a brief discussion of the implications of this research for understanding contemporary configurations of policy, commerciality, and expertise in rendering complex new issues governable (Sect. 6).

Climate Adaptation Policy and Its Advisory Industries

Climate change adaptation refers to the process of adjusting to actual or expected climate and its effects (IPCC, 2013). The scale and scope of the global adaptation task is becoming ever more urgent and extensive as the world's largest polluters fail to rein in global emissions (UNEP, 2019): under current policy commitments, we remain on track to experience on average 3 °C of global warming by 2100, far exceeding the globally agreed goal of 1.5 °C and target of 2 °C (Climate Action Tracker, 2019). Public policy has long been identified as an important mechanism to support effective and fair adaptation across multiple scales (Burton et al., 2002; Berrang-Ford et al., 2014; IPCC, 2014) and in the past two decades, climate change adaptation has emerged as a distinctive new field of public policymaking (Massey and Huitema, 2013). In particular, it is seen as a necessary enabling activity of government in order to overcome barriers to autonomous adaptation by individuals and organizations (Henstra, 2016).

Adaptation policy has changed substantially over that time, evolving from its earliest incarnations of awareness-raising and impact assessment to outlining programs of adaptive action and more recently to promoting innovation, marketization, and urban infrastructural renewal (Burton et al., 2002; Henstra, 2016; Keele, 2018). Contemporary adaptation policy varies across socio-political contexts but typical elements include: the provision of information about climate impacts to assist decision-making; the establishment of regulatory and other settings to encourage adaptive actions by individuals, communities, organizations, and markets; the management of climate impacts on public goods such as national parks, national security, and emergency management; and the provision of various types of welfare support to assist more vulnerable groups to adapt.

Adaptation policymaking is, however, notoriously fraught. Tangney (2017, 8) identifies four key reasons: "the complex, uncertain, multi-level and highly interconnected nature of individual adaptation problems; the pressing need to value future as well as present needs; the interdependence of climate adaptation policymaking with a broad range of concurrent policy priorities; and, the degree of political conflict climate adaptation issues provoke as a result of these characteristics." Given the inherent difficulties in projecting future socio-economic development pathways and future climatic changes, not to mention the downscaling of those projections to local scales, climate change adaptation also demands new ways to think about policymaking under conditions of extreme uncertainty (Buurman and Babovic, 2016).

The importance of knowledge—particularly expert scientific knowledge—in supporting evidence-based and effective climate policymaking has been a core principle of climate change research and communication efforts. Climate policymaking addresses a highly complex collective action problem and has been heavily predicated on complex social, environmental, and economic modeling tools and scenarios. Substantial funding and organizational efforts have been made by governments around the world to better bridge the science–policy divide and ensure salient, credible, and legitimate information is available (or even better, co-produced) with policymakers (Cash et al., 2003; Kirchhoff et al., 2015). This has culminated in recent efforts to drive a paradigm shift in climate knowledge systems from more linear models where information is "pushed out" to policymakers or "pulled in" from scientists to more iterative "service-based" models where climate intelligence is co-produced and closely reflects the needs of end-users (World Meteorological Association, 2011; Lourenço et al., 2016; Keele, 2019). In many parts of the world—particularly in advanced liberal democracies and at the international level, but increasingly in emerging economies of Asia, the Middle East, South America, and Eastern Europe—governments are turning to the private sector to provide these new "climate services" (Webber and Donner, 2017).

The advisory industry has arguably been one of the earliest "winners" from the rapidly emerging and hugely contested domain of climate policy. Professional service firms—from the Big Three management consultancies (McKinsey, Boston, and Bain) to the Big Four accounting and auditing firms (KPMG, Deloitte, EY, and PWC) as well as large design and engineering consulting firms (AECOM, Arup, Jacobs, GHD, and others)—have been early entrants and prominent players in the nascent climate services industry, and continue to actively shape the emergence of downstream markets (Lovell and Ghaleigh, 2013; EBI, 2015; Keele, 2018). A

2011 report on commercial opportunities arising from climate adaptation found, for example, that of the four sectors surveyed, professional services and consulting were stand-out beneficiaries, with almost a quarter of firms generating revenue in climate adaptation (EIU, 2011). The industry sits on the cusp of a major expansion, particularly in the context of unprecedented climatic extremes and impacts especially on coastal assets and other major economic sectors; the resurgent commitment to sustainable development goals, energy transitions, and infrastructure investment; and of course the tectonic shifts underway in corporate climate risk disclosure and financial practices (TCFD, 2019).

Consultants—for-profit, non-state actors selling their advisory services to clients on a fee-for-service basis typically under confidential contractual terms—offer a window into the unfolding interactions between private sector expertise and public policymaking. The global climate services industry is estimated to be worth in the order of US$3.55 billion globally (EBI, 2015). This is concentrated particularly in the USA, United Kingdom, parts of Europe, Canada, Australia, and New Zealand (Saint-Martin, 2012; IBISWorld, 2016a, 2016b) but professional service firms are also deeply embedded into international climate and development apparatuses (Donner and Webber, 2014). Detailed and comparative evidence of the extent of consulting usage is not yet available, but recent painstaking forensic accounting work found that upward of 10% of the UK's foreign aid budget earmarked for climate change went to western consultants, exceeding more than £875 million since 2011 (Apparicio, 2018) and similar questions could be asked about international programs funded by the Rockefeller Foundation, the World Bank, the Green Climate Fund and others.

The Spatial Politics of (Privatized) Expertise and Rule

Climate consulting remains virtually unstudied by scholars, with few exceptions. In the United Kingdom, Webb (2011) documented the use of risk assessment techniques procured from private sector consultants to formulate the country's first climate change adaptation plan. In India, Bahadur and Tanner (2014) revealed the tensions arising from two distinct epistemic communities, each containing a different consultancy firm, implementing global urban resilience programs in local places. Donner and Webber (2014) and Webber and Donner (2017), meanwhile, have conducted empirical work in the Pacific to trace the circulation of climate services and the implementation of adaptation aid programs by research agencies and consultants. While none of these studies foreground the work of consultants, the impact of geographical institutional logics on the usage and access of consultants to public policymaking is evident—whether that be through prevailing advanced liberal bureaucratic cultures, the legacy of colonialism, or the spatial dependencies fostered by international flows of aid.

Geographical perspectives make visible the ways in which space, and spatiality, is integral to the use and influence of private sector expertise in public policymaking, and in particular, to the way power is exercised in the co-constitution of expertise and rule (Larner and Walters, 2004; McCann, 2008; Prince, 2014a; Peck and Theodore, 2015). Political geographer John Allen (2003, 2004, 2009) provides a useful conceptual framework for organizing these relationships and effects based on three "spaces of power"—bounded territories, networked flows, and topological ties—that are each associated with different spatial vocabularies of power (see Allen, 2009 for further elaboration).

Territorial vocabularies of power are perhaps the most familiar to policy studies, predicated on the ways in which territories (such as the nation state) "contain" power, impose boundaries and borders, and operate in a tiered hierarchy of jurisdictional authority from the global to the local. This spatial vocabulary of power is evident, for example, in studies of multi-level policymaking and associated policy advisory communities (e.g. Howlett and Newman, 2010; Mavrot and Sager, 2018) or of the co-locational benefits and "buzz" of professionals with their clients particularly in urban agglomerations (e.g. Bathelt et al., 2004; Isaksen, 2004; Tether et al., 2012).

Networked vocabularies of power are widely used in studies of expertise and professional service firms, grounded in the growing influence of private sector actors and their ability to access horizontal networks across traditional territorial boundaries, reaching into other countries and other sectors (e.g. McCann, 2008; Peck and Theodore, 2010; Boussebaa et al., 2014). This form of inquiry is particularly attentive to the mobility of private sector experts (e.g. Larner and Laurie, 2010) and their role in the movement of policy ideas and tools, including policy failures (e.g. Lovell, 2019). A networked vocabulary of power also resonates through the importance of professional service firms' networked reputation in the purchasing behavior of clients (e.g. Glückler and Armbrüster, 2003; see

Volkova in this volume) or the way knowledge "pipelines" operate in the knowledge economy (e.g. Bathelt et al., 2004).

Topological vocabularies of power, by contrast, challenge the more fixed, topographical, conceptions of space articulated in territorial and networked power geometries. Topological vocabularies highlight how otherwise distant places can be made more proximate by establishing relations of "connection and simultaneity" (Allen, 2009, 17). Geographers have shown how the technocracy, including many professional service firms, is instrumental to achieving topological ties through their calculative practices of measurement (that inform or evaluate policy, for example) and their claims to a "certain disembodied, universal rationality" that is "abstract, apolitical and technical" (Prince, 2016, 2). These knowledge practices and rationalities create new spaces of global competition and comparison (Larner and Le Heron, 2002), and allow some places to loom larger in policymaking while others recede into obscurity (Prince, 2014a).

Private sector experts like consultants rarely operate in a single spatial register of power. Indeed, their blurred structural position and fluid hybridity as professionals, experts, practitioners, managers, business people, and/or contracted labor allows them to enact different spatial relations of power to their advantage, or to that of their clients. To illustrate this conceptual framework, this chapter studies adaptation policymaking as a governmental activity that is constituted by (and in turn constitutes) recognizable political rationalities; a range of expert practices and technologies; adaptive expert or bureaucratic subjects as much as adaptive citizens and natures; alongside specific spatial imaginaries and vocabularies of power.

The empirical analysis presented in the next section highlights these three forms of spatiality—territorial, networked, and topological—in the ways that climate consulting has shaped adaptation policymaking, and benefitted in return. To do so, it draws from a larger program of research that combined an historical analysis of climate adaptation policy consulting over a period of two decades with an institutional ethnography of the climate consulting industry as it unfolded over a two-year period (Keele, 2018). The study constructed a genealogical "analytic of government" (Dean, 2010) that traced key shifts in the underlying rationalities, technologies, and spatial imaginaries of climate adaptation policy and its principal evidence bases. The study complemented this by tracing the practices, stories, tools, and collaborations (Li, 2007) through which consultants advised governments on adaptation policy and programs.

Multiple sources of data were used in the study, including more than 150 hours of participant-observation during a regional climate adaptation consulting project; 23 days of observation at adaptation conferences and events; 45 semi-structured interviews with adaptation consultants, government clients, and other key informants (e.g. from industry associations); plus more than 400 documents from public adaptation policy, government procurement, and individual consultancy firms (see Keele, 2018 for full methodology).

Australia: A Global Leader in Adaptation Planning and Consulting Use

The research informing this chapter turned to Australia to examine the role and influence of consultants in policymaking. Three features of the Australian context make it a highly instrumental case study. The first is its stark climate change vulnerability. Australia is one of the most at-risk developed countries in the world to the impacts of climate change; a condition exacerbated by Australia's already highly variable climate regime, its expensive (and largely coastal) infrastructure systems, its economic dependence on natural resource-based industries (e.g. agricultural production, mining, and tourism), and its natural limits to adaptation (particularly in its alpine, reef and hydrological systems) (Reisinger et al., 2014). A series of unprecedented climatic disasters over the past two decades, beginning with the Millennium Drought (1998–2009) and culminating in the continental-scale bushfires in 2019–2020, have given shocking immediacy to potentially catastrophic climate futures.

The second reason is a widespread commitment across all Australian states and territories and through all levels of government to support climate change adaptation together with the use of diverse policy instruments to enact those commitments. Set in contrast to Australia's highly partisan and contested politics of greenhouse gas mitigation that makes it a global laggard in tackling climate change (GermanWatch, 2020), adaptation has emerged as a more stable object of climate policy and funding. All states and territories have active adaptation policies and plans; three states have passed climate legislation supporting the consideration of climate in public decision-making; federal and state governments have funded multiple programs to support the vast majority of c.550 local governments to carry out climate risk assessments and adaptation plans (Webb and Beh, 2013); and between 2008 and 2013 the Australian

Government funded one of the world's most prolific applied adaptation research facilities (National Climate Change Adaptation Research Facility). More recently, climate adaptation policy has become closely entangled with national reforms to disaster risk reduction and the international urban resilience agenda.

The third reason for selecting Australia is its remarkably high dependence on consulting services. Australian governments are reported as the world's second highest users of consultants (Creighton, 2014) with annual spending of close to $1bn representing almost a quarter of spending on consultants by Australian governments and businesses (Creighton, 2015). Over two decades public sector reform has contributed to a bureaucratic culture that aspires to best value procurement, evidence-based policymaking, and a lean public service (Orchard, 1998; O'Flynn, 2007). This trend has attracted significant scrutiny and debate in recent years, with two auditor-general reports and a senate inquiry drawing attention to the widespread use of professional service firms and highlighting critical problems with defining, reporting, and validating consulting procurement data (Auditor-General, 2017; NSW Auditor-General, 2018). This prompted public debate about impacts on the capacity and independence of Australian public services (e.g. Tadros and McIlroy, 2018).

Consulting on Adaptation Policy

Over the past decade and a half, Australian governments in all states and territories have progressively turned to private sector consultants as important providers of climate adaptation advice, products, and services. The ecosystem of consultancy actors that has emerged to meet (and cultivate) this growing demand for adaptation consulting is unusually diverse, with all major types of consulting firms represented in the field. In particular, it is a policymaking sphere where both auditing/accounting consultancies (KPMG, EY, PWC, and Deloitte) and engineering/design consultancies (AECOM, GHD, Arup, Jacobs, WSP, and others) are active competitors alongside a suite of smaller economic, public policy, environmental and other specialist firms (such as Marsden Jacob Associates, SGS Planning, Climate Risk, ERM, Seed Consulting, Edge Environment, and others) (Keele, 2018).

The types of policy work outsourced to the private sector have been diverse: from conducting climate risk and vulnerability assessments to collating best practice case studies; from preparing methodological guidance documents to developing decision support software tools and new rating schemes. This indicates both the breadth of techno-managerial instruments—models, maps, indicators, codes, and training—used to shape adaptation policy and practice as well as the extent of private authority—those aspects of adaptation planning that the Australian public sector appears *able* (accountably and transparently) to procure from consultants, and/or for which consultants are seen as *suitable* (credible and efficient) sources of such advice—operating in climate policymaking.

Territorial Effects: Accomplishing Multi-Scalar Climate Governance

A longitudinal study of the use of consulting in adaptation policymaking shows how this mode of advisory work was used to enact relations of power that simultaneously expanded the reach of consultants and entrenched a nested, multi-scalar arrangement of governing climate change. This has partially shifted responsibility but not necessarily commensurate authority to other scales of government, allowing federal and state governments to continue to "govern at a distance" (Rose and Miller, 2010, 282). These territorial politics of climate change have unfolded in part due to the nature of consulting work but also to the specific histories of State restructuring and environmental governance in Australia. Three brief examples illustrate this.

In 2004, a well-known Australian economic and public policy consulting firm, Allens Consulting, was engaged by the federal government for the first major adaptation consultancy commission in Australia. The consultants were engaged to "provide a high-level strategic risk and vulnerability assessment of climate change impacts for Australia" (Allen Consulting Group, 2004, 2). This consulting work was pivotal in translating climate change from a science problem to a policy problem: the resulting "Allens Report" became the principal evidence base informing the Australian Government's first coordinated *National Climate Change Adaptation Programme* in 2005. A key outcome of the consultancy task was to articulate and substantiate the national strategic (economic) importance of unavoidable climate change. The use of this spatial imaginary, along with associated discursive frames and modeling techniques, legitimized the federal government's sovereignty over these issues and authorized the subsequent allocation of federal funds to direct national adaptation efforts via policy, regulation, funding inducements, and new national research collaborations. This maneuver unfolded in the context of a longer history of political and constitutional struggle between the Australian states and the federation on issues of environmental policy, and further entrenched a trend in recent decades of centralizing environmental governance (Hollander, 2010).

The subnational spatial category of the "region" has also become a core organizing unit for adaptation planning and policy in Australia. The framing of the region as an appropriate scale at which to evaluate the relative importance of climate impacts had been established in the Allens Report (2005). However, subsequent consultancy commissions became instrumental in operationalizing, disseminating, and institutionalizing that approach. By way of example, a public–private research collaboration between government-consulting science agency in the state of South Australia produced an influential adaptation planning methodology in 2011 that focused on the socio-ecological region (i.e. defined by natural resource management boards or economic development agencies) to conduct integrated climate risk and vulnerability assessments and regional adaptation plans. This collaboration catapulted two consultancy firms—one local, one national—to the forefront of this market for a period of time, before being mobilized across jurisdictions to other parts of Australia, encouraging alliances of local governments into regional-scale governance arrangements (while also increasing their purchasing power for large consultancy firms). Australia's great experiment with regionalism has been well documented (e.g. Wallington et al., 2008; Curtis et al., 2014); however, what has received less attention has been the role that "floating" actors like private sector experts have played in facilitating and legitimizing this regionalism. The lack of existing strong governance capacity at the regional level helped to cultivate a demand for independent facilitators and technical advisors.

The most local layer of government in Australia—councils—was also enrolled in climate risk assessment methodologies and adaptation planning processes through a series of federal and state funding programs. These programs created conditions highly conducive to the use of private sector experts and in fact the earliest incarnations—including the Integrated Assessments on Human Settlements Sub Program and the Local Adaptation Pathways Program—stipulated both the risk-based methodology that councils were required to follow (developed in a consultancy commissioned by the federal government) and the use of a consultant advisor from a pre-selected panel (to which the authors of the methodology were appointed). Altogether, close to a dozen programs have used public funding to catalyze the private adaptation consulting industry—in essence facilitating "rent extraction" (Barnett, 2020)—and enabling an additional cohort of environmental, design, and management consultancy firms in bidding for this work and building their track record. These programs also altered the spatial reach of these consultancy firms, with many utilizing these opportunities to capitalize on "local" knowledge and networks but also to then leverage existing experience into new areas.

Network Effects: Competitive Collaborations and Showcase Events

The multi-sited ethnographic study of consulting also revealed how private sector advisors were able to create models of adaptation policymaking from publicly funded pilot projects and circulate them through practitioner networks, expanding their reach into new markets and normalizing public–private partnerships as an appropriate model for adaptation policymaking. Emphasis is also given here to the role of conferences in convening network participants in space and time (including virtually, through social media) and creating opportunities for consultants (and their clients) to showcase adaptation policy or planning projects to build credibility and facilitate their mobility.

Government clients routinely cited consultants' ability to access knowledge networks (whether that be from other countries, other cities, other industries) as one of the key reasons to outsource for specialist advice. The international and cross-sectoral reach of consultancy firms together with their internal knowledge management practices (Amin and Cohendet, 2005) are seen to give consultants a unique ability to find and combine different types of inputs for adaptation policymaking. The additional ability of private sector advisors like consultants (Freeman, 2007) to synthesize diverse types of technical knowledge (e.g. climatic, ecological, economic, demographic, engineering, and others) to produce politically palatable options and recommendations is another justification for governments seeking policy advice from the private sector.

One of the most notable features of climate policy consulting in the past two decades has been the influential iteration between discrete advisory projects and the circulation of learnings (often as products) through wider networks: as Grabher (2004) has neatly summarized, we have witnessed "learning in projects, remembering in networks." Consultants have been a key driver and beneficiary of the projectification of climate adaptation, including the projectification of policy development. Time and again, influential climate adaptation planning methodologies have been produced in innovative, pilot, or seed projects involving government and consultants (and sometimes other organizations from the research or community sectors), presented at climate adaptation practitioner conferences, and then observed circulating into new councils, new regions, and new sectors.

One such example is AdaptWater™, an award-winning climate adaptation decision support software tool for the water sector. This was initially co-developed by a water utilities association and a niche climate change consultancy firm in a pilot project. Semi-privatized corporate information about public water management infrastructure and public climate change science were collated by the consultant, in collaboration with the wider project team, and used to develop a customized climate change risk assessment software tool. This tool received an award in 2011 from the national adaptation research facility and was presented at multiple adaptation practitioner events in subsequent years. At the 2014 national climate adaptation conference, for example, the consultancy firm hosted a free showcase of AdaptWater™ in partnership with their (quasi-public sector) client. The showcase was pitched at giving delegates a "more detailed understanding of how the tool works and the potential for application within their own organization," thereby exposing a new audience of potential clients to the tool and gathering valuable industry intelligence. This session was complemented by a session the next day offering a free training session in a spinoff tool AdaptInfrastructure™ which has been "diversified for other sectors." Since then, this tool has been circulated across multiple water utilities in Australia, its scope has been broadened to encompass other linear infrastructure asset classes, and the software-as-service offering has been mobilized through practitioner networks, transgressing both public–private and territorial boundaries. In a recent development the consultancy firm has partnered with a former climate policymaker-turned-consultant to launch next generation decision support software capable of producing "investment grade analysis of physical climate risk," which has in turn been circulated internationally through the networked relationships of these consultancy firms with international agencies, multilateral banks, and global reinsurance companies.

These twinned abilities to access, combine, and localize knowledges through multiple horizontal and networked flows of information and experience also position consultants as credible convenors across stakeholder groups (and their associated knowledge bases), particularly between government and business. Consultants have proven highly influential intermediaries in bringing together public and private dimensions of climate change adaptation (Tompkins and Eakin, 2012), in performing adaptation policymaking that operationalizes public–private partnerships and in entrenching these as the most appropriate models to tackle the impacts of climate change. This has shaped the role for the State as well as cultivating ongoing roles for consultants and other private sector actors. A good example of this has been the collaborative work of consultants, professional associations, government, and the built environment industry to develop and deliver the nation's pre-eminent professional development in climate change adaptation (through the *Learn to Adapt* program). This networked collaboration not only entrenches private authority in climate-proofing public infrastructure projects but it also creates new opportunities for competitive policy advisory work for the consultants who have donated time and expertise to develop the climate adaptation planning guidelines, training manuals, and rating schemes. Consultants have been highly successful in exploiting the productive tension between collaboration and competition across professional service firms.

Topological Effects: Creating Value Between Universality and Specificity

Interrogating the policy work of climate consultants also reveals how these private sector actors sustain claims to "universal" knowledges and actively work to establish new forms of calculation and measurement (such as global league tables of adaptation action or catalogs of international best practice in adaptation). This work has the effect of placing Australian adaptation policymaking into new global relations of comparison and enrolling Australian places and communities in new spaces of competition on the basis of their climate vulnerabilities, risks, and adaptations. It also has the effect of creating a role for consultants to generate "value" in the re-localization of these so-called universal knowledges in the preparation of context-specific of advice. These claims and techniques of universal knowledge have proven particularly easy to package and circulate through "fast policy networks" (Peck and Theodore, 2015) or through "global policy assemblages" (Prince, 2010), creating pathways for consultancy brands and reputations to follow that overflow bounded territories or even established public–private networks.

Widely sold adaptation consulting services—including physical or transition-risk matrices or coastal inundation models or disclosure regimes based on international standards, for example—are grounded in claims and techniques of techno-managerial "universality" (Thrift, 1997), and have been highly influential in shaping adaptation policy in Australia (and elsewhere). Consultancy firms of different hues—management, economic, engineering, and environmental—have all been quick to repurpose existing calculative tools and products to evaluate climate risks and adaptation options. Another form of climate consulting—procedural advisory services such as techniques of stakeholder consultation, vulnerability assessment, or scenario planning—is often overlooked but similarly lays claim to universality, particularly when these techniques are abstracted, codified, and commodified by private sector experts (Suddaby and Greenwood, 2001) and then stipulated as globally applicable indicators of "good governance" or "participatory policymaking." These too have been rapidly developed by consultancy firms with stakeholder consultation, impact assessment, and project management experience.

In several influential commissions shaping adaptation policy, consultants have actively worked to develop conceptual models and assessment techniques that attempt to erase geographical difference and distance. One example is global design firm Arup's work with the Rockefeller Foundation to produce a City Resilience Index that can "land" in any city in the world and is used to evaluate the climate resilience of the urban system or to compare and contrast cities globally: as Arup has written, the "international and flexible nature of the index enables a wider understanding beyond that of the usual local or national approach" (Arup, 2017, np). Of course, in practice, the actual application of this "relevant, robust, and globally applicable" index to local contexts involves substantial translation work, which has been managed by "Strategy Partners" funded by the Rockefeller Foundation through the 100 Resilient Cities program. The majority of these Strategy Partners were large consultancy firms like AECOM, Arup, Buro Happold, and others. This is a well-known model for revenue generation: as one interviewee described: "From a consultant's point of view, if you can have a tool which is proprietary but is reputable and you can use, and then train people how to use the tool and so on…there's a whole downstream service there."

In another example, geographic distance is not so much erased as re-folded into new lines of proximity (Prince, 2016). The *Climate Adaptation Manual for Local Government: Embedding Resilience to Climate Change* was developed for the Australia Centre of Excellence for Local Government (ACELG) by an international engineering and resource management consultancy firm. The manual claims to "gather leading practice within local government… [to develop] a categorization and definition of five different [adaptation] embedding approaches or models, and a step-by-step framework for effectively embedding resilience to climate change into council operations" (Inglis et al., 2014, 2). The models and framework reveal strong managerial technologies, based around stock-taking, goal-setting, gap analysis, and pathway planning. These process standards are demonstrated through a number of illustrative case studies, "selected for inclusion based on their transferability" (Inglis et al., 2014, 3), and they bring into the Australian local government sector a number of examples from appropriately "similar" cities overseas (including from Canada, the USA, Mexico, the Netherlands, and the United Kingdom).

In products such as this, narratives and other heuristics about organizational learning are constructed, formalized, and circulated—not so much abstracted in the same sense that an economic model abstracts and simplifies the world, but an abstraction nonetheless (Paschen and Ison, 2014). What becomes commodified by consultants is the insider knowledge, the enacted practice, and the international linkages that they have accrued in delivering the initial project, which can then be made available to other clients or even to other consultants elsewhere. These commodities powerfully shape what "good" adaptation planning is understood to involve and position consultants as credible purveyors of these truths. They are also underpinned by a spatial logic that establishes the commensurability of local government organizations in different places (Bulkeley, 2005; Prince, 2012) and brings these into spaces of (competitive) comparison (Larner and Le Heron, 2002; Kantola and Seeck, 2011). This is not achieved through traditional calculative practices, but rather through the logics of managerialism and attempts to inculcate new norms for leading adaptation planners.

Conclusions

The chapter has argued that environmental and sustainability issues represent a difficult, yet increasingly important, domain for government and business. Policymaking in these spheres demands new forms of advice, often provided by private sector experts—technocrats drawing on the credibility and calculative practices of the natural, economic, engineering, and social sciences but simultaneously commercial actors in the business of selling ideas for profit. Evidence suggests that the work of consultants has been crucial to the ability of governments to render complex issues like adapting to climate change governable. Climate adaptation consulting is a rapidly emerging and diversifying market—it is naturally expansive and is a key part of the way governments (and business) formulate responses to this pressing issue. In particular, consultants have been highly influential in their ability to translate unfamiliar problems like climate change adaptation into familiar (techno-managerial) concepts that can be operationalized as tools then circulated, commercialized, and ultimately used by governments and businesses to tame the existential threats posed by dangerous climate change.

At the same time, this chapter has highlighted how public policymaking—whether for climate adaptation or other issues—produces and is produced by spatial processes, categories, and effects. The privatization of policy advice, and the reliance of governments on actors like consultants, has introduced and legitimized new forms of spatiality into our policy responses to a changing climate. Consultants have actively helped to construct the spatiality of the climate governance regime in Australia, simultaneously embedding themselves deeply into the multiple spatial relations that characterize adaptation policy—whether territorial, networked, or topological. Through its illustrative examples, this chapter has identified different ways in which consultants have been enrolled—through their contractual conditions, their reputations, their mobilities, and their knowledge products—in allocating roles and responsibilities for climate change adaptation across multiple levels of government as well as in creating new patterns of collaboration and competition as cities and other places race to report on their climate risks and their adaptation planning actions. Scrutinizing their involvement in policymaking for this complex collective action problem helps to explain the shifting and blurring of boundaries between public and private, and opens up new ways of seeing how power operates over different spatial scales. It also makes visible the practices that cultivate demands for the blended expertise and cross-sectoral reach that consultants provide and legitimize climate policy problematizations and interventions rendering cities, infrastructure, coastal communities, and other socio-spatial categories legible for "climate-proofing" investment.

Acknowledgements I would like to acknowledge the receipt of an Australian Postgraduate Award along with the supervisory guidance of Professor Ruth Fincher, Associate Professor Lauren Rickards, and Dr. Sonia Graham that supported the research project underpinning this chapter. This article has benefitted from generous readings by Dr. Elissa Waters, Professor Andrew Sturdy, Professor Anne Vogelpohl, and Associate Professor Chris Hurl although all errors remain the author's own.

References

Allen Consulting Group (2004) *Responding to Climate Change: An Issues Paper*, Canberra: Allen Consulting Group, p. 19.

Allen Consulting Group (2005) *Climate Change Risk and Vulnerability—Promoting an Efficient Adaptation Response in Australia: Final Report*. Australian Greenhouse Office. Canberra: Commonwealth of Australia, p. 159.

Allen, J. (2003) *Lost geographies of power*. Malden, MA: Blackwell.

Allen, J. (2004) 'The whereabouts of power: Politics, government and space', *Geografiska Annaler: Series B, Human Geography* 86(1): 19–32.

Allen, J. (2009) 'Three spaces of power: Territory, networks, plus a topological twist in the tale of domination and authority', *Journal of Power* 2(2): 197–212.

Amin, A. and Cohendet, P. (2005) 'Geographies of knowledge formation in firms', *Industry and Innovation* 12(4): 465–486.

Apparicio, S. (2018) *One Tenth of UK Climate Aid Spent Through Western Consultants*. Climate Home News. London: Climate Home News.

Arup (2017) *Facing up to the future: The City Resilience Index*, https://www.arup.com/perspectives/city-resilience-index, accessed 26 October 2020.

Auditor-General (2017) *Australian Government Procurement Contract Reporting*. Information Report. Barton, ACT: Australian National Audit Office. ANAO Report No. 19 2017–18.

Bahadur, A. V. and Tanner, T. (2014) 'Policy climates and climate policies: Analysing the politics of building urban climate change resilience', *Urban Climate* 7: 20–32.

Barnett, J. (2020) 'Global environmental change II: Political economies of vulnerability to climate change', *Progress in Human Geography* 44(6): 1172–1184.

Bathelt, H., A. Malmberg, A. and Maskell, P. (2004) 'Clusters and knowledge: Local buzz, global pipelines and the process of knowledge creation', *Progress in Human Geography* 28(1): 31–56.

Berrang-Ford, L., Ford, J.D. Lesnikowski, A., Poutiainen, C., Barrera, M. and Heymann, S.J. (2014) 'What drives national adaptation? A global assessment', *Climatic Change* 124(1): 441–450.

Bock, S. (2014) 'Politicized expertise—An analysis of the political dimensions of consultants' policy recommendations to developing countries with a case study of McKinsey's advice on REDD + policies', *Innovation: The European Journal of Social Science Research* 27(4): 379–397.

Boussebaa, M., Sturdy, A. and Morgan, G. (2014) 'Learning from the world? Horizontal knowledge flows and geopolitics in international consulting firms', *International Journal of Human Resource Management* 25(9): 1227–1242.

Bouteligier, S. (2011) 'Exploring the agency of global environmental consultancy firms in earth system governance', *International Environmental Agreements-Politics Law And Economics* 11(1): 43–61.

Bulkeley, H. (2005) 'Reconfiguring environmental governance: Towards a politics of scales and networks', *Political Geography* 24(8): 875–902.

Burton, I., Huq, S., Lim, B., Pilifosova, O. and Schipper, E.L. (2002) 'From impacts assessment to adaptation priorities: The shaping of adaptation policy', *Climate Policy* 2(2): 145–159.

Buurman, J. and Babovic, V. (2016) 'Adaptation pathways and real options analysis: An approach to deep uncertainty in climate change adaptation policies', *Policy and Society* 35(2): 137–150.

Cash, D.W., Clark, W.C., Alcock, F., Dickson, N.M., Eckley, N., Guston, D.H., Jäger, J. and Mitchell, R.B. (2003) 'Knowledge systems for sustainable development', *Proceedings of the National Academy of Sciences* 100(14): 8086–8091.

Climate Action Tracker (2019) *Global Warming Projections: Global Update*. Climate Action Tracker, https://climateactiontracker.org/, accessed 30 March 2020.

Creighton, A. (2014) 'Australia second only to Britain in use of consultants', *The Australian*, Sydney, Australia: News Corp Australia.

Creighton, A. (2015) 'Governments spend near $1bn a year on consultants', *The Australian*, Sydney, Australia: News Corp Australia.

Curtis, A., Ross, H., Marshall, G., Baldwin, C., Cavaye, J., Freeman, C., Carr, A. and Syme, G.J. (2014) 'The great experiment with devolved NRM governance: lessons from community engagement in Australia and New Zealand since the 1980s', *Australasian Journal of Environmental Management* 21(2): 175–199.

Dean, M. (2010) *Governmentality: Power and Rule in Modern Society London*, Thousand Oaks, CA: Sage.
Donner, S.D. and Webber, S. (2014) 'Obstacles to climate change adaptation decisions: A case study of sea-level rise and coastal protection measures in Kiribati', *Sustainability Science* 9(3): 331–345.
EBI (2015) *Climate Change Industry Business Segment Review Report 4900: Climate Change Consulting*, San Diego: Environmental Business International, p. 306.
EIU (2011) *Adapting to an uncertain climate: A world of commercial opportunities*, UK: UK Trade & Investment.
Freeman, R. (2007) 'Epistemological bricolage: How practitioners make sense of learning', *Administration & Society* 39(4): 476–496.
GermanWatch (2020) *Climate Change Performance Index*, https://www.climate-change-performance-index.org/, accessed 30 March 2020.
Glückler, J. and Armbrüster, T. (2003) 'Bridging uncertainty in management consulting: The mechanisms of trust and networked reputation', *Organization Studies* 24(2): 269–297.
Grabher, G. (2004) 'Learning in projects, remembering in networks? Communality, sociality, and connectivity in project ecologies' *European Urban and Regional Studies* 11(2): 103–123.
Henstra, D. (2016) 'The tools of climate adaptation policy: Analysing instruments and instrument selection', *Climate Policy* 16(4): 496–521.
Hollander, R. (2010) 'Rethinking overlap and duplication: Federalism and environmental assessment in Australia', *Publius* 40(1): 136.
Howlett, M. and Newman, J. (2010) 'Policy analysis and policy work in federal systems: Policy advice and its contribution to evidence-based policy-making in multi-level governance systems', *Policy and Society* 29(2): 123–136.
IBISWorld (2016a) *Engineering Consulting in Australia: M6923*. IBISWorld Industry Report: 35.
IBISWorld (2016b) *Management Consulting in Australia: M6962*. IBISWorld Industry Report: 32.
Inglis, J., Whittaker, S. Dimitriadis, A. and Pillora, S. (2014) *Climate Adaptation Manual for Local Government: Embedding Resilience to Climate Change*, Sydney: University of Technology, p. 66.
IPCC (2013) *Summary for Policymakers: Climate Change 2013: The Physical Science Basis*. Contribution of Working Group I to the Fifth Assessment Report of the Intergovernmental Panel on Climate Change. Cambridge, UK and New York, NY, USA: Cambridge University Press.
IPCC (ed) (2014) *Summary for Policymakers: Climate Change 2014: Impacts, Adaptation, and Vulnerability*. Contribution of Working Group II to the Fifth Assessment Report of the Intergovernmental Panel on Climate Change. Cambridge, UK and New York, NY, USA: Cambridge University Press.

Isaksen, A. (2004) 'Knowledge-based clusters and urban location: The clustering of software consultancy in Oslo', *Urban Studies* 41(5–6): 1157–1174.

Kantola, A. and Seeck, H. (2011) 'Dissemination of management into politics: Michael Porter and the political uses of management consulting' *Management Learning* 42(1): 25–47.

Keele, S. (2018) 'Outsourcing adaptation: Examining the role and influence of consultants in governing climate change adaptation', PhD, University of Melbourne.

Keele, S. (2019) 'Consultants and the business of climate services: Implications of shifting from public to private science', *Climatic Change* 157(1): 9–26.

Kirchhoff, C.J., Lemos, M.C. and Kalafatis, S. (2015) 'Narrowing the gap between climate science and adaptation action: The role of boundary chains', *Climate Risk Management* 9: 1–5.

Larner, W. and Laurie, N. (2010) 'Travelling technocrats, embodied knowledges: Globalising privatisation in telecoms and water', *Geoforum* 41(2): 218.

Larner, W. and Le Heron, R. (2002) 'The spaces and subjects of a globalising economy: A situated exploration of method', *Environment & Planning D: Society & Space* 20(6): 753.

Larner, W. and Walters, W. (2004) *Global Governmentality: Governing International Spaces*, New York, NY: Routledge.

Li, T.M. (2007) 'Practices of assemblage and community forest management', *Economy and Society* 36(2): 263–293.

Lourenço, T.C., Swart, R., Goosen, H. and Street, R. (2016) 'The rise of demand-driven climate services', *Nature Climate Change* 6(1): 13.

Lovell, H. (2019) 'Policy failure mobilities', *Progress in Human Geography* 43(1): 46–63.

Lovell, H. and Ghaleigh, N.S. (2013) 'Climate change and the professions: The unexpected places and spaces of carbon markets', *Transactions of the Institute of British Geographers* 38(3): 512.

Massey, E. and Huitema, D. (2013) 'The emergence of climate change adaptation as a policy field: The case of England', *Regional Environmental Change* 13(2): 341–352.

Mavrot, C. and Sager, F. (2018) 'Vertical epistemic communities in multilevel governance', *Policy & Politics* 46(3): 391–407.

McCann, E.J. (2008) 'Expertise, truth, and urban policy mobilities: Global circuits of knowledge in the development of Vancouver, Canada's 'four pillar' drug strategy', *Environment and Planning A* 40(4): 885–904.

NSW Auditor-General (2018) *Procurement and Reporting of Consulting Services*, Sydney, NSW: Audit Office of NSW, p. 49.

O'Flynn, J. (2007) 'From new public management to public value: Paradigmatic change and managerial implications', *Australian Journal of Public Administration* 66(3): 353–366.

Orchard, L. (1998) 'Managerialism, economic rationalism and public sector reform in Australia: Connections, divergences, alternatives', *Australian Journal of Public Administration* 57(1): 19–32.

Paschen, J.-A. and Ison, R. (2014) 'Narrative research in climate change adaptation—Exploring a complementary paradigm for research and governance', *Research Policy* 43(6): 1083–1092.

Peck, J. and Theodore, N. (2010) 'Mobilizing policy: Models, methods, and mutations', *Geoforum* 41(2): 169–174.

Peck, J. and Theodore, N. (2015) *Fast policy: Experimental statecraft at the thresholds of neoliberalism*, Minneapolis: University of Minnesota Press.

Prince, R. (2010) 'Policy transfer as policy assemblage: Making policy for the creative industries in New Zealand'. *Environment and Planning A* 42(1): 169–186.

Prince, R. (2012) 'Policy transfer, consultants and the geographies of governance', *Progress in Human Geography* 36(2): 188–203.

Prince, R. (2014a) 'Calculative cultural expertise? Consultants and politics in the UK cultural sector', *Sociology* 48(4): 747–762.

Prince, R. (2014b) 'Consultants and the global assemblage of culture and creativity', *Transactions of the Institute of British Geographers* 39(1): 90–101.

Prince, R. (2016) 'The spaces in between: Mobile policy and the topographies and topologies of the technocracy', *Environment and Planning D: Society and Space* 34(3): 420–437.

Reisinger, A., Kitching, R.L., Chiew, F., Hughes, L., Newton, P.C.D., Schuster, S.S., Tait, A. and Whetton, P. (2014) *Australasia. Climate Change 2014—Impacts, Adaptation and Vulnerability: Part B: Regional Aspects: Working Group II*, Contribution to the IPCC Fifth Assessment Report: Volume 2: Regional Aspects. C. Intergovernmental Panel on Climate, Cambridge: Cambridge University Press, 2, pp. 1371–1438.

Rose, N. and Miller, P. (2010) 'Political power beyond the State: Problematics of government', *British Journal of Sociology* 61: 271–303.

Saint-Martin, D. (2012) 'Governments and management consultants: Supply, demand, and effectiveness', in M. Kipping and T. Clark (eds). *The Oxford Handbook of Management Consulting*, Oxford: Oxford Publishing, pp. 447–464.

Scott, T.A. and Carter, D.P. (2019) 'Collaborative governance or private policy making? When consultants matter more than participation in collaborative environmental planning', *Journal of Environmental Policy & Planning* 21(2): 153–173.

Suddaby, R. and Greenwood, R. (2001) 'Colonizing knowledge: Commodification as a dynamic of jurisdictional expansion in professional service firms', *Human Relations* 54(7): 933–953.

Tadros, E. and McIlroy, T. (2018) *MPs Alarmed at Government Consultancy Spending*, Australian Financial Review: Nine Publishing.
Tangney, P. (2017) *Climate Adaptation Policy and Evidence: Understanding the Tensions Between Politics and Expertise in Public Policy*, Abingdon, Oxon; New York, NY: Routledge.
TCFD (2019) *Taskforce on Climate-Related Financial Disclosures: Status Report*, Switzerland: Financial Stability Board, p. 144.
Tether, B.S., Li, Q.C. and Mina, A. (2012) 'Knowledge-bases, places, spatial configurations and the performance of knowledge-intensive professional service firms', *Journal of Economic Geography* 12(5): 969–1001.
Thrift, N. (1997) 'The rise of soft capitalism', *Cultural Values* 1(1): 29–57.
Tompkins, E.L. and Eakin, H. (2012) 'Managing private and public adaptation to climate change', *Global Environmental Change* 22(1): 3–11.
UNEP (2019). *The Emissions Gap Report 2019*, Nairobi: United Nations Environment Programme.
Wallington, T., Lawrence, G. and Loechel, B. (2008) 'Reflections on the legitimacy of regional environmental governance: Lessons from Australia's experiment in natural resource management', *Journal of Environmental Policy and Planning* 10(1): 1–30.
Webb, J. (2011) 'Making climate change governable: The case of the UK climate change risk assessment and adaptation planning', *Science & Public Policy* 38(4): 279–292.
Webb, R.J. and Beh, J.L. (2013) *Leading Adaptation Practices and Support Strategies for Australia: An International and Australian Review of Products and Tools*, Gold Coast: National Climate Change Adaptation Research Facility, p. 118.
Webber, S. and Donner, S.D. (2017) 'Climate service warnings: Cautions about commercializing climate science for adaptation in the developing world', *Wiley Interdisciplinary Reviews: Climate Change* 8(1): 1–8.
World Meteorological Association (2011) *Climate Knowledge for Action: A Global Framework for Climate Services—Empowering the Most Vulnerable*, Geneva: WMO.

Advising Cities

Who Drives India's Smart Cities? Understanding the Role of Consulting Firms in the Smart Cities Mission

Uttara Purandare

Introduction

This chapter looks at the relationship between private and public actors under India's Smart Cities Mission (SCM), a policy aimed at transforming 100 cities across India into smart cities. While a number of authors have discussed the role of technology firms, such as IBM or Cisco, in building smart cities, this contribution focuses on another private sector actor, the management consulting firm. Consulting firms are becoming increasingly influential in India's policy landscape, from the federal to the local level, and in different policy arenas. However, the role of these firms and the real and possible impacts of their involvement in policymaking have not yet been studied in great detail in the Indian context (for studies in other countries see Vogelpohl, 2018, 2019; Vogelpohl and Klemp, 2018; Raco et al., 2015; Klauser, 2011). By accelerating the speed of the policymaking process and mobilizing policy information in new ways across space, this chapter demonstrates that consultants have transformed urban governance, with significant implications for urban democracy.

U. Purandare (✉)
IITB-Monash Research Academy, Mumbai, Maharashtra, India

C. Hurl and A. Vogelpohl (eds.), *Professional Service Firms and Politics in a Global Era*, https://doi.org/10.1007/978-3-030-72128-2_4

The smart city, which depends heavily on the use of information and communication technologies (ICTs) and collection of data, has been conceived to a large extent in the private sector by firms like IBM, Cisco (Townsend, 2013; Söderström et al., 2014; McNeill, 2015), and more recently Google and Microsoft (Luque-Ayala and Maia, 2018). Policymakers are attracted to this model as a means of achieving economic growth by attracting private capital and businesses. The private sector itself has been employed to help achieve this—through drafting policy documents, providing advisory services and expertise, and developing new technologies. Alongside the technology sector, this chapter attempts to demonstrate that management and "strategy" consultants have also played a pivotal role in the design of the smart city but are, by design, rendered invisible in the policymaking process.

Why do these trends require greater scrutiny? For one, it is important to understand whether the outsourcing of policymaking dilutes democratic processes and reduces citizen participation (see Vogelpohl, 2017, 2018, 2019; Townsend, 2013; Green, 2019). Does the dependence on management consultants centralize power rather than empower local governments? Furthermore, does this dependence help to reify the smart city as well as entrench the position of consultants as policy experts? This chapter aims to answer these questions by studying the Smart Cities Mission.

The following section will discuss the smart city concept and some of its core characteristics. This will draw from the policy mobilities literature which will help us understand how the concept has spread and mutated, and how it is amenable to mobilization across urban contexts. Through its framing as a product of technical fine-tuning, rather than political deliberation, I will show that the smart city concept lends itself to corporate governance and the rise of a "consultocracy" (Saint-Martin, 1998). The second section will further examine these dynamics, looking at how the nodal Ministry which coordinates the Mission, the Ministry of Housing and Urban Affairs (MOHUA) at the federal level, encourages city governments to work with management consultants to draft their smart policies. The third section explores how India's federal government has helped to build a consultocracy, how consultant-driven processes compress policymaking in time, and how political decisions are transformed into technical ones within the smart city paradigm. This analysis draws on some examples of smart city projects, with a focus on Pune, and also looks at the role of consultants at the nodal Ministry. It shows how a consultocracy entrenches the smart city concept and confirms consultants as experts. Since the Mission is still a work-in-progress, the analysis is based on the study of various SCM documents, including the Mission guidelines, smart city plans drafted by selected cities, and Pune's annual reports. The concluding section will talk more about the implications of this consultocracy and discusses some further avenues for research.

Urban Policy Mobilities and the Smart City

Over the past decade, the smart city has become an increasingly ubiquitous concept in urban policy. Smart city policies are characterized by the use of information and communication technologies (ICTs), data-informed policymaking, the rise of a technocracy, and the increasing privatization of urban services. Framed as a matter of technological fine-tuning by a specialized class of engineers, the "smart city" is often treated as an "apolitical" endeavor (Kitchin, 2015). As former IBM CEO Samuel Palmisano notes, "Building a smarter planet is realistic precisely because it is so refreshingly non-ideological" (cited in Hollands, 2015, 64). Smart city proponents suggest that all urban problems can be measured; or they can be broken down enough so their constituent parts can be measured and then solved, often using ICTs (Kitchin, 2014).

It is notable how popular such ideas have become in recent years, though the manner in which they are taken up varies across regions and institutional settings. In some cases, these policies have emerged at the city level itself, often spearheaded by mayors or specific departments, as in Rio de Janeiro (Townsend, 2013). In others, like India, national-level policies have been introduced that encourage cities to develop smart city policies (see Sami and Anand in this volume). In a handful of cases, there has been an attempt to build new "greenfield" smart cities like New Songdo, South Korea, or Masdar City, UAE. Alongside national and local governments, international bodies like the UN are also playing a pivotal role in promoting the smart city as *the* solution to complex urban problems in the Global North and South (UN, 2015).

How do we understand the way in which smart city ideas and discourses spread across jurisdictions? The recent policy mobilities literature is helpful in understanding the proliferation of the smart city in different contexts. McCann (2011, 109) defines urban policy mobilities as "socially produced and circulated forms of knowledge addressing how to design and govern cities that develop in, are conditioned by, travel through, connect, and shape various spatial scales, networks, policy communities, and institutional contexts." The policy mobilities approach helps us understand that the proliferation of policy ideas or models is not a natural one but a deliberate one, initiated by a variety of policy actors. "*People move them around* for particular purposes" (Temenos and McCann, 2013, 344; emphasis in original). It further critiques the idea that certain policies move or are moved from one place to another without being modified by local contexts. While certain policy aspects remain the same or similar, others change. This makes it important to study such policies conceptually in order to understand their core characteristics, and also locally to understand how the policy has mutated—rather than converged—and how these mutations are contextually determined. As Peck and Theodore (2015, xvii) point out, "while some aspects of the policymaking process, like the generation of codified institutional designs and models, seem to be built for travel, there is much that cannot be so easily bottled for export."

Temenos and McCann (2013) discuss urban policy mobilization in two ways. First, certain policy models can be thought of as assemblages, or bundles of knowledge, interventions, and practices. Second, the city itself can be thought of as an assemblage of "policy models and expertise drawn out of circulation and gathered in local contexts" (ibid., 347). The smart city is a prime example of how both these tendencies come together. While most smart cities include ICT interventions and attempt to expand their ability to collect and analyze data (Kitchin, 2014), the concept includes an entire range of other interventions that city governments can choose to apply while keeping the "smart" label. Some cities might focus on improved energy efficiency, others might choose safety or public transport or improved e-governance. All these come under the umbrella of "smart" and tend to share a number of commonalities, like the use of ICTs and Big Data, environmental sustainability, and economic growth. In other words, the smart city concept is not a fixed bundle of interventions. Instead, interventions are often introduced by policymakers in a piecemeal manner. The smart city plays out differently not only because of underlying contextual differences but also because city officials choose interventions that suit them, that are required, and that might have a greater chance of success.

The smart city concept has spread to cities across the world in different ways. The UN's (2017) commitment in the New Urban Agenda and its discussion paper on the topic is one way. Further, smart city policies have often moved from city to city rather than being mobilized at the national level. Individual cities are studied as models and city officials travel there to learn best practices, engaging in what is known as policy tourism (McCann, 2011; Clarke, 2011). One measure of success in the smart city paradigm is whether or not cities become models for other cities. India's SCM guidelines, for example, encourage the selected cities to "create a ***replicable model which will act like a light house*** [sic] ***to other aspiring cities***" (MOUD, 2015, 5; emphasis in original).

Policy actors have also played a role in the spread of the smart city. A number of studies have already noted the significance of technology firms in mobilizing smart city ideas across contexts. For instance, IBM has offered cities pro bono consulting services to introduce smart initiatives (Townsend, 2013, 65). Google has worked with local governments on different projects in cities as diverse as New York (Green, 2019), Rio de Janeiro (Luque-Ayala and Maia, 2018), and Pune (Indian Express, 2018). As with technology firms, consulting firms are becoming increasingly pivotal in mobilizing the smart city concept. McKinsey's research wing and think tank, McKinsey Global Institute (MGI), has published multiple reports, discussion papers, and articles on smart cities. Firms like McKinsey and PwC, as will be discussed below, also work directly with national and local governments on smart city projects, providing various forms of expertise.

In order to design smart city policies, or administer these policies once they have been introduced, governments tend to employ experts or technocrats with different expertise; they might advise on technology deployment and data analysis, or, as is increasingly case, assist in drafting city policies (Townsend, 2013; Vogelpohl, 2018). As the literature suggests, many of these experts may have worked on smart city projects elsewhere but may have no prior knowledge of the city in question. Nevertheless, they help determine which problems are considered, how these are measured, and in finding and applying appropriate solutions which are often derived from other contexts. They also play a pivotal role in presenting the smart city as an opportunity for private investment drawing on corporate language and imagery (Söderström et al., 2014).

This growing use of consultants has significant implications for urban democracy. The extensive use of expert knowledge, and of data, is sold by smart city proponents as "creating technologies, techniques, and visions that are scientific, objective, commonsensical and apolitical" (Kitchin, 2015, 132). This leads us to believe that the way decisions are made, resources are distributed, and avenues for development are selected in smart cities are based on evidence, rationality, and a scientific approach, as opposed to ideology and bias in the "old" approach. This is a form of corporate storytelling that makes politics, history, and even elected representatives superfluous to urban governance (Söderström et al., 2014). Green (2019, 46–47) points to the "information fallacy" of the smart city, the belief that most urban problems stem from a lack of information and can be solved by gathering more data. He argues that such an approach casts "political problems... as coordination problems" which can overlook inequalities and contextual differences. This can have far-reaching consequences, as will be demonstrated below, including changing the distribution of resources, privileging certain groups or sectors, and overlooking policies that might emerge locally—outcomes that are far from apolitical (Green, 2019).

India's Smart Cities Mission

The Indian Smart Cities Mission was launched by the federal government in June 2015 with the aim of transforming 100 Indian cities spread across the country into "smart" cities. The Mission guidelines state, "the purpose of the Smart Cities Mission is to drive economic growth and improve the quality of life of people" (MOUD, 2015, 6). The Mission has been rolled out by high ranking officials working with the Ministry of Urban Development (MOUD), now the Ministry of Housing and Urban Affairs (MOHUA), who actively set out to coordinate the implementation of the SCM in cities across the country. As part of this, the federal government has laid down a process by which cities can become eligible for funding. Until they fulfill the federal government's criteria, even cities selected under the Mission cannot access SCM funds. All 100 selected cities are required to submit a smart city proposal (SCP). On the one hand, the SCM guidelines encourage cities to define their own parameters for "smart" and design their interventions accordingly. On the other, the guidelines provide detailed checklists of interventions that each city has to introduce and sectors that the city has to develop.

It is at the SCP-drafting stage that management consultants begin working with cities. The Mission guidelines (MOUD, 2015, 9) direct city governments to approach consulting firms or "handholding agencies" (this includes foreign governments and international institutions like the World Bank, UN Habitat, etc.) to help draft their smart city proposals.

Consulting firms are expected to draw up the proposals while other agencies and foreign governments can offer "technical assistance support" (MOUD, 2015, 10). The guidelines state, "it is realized that the task of preparing the SCPs is quite challenging and States/ULBs [Urban Local Bodies] will require assistance of experts" (ibid.). Rather than engaging in policy tourism and traveling to learn from other cities, the SCM thus invites "experts" to give advice on what would work best for Indian cities and how these interventions can be designed. Indeed, external expertise tends to be privileged over democratically elected representatives. Under the 74th Constitutional Amendment Act, urban planning is the responsibility of local governments (GoI, 1992) which draft city development plans. Experts such as urban planners have also been part of the process, as have civil society representatives, but city officials led these processes. The SCM suggests, as reflected by the above quote, that smart city development is inherently different, requiring skills not found within city governments. On this basis, consulting firms are expected to draw up the proposals with the support of other agencies and foreign governments.

The Mission pre-approved close to 50 consulting firms that cities were free to engage with (MOUD, 2016a). These included management consultants like PwC, Deloitte, KPMG, CRISIL, and McKinsey; technology firms like Cisco, SoftTech Engineers, and Infosys; and financial institutions like Genesis Finance. The guidelines lay out the "scope of work" for these firms. This has included citizen consultations, identification of urban challenges, a review of previous urban plans and coordination with other urban policies, and the drafting of the SCP itself (MOUD, 2015, 21–22). The SCP identifies the areas of the city that should be selected for pilot projects, where approximately 80% of smart city funds are concentrated, as well as those projects that are deemed to benefit the entire city (pan-city interventions). Importantly, the firms have been expected to lay out the financial plan for the entire SCP, including "identify[ing] internal (taxes, rents, licenses and user charges) and external (grants, assigned revenues, loans and borrowings) sources of mobilizing" (MOUD, 2015, 21). In this way, cities are encouraged to outsource the entire process of devising, prioritizing, and financial planning to external consultants. The consultants in turn are expected to follow the guidelines laid down by the nodal Ministry. In their study, Praharaj and Han (2019) highlight the central role of private firms in driving the process. As they note, "unique collusion between these influential companies and the public-sector leadership was observed, which...

places global corporations in charge of devising the smart city plans in selected cities" (ibid., 9).

Private sector involvement has not been restricted to the designing of smart cities but continues into their administration and governance. Smart city interventions are governed by special purpose vehicles (SPVs) which each selected city is required to set up. The SPV is a quasi-governmental structure that is separate from and runs parallel to the existing ULB. It is incorporated as a company and up to 40% of the SPV can be privately owned; it can also be headed by someone who is not an elected representative or a bureaucrat (MOUD, 2015). Pressing questions have been raised about the functioning of the SPV and how such bodies can weaken local governments and urban democracy. As Khan et al. note (2018, 86), the SPV has "the power to collect royalties and taxes and to own the assets created, thereby undermining the autonomy of public organisations."

The shift to private administration of smart cities is justified by the argument that when policies are based on data and evidence, the policymaking process is scientific rather than political and can therefore be carried out by so-called experts. Moreover, it is argued that these actors may even be superior to governments in the administration of smart cities given their capacity to produce plans and material that speak the language of corporate asset management, promoting private investment in these projects. As Söderström et al. (2014, 313) note, consultants help the city to "speak the language of IBM." However, significant questions remain about the appropriateness of hiring consulting firms and other experts unfamiliar with the context of the city to plan that city. Not only are these questions related to "who is an expert" and what form of expertise is privileged (Vogelpohl, 2019), but also why the speed of decision-making is given greater credence as compared to inclusion or sustainability of the policy. In the next section I will discuss the role of consulting firms in building Indian smart cities and the blurring between public and private sectors across space and over time.

The Smart City Mission's Consultocracy

The smart city is a "fast policy," which refers not only to the speed at which policies move across geographies but also how closely connected these policies are (Peck and Theodore, 2015; Vogelpohl, 2017, 66). Peck and Theodore (2015, xvii) refer to this as involving "increasingly *compressed* policymaking moments." We have seen that the SCM hires consultants not just as external advisors but as essential actors in designing and administering smart cities across India. These actors play a central role in mobilizing the smart city concept and getting it off the ground across jurisdictions. Vogelpohl (2019, 106) discusses this form of "networked knowledge" as a way by which these firms entrench their expertise. In this section I will discuss in more detail how the policymaking process in Indian smart cities is compressed by consultants, the role of the federal government in fostering a consultocracy, and how such a consultocracy has become entrenched in government.

Building a Consultocracy: Role of India's Federal Government

In the previous section I discussed how smart city policies are often mobilized at the city level. However, India's approach has also been coordinated from above by the federal-level Ministry of Housing and Urban Affairs (MOHUA). The Ministry drafts the various smart city policy guidelines, keeps track of the cities' progress, and ranks the 100 cities along various indexes. The guidelines underscore the importance of working with "experts" and hasten the process of hiring consultants. The MOHUA itself works closely with various consulting firms. For example, Cisco and Quantela are two of the Ministry's partners in the India Urban Observatory (IUO), "a data analysis and management hub" launched in 2019 (MOUHA, 2020). A video on the MOHUA website presents the IUO as a central node from which data and information from cities are collected and analyzed, and from which decisions on local projects are made. This means that consulting firms are not only accessing vast amounts of city-level data but also playing a role in analyzing the data, making decisions, and implementing these decisions in the 100 smart cities. Dangerously, there is little publicly available information on the nature of these public sector–private sector relationships. The IUO website does not describe the roles of each partner nor does it publish the contracts drawn up between the Ministry and the various firms.

Some information can be gleaned from the firms themselves. In a publication entitled "Urban development and reforms: Advisory solutions for urban problems" [in India], PwC lists smart cities as one of its five "key urban domains" for which it provides "a holistic range of advisory services" (2019, 2). The document goes on to detail how it has contributed to the SCM, the cities it has worked with, and the breadth of its expertise. The latter spans from "policy formulation and governance assistance" to "preparation of smart city plans," "SPV organization structuring" and "financing strategies and financing plans" (PwC, 2019). Technology firms like Cisco have also attempted to integrate their own technologies into India's cities (ETCISO, 2019). Praharaj and Han (2019, 4) write that the company announced a plan to invest 100 million USD in digital initiatives across the country "with the solid backing of the state." Firms like PwC, McKinsey, and Deloitte, on the other hand, are playing a role in steering the design and implementation of policies like the SCM, in "setting the tone of the smart city discourse" (ibid.), again working closely with the federal government.

By pushing cities to employ the services of consultants and follow the interventions laid out in their guidelines, the federal government has contributed to the entrenchment of private firms in urban governance, weakening local governments, and undermining locally-based decision-making. Moreover, the federal government itself has outsourced certain governance functions to consultants, contributing to the entrenchment of consultants at the national level.

Policy Compression Over Time as a Driver for Consultocracy

The smart city is not only a fast policy in terms of how it moves from city to city or country to country, but also in terms of how quickly policy decisions are made. Vogelpohl (2018) points out that the employment of consultants and their assumed expertise allows for decisions to be taken quickly and without much debate. If looked at closely, however, this expertise might not be particularly meaningful given that consultants may not have the time, ability, or resources to adequately understand the local context.

This can be seen in terms of the intensified speed of policymaking at the local level. Of the 100 SCPs submitted to the MOHUA in 2016, the city of Pune was ranked second (MOHUA, n.d.). McKinsey was hired by the city government in November 2015 to draft its SCP. The firm was expected to complete this job in just 100 days (PMC, 2015, 23) and was paid a hefty sum of Rs. 20 million (approximately USD 300,000) (TOI, 2015). Not only is this a very short amount of time to design a policy of this scale and significance, but it also shows that governments are diverting funds to the private sector that could be used to improve the capacity of local governments.

Different teams from the same firm can work with different cities simultaneously—given that SCPs had to be submitted within certain time-frames, this a likely possibility. This might also lead to firms applying the same models in different cities—presented as "best practices"—without much consideration for local actors or contexts. Importantly, and as discussed above, the Mission guidelines lay out what a smart city must look like. This raises the question about what input the consultant provides apart from pre-packaged infographics and reports. We see this clearly in the similarity of interventions across cities. For instance, 83 cities include some form of a "command and control centre" (Praharaj and Han, 2019, 4). Taraporevala (2018) has looked at the kinds of smart interventions introduced in the first 60 selected cities. She found that across the board, the five categories of transport, energy and ecology, water and sanitation, housing, and economy form 80% of smart city budgets. Most of these categories contain ICT interventions like digital meters for water and electricity, and traffic management systems. Looking at a selection of SCPs, I have found that most pan-city interventions are ICT-based, as required by the Mission guidelines (MOUD, 2015, 8). Many include providing public Wi-Fi and designing city apps and dashboards.

Transforming Political Decisions into Technical Ones

Closely related to the increased speed of policymaking, as well as its acceptance, is the framing of political decisions as technical ones, and a superficial approach to public consultation and inclusion. For instance, in Pune, external consultants were expected to draft their proposal while familiarizing themselves with the city. The proposal aimed at identifying the city's unique strengths and weaknesses, selecting neighborhoods for pilot projects, and preparing how funds should be distributed. The result of this for a city like Pune is a generic document using the keywords and standard interventions found in the Mission guidelines. Like the cities discussed above, Pune also proposes a command and control center, improved urban mobility and traffic management, and apps to assist in governance and service delivery as pan-city plans. Further, the area selected for the majority of smart city implementation in Pune is a very small part of the city. The Housing and Land Rights Network report states, "76% of the total funds will be channelized into… approximately only 1% of the total city area" (HLRN, 2018, 18). While the SCP claims that this area of the city emerged as the "democratic and rational choice" (MOUD, 2016b, 26), it fails to demonstrate how. For example, it does not detail how the "objective criteria" for its decision-making was drawn up, what some of the criteria like "scope for inclusive transition" or "criticality to the city" entail, or on what basis the most popular area of Pune was selected for development rather than the least.

While the SCM guidelines as well as Pune and McKinsey's contract state that it is necessary to gather inputs from citizens for the SCP, for many cities this exercise was often what Khan et al. (2018, 84) refer to as "cosmetic." Looking at 60 of the 100 smart cities, they find that "each city claims to have engaged in deep civic participation; however this is not corroborated by the descriptions of this participation in the proposals themselves" (ibid., 83). Of the top 60 cities, they note that only two-thirds could demonstrate non-digital methods of outreach and feedback, and even fewer could demonstrate using digital means. This superficial fulfilling of citizen participation can be attributed to a number of factors. Since consultants lead the drafting of the SCP, they may not be familiar with local politics and may not know what city networks to tap into. Furthermore, if they are given a short time frame in which to complete the SCP, only a small portion of that can be spent on ensuring meaningful participation. The authors also found that cities often used only limited avenues to gather feedback, inevitably excluding large sections of the population from contributing to the SCP (ibid.).

The Pune SCP details to some extent the ways in which citizens participated in the envisioning of the smart city. It claims that 50% of Pune's households were reached out to and more than 3.5 million inputs were received (MOUD, 2016b, 19). The SCP also details the various ways in which citizens were invited to collaborate, from the use of social media to door-to-door campaigns and hackathons (ibid., 20). The proposal offers some data on input from citizens but it does not offer much input on the process of citizen participation. Were these interactions with citizens one-off or did they continue over a period of time? What kinds of questions were asked in surveys? Did the surveys ensure the capture of various demographics? Did citizens get a chance to interact with one another and ask questions of policymakers? While the numbers might sound impressive, they do not give us a sense of the depth of participation; rather they are a fairly superficial measure of participation, wrapped in corporate-speak and infographics. HLRN (2018, 32) further points out that the Pune proposal does not specify whether "any steps were taken to engage with marginalized sections and low-income groups in the preparation of [its] proposal." Praharaj and Han (2019, 4) further assert that the inputs of local stakeholders and politicians were "suppressed."

Conclusion

From the above discussion we see how the same consulting firm can work with different entities in different capacities. We see that firms can have their fingers in a variety of pies, many of which are related to core governance functions. Firms act, simultaneously, at various levels—international, federal, and local—in different geographies and for different clients. For instance, apart from working directly with the MOHUA, PwC has also worked with more than 20 Indian smart cities as a "strategy consultant" or as project management consultant. Moreover, the 2019 report mentions that PwC has conducted "research on smart cities and investment opportunities in India" for the Japan Bank for International Cooperation (PwC, 2019).

We also see that most decisions are taken by the federal government and consulting firms while local governments are largely excluded. At the local level we see how local politics and consensus-building are diluted due to increased speed and urgency in the policymaking process, and due to the assumed rationality in decision-making if seemingly objective criteria are applied. This ensures that smart city ideas are implemented faster and with greater authority. Furthermore, by pushing local governments to employ consultants, as the SCM does, and normalizing their role in policymaking, city governments are no longer incentivized to build their own capacities, further entrenching the role of the consultant.

Consulting firms, on their part, use their various roles to further build their networked knowledge and expertise. The increased spread and popularity of these interventions, seemingly confirms them as best practice (Vogelpohl, 2019, 106) and even though the consulting firm may not provide significant input, its so-called expertise is confirmed by its presence. It is interesting that the role of these firms and consultants, and the extent to which they contribute to the policy process and design is not made transparent. For example, the Pune Smart City Corporation's Annual Report does not mention which consulting firms it works with. Instead it refers to working with "general consultants" who are "responsible for technical and project management support" (PSCDCL, 2018, 7), and specialist and advisory firms (ibid., 14). This means that consulting firms speak in the voice of government bodies, and citizens are unable to distinguish between government and consulting firm—while the latter continue to be unaccountable to the public. As governments cede decision-making, accountability becomes convoluted and diminishes.

This outsourcing of policy design and decision-making can have serious impacts on local democracy in India and on the future of its cities. To begin with, India has repeatedly failed to decentralize power and strengthen local government (Vaddiraju, 2016). The extent to which private consulting firms are now playing a role in core governance functions like policy and project design further weaken city governments. An activity like city planning which usually goes through multiple drafts and is always a work-in-progress, has been reduced to a short-term project which has to check a list of boxes and compete with other cities for government resources and private investment. By bringing in consultants, the policy process has been abbreviated and presented as an apolitical activity. This tends to hide the power relations that exist between people and groups, thereby strengthening the status quo. This is one of the reasons the smart city has been criticized for increasing inequity and deepening social fissures (Datta, 2015). Additionally, by hiring external experts and out-sourcing governance, the capacity of local government remains untapped and underdeveloped. This further increases the dependence on "experts" and consultants, and diverts funds that could be used for urban development toward the private sector.

This impacts democracy and citizen participation. As Vogelpohl (2018, 1347) notes, the shrinking space for public officials in public life has caused "not only a lack of transparency in political processes, but also strengthened the power of non-elected organizations, and thus of arbitrary, hardly retraceable decisions." She discusses how consensus from citizens is manufactured by simplifying complex urban issues and reducing them to narrow ideas that would not be opposed—like safety or environmental sustainability. In India's case, we have seen how the majority of SCM funds are concentrated in small parts of the city while pan-city projects are focused on board interventions like improved connectivity and traffic management. By putting efficiency and economic growth at the center of urban planning and policy—as smart city consultants do (Green, 2019, 50)—citizens are made "passive passengers" (Vogelpohl, 2018, 1361) on the smart city ride. This cannot be rectified by an e-governance app but needs citizens and local governments to reclaim their democratic spaces.

Usually, consultants and experts work behind the scenes. When one looks at cities' SCPs, it is not clear that management consultants have drafted the document. No doubt city officials also play a role in designing these policies but it is impossible to gauge the influence of consultants and experts, or their interests. This influence on decision-making and the pressure to show results also impacts which urban problems are chosen to "solve". I have also demonstrated a lack of transparency in how decisions are made.

This chapter has attempted to underscore the role that government has played in allowing this to happen, indeed ensuring that it does. This push away from democratization and decentralization has been spearheaded by federal and regional governments. Rather than bring democracy closer to citizens, policies like the SCM ensure that power remains concentrated at the top. Further research in this field will have to consider why governments participate in the smart city smoke and mirrors, and the ways in which their interests align with the private sector's or vice versa.

References

Clarke, N. (2011) 'Urban policy mobility, anti-politics, and histories of the transnational municipal movement', *Progress in Human Geography* 36(1): 25–43.

Datta, A. (2015) 'New urban Utopias of postcolonial India: 'Entrepreneurial urbanization' in Dholera smart city, Gujarat', *Dialogues in Human Geography* 5(1): 3–22.

ETCISO. (2019) 'MoHUA, Cisco launches urban observatory to improve productivity of cities', *ETCISO*, 13 March.

Government of India (GoI). (1992) *The Constitution (74th Amendment) Act, 1992*, New Delhi, India: Government of India.

Green, B. (2019) *The Smart Enough City*, Cambridge, Massachusetts: The MIT Press.

Hollands, R.G. (2015) 'Critical interventions into the corporate smart city', *Cambridge Journal of Regions, Economy and Society* 8: 61–77.

Housing and Land Rights Network (HRLN). (2018) *India's Smart Cities Mission: Smart for Whom? Cities for Whom?* New Delhi, India: HRLN Update 2018.

Indian Express. (2018) 'Google Station free WiFi moves to smart cities, 150 hotspots to go live in Pune', *Indian Express*, 31 January.

Khan, S., Taraporevala, P. and Zerah, H. (2018) 'Mission impossible: Defining Indian smart cities', *Economic and Political Weekly* 53(49): 80–49.

Kitchin, R. (2014) 'The real-time city? Big data and smart urbanism', *GeoJournal* 79: 1–14.

Kitchin, R. (2015). Making sense of smart cities: Addressing present shortcomings. *Cambridge Journal of Regions, Economy and Society* 8(1): 131–136.

Klauser, F. (2011) 'The exemplification of 'fan zones': Mediating mechanisms in the reproduction of best practices for security and branding at Euro 2008', *Urban Studies* 48(15): 3203–3219.

Luque-Ayala, A. and Maia, F.N. (2018) 'Digital territories: Google maps as a political technique in the re-making of urban informality', *Environment and Planning D: Society and Space* 37(3): 449–467.

McCann, E. (2011) 'Urban policy mobilities and global circuits of knowledge: Toward a research Agenda', *Annals of the Association of American Geographers* 101(1): 107–130.

McKinsey Global Institute (MGI). (n.d.) *Smart cities*. McKinsey & Company, https://www.mckinsey.com/search?q=smart%20cities, accessed 12 September 2020.

McNeill, D. (2015) 'Global firms and smart technologies: IBM and the reduction of cities', *Transactions of the Institute of British Geographers* 40(4): 562–574.

Ministry of Housing and Urban Affairs (MOHUA). (2020) *India Urban Observatory*. New Delhi, India: Ministry of Housing and Urban Affairs, Government of India, https://iuo.mohua.gov.in/portal/apps/sites/#/data/pages/iuo, accessed 27 July 2020.

Ministry of Housing and Urban Affairs (MOHUA). (n.d.) *City Challenge*. New Delhi, India: Ministry of Housing and Urban Affairs, Government of India, http://smartcities.gov.in/content/city_challenge.php, accessed 01 September 2020.

Ministry of Urban Development (MOUD). (2015) *Smart Cities: Mission Statement and Guidelines*. New Delhi, India: Ministry of Urban Development, Government of India.

Ministry of Urban Development (MOUD). (2016a) *Name and Address of Shortlisted Firms for Smart Cities Proposal*. New Delhi, India: Ministry of Urban Development, Government of India.

Ministry of Urban Development (MOUD). (2016b) *Smart City Challenge Stage 2: Smart City Proposal Pune*. New Delhi, India: Ministry of Urban Development, Government of India. Smart City Code: MH-02-PUN.

Peck, J. and Theodore, N. (2015) *Fast Policy: Experimental statecraft at the Thresholds of Neoliberalism*, Minneapolis: University of Minnesota Press.

Peck, J., Theodore, N. and Brenner, N. (2009) 'Neoliberal Urbanism: Models, Moments, Mutations', *SAIS Review* 29(1): 49–66.

Praharaj, S. and Han, H. (2019) 'Cutting through the clutter of smart city definitions: A reading into the smart city perceptions in India', *City, Culture and Society* 18: 100289.

PwC (2019) *Urban Development and Reforms: Advisory Solutions for Urban Problems*. India.

Pune Municipal Corporation (PMC). (2015) *Preparation of Proposal for Assisting Pune City to Participate in the Smart Cities Challenge*. Pune, India: Pune Municipal Corporation. RFP No.: CBUD/UP /50 /6/L53 /Pune.

Pune Smart City Development Corporation Limited (PSCDCL). (2018) *1st Annual Report 2016–17*. Pune, India: Pune Smart City Development Corporation Limited.

Raco, M., Street, E. and Freire-Trigo, S. (2015) 'The New Localism, Anti-Political Development Machines, and the Role of Planning Consultants: Lessons from London's South Bank', *Territory, Politics, Governance* 4(2): 216–240.

Saint-Martin, D. (1998) 'The New Managerialism and the Policy Influence of Consultants in Government: An Historical–Institutionalist Analysis of Britain, Canada and France', *Governance: An International Journal of Policy and Administration* 11(3): 319–356.

Söderström, O., Paasche, T. and Klauser, F. (2014) 'Smart cities as corporate storytelling', *City* 18(3): 307–320.

Taraporevala. P. (2018) *Demystifying the Indian Smart City: An Empirical Reading of the Indian Smart Cities Mission*. New Delhi, India: Centre for Policy Research. Working Paper.

Temenos, C. and McCann, E. (2013) 'Geographies of Policy Mobilities', *Geography Compass* 7(5): 344–357.

Times of India (TOI). (2015) 'Funds no barrier as McKinsey chosen to draft smart city plan', *Times of India,* 2 September.

Townsend, A. (2013) *Smart Cities: Big Data, Civic Hackers, and the Quest for a New Utopia*, New York: W. W. Norton & Company.

United Nations. (2015) *Smart Cities*, New York, USA: Habitat III. Habitat III Issue Papers 21.

United Nations. (2017) *New Urban Agenda*, Nairobi, Kenya: United Nations.

Vaddiraju, A.K. (2016) 'Urban Governance and Right to the City', *Economic and Political Weekly* 51(32): 21–23.

Vogelpohl, A. (2017) 'Consulting completed: Temporal aspects of expertise in urban development during times of fast policies', *Geographica Helvetica* 72: 65–76.

Vogelpohl, A. (2018) 'Consulting as a threat to local democracy? Flexible management consultants, pacified citizens, and political tactics of strategic development in German cities', *Urban Geography* 39(9): 1345–1365.

Vogelpohl, A. (2019) 'Global expertise, local convincing power: Management consultants and preserving the entrepreneurial city', *Urban Studies* 56(1): 97–114.

Vogelpohl, A. and Klemp, F. (2018) 'The creeping influence of consultants on cities: McKinsey's involvement in Berlin's urban economic and social policies', *Geoforum* 91: 39–46.

Boutique Consultancy and Personal Trust: Advising on Cities in Moscow

Daria Volkova

Introduction

Over the past decade, the sphere of urban planning in Russia, and in Moscow in particular, has changed. Since 2010, public spaces have become a major focus of urban policy. Claiming to be on the path to a "city of people," Moscow's public authorities and experts fostered the idea of what they called the "comfort environment" (Kalyukin et al., 2015). As a part of this plan, Moscow authorities supported the idea of renewal, mostly through redeveloping old factories and renovating parks and streets. Through the success of such projects, a whole field of new urban planning has emerged in public discourse, as well as a whole infrastructure for urban planning professionals to communicate and present their ideas (Argenbright et al., 2019).

In this chapter, I will show how these changes were facilitated by private planners and specialists in Russia who are gaining more power in the traditionally state-centered policy process. Two decades ago, urban planning was the sole prerogative of state planners. Today, new types of consultancies operate within this system, drawing on knowledge from

D. Volkova (✉)
Urban Sociology, HSE University, Moscow, Russia
e-mail: volkova.daria.v@gmail.com

C. Hurl and A. Vogelpohl (eds.), *Professional Service Firms and Politics in a Global Era*, https://doi.org/10.1007/978-3-030-72128-2_5

the private sector. In Moscow, I argue, their influence in urban development is based on three types of strategies—building trust through personal contacts, establishing credibility through professional networks, and through public performances of expertise. Through the continued predominance of personal networks, I show how access to urban policymaking has been restricted to an approved class of consultants. This results in what I frame as "boutique consultancy" which is characterized by a select group of smaller scale and more individualized projects spearheaded by local consultants and firms. Such consultants have generated influence through establishing and consolidating exclusive public forums, through public lectures and events on urbanism, and university programs that have generated the discursive underpinning of new models of urban development in Moscow (Abashev et al., 2020).

The new knowledge produced in this system has not only changed the public discourse, but also influenced political decision-making. Planning consultants have contributed to the neoliberal restructuring of the city (Kalyukin et al., 2015) by focusing on commercialization and aesthetic politics that emphasize changes to the physical environment as a means of reform. In Moscow, these expert ideas were taken up by the new mayor Sobyanin (in office since 2010) who has emphasized policies of the comfort city and commercialization—addressing middle-class needs and businesses (Büdenbender and Zupan, 2017). These policies have not only excluded broader social or political issues, such as income inequality and freedom of speech, from public debates; they have also excluded broader groups of citizens from the planning process.

The policies developed in Moscow have been very influential and have come to shape the urban reform agenda at the national level. In 2019, the federal government drew from this model in introducing the program "Housing and City Environment" with special attention to the "comfortization" and beautification of cities. Planners and consultants have shaped this process through various projects including indexes measuring the level of urban development throughout the country (Department of Construction, 2020), strategies for city development (Novaya Zemlya, 2019), and educational programs for Moscow authorities and for regional actors (Faculty of Urban and Regional development, 2020). Thus, private consultancy firms have not only participated more actively in the urban planning system in Moscow, but they have succeeded in positioning themselves as experts in urban development more broadly across Russia.

My research traces the process of creating such firms, the institutionalization of the urban consultancy sphere, and how consultants have gained and exercise power over urban governance. To sharpen the focus on the structure of knowledge production, I examine both the actors involved and the system of advising (Commenges et al., 2017; Krick, 2015; McCann, 2008). Rather than looking at the particular advice given, I am more interested in different practices through which knowledge is produced, how these practices have been refined over time, and what opportunities there are for consultants to influence the policymaking process.

I focus on the peculiarities of knowledge production in Moscow, in which municipal independence and the free market in urban consultancy still rely on dominant local actors. The second part of the paper describes the general role and structure of expertise and knowledge production of urban planning consultants. The third part explains the methodology, describing the peculiarities of the role of local firms and individual experts in urban consultancy in Moscow. My research is based on interviews with the owners and founders of consultancies, who are based in Moscow and who are active advisers on urban development issues. The fourth part focuses on how the field of urban consultancy was established in Moscow, the differentiation of companies and the possibility to compete, and how consultants present themselves publicly. The conclusion summarizes how, in this specific environment of urban governance, the production of expert knowledge influences political decisions, how consultants build up their power through networking, and how they use publicity for the institutionalization of such relationships.

Experts in City Development

While global consultants are central actors in advising cities in many parts of the world, in Moscow they have had a limited influence. Although international consultancy firms and architects are taken up in the development sector and architecture, the major issues in urban governance are mostly handled by local experts. Through their knowledge production practices, local consultants, urban experts, and professional service firms operating in the urban sphere have created new rules and norms for urban development (Carr, 2010). Here, I describe some peculiarities of this type of knowledge production and outline the issues on which I focused.

Given the variety and complexity of issues covered in urban planning—including everything from beautification and public health to security and policing—a variety of actors from different backgrounds and operating at different levels have been able to claim membership in the emerging field of knowledge known as "urbanism" in Russia. However, generating urban knowledge has increasingly come to rely on professional expertise (Allmendinger and Haughton, 2012; see Linovski in this volume), leaving citizens and non-expert groups with only limited and partially effective tools for participation, including public hearings and participatory practices. In practical decision-making, expert knowledge in urban planning and governance is weighted over local knowledge (Hordijk and Baud, 2006).

Drawing from their claims to expertise, private consultants have played a key role in legitimizing political decisions (Moser, 2013). For public officials, engaging consultants has become a viable means to establish a reassuring narrative attesting to the credibility of their ideas (Faust, 2012, 8; Faulconbridge and Jones, 2012). In understanding how this plays out in the policymaking process, I identify three analytical dimensions that help to chart the way in which consultants position themselves: (1) access to the policymaking field, and relationships with public officials; (2) access to the professional field, and relationships with other experts in urbanism; (3) and access to the public, and relationships with citizens. Each of these dimensions reveals the power distribution between the actors in the knowledge structure, with consultants achieving varying degrees of access to public officials, professional networks, and public audiences (Faust, 2012).

In Russia, access to the field has initially depended on building the trust with clients (public authorities and private clients). This very often involved drawing from personal connections, networks, and relationships. At the earliest stages, consultancies were limited to the trust gained from an inner circle. Later, as consultants established personal networks, their client base could be broadened by word of mouth, and eventually be extended through public recognition and reputation.

However, as the discipline of urban consulting has consolidated in Russia, access to the field has also increasingly depended on professional identities. Within the professional field, consultants have come to manage their socialization as experts inside and outside the national sphere through education and various institutions that define the scope of knowledge and establish professional language in the sphere (Carr, 2010).

Knowledge is transferred through different media (books, lectures) (Khirfan et al., 2013), and established on different platforms, both private and public, through negotiation within expert and consultancy groups (Krick, 2015). Thus, experts and consultants themselves legitimize knowledge and expertise in interactions with each other (Commenges et al., 2017), and through credentials and social connections.

Furthermore, consultants have set out to position themselves as reputable actors through presenting themselves in media, though the extent and nature of public performance are variable and shaped by the access of consultants to clients through personal networks and professional associations. If a firm is close to the government, they may not need to present their work publicly. However, if they have weaker ties with clients or professional associations and network, they may need to rely more on performative elements of the production of knowledge, for example, by giving lectures, writing books, or participating in professional events (Hordijk and Baud, 2006; see McCann and Mahieus in this volume).

Drawing from this framework, I will explore the emergence of the field of urban consultancy in Moscow, while at the same time locating consultants in the field of knowledge production. In understanding the positionality of various consultants, I ask: How do consultants and firms access the field and gain power? How are relationships between actors structured? And how do they legitimize their knowledge in public and private? As will be demonstrated below, the influence of urban consultants in Russia is much more dependent on access to public officials through personal networks, than it is based on professional associations or public reputation, which explains, in part, why boutique consultancies remain dominant in the market.

Methodology

Expert knowledge is often problematized for being exclusionary and technocratic, structurally deepening the democratic deficit. It is worth noting, however, that the knowledge practices of different experts vary, depending on the envisioned project and types of instruments employed, in the way they treat local knowledge, and the extent to which they include laypeople or communicate with their clients (Özdemir, 2019). Analytic precision is needed here, even when looking at the same group or organization: the different components of the process can invoke different usages of expertise and research (Boswell, 2008). The sphere of urban consultancy in Russia is indeed heterogeneous and includes many professionals with different backgrounds in transport, regional studies, economics, etc., and varying influence across regions and domains. Acknowledging this heterogeneity, my research focuses solely on private firms and consultants in Moscow who are involved in advising city governments in the urban planning sphere. The consultants included in this study know each other, began their work at approximately the same time, and have also managed to gain some symbolic capital at the present moment.

My analysis is based on six in-depth interviews with the experts, founders, and CEOs of planning firms in Moscow. While some of these consultants own firms that employ other people (established mostly in the last decade), others act as individual consultants. The sample was drawn from firms and consultants with the highest number of projects implemented across the country. All the firms act as consultancies not only in strategic urban development, but also in beautification projects, architecture, and planning. But their principle area of activity, as stated by the interviewees, is as consultants and intermediaries between the client (government, business) and planners or architects, who, in the end, are charged with implementing the vision. The firms operate not only in Moscow but also in other regions of Russia.

The interviews were conducted in Russian in 2020. The interviews consisted of three parts: (a) how did consultants establish their firm at the beginning: how did they recruit employees, what were their first projects; (b) what is the current status of the firm, how have they developed their business; (c) and what is their opinion on the profession of the urbanist and on the market for consultancy in urban development and public policymaking. I supplemented this with an analysis of publicly available sources, including media interviews with other consultants. Additionally, I analyzed publicly available descriptions of their projects, listed on consultant's websites, which helped to sort out which projects were valuable to them and how they represent themselves publicly. The analysis is focused on the field of knowledge production, understood as system of actors and interactions that includes a set of rules and common practices, power arrangements between actors, and the predominance of particular interests and styles of consulting as hegemonic.

Urban Consulting in the City of Moscow

The Prevalence of Personal Trust

In Russia, the sphere of urban planning and governance was a relatively opaque and state-run profession until the early 2010s. It had not achieved the same public status as it has today. Masterplans and strategies for urban development, created by state-employed public planners, were not widely discussed in public (Golubchikov, 2004). Over the last two decades, however, private individual actors and companies entered the scene of urban consultancy in cities across Russia, including Moscow. Here I trace how these actors gained access to the field, and whether access has changed with the increased professionalization of the sphere.

Access to the field and gaining trust. For the majority of the consultants who are now visible as experts in the field, their careers got started in spheres connected with governmental structures. Before becoming consultants, the majority had already established a wide web of contacts with the Moscow authorities and federal government and gained a reputation through different pathways: business, economics, architecture, and the university sphere. Some of them had experience working inside the president's analytical center developing strategies for regional development in Russia during the 1990s. Others consulted the deputies of the State Duma on the legal process during the 2000s. Networking, as described by the interviewees, was one of the primary strategies deployed in setting out to establish firms and build a client base, and continues to be an important strategy today. Prior to becoming consultants, the founders of KB Strelka—the most famous and largest Moscow-based consultancy, founded in 2013—were influential private actors and had contacts with high-level government officials, including federal ministries (Suvorova and Mudryi, 2017). Another prominent example is the Institute for Urban Economics, a NGO, which, since the mid-1990s, has attracted a number of specialists in economics and geography and "consults on socio-economic development, participates in law-making, and provides independent evaluation" (Institute for Urban Economics, 2020). The Institute's projects built a bond of trust between the government and its specialists, some of which have managed to become private consultants due to these established networks. Some also joined universities as professors or lecturers, drawing from professional associations as a means of generating credibility. The Institute still plays an important role in urban consultancy, providing advice on the housing system, and various laws and regulations in the sphere of urban planning and infrastructure development.

For each firm and for every consultant, their initial projects were acquired through personal contacts with both government and private firms. In this context, consultants had to carve out a niche for themselves. The formation of a firm and the initial difficulties it encountered were often related to the idea that each firm must provide a unique service, one which was not common before. Notably, the capacity for consultants to build trust and credibility in speaking to a new field of knowledge initially depended on personal networks. Consultants needed to convince clients that there was a need for their advice and that implementing their ideas would make the public or commercial space better, which, for public officials, meant that these spaces would be more profitable. Personal trust in the firm's leaders stimulated the trust in such new initiatives:

> When we just began, this sphere was not defined. It was not clear who is an urbanist: many thought that it is something close to hipster, but who is a hipster was not clear for everyone either. And probably, in the first stages, the most difficult thing was to translate from language to language. But it absolutely does not mean that the market had its own language and you simply could translate it. No, different clients had completely different coordinate systems. <…> And then, using the common "non-professional" language, we needed to explain how it is working, what is your property, what do you actually have, what is its value which often was not seen.
>
> [Head of planning firm, 2]

As the quotation makes clear, consultants often initiated their careers by promoting new, market-based ideas in urban development, such as increasing the effectiveness of the space usage. However, they could only establish credibility to the extent that they had already established trust with clients through their work in other spheres. The reputation of the consultants was built up in other areas, before they got to urbanism. Rather than drawing on professional affiliations or public reputations, the majority of the firms relied on relations of personal trust.

Through fostering long-standing relationships with the same clients, personal contacts have been central to helping urban consultants set up and maintain business. For example, it is not unusual for regional governments or corporations to commission the same urban experts for different projects, developing enduring relationships over time. For example, the consultancy firm Novaya Zemlya has long developed different types of projects and urban strategies in cooperation with the Metalloinvest, one of the largest mining and metallurgical holdings (Novaya Zemlya, 2020). The consultancy firm plans projects in cities where the holding company conducts its business and has its financial investments. In this context, long-term trust-based relationships with the same client are the primary source for business.

While a market for urban consultancy has taken shape in Russia, the field remains quite unstable. As one consultant notes: "this sphere can't be called a sustainable market, because it is based on the budget cycle" [interview 1] of the government. In spite of instability, a market for urban consultancy has gradually consolidated in Russia to the point where some firms can now choose between clients and the projects they work on. As my interviews show, some of them work more with private clients (such as a large business) because the projects with public authorities are more demanding (involving more communication with the client, editing, approval of the client) and entail more risks in terms of the final result and responsibility. Other firms work more on projects for public authorities on different levels of power. However, regardless of the type of the client, the consultancy field remains dependent on personal contacts, especially between the client and the owner or the main expert in the firm: personal participation in a project by the firm's top executives remains very important.

Professionalization of the sphere. Reputations built from personal networks have been further consolidated through support from the federal government, which came to promote urbanism as an emerging field in the 2000s, especially in the city of Moscow, where they helped to establish the infrastructure necessary to consolidate urban consultancy as a distinctive profession. Examples of state-backed initiatives include the Moscow Urban Forum, an annual international forum for urban issues established with federal support for the development of new educational programs in urbanism. However, it cannot be said that government initiatives themselves led to the rise of the expertise and consultancy in the urban sphere; rather, the government supported its rise and shaped its cornerstones through funding the necessary infrastructure: forums, conferences, governmental programs.

While personal networks remain prominent drivers of urban consultancy, influence in the field has more recently been shaped by professional associations, including new educational programs in urban planning and architecture. With the founding of major urbanism-oriented institutions, the consolidation of urban consultancy as a professional field in its own right, and the emergence of a new type of "urban planner," access to the field is no longer so strictly dependent on personal connections within the inner circle of urban planners.

Various educational programs and other initiatives support the expertise in this sphere. The largest and most influential universities in Moscow have developed Masters programs that are focused not only on planning and architecture, which had been the previous educational approach mostly inherited from the Soviet Union. Some universities, such as Higher School of Economics, set up bachelor programs, which gained a lot of attention. In 2019, a public initiative aimed mostly at students and devoted to planning and beautification was financially supported by the government and spread its network to the whole country (City Renovations, 2020). That initiative provides the opportunity to students and young professionals to take an internship and participate in many research projects, events, and forums, with the support of professional associations and governmental structures (ministries, presidential grants, Federal Council).

However, the profession of the new independent consultant on city development is only in its nascent stage and personal trust remains important in the sphere of urban consultancy. This is mirrored in the process of recruiting, too. Consultants consider hiring new members mostly through Russia's largest universities: the Moscow State University, the leading institution of higher education in Russia, and the Higher School of Economics, a national research university. These sources are claimed to be the main supply for new recruits because of the trusted expertise of the creators, lecturers, and professors in these programs. However, each expert I interviewed stressed the difficulty of finding staff due to the importance of recommendations. They hire through networking:

> I think, we always keep our vacancies on HeadHunter[1] open, but the rest is totally word of mouth and recommendations. If I speak honestly, the topics in the sphere is so unique, so it is quite impossible to use the other sources [for hiring].
>
> [Head of planning firm, 4]

[1] The largest headhunter website in Russia.

Thus, while access to credentials (university programs, professional experience) is gaining importance in the sphere of consultancy, personal trust and networks still play a crucial role in access to the field and in the life of the consultancy bureau, outweighing the importance of credentials.

Networked Reputation and Ambivalences of Competition and Collaboration

Beyond looking at how firms are able to access the field of urban consultancy, it is also important to consider how different consultancy firms relate to each other, exploring the possibility of competition between different firms, the role of alliances and collaborations between them, and how they differentiate themselves from one another. While consultants stress the differences between each other, competition remains limited.

Specialization based on clients. Consultants often describe their firms as a "boutique consultancy." Such a definition relies on the individuality of their projects:

> We did not choose the way of mass-market, but more the way of a boutique company, where each project is individual -- it is characterized by individual development, starting with methodology and ending with the scheme of realization.
>
> [Head of planning firm, 2]

Each firm emphasizes that it creates unique projects. Claims of individuality are common for many companies and consultants. However, here it is related to the fact that such firms claim to "create a new thing every time" and to "resolve the specific issues of particular clients in particular moment" [interview 1]. It does not only emphasize the specifics of the certain firm, but also the relevance of the particular client for the outcome, as well as the novelty and uncertainty of the sphere itself.

Meanwhile, many consultants admit that beautification projects, which could be described as architectural solutions and often cannot be addressed as unique products per se, provide the largest percentage of the contracts. In such projects, the firm oversees projects for local parks, streets, or public spaces. Such planning projects help them to establish trust and gain reputation: they become the intermediaries between the authorities and the builders, establishing a relationship with the clients.

Furthermore, as stressed by the consultants, they aim to gain greater expertise that goes beyond merely working on physical public spaces, moving toward strategic planning and policy advice.

Claiming that there is a lack of competition does not mean that there is a high degree of specialization: firms will often take on a variety of projects. One of the main requirements for consultants in this sphere is that "they need to work with every problem in any city, as if dropped out there by a helicopter" [interview 1]. Regarding their skills and knowledge, some of the companies claim to be ready for any type of consultancy project. The differentiation between the approaches is not entirely visible from the outside, especially given the number of planning projects and public space developments performed by each company. At the same time, each consultant struggles to name the competitors in the sphere. Speaking to the lack of competitors, some of them emphasize, that "we can develop the most difficult projects, which are very risky" [interview 1], some describe their tasks as to "deal with multifunctionality" [interview 5], which was not for everyone. They do not feel a lot of pressure from consultants within the same field. Because access to the projects is structured through networking and personal trust, there is no need for consultants to compete for the projects openly.

Asymmetric competition. The firm that is unsurpassed in terms of success and competition, and mentioned by almost all respondents, is KB Strelka. Consultants sometimes criticize it for its standardized approach and monopolistic influence. For example, Strelka participated in developing new housing standards, which were adopted across the country. Strelka is the only firm that has the capacity for large-scale projects. It does not fit the definition of a boutique consultancy. Instead, it is able to hire substantial personnel and establish various departments, including urban anthropology and urban economics. Thus, Strelka has become the dominant competitor, having solidified its reputation and developed expertise in every sphere of urban knowledge. The firm is most often approached by the authorities to cooperate on numerous programs. Also, Strelka's huge projects denote the importance of personal trust in consultancy. These projects become possible due to the long-time relationships of the Moscow authorities with Strelka, which strengthened the trust between them. By contrast, a consultant of a boutique firm states:

> We rarely can, we do not have much power to contact the cities or governors and communicate with them somehow. It is a long process and completely different people and realities. It does not mean that they are bad clients though, you simply need to communicate with them longer, they represent the interests of the whole society, they have law regulations, etc. Thus, only a huge organization with ultimate powerful support as Strelka can take this on. We can't do that at all.
>
> [Head of planning firm, 3]

One of the simple ways to cope with such an obstacle is gaining support through a consortium. Thereby, firms bundle resources to take part in long-term projects which require complex expertise. This form of collaboration, having emerged only recently, is used most often in public competitions. However, boutique consultancies do not mention such forms as a way for increasing competition, rather as another way to get larger contracts.

Competition is limited not by the differentiation of the market spheres and different services which each consultant provides. The lack of competition is predefined by the structural peculiarities of the network structure where each company is significantly limited by the number of clients and authorities they have a routinized working relationship with.

The Role of Publicity for a Professional Reputation

In Moscow, consultants manage their publicity to augment their personal networks with clients and reputation within the professional field. Urbanism has become a popular topic in public discourse, with a wide array of new public figures—such as bloggers, activists, and academics—claiming credibility in speaking to urban issues (Abashev et al., 2020). Consultants have responded to the growing popularity of such figures by emphasizing their specialized expertise. Through the public performance of professional identity, they try to differentiate themselves, maintaining a niche for their services.

Maintaining expertise. Over the past 10 years, many experts, including those I interviewed, have attempted to gain public recognition by promoting their expertise through public forums, presentations, speeches, lectures, books, podcasts, etc. They often comment on issues in the media, being presented as experts in the urban sphere.

One of the most significant expressions of publicity is pro bono projects. Some consultants accept offers to participate in projects which are not explicitly profitable due to the "pure interest" of being involved in cultural production. Pro bono projects are sought for the sake of the R&D model for the business: "we can do the project for a little money if it is super-interesting, iconic, and cool cultural project, which we can perform with pleasure" [interview 4]. For consultants, the audience for such projects is primarily the professional community, not the general public.

The presentation of projects to the general public is not important to secure contacts. Companies can refrain from public engagement and still run projects and gain fame in the professional community. For example, the Moscow Center of Urbanism has recruited a number of young professionals for their consultancy projects, but, for a while, did not even have a public website. Nor did they mention their main expert—Sergey Kapkov, a former government official, who is very famous for his work on the Gorky Park project, the first prominent redevelopment of a Soviet park. This further demonstrates the importance and priority placed by consultants on personal connections: the main expert of the firm does not need to be mentioned publicly as affiliated with the firm as contracts are arranged through networks. Publicly accessible websites with project descriptions and ideas are of little importance for the other experts as well: as stated by the consultants, clients hardly use them, preferring to address their network. Thus, firms do not get much capital from them. This also applies to the largest consultancy bureau KB Strelka. While Strelka Institute initiates events, public talks, and lectures, the bureau does not explicitly present its projects on its website, mentioning only briefly some of them on a landing page (Strelka, 2020). Thus, for the sake of business development, there appears to be no need to be particularly visible to a wider audience.

Public experts vs. consultants in practice. However, consultants are not the only ones to exercise their expertise publicly. In the 2010s, the sphere of urbanism and city development was one of the main topics across the media landscape. During this time, numerous bloggers, activists, and critics became popular expressing their opinions on various urban issues through different media. The most famous of them are located in Moscow (Varlamov, The Village). Although many have no formal education in planning or architecture or professional networks, as consultants do, they have captured the attention of a wider audience.

This popular discourse has provoked controversies among professional consultants who see themselves forced to acquire their own public reputation. Some of them claimed that popular knowledge should be distinguished from professional expertise. Speaking about one famous blogger, a private consultant said that "he is good at being a publicist in the sphere of talking about the cities" [interview 5]. However, the interviewee points out, that "this is not the professional job," marking the distance between experts and publicists. In an index which orders the experts in urban sphere, professionals do not rank the bloggers as highly as their more structurally positioned and recognized colleagues, but accept their rising popularity (CPK, 2020).

Others explained this as a process, which is indirectly important for their work:

> This is absolutely important, because this is an opportunity to hear, even if poorly formulated, some pain, to understand how the physical environment which is made by the planner is perceived, why, etc. This is definitely super important.
>
> [Head of planning firm, 3]

In this quotation, the consultant relies on public opinion as an indicator: the public reaction to the projects could be either good or bad, but the only post-factum reaction is possible. The initial advice on city development is neither articulated nor publicly discussed. Instead, this is a sphere for the expression of expert knowledge. Thus, the consultants become intermediaries between the government, business, media, and the contractors (e.g. architects). Being very close to the authorities, private and small consultancy firms rely on publicity only for building up symbolic capital among experts and public reputation. Public expressions of knowledge are only of minor importance for the business itself. Thus, the system of knowledge production promotes the role of particular experts, more often than not—the leaders of the firms.

Conclusion

This chapter addressed consultants' influence on knowledge production in urban development. In the context of Moscow, I have demonstrated that such consultants operate in relatively closed environments, which are not particularly open to public discussion, despite the wide publicity of the main experts and the popularity of the sphere. Drawing from personal networks, consultants entered the field of urban consultancy from positions already close to prominent decision-makers. This helped them to secure their first projects and then to gain more trust with businesses and authorities. Thus, knowledge production has depended most prominently on relationships of personal trust.

Access to the field is broadening due to the emergence of new avenues for institutionalization, including new academic faculties, countless forums and books, and the increasing popularity of the topic in the public. Consequently, a tension has emerged between consultants and outsiders, who are deemed to lack sufficient credentials to speak to urban issues. However, the inner circle of the main consultants is still well-managed: most consultants view bloggers who work on urbanism as only providing a platform for testing and discussing ideas brought forward by urban consultants, or as a popular phenomenon, irrelevant to their profession.

Due to the limited influence of the public on the decisions implemented by the consultants, public performance remains a subordinate strategy in generating credibility. Rather than seeking to influence the general public through their performances, consultants have instead adopted publicity strategies with the aim of influencing public officials and other professionals. Pro bono projects or forums, books, and collaborations play a greater role for the consultants because of the prestige and expertise gained in the eyes of the authorities or corporations, which allow them to grow the networks further.

In the case of Moscow, the manner in which actors have been able to access the field of urban consultancy is a central factor in shaping their career prospects in urban development. More broadly, exploring the different ways in which consultants make claims to credibility—through personal networks, professional associations, and public performances—can further the research on role and influence of consultants in public policymaking.

References

Abashev, V.V., Vlasova, E.G., Pechishhev, I.M., Pustovalov, A.V. and Kurbanova, R.F. (2020) *Urbanizm i urbanisty v rossijskih setevyh izdanijah 2010-h godov*, Perm': Permskij gosudarstvennyj nacional'nyj issledovatel'skij universitet.

Allmendinger, P. and Haughton, G. (2012) 'Post-political spatial planning in England: A crisis of consensus?', *Transactions of the Institute of British Geographers* 37(1): 89–103.

Argenbright, R., Bityukova, V.R., Kirillov, P.L., Makhrova, A.G. and Nefedova, T.G. (2019) 'Directed suburbanization in a changing context: "New Moscow" today', *Eurasian Geography and Economics* 61(3): 211–239.

Boswell, C. (2008) 'The political functions of expert knowledge: Knowledge and legitimation in European Union immigration policy', *Journal of European Public Policy* 15(4): 471–488.

Büdenbender, M. and Zupan, D. (2017) 'The evolution of neoliberal urbanism in Moscow, 1992–2015: The evolution of neoliberal urbanism in Moscow', *Antipode* 49(2): 294–313.

Carr, E. S. (2010) 'Enactments of expertise', *Annual Review of Anthropology* 39(1): 17–32.

Commenges, H., Tomasoni, L., Seigneur, C., Bonin, O., Leurent, F., Bonhomme, C. and Deroubaix, J.-F. (2017) 'Who is the expert? Integrated urban modeling and the reconfiguration of expertise', *Journal of Urban Technology* 24(2): 89–108.

City Renovations. (2020) *Renovations.* https://urbanrenovation.ru/renovation/, accessed 4 September 2020.

CPK. (2020) *Ranking of the experts in the field of urbanism.* 8 July, https://cpkr.ru/issledovaniya/budushchee/reyting-ekspertov-v-sfere-urbanistiki/, accessed 4 September 2020.

Department of Construction. (2020) *Index of quality of the city environment.* https://xn----dtbcccdtsypabxk.xn--p1ai/#/, accessed 4 September 2020.

Faculty of Urban and Regional development. (2020) *HSE experts took part in creating an educational program for city managers.* 22 July, https://gorod.hse.ru/news/381345159.html, accessed 4 September 2020.

Faulconbridge, J. and Jones, A. (2012) 'The geographies of management consultancy firms', in T. Clark and M. Kipping (eds). *The Oxford Handbook of Management Consulting*, Oxford: Oxford University Press, pp. 225–246.

Faust, M. (2012) 'Sociological perspectives on management consulting', in *The Oxford Handbook Of Management Consulting.*

Golubchikov, O. (2004) 'Urban planning in Russia: Towards the market', *European Planning Studies* 12(2): 229–247.

Hordijk, M. and Baud, I. (2006) 'The role of research and knowledge generation in collective action and urban governance: How can researchers act as catalysts?', *Habitat International* 30(3): 668–689.

Institute for Urban Economics. (2020) *About us*. http://www.urbaneconomics.ru/o-nas, accessed 4 September 2020.

Kalyukin, A., Borén, T. and Byerley, A. (2015) 'The second generation of post-socialist change: Gorky Park and public space in Moscow', *Urban Geography* 36(5): 674–695.

Strelka. K.B. (2020)*About the company*. https://strelka-kb.com/, accessed 4 September 2020.

Khirfan, L., Momani, B. and Jaffer, Z. (2013) 'Whose authority? exporting Canadian urban planning expertise to Jordan and Abu Dhabi', *Geoforum* 50: 1–9.

Krick, E. (2015) 'Negotiated expertise in policy-making: How governments use hybrid advisory committees', *Science and Public Policy* 42(4): 487–500.

McCann, E. J. (2008) 'Expertise, truth, and urban policy mobilities: Global circuits of knowledge in the development of Vancouver, Canada's 'four Pillar' Drug strategy', *Environment and Planning A: Economy and Space* 40(4): 885–904.

Moser, P. (2013) 'Integrating urban knowledge', in H.T Andersen and R. Atkinson (eds.) *Production and Use of Urban Knowledge,* Dordrecht: Springer, pp. 17–34.

Novaya Zemlya. (2019) *GIS-integrated infrastructure index for the Izhevsk development strategy 2030*. http://novaya-uk.com/gis-integrated-infrastructure-index-for-the-izhevsk-development-strategy-2030/, accessed 4 September 2020.

Novaya Zemlya. (2020) *The best solutions for spatial, socio-economic development of cities and territories*. https://www.nzemlya.com/main, accessed 4 September 2020.

Özdemir, E. (2019) 'The role of the expert knowledge in politicizing urban planning processes: A case from Istanbul', *Planning Theory* 18(2): 237–259.

Suvorova, N. and Mudryi, S. (2017) 'Issledovanie: kak ustroen biznes «Strelki»', 2 November, Inc. https://incrussia.ru/fly/issledovanie-kak-ustroen-biznes-strelki/, accessed 4 September 2020.

Everywhere from Copenhagen: Method, Storytelling, and Comparison in the Globalization of Public Space Design

Eugene McCann and Lise Mahieus

Introduction

Sydney, Hamburg, New York, Chongqing, Sao Paulo, Amman, Moscow, Mexico City, Toronto, Kilmarnock. The "Our Approach" section of the Copenhagen-based architecture firm Gehl Architects' website, includes an introductory video displaying forty cities and towns, which, it soon becomes clear, are some of the places the company has worked since its founding in 2000 (Gehl Architects, n.d.-a). The video's narrative explains,

> we approach our work both as social scientists and architects, spending days, weeks, months, and years investigating the interconnected loop between life and form in cities throughout the world. As social scientists

We would like to thank Chris Hurl and Anne Vogelpohl for their valuable comments on earlier drafts of this chapter.

E. McCann (✉) · L. Mahieus
Simon Fraser University, Burnaby, BC, Canada
e-mail: emccann@sfu.ca

L. Mahieus
e-mail: lise_mahieus@sfu.ca

C. Hurl and A. Vogelpohl (eds.), *Professional Service Firms and Politics in a Global Era*, https://doi.org/10.1007/978-3-030-72128-2_6

> we observe how people use their environments and how they contribute to people's quality of life and lifestyle. As architects we are concerned with the form of the built environment in response to people's uses and needs.

As might be expected of a firm whose focus is the design of streets, plazas, and "life between buildings" (Gehl, 2011), the firm's observational method tends to address relatively small urban spaces. Yet, at the same time, as the video makes clear, the firm's scope is global, with offices in Copenhagen, New York, and San Francisco offering cities insights into "improving quality of life for people … [by] pairing people's needs, values, and principles with beautiful, useable, intelligent spaces" (Gehl Architects, n.d.-a).

Gehl Architects is a global design consultancy closely associated with Jan Gehl, a Danish architect, academic, and urban designer who co-founded the firm with fellow architect, Helle Søholt, in 2000. Gehl is a prominent global figure in a planning movement called "placemaking," an approach that emphasizes collaborative community planning to redesign public spaces (Project for Public Spaces, 2007). His time as an academic architect, early in his career, as well as his work in practice has afforded him substantial credibility as a purveyor of his brand, or model, of public space design.

In this chapter, we follow the work of Vogelpohl (2019, 98) and others, who point to the way in which global professional service firms act to shape cities and urban policy "through methodical standards, to solidify competitive thinking through comparisons and networked knowledge as well as data sets, and to expect solutions through their prestigious name and external perspective" (see also Bok and Coe, 2017). We consider Gehl and his firm as a particular case of a professional service firm that acts as a transnational policy actor, what the policy mobilities literature calls a global "transfer agent," to create and mobilize models of "best practice" in urban policy (McCann, 2011; Ward, 2018; Temenos et al., 2019). Understanding Gehl helps us understand the ideas and practices of a wider set of "placemakers" who increasingly hold the center of debates about the future of urban design and planning. Our discussion also deepens an underdeveloped element of the policy mobilities literature: the study of private corporate actors in the circulation of policy models. Gehl Architects trades in a certain type of urban expertise as a product, represented by the firm's credo, "first life, then space and finally buildings" (Gehl Article, n.d.-b). By circulating its version of placemaking among cities, the firm has created and benefits from a market for its ideas and the Gehl brand.

We argue that Gehl generates credibility from a carefully curated image as a committed devotee of straightforward observational methods, like notetaking and counting people in public spaces, and the firm's centering of what they call "architectural ethnography" (Gehl Architects, 2019) in their approach. These methodological attributes are selling points that drive the travels of the Gehl approach among cities. The methodological orientation gives the firm distinctiveness and gravitas. It positions Gehl as an experienced and meticulous expert; a serious force of change.

This discussion of urban design ideas in motion is part of our larger research project on how urban public space is globalized through the circulation of design models. In this paper we provide a preliminary account, drawing on our critical analysis of Gehl Architects' website, supplemented by Jan Gehl's books and other related media, to identify the key elements of the practice's approach to public space.

In the following sections, we will first elaborate on the geographies of policy mobilities, as evident in Gehl's approach: the way consultants establish credibility, construct a story of a better urban future, and create markets for their intellectual products; and the role of methods, and persuasive storytelling in consultants' work. We will detail Gehl's approach to public space and unpack his firm's methodology and methods, with an eye to the assumptions that underlie the approach and questions they raise about the way design-oriented "placemaking" tends to address only a superficial level of urban life and space. We will also contrast Gehl's tendency to invoke a singular, undifferentiated "public" for whom space should be designed to how critical social scientists theorize public space, not simply as a matter of design and planning, but as constituted by multiple publics, conflicts, and tensions.

Policymaking and Public Space in the Urban-Global Context

How might we think about private consultants circulating their vision of public space among cities across the globe? What are the implications of their involvement in urban policymaking? The policy mobilities literature provides a number of insights (McCann, 2011; Temenos and McCann, 2014; Ward, 2018), as does the critical literature on publics and public spaces (Bodnar, 2015; Mitchell, 1995, 2017; Nowicka, 2020; Valentine, 2008).

Policy Mobilities

For our purposes, three themes are particularly relevant. First, the policy mobilities literature discusses "transfer agents" (Stone, 2004) as a "specialist elite" (Larner, 2002, 663) who work through various networks to circulate "best practice" models for urban governance and design among cities. The global consultancy industry, from global firms (Chang, 2017; Rapoport and Hult, 2017; Vogelpohl, 2019, see Purandare in this volume) to "middling technocrats" (Larner and Laurie, 2010), to lone gurus (Peck, 2005; McCann, 2008, see Volkova in this volume), is one iteration of this type of transfer agent. Consultants promote their models as ideal "solutions," ready for adoption by a wider variety of clients. In this process, credibility must be established: the transfer agent must show that they have done the work and often personally developed a model approach to a specific problem. They must also shape a narrative about their approach, drawing on successful case studies in various locations. Crucially, they must tell these place-specific stories with enough generality that they are seen by policy actors elsewhere as being applicable to their own particular circumstances and the consultants must make it clear that the lessons from the distant case studies can be adapted to different and changing circumstances. Consultants work not only to solve policy problems, then, but also to create markets for their solutions (Baker et al., 2016).

In turn, a second insight—the role of metrics and measures—has been developed by policy mobilities scholars. They argue that these calculative and comparative technologies are a necessary factor in the mobilization of policy models. "Labour such as the generation of indicators or benchmarks … becomes necessary for the translation process as it creates consensus over differences" (Adscheid and Schmitt, 2019, 5). As Larner and Le Heron (2002, 761) argue, technologies such as calculations make the "incommensurable commensurable." Metric-making thus facilitates market-making and circulation by creating equivalencies and comparable cases among otherwise distinct cities.

A third theme in the literature addresses the role private consultants play in narrating and legitimating specific visions or agendas in debates over the future of cities (McCann, 2011; Jokinen et al., 2018; Montero, 2019; Franco and Ortiz, 2020). There are at least two elements to this storytelling that are relevant to the work of placemaking consultants like Gehl. First, when a policy receives global awards and recognition as a "best practice," its entry into a new city comes wrapped in that story of success and plaudits. As a result, it can be difficult for groups who are skeptical of a new policy to challenge it since it is narrated as a globally accepted "best practice." Second, as consultants narrate their strategy for overcoming complex policy and political problems in a city, their storytelling tends to involve a form of "post-political" simplification and technicalization (Swyngedouw, 2009). They need to "boil down" complex issues within cities and profound differences among cities in order to create a ready market for their policy products.

In this way, planning and design consultants like Gehl fit neatly in a long tradition of persuasive storytelling in urban planning. Indeed, this tradition is so central to the discipline that Throgmorton (2003, 126) defines planning as "persuasive and constitutive storytelling about the future." As Söderström et al. (2014), drawing on Sandercock (2003) and Throgmorton (2003), argue, storytelling is crucial to a future-oriented discipline like planning, while we would add that the architecture and design professions find it similarly crucial. As Throgmorton (2003, 128, our emphasis) continues, "*stories cannot tell themselves*. Rather, they must be transformed into narratives and then be told. That act of construction is necessarily selective and purposeful."

> Through emplotment, characterizations, descriptions of settings, and rhythm and imagery of language, such 'planning stories' unavoidably shape the readers' attention, turning it this way instead of that. (ibid., 127)

Planning as storytelling is about power—the power to name, to make and affix meaning, and to shape urban politics (Söderström et al., 2014). In planning, "it is not merely the individual stories that count, but *storytelling* and the complex social networks, physical settings, and institutional processes in which those stories are told" (Throgmorton, 2007, 250, quoted in Van Hulst, 2012, 301; italics in the original). Moreover, this narrative power is not simply localized: "[C]ities and their planning-related organizations can be thought of as nodes in a global-scale web, a web that consists of a highly fluid and constantly (albeit subtly) changing set of relationships" (Throgmorton, 2003, 130). We suggest that these relationships are built, maintained, and extended by private planning, architecture, and design consultants like Gehl and other placemakers. Yet, whether operating in local contexts or in wider networks, placemakers' narratives are what Van Hulst (2012, 302, following Forester, 1993) calls storytelling as "organizing attention." They direct focus to certain aspects of public space and, deliberately or not, away from others. We unpack this issue in the following section.

Critical Approaches to Public Space

Gehl's ideal of urban public space is a liberal consensual one—a singular convivial place for a singular public. This can, if not approached carefully, divert attention from a critical understanding of public space as rife with exclusions and injustices that cannot be simply remedied through design, even while design exacerbates them. The liberal consensual ideal also draws attention away from a more progressive ideal of public space as multiple, complex, and open to dissensus. The long-standing critical urban public space literature (see Bodnar, 2015 for a review) contrasts with and highlights the elisions in placemakers' vision.

This literature shows that public space reflects and reproduces the social inequalities of contemporary society, while also providing a setting in which people express their political positions (Terzi and Tonnelat, 2017). It is simultaneously a space of inclusion and exclusion, conformity and subversion, characterized by various and often incompatible uses (Parkinson, 2013; Bodnar, 2015). This is why "public spaces are absolutely essential to the functioning of democratic politics" (Mitchell, 1995, 115).

Not only is public space essential to political expression, but it is also where political identities can be formed with or against the strangers one encounter (Young, 1986; Bodnar, 2015). For Young (1986), the "being together of strangers" generally encourages openness to unassimilated others, ideally leading to a less oppressive city and a progressive politics of difference. In this sense, public space is not only a site of protest and other explicitly political expressions. It is also a site of and stake in the quotidian negotiation of living together (Massey, 2005).

Yet, public space should not be romanticized as an entirely positive space, even when well-designed. First, it is not equally welcoming or accessible to all. It is frequently the site and object of securitization and surveillance practices that differentially target racialized, classed, and stigmatized people, while it is also frequently less accessible to people who are disabled and the elderly than to more physically able people. Second, not everyone has the choice of whether or how to participate in public space. While being in public is a choice for many, it is a necessity for people who are homeless or whose housing is so cramped or inadequate that they must spend large portions of their days in public, often performing private acts, like bathing. Third, proximity does not always lead to "meaningful contact" (Valentine, 2008, 334) and, indeed, frequently involves violence (Catungal and McCann, 2010). Groups who exist together in public space frequently do not mix together in any meaningful way. Fourth, proximity can breed defensiveness. Convivial interactions in public can be superficial displays of urban etiquette—which do not always equate to lessening of prejudice or overcoming social distance (Valentine, 2008; Nowicka, 2020).

Superficial forms of encounter in public space may maintain the social order by creating the expectation that people will suppress differences in their interactions. Nowicka (2020) warns against mistakenly adhering to a "fantasy of equality" (Nowicka, 2020, 32). She calls for greater attention to how the prevalent belief in equality obscures, rather than corrects, injustices. The critical question applies: who is public space for? It cannot be conceptualized as an apolitical place of peaceful and convivial interactions, but as a "battleground where different hegemonic projects are confronted" (Mouffe, 2007, 3). Indeed, as Mouffe (2005) argues, conflicts are ineradicable in politics and social life. Therefore, aiming for consensual definitions of publicness and public space can obscure injustices and tensions instead of giving them a place to be addressed, which leads to the emergence of antagonisms (Fraser, 1990).

Clearly, then, public space is complex and political. Yet, it is the very simplicity and unitary ideal espoused by placemakers like Gehl—an ideal of a singular public whose relationships to space can be grasped through observational measurements and enhanced through design interventions—that attracts local governments intent on adopting relatively anodyne and uncontroversial solutions. The model circulates among cities as a result of its elision of unequal power relations among publics.

"Cities for People": Gehl's Diagnosis, Prescriptions, and Influence

Combining his academic pursuits with the work his firm has done since its founding in 2000, Gehl has become a *bona fide* global policy guru—a transfer agent of urban design and public space planning. His firm has expanded internationally, creating markets as it grows. Gehl and his firm are skilled in packaging and presenting their ideas in a way that is persuasive to their intended audiences, including city governments and others who buy, literally and figuratively, into their model. This vision of a walkable, "human-scale" city "for people" (Gehl, 2010), as represented in his academic background and his prolific output of books, lectures, workshops, and masterclasses that describe the successes and lessons of his consulting contracts with 250 cities, is a particular form of persuasive storytelling. Using carefully crafted stories that "[set] out a view of what is wrong and what needs fixing" (Van Hulst, 2012, 300, quoting Schön, 1979, 144), private consultants create the conditions for their ideas to be persuasive and mobile: they combine diagnoses of problems and prescriptions of solutions into an influential story. In Gehl's case, as we will explore below, appeals to unitary conceptions of "people" and "public" and to comparison and competition conditions audiences and markets to accept his vision of better urban spaces.

Diagnoses and Prescriptions Framing Discussion and Action

For Gehl, the problem with cities is the legacy of postwar modernist, automobile-oriented planning, leading to the "gradual breakdown of the opportunities of city space to function as a meeting place" (Gehl, 2010, 25). Having defined the problem, consultants must identify a solution and provide the data and principles necessary to achieve it. Drawing on a long lineage of architects and planners, and critics, including Jane Jacobs, William H. Whyte, Donald Appleyard, and Allan Jacobs, who he and Svarre profile in a chapter of *How to Study Public Life* (2013), Gehl's cure to the ills of the contemporary city is to study, then plan, "the city at eye level … the human landscape" in order to design spaces that will attract pedestrians and diverse social activity (Gehl, 2010, 195). Thus, Gehl's first book, *Life between buildings: Using public space*, originally published in Danish in 1971 and updated in new editions in various languages in the subsequent years (Gehl, 2011), emphasizes the necessity for planners and designers to focus primarily on creating cities where people want to congregate and encounter each other. These encounters are always envisioned as convivial, not conflictual.

Local Testimonials Highlighting Influence

Gehl's ideas have led to numerous commissions and are the subject of many laudatory comments from journalists and from planners in cities where his firm has worked. For example, recent media comments relating to his work in Toronto and elsewhere in Canada encapsulate the balance that consultants must find between personal approachability and a clear narrative of credible analysis. "Gehl is the demigod of urban planning," one senior planner exclaims, "We all have his books on our shelves" (quoted in Warren, 2009), while another publication continues the messianic theme while also emphasizing the alluring simplicity of Gehl's methods: "The Gospel of Jan Gehl, spread around the globe by a staff of 35, is so commonsensical it seems obvious" (Hume, 2012).

How to Study Public Life (Gehl and Svarre, 2013) catalogs many of the more significant commissions Gehl and his firm have had from cities. Copenhagen, Melbourne, and New York feature prominently as exemplars of this influence. On their website, the firm quotes Tina Saaby, Copenhagen's former Chief City Architect: "From Politicians to Department Heads, Project Managers and citizens – [Gehl's] notion of People First and Life, Space, Buildings has infiltrated all aspects of making Copenhagen what it is today" (quoted in Gehl Architects, n.d.-j) and they argue that, by 2014, "the new National Architecture Policy for Denmark emphasizes the need for a 'putting people first' approach to architecture, thereby making it a national political goal" (Gehl Architects, n.d.-k).

In Melbourne, where the firm has worked since the early 1990s to revitalize the urban core in the face of suburban flight (City of Melbourne, 2015), Gehl's methods of surveying and measuring the liveliness of urban public spaces have been internalized by the city's planning department. The city now conducts Gehl-style research, building on the consultant's earlier iterations. The firm, in turn, uses their work in Melbourne as a selling point when engaging with other cities, dubbing it the "Melbourne Miracle" (Gehl Architects, n.d.-i). A more recent engagement with New York City, beginning in the mid-2000s as part of its *PlaNYC* and Sustainable Streets programs, produced the *World Class Streets* report (Gehl Architects and NYC DOT, 2008) and pilot projects, including a temporary pedestrianization of Times Square, Broadway, and Herald Square (Gehl Architects, n.d.-l). Indeed, the firm argues that its influence goes further: they "trained the city" (Gehl Architects, n.d.-m) to follow their methods of surveying, data collection, and ongoing communication among stakeholders. Gehl's influence on planners and local politicians is not only built on his diagnosis of contemporary problems and his vision of a "people-centered" future. It is also legitimized by the evidence he develops from his particular way of studying public spaces.

"Taking a Good Look": Gehl on the Street

As we have argued, the process of generating credibility and mobilizing a model of expertise across geographically dispersed cities involves persuasive storytelling about the foundations and principles upholding the model. It also involves the development of methods and measures that emphasize the model's scientific, factual, or quantitative credibility and objectivity. If those methods can make it easier for potential customers or adopters to compare their situation to that of others elsewhere, through the creation of comparable measures and equivalences, all the better.

Gehl's professional "origin story" as a practitioner who has long combined on-the-ground experience with academic analysis is central to his credibility. A study trip took Gehl and his wife, psychologist Ingrid Gehl, to Italy in 1965. "While in Italy, they amass and observe many 'best practice' examples and gain inspiration away from the newly built 'lifeless' suburbs which were emerging in Denmark" (Gehl Architects, n.d.-c). While observing interactions in the *strate* and *piazze*, Ingrid Gehl insisted that "human behavior should be considered and used as the starting-point for architecture" (Gehl Architects, n.d.-d). They returned to Copenhagen and used the city as a "laboratory" for their ideas through the subsequent decades.

In response to their diagnosis of the lifelessness of the modernist car-oriented city, Gehl's firm is intent on "recording the 'life' that occurs in our study areas, as well as the qualities of the surrounding 'space'" (Gehl Architects, n.d.-a). Indeed, for a number of years until at least October 2019, its website noted that,

> At Gehl we use *architectural ethnography* [our emphasis] as a tool to understand the context, culture and behavior of people in the cities that we work with. These findings form the foundation of our project work and allow for long-term collaborations with our clients. (Gehl Architects, 2019)

The firm emphasizes the time invested in surveying and understanding the public spaces they work on. They discuss "spending days, weeks, months and years" (Gehl Architects, n.d.-a) to develop "the 'Gehl way of seeing'" (2019). They claim that their methods, geographic scope, and longitudinal studies provide them with "a huge pool of knowledge that allows us to compare how people interact and behave in cities all around the world" (Gehl Architects, n.d.-a). This knowledge pool is traced back to the Gehls' Italian sojourn its expansion beyond Copenhagen and into practice (as opposed to academia) is defined by Gehl's 1986 "Public Space Public Life (PSPL)" survey in Copenhagen (Gehl Architects, n.d.-e).

The firm surveys public life for two stated reasons: First, "making people count by making them visible for decision makers in planning and design processes" (Gehl Architects, n.d.-f) and, second, to make "the entire municipal government more people-focused and more evidence driven." The following section highlights how method, measurement, evidence, and comparison are central to this surveying practice.

Methods for Studying Public Life

Gehl's co-authored book, *How to Study Public Life* (Gehl and Svarre, 2013), codifies the firm's method and is billed as a "how to" guide that provides "concrete tools and stories ... about the interaction between life and the built environment" (Gehl Architects, n.d.-h). The book's preface outlines his methodology: "Public life studies are straightforward. The basic idea is for observers to walk around while taking a good look. Observation is the key and the means are simple and cheap" (Gehl and Svarre, 2013, xii). Appeals to the straightforward, the simple, the basic, to low-tech visual observation and to "manual methods" pervade the book's descriptions of Gehl's method: "using one's senses, common sense and simple registration techniques with pen and paper" (ibid., 6).

"[G]eneral study questions: how many, who, where, what, how long?" (ibid., 11) guide the approach and frame a set of methods: counting, mapping activities, tracing lines of movement, tracking (following) people, photographing (including time-lapse and video, a la Whyte [1980]), keeping a diary to note "details and nuances" as a "qualitative supplement to ... elucidate hard [quantitative] data," and test walks to immerse the observer in the study environment (ibid., 22–35).

It might seem odd that a private firm would freely share their methodology. Why would they not control and monetize it through proprietary protection? We suggest two reasons: (1) placemaking consultants genuinely want to improve cities and they believe their methods are fit-for-purpose, so they are willing to share for the greater good; and (2) the methods are so tied to the experience and reputation of Gehl and his firm that, even though they describe them openly, clients still see the architects' direct involvement in the implementation and interpretation of the study techniques (e.g., Gehl's name on the published report) as worth employing the firm. In many ways, consultancy is an industry built on networking and branding although, as one of this book's editors pointed out, the reliance on a personal brand (e.g., Gehl's) may be a different mode of operation than that of the Big Four accounting firms, which tend to downplay personal discretion in their metrics.

"Public Space Public Life" as a Key Consulting and Branding Tool

The "Public Space Public Life" study or survey (PSPL) is the core product of the firm's consultancy business, with versions having been produced for clients across the world. These studies combine the methods described above that are intended to provide a comprehensive understanding of the character of "public life" in a specific street, neighborhood, or district, town, or city. Some of the elements of the studies "are constant, such as counting pedestrians and registering stationary activities," but the combination and focus of each study is molded to the local context through "a close dialogue with local partners" over a long period of time, sometimes extending across decades (Gehl and Svarre, 2013, 126).

"Long-term" is a crucial word in the Gehl method. The first study in Copenhagen was undertaken in 1986, with follow-up surveys in 1996 and 2006 charting the gradual increase in both the amount of car-free space in the city center and also the number of people engaged in "stationary activities," as opposed to simply traversing the space (Gehl and Svarre, 2013, 126). This longitudinal approach has been replicated elsewhere. In Melbourne, for example, an initial study in 1994 served as a baseline against which to measure interventions aimed at changing the character of that city center. In the next decade, initiatives including, "narrow passageways through blocks of buildings were converted into attractive places for staying and sauntering. ... [and make] downtown Melbourne a more attractive place to live and to visit – by day and by night." Gehl's 2004 survey showed a growth of 71% in the amount of publics space in which people could stay and a 98% increase in pedestrian traffic in the area (ibid., 31). While acknowledging that these changes were the result of the collaboration of various actors and interests, they argue that, "having a public space-public life study as a tool in the process increased understanding of the importance of providing quality space" for people (ibid.). Repetition over years provides "a clear picture of what's working and what's not, and [allows planners] to track long-term development" (Kielgast, n.d.).

According to Gehl Architects (Copenhagen) Associate, Louise Vogel Kielgast, the long-term nature of PSPL projects is complemented by data it produces and the utility of that data for cross-city comparison. "[T]his is … the magic of the PSPL methodology!" she suggests,

> We know that data and numbers are things that you can agree on objectively, a layer underneath the subjective feeling and opinion of place, and this is important when planning decisions have to be made – to have the hard numbers.

Yet, we suggest that the apolitical and (ironically) asocial appeals to "people" and "the public" in the work of placemakers like Gehl and related appeals to uncomplicated counting or "registering" (Gehl and Svarre, 2013, 22) methods, largely based on detached observations in public spaces offer a superficial understanding of public space. Appeals to objective data elide, or "bracket" (cf. Fraser, 1990), the range of inequities, feelings, and opinions that constitute publics as differentiated and conflictual producers of public spaces. Work by Valentine (2008), among others, suggests that the detached observation of fleeting moments in urban public space tends to capture thin gestures of urban etiquette, rather than any kind of deep (dis)connection among users. We argue that policymakers may be attracted to the "cleanness," or clarity, of the Gehl method, its results, and the directions for change that it prescribes precisely because of its apolitical character. Moreover, as time goes on and the model travels, local governments are attracted to tales of success from elsewhere. They hope to "Copenhagenize" (Colville-Andersen, 2018) their cities, so to speak. In doing so, they validate and reinforce a "common sense" among placemakers about what makes a vibrant and attractive public space and for whom that space is to be made.

Comparative and Competitive Stories Creating Markets

Hard data not only overcomes subjectivity, according to the firm, but it also positions a city to compare and compete with others. For Gehl and Svarre (2013),

> Given the fact that a number of cities around the world have carried out PSPLs, we have a substantial amount of data that we can draw upon, to identify common patterns in human behaviours according to spatial design. This gives cities comparable data, to understand how your city performs in relation to public space and public life in other cities.

As the policy mobilities literature argues, comparison through metrics often involves ranking and competition under neoliberal urbanism. The treadmill of competition compels most urban business and political elites to emulate other cities' successes in order to outperform and outcompete them in a zero-sum game of interurban competition (McCann, 2004, 2013). As Gehl and Svarre (2013, 3) note in their book's introduction, from the late 1980s onwards, "[c]ity planners and politicians wanted to make conditions better for people in order to have an edge in inter-city competition. It became a strategic goal to create attractive cities for people." Tellingly, it is on this theme of competition that they also conclude their book:

> Copenhagen and Melbourne [among others] show how research, public space-public life studies, visions, political will and action can put cities on the world-class map … On lists of the "World's Most Livable Cities in the 21st century, it is no surprise that year after year Melbourne and Copenhagen continue to rank among the best." (ibid., 159)

Thus, a model like Gehl's is performative in that it sets the terrain for its own adoption and circulation through its provision of comparative—and competitive—techniques and technologies.

Discussion

In this chapter, we have used a study of Gehl Architects to highlight some of the ways in which private consultancies create markets for and circulate their products. In Gehl's case, and the case of other urban planning and design consultants, their products are intellectual and methodological, as much as physical. They must persuade potential clients that their models and the research metrics and methods underpinning them are valid, locally appropriate, and globally tested. As we have suggested, however, these products, or traveling models, embody assumptions about, and elisions of socio-spatial power relations. These forms of placemaking storytelling organize attention and tend to reinforce hegemonic notions of the public and desirable public life. Thus, the models are particularly attractive as technical, apparently apolitical, "solutions" to narrowly defined urban problems.

Analyzing Gehl's writings and Gehl Architects' website in the light of the long-standing critical social science literatures on public space emphasizes Gehl's undifferentiated and apolitical notions of "public space" and "the public." Both the firm and Gehl, himself, in his writing, emphasizes that they plan for "the public" and that cities should be "for people." Yet, they rarely unpack to whom these labels refer, apart from a few references to gender and age. This critique is particularly apropos in the dual contexts of the Covid-19 pandemic and the worldwide Black Lives Matter protests of 2020. On the one hand, "placemakers" and "urbanists," including Gehl, have been vocal in their proposals for modeling changes to the future design, funding, use, and regulation of temporarily car-free streets (McCann, 2020). Many of their ideas are attractive to politicians and planners because they are couched at a level of analysis where "the public" remains a unitary category, but, on the other hand, the murder of George Floyd has catalyzed a debate among planners about whether "urbanism" is for *all* people equally or whether the blind spots of what some critics refer to as hegemonic "white urbanism" are founded upon and also perpetuate long-standing inequalities, exclusions, and violence in the urban built environment. As planner Amina Yasin (2020) recently put it,

> Given the number of Black people profiled and murdered on our streets, how can urbanists remain singularly focused on fighting inanimate objects — like cars — while actively ignoring human rights, and silencing advocates who point out that streets aren't in reality for everyone? Perhaps systemic racism, in which ableism is entrenched, is the greatest enemy to cities and not cars? (see also Walker 2020a, 2020b)

Certainly, this caution resonates strongly with critical social scientists' arguments about the inequalities and exclusions that parallel and frequently overwhelm the political and social benefits of public space, as traditionally conceived. This homogenized conception of the public resonates with what Nowicka (2020, 32) calls the "fantasy of equality," which clouds the perception of, and stymies efforts to overcome, spatial injustices.

References

Adscheid, T. and Schmitt, P. (2019) 'Mobilising post-political environments: tracing the selective geographies of Swedish sustainable urban development', *Urban Research and Practice*, https://doi.org/10.1080/17535069.2019.1589564.

Baker, T., Cook, I.R., McCann, E., Temenos, C. and Ward, K. (2016) 'Policies on the move: The transatlantic travels of tax increment financing', *Annals of the American Association of Geographers* 106(2): 459–469.

Bodnar, J. (2015) 'Reclaiming public space', *Urban Studies* 52(12): 2090–2104.

Bok, R. and Coe, N.M. (2017) 'Geographies of policy knowledge: The state and corporate dimensions of contemporary policy mobilities', *Cities* 63: 51–57.

Catungal, J.P. and McCann, E.J. (2010) 'Governing sexuality and park space: Acts of regulation in Vancouver, BC', *Social and Cultural Geography* 11(1): 75–94.

Chang, I.C.C. (2017) 'Failure matters: Reassembling eco-urbanism in a globalizing China', *Environment and Planning A: Economy and Space* 49(8): 1719–1742.

City of Melbourne (2015) *Places for people: Establishing a platform of evidence to share Melbourne's future*, October, https://s3.ap-southeast-2.amazonaws.com/hdp.au.prod.app.com-participate.files/1114/4618/1290/Places_for_People_Strategy_pt1.pdf, accessed 30 September 2020.

Colville-Andersen, M. (2018) *Copenhagenize: The definitive guide to global bicycle urbanism*, Washington: Island Press.

Forester, J. (1993) 'Practice stories: The priority of practical judgment', in F. Fischer and J. Forester (eds). *The Argumentative Turn in Policy Analysis and Planning*, London: Duke University Press, pp. 186–210.

Franco, I.D. and Ortiz, C. (2020) 'Medellín in the headlines: The role of the media in the dissemination of urban models', *Cities* 96: 102431.

Fraser, N. (1990) 'Rethinking the public sphere: A contribution to the critique of actually existing democracy', *Social Text* 25/26: 56–80.

Gehl Architects (2019) *Benefits of working with Gehl*. Archived (June 2016–October 2019) on the Internet Archive Wayback Machine, https://web.archive.org/web/20191024054445/https://gehlpeople.com/work/services/, accessed 11 August 2020.

Gehl Architects (n.d.-a) *Our approach*, https://gehlpeople.com/approach/, accessed 11 August 2020.

Gehl Architects (n.d.-b) *Change making*, https://gehlpeople.com/services/process-facilitation/, accessed 10 August 2020.

Gehl Architects (n.d.-c) *1965: Observing people in Italy*, https://gehlpeople.com/story-article/observing-people-in-italy/, accessed 11 August 2020.

Gehl Architects (n.d.-d) *1970: Architecture, psychology and urban planning*, https://gehlpeople.com/story-article/architecture-psychology-and-urban-planning/, accessed 11 August 2020.

Gehl Architects (n.d.-e) *1987: 'Public Space Public Life' survey in Oslo*, https://gehlpeople.com/story-article/public-space-public-life-survey-in-oslo/, accessed 11 August 2020.

Gehl Architects (n.d.-f) *Services—Public life*, https://gehlpeople.com/services/pilot-projects/, accessed 11 August 2020.

Gehl Architects (n.d.-g) *Services—Active engagement and process leadership*, https://gehlpeople.com/services/process-facilitation/, accessed 11 August 2020.

Gehl Architects (n.d.-h) *2013: How-to guide book*, https://gehlpeople.com/story-article/how-to-guide-book/, accessed 11 August 2020.

Gehl Architects (n.d.-i) *The Melbourne miracle*, https://gehlpeople.com/projects/melbourne-australia/, accessed 30 September 2020.

Gehl Architects (n.d.-j) *A metropolis for people*, https://gehlpeople.com/story-article/a-metropolis-for-people/, accessed 30 September 2020.

Gehl Architects (n.d.-k) *A people focused national architecture policy*, https://gehlpeople.com/story-article/a-people-focused-national-architecture-policy/, accessed 30 September 2020.

Gehl Architects (n.d.-l) *New York City ready for change*, https://gehlpeople.com/story-article/new-york-city-ready-for-change/, accessed 30 September 2020.

Gehl Architects (n.d.-m) *Unrolling a welcome mat for the people of New York*, https://gehlpeople.com/projects/new-york-usa/, accessed 30 September 2020.

Gehl Architects and NYC DOT (2008) *World class streets: Remaking New York City's public realm*, https://issuu.com/gehlarchitects/docs/issuu_561_new_york_world_class_stre, accessed 30 September 2020.

Gehl, J. (2010) *Cities for People*, Washington: Island Press.

Gehl, J. (2011) *Life Between Buildings: Using Public Space*, Washington: Island Press.

Gehl, J., & Svarre, B. (2013) *How to Study Public Life*, Washington: Island press

Hume, C. (2012) 'Building bridges across city's Islands', *Toronto Star*, 6 July, http://proxy.lib.sfu.ca/login?url=https://www-proquest-com.proxy.lib.sfu.ca/docview/1023748463?accountid=13800, accessed 30 September 2020.

Jokinen, A., Leino, H., Bäcklund, P. and Laine, M. (2018) 'Strategic planning harnessing urban policy mobilities: The gradual development of local sustainability fix', *Journal of Environmental Policy and Planning* 20(5): 551–563.

Kielgast, L.V. (n.d.) *Public space public life —Q&A with Louise Vogel Kielgast*, https://gehlpeople.com/announcement/public-space-public-life-qa-with-louise-vogel-kielgast/, accessed 11 August 2020.

Larner, W. (2002) 'Globalization, governmentality and expertise: Creating a call centre labour force', *Review of International Political Economy* 9(4): 650–674.

Larner, W. and Laurie, N. (2010) 'Travelling technocrats, embodied knowledges: Globalising privatisation in telecoms and water', *Geoforum* 41(2): 218–226.

Larner, W. and Le Heron, R. (2002) 'The spaces and subjects of a globalising economy: A situated exploration of method', *Environment and Planning D: Society and Space* 20(6): 753–774.

Massey, D. (2005). *For Space*, London: Sage.

McCann, E. (2004) ''Best places': Interurban competition, quality of life and popular media discourse', *Urban Studies* 41(10): 1909–1929.

McCann, E. (2008) 'Livable city/unequal city: The politics of policy-making in a «creative» boomtown', *Revue Interventions économiques* (37), https://doi.org/10.4000/interventionseconomiques.489.

McCann, E. (2011) 'Urban policy mobilities and global circuits of knowledge: Toward a research agenda', *Annals of the Association of American Geographers* 101(1): 107–130.

McCann, E. (2013) 'Policy boosterism, policy mobilities, and the extrospective city', *Urban Geography* 34(1): 5–29.

McCann, E. (2020) 'Spaces of publicness and the world after the coronavirus crisis', *Society and Space Magazine*, https://www.societyandspace.org/articles/spaces-of-publicness, accessed 28 September 2020.

Mitchell, D. (1995) 'The end of public space? People's Park, definitions of the public, and democracy', *Annals of the Association of American Geographers* 85(1): 108–133.

Mitchell, D. (2017) 'People's Park again: On the end and ends of public space', *Environment and Planning A: Economy and Space* 49(3): 503–518.

Montero, S. (2019) 'Enacting persuasion: Storytelling, emotional artefacts and face-to-face encounters as key actions behind policy circulation', in T. Baker and C. Walker (eds). *Public Policy Circulation*, Edward Elgar Publishing, pp. 161–179.

Mouffe, C. (2005) *On the Political*, London: Routledge.

Mouffe, C. (2007) 'Artistic activism and agonistic spaces', *Art and Research* 1(2): 1–5.

Nowicka, M. (2020) 'Fantasy of conviviality: Banalities of multicultural settings and what we do (not) notice when we look at them', in O. Hemer et al. (eds). *Conviviality at the Crossroads*, Cham: Palgrave Macmillan, pp. 15–42.

Parkinson, J.R. (2013) 'How is space public? Implications for spatial policy and democracy', *Environment and Planning C: Government and Policy* 31(4): 682–699.

Peck, J. (2005) 'Struggling with the creative class', *International Journal of Urban and Regional Research* 29(4): 740–770.

Project for Public Spaces. (2007) *What is placemaking?* https://www.pps.org/article/what-is-placemaking, accessed 10 August 2020.

Rapoport, E. and Hult, A. (2017) 'The travelling business of sustainable urbanism: International consultants as norm-setters', *Environment and Planning A: Economy and Space* 49(8): 1779–1796.

Sandercock, L. (2003) 'Out of the closet: The importance of stories and storytelling in planning practice', *Planning Theory and Practice* 4(1): 11–28.

Schön, D. A. (1979) 'Generative metaphor: A perspective on problem-setting in social policy', *Metaphor and Thought* 2: 137–163.

Söderström, O., Paasche, T. and Klauser, F. (2014) 'Smart cities as corporate storytelling', *City* 18(3): 307–320.

Stone, D. (2004) 'Transfer agents and global networks in the "transnationalization" of policy', *Journal of European Public Policy* 11(3): 545–566.

Swyngedouw, E. (2009) 'The antinomies of the postpolitical city: In search of a democratic politics of environmental production', *International Journal of Urban and Regional Research* 33(3): 601–620.

Temenos, C., Baker, T. and Cook, I.R. (2019) 'Inside mobile urbanism: Cities and policy mobilities', in T. Schwanen and R. van Kempen (eds). *Handbook of Urban Geography*, Cheltenham: Edward Elgar, pp. 103–118.

Temenos, C. and McCann, E. (2014) 'Policies', in P. Adey et al. (eds). *The Routledge Handbook of Mobilities*, London: Routledge, pp. 595–604.

Terzi, C. and Tonnelat, S. (2017) 'The publicization of public space', *Environment and Planning A: Economy and Space* 49(3): 519–536.

Throgmorton, J. A. (2003) 'Planning as persuasive storytelling in a global-scale web of relationships', *Planning Theory* 2(2): 125–151.

Valentine, G. (2008) 'Living with difference: Reflections on geographies of encounter', *Progress in Human Geography* 32(3): 323–337.

Van Hulst, M. (2012) 'Storytelling, a model of and a model for planning', *Planning Theory* 11(3): 299–318.

Vogelpohl, A. (2019) 'Global expertise, local convincing power: Management consultants and preserving the entrepreneurial city', *Urban Studies* 56(1): 97–114.

Walker, A. (2020a) 'Coronavirus is not fuel for urbanist fantasies', *Curbed*, 20 May, https://www.curbed.com/2020/5/20/21263319/coronavirus-future-city-urban-covid-19, accessed 8 October 2020.

Walker, A. (2020b) 'Urbanism hasn't worked for everyone', *Curbed*, 16 June, https://www.curbed.com/2020/7/16/21315678/city-racism-urbanism-atlanta-beltline, accessed 8 October 2020.

Ward, K. (2018) 'Policy mobilities, politics and place: The making of financial urban futures', *European Urban and Regional Studies* 25(3): 266–283.

Warren, J. (2009) 'Saskatoon has potential: Gehl', *Saskatoon Leader Post*, 1 September, http://proxy.lib.sfu.ca/login?url=https://www-proquest-com.proxy.lib.sfu.ca/docview/350144154?accountid=13800, accessed 30 September 2020.

Whyte, W.H. (1980) *The Social Life of Small Urban Spaces*, New York: Conservation Foundation.

Yasin, A. (2020) 'Whose streets? Black streets', *The Tyee*, 18 June, https://thetyee.ca/Analysis/2020/06/18/Whose-Streets-Black-Streets, accessed 8 October 2020.

Young, I.M. (1986) 'The ideal of community and the politics of difference', *Social Theory and Practice* 12(1): 1–26.

Finance and Financialization

International Consultancy Firms and African States: New Debt Bonds

Janet Roitman

Introduction

Over the past decade, a tide of financial analysis has washed over the African continent. These widely circulated reports are the work of international management consultancies, such as McKinsey & Company and Deloitte. This surge of interest in finance on the African continent is indicative of the decline in bilateral and multilateral foreign aid, which increasingly has been displaced by foreign direct investment and private capital markets (Hou et al., 2013; Sy and Rakotondrazaka, 2015; Kvangraven, 2016). It also reflects a shift in the role of private consultancies: from a focus on management to a focus on building global capital and private equity markets. That role has evolved over the course of the twentieth century: from a concern with cost accounting implemented by "management engineers," to elaborating the "multidivisional model" of the firm and the practice of strategic management, to concocting the notion of "corporate culture," to embracing the notion of shareholder value and the influence of private equity (McKenna, 2006; Kiechel,

J. Roitman (✉)
The New School, New York, NY, USA
e-mail: RoitmanJ@newschool.edu

C. Hurl and A. Vogelpohl (eds.), *Professional Service Firms and Politics in a Global Era*, https://doi.org/10.1007/978-3-030-72128-2_7

2010).[1] One might interpret these shifts in terms of a history of ideas and thus conclude that the meaning of management has changed over time. But the contemporary practices of these international firms suggest that management itself—as the defining core competency and service of the international consultancies—has been displaced by other forms of knowledge and practice. In significant ways, the international consultancies have become agents of financialization, facilitating the development and extension of new financial assets, products, and markets.

Today, management consulting includes both audit and advisory services, though the distinction has become increasingly unclear as firms engage in practices such as advising auditors, raising potential conflicts of interest which have come under increasing regulatory scrutiny (Kinder, 2019; see Sturdy in this volume). In fact, the large consultancies no longer primarily intervene at the level of management practice. In that sense, they are in step with elite business schools, which now hire engineers, as opposed to economists or MBAs, as high-level administrators because, as those administrators note, today data science is as important as management science (Moules, 2019). Indeed, the term management has virtually disappeared from the ambit of much consultancy work, as the international consultancies increasingly provide research services and thus build out full-fledged research organizations, such as McKinsey & Company's in-house international think tank, McKinsey Global Institute, which provides in-depth analysis of a range of industries and countries.[2]

[1] McKenna (2006, 49) notes, "Contrary to popular assumptions, Taylorism was not the predominant influence on the development of consulting firms." Indeed, "Firms like McKinsey & Company largely replaced Taylorist consultancies in America during the 1930s…" (169). His argument is that management consultancy achieved full professional status in the twentieth century largely as a result of state regulation—or specifically, antitrust regulations of the 1930s, such as the Glass-Steagall Act, which targeting price-fixing stratagems and banker-led cartels. This jurisdictional void paved the way for the development of management consulting (20–15). In McKenna's words, management consulting was "the regulatory solution to monopoly" (43). This historical point has potential relevance for the realm of consultancy practice today (see the exceptional reporting by Bogdanich et al. [2019], published by *The New York Times*, cited below).

[2] This is a potentially expanding field of competition: a recent shift in the regulatory regime requires private banks to charge investors for research provision instead of including the cost in commissions for trading, which has led Wall Street banks (Goldman Sachs, Morgan Stanley) to compete with the international consultancies, entering the market as research service providers to firms as a way to offset lost business in asset management (Wigglesworth, 2019).

Alongside the turn to the provision of research services, the international consultancies have developed offshore services delivery and the outsourcing of contracts, much of which relates to the assessment and development of consumer markets, capital markets, and financial markets. And this has given rise to new practices, new targets of intervention, and new clients, including African governments and state agencies.[3] Beyond providing management advice for specific public and private-sector clients, the consultancy firms increasingly serve as intermediaries: on the one hand, they devise strategies for international private investors that locate market and asset opportunities in Africa; and, on the other, they advise African governments regarding ways to access international capital markets by means of particular financial assets and techniques. Through this, they participate in the development of new trends in finance in Africa.

As will be shown below, in their role as intermediaries between international private investors, national development banks, and the African diaspora, international consultancy firms have become agents of financialization in many African settings. Rather than simply describing or advising on African markets, they have actively promoted the definition and development of new asset classes, which are the bases for the development of investment-grade financial products and secondary capital markets. With the goal of providing new financial products to international institutional investors, such as pension funds and private equity firms, this intermediary role contributes to the extension of international capital markets and financial practices. These financial practices are intensifying, leading to the further integration of African capital markets and international financial markets, as well as increased debt-servicing costs.

[3] The South African government and the state-owned utility, Eskom, recently made headlines for its relationship to both KPMG and McKinsey, both mired in impropriety (Gapper, 2017; Groenewald, 2017; Bogdanich and Forsythe, 2018a; see also the extremely informative series of *New York Times* articles on McKinsey's relationship to authoritarian regimes and particular industries and executives: Bogdanich and Forsythe, 2018b; and Bogdanich et al., 2019).

"Africa Rising"

The influence of transnational professional service firms, such as the McKinsey Global Institute, is manifest in their predictions of immense economic transformation across the African continent over the coming decades. These forecasts are predicated on the development of consumer markets and an emergent middle class—or what has been dubbed "Africa Rising." Most notable and oft-cited is the 2010 report published by the McKinsey Global Institute entitled "Lions on the Move: The Progress and Potential of African Economies" (McKinsey Global Institute, 2010). And just thereafter, in 2012, the private consultancy, Deloitte, produced a report called "The Rise and Rise of Africa's Middle Class" (Chimhanzi and Gounden, 2012). These proclamations were echoed in the popular press, including *The Economist* (2011) and *Time Magazine* (Perry, 2012). The exuberant consultancy and media reports precipitated events that explored private–public partnerships, such as the 2012 Annual African Economic Forum at Columbia University, which convened investment bankers, economists, World Bank officials, and heads of private equity firms for the "Roaring Giant" conference. Ultimately, this spate of news about economic growth and financial opportunity in Africa was riding the commodities boom of the early 2000s and consequential rising GDP for many Sub-Saharan African countries (Taylor, 2014).

Oddly, at the time of publication, the consultancy reports ignored the fact that a similar prognosis had been proclaimed already twenty years prior, in a *Time* magazine feature article entitled "Africa Rising" (McGeary and Michaels, 1998). And, perhaps more significantly, the research emanating from both Deloitte and McKinsey Global Institute also ignored nascent debates among development economists and social scientists regarding the validity of claims regarding a new middle class (Ncube and Shimales, 2013; Ncube and Lufumpa, 2015; Wohlmuth, 2014; Resnick, 2015; Chitonge, 2015; Johnston and Abreu, 2016; Stoffel, 2016; Southall, 2016; Melber, 2016; Lentz, 2016). Either oblivious or unfamiliar with contemporaneous research on the validity and implications of observations regarding rising GDP and the expansion of consumer markets in Africa, in June 2015, Deloitte published, "Competitiveness: Catching the Next Wave. Africa," claiming that "The pace of growth in sub-Saharan Africa could easily surpass most regions of the world" (Deloitte, 2015, 3). And in September 2016, McKinsey Global Institute published "Lions on the Move 2," which projected that business spending would grow from US$2.6 trillion to US$3.5 trillion by 2025, thus, again, documenting—or forecasting?—opportunities for financial investment on the continent.[4]

The Africa Rising narrative directed international investors' attention to the potential of consumer markets on the continent. But Africa Rising didn't end in the shadow of shopping malls. In predicting and promoting this vision, the consultancy firms have set sights on consumer markets as well as financial markets. In particular, they have focused on two specific realms of finance: the development of new asset classes for private-sector investment, on the one hand, and the potential role of the private sector for public financing, on the other.[5] At first glance, consultancy firms appear to be focused on new investment opportunities associated with growing middle-class consumer demand, such as consumer retail and real estate markets. However, the focus on emerging trends in demand is not necessarily or primarily a question of the aggregate demand *of African consumers*. Instead, the focus is on investors' demand—or *the demand of institutional investors and private equity funds for financial products in Africa*.

Indeed, a recent *Financial Times* "This is Africa" report on East African capital markets noted that the main goal for institutional investors is "to develop the buy side" (Irving, 2017). What is the buy side? This refers to investment products, as explained by the report's author in response to the problem of low levels of investment in private capital markets in Africa: "Mostly, however, the findings point to a lack of investable products and capacity constraints rather than a lack of demand as an explanation for the relatively low investment in private sector securities." Note that "demand" here does not refer to African middle-class *consumers*. What is at stake is demand on the part of institutional investors in Europe, Russia, China, and South Africa, who seek investment-grade financial products. Therefore, the challenge is supply, or to devise those investment-grade products in Africa (setting aside the mining and oil/gas

[4] See also McKinsey Global Institute's (2017) report, titled "Lions (still) on the Move: Growth in Africa's Consumer Sector."

[5] Asset classes have been defined traditionally as equity (stocks), fixed income (bonds), property, and cash (money market instruments); today, they include commodities, futures, financial derivatives, cryptocurrencies. What is significant for the present discussion is the revenue stream generated by the asset class.

sectors). This is not to say that financial firms are not interested in developing domestic consumer markets and the consumer financial sector in Africa. But establishing markets for financial products means developing globally integrated markets. So while there are efforts to cultivate the middle class as a domain of actual and potential demand—in shopping malls, for instance—the goal is equally to develop financial products, such as corporate bonds, for international private equity funds and institutional investors.

Future Flows: Private Finance and Public Debt

How are investment-grade financial products developed in a context of limited domestic capital markets and sovereign debt ratings that are below investment grade? During the early 2000s, and in direct response to the Africa Rising narrative, private equity funds increased their investments in Africa, and diversified out of South Africa (White & Case, 2017, 8). But recently, sharp declines in the price of oil and other commodities resulted in currency depreciations, which impacted these investments negatively, leading to financial losses and significantly increased risk premiums on investments. In this challenging context, transnational professional service firms have sought to forge a pathway that draws together governments and investors by marketing new financial asset classes (see also Möller in this volume). For instance, a premier international law firm that serves as counsel to private companies, governments, and financial institutions published a report in 2017 that reviews the potential bases for asset-class formation and private equity fund investment, with specific reference to a Boston Consulting Group 2016 report, "Why Africa Remains Ripe for Private Equity" (BCG, 2016). The main subject of this and other consultancy reports is the development of private-sector financing for public infrastructure projects: "Private sector financing forms a large part of the answer in closing the funding gap [in African infrastructure projects] in the form of private equity, debt and the relatively untapped resources of pension funds and capital markets" (White & Case, 2017, 2). The two main barriers to these investments—or what makes the risk premium unacceptable—are foreign exchange risk and the sovereign debt rating. While the foreign exchange risk can often be hedged or offset, speculative-grade sovereign debt ratings have thwarted the issuance of public debt in Africa.

In this apparent sand trap of sub-investment-grade sovereign bond ratings, certain global management consultancies have promoted "innovative development financing" as a means to tread through this intractable problem. This strategy, first put forth by development economists and then disseminated by international consultancy firms, involves the capture of international cross-border remittances and the promulgation of a new asset class (Ketkar and Ratha, 2001, 2009; Sy and Rakotondrazaka, 2015; Chimhanzi and Gounden, 2012; McKinsey & Company, 2013). Before explaining the motivations of this strategy, which facilitates the creation of investment-grade asset classes as the basis of financial securities, it is important to highlight the significance of remittance transfers to Africa so as to understand how they are figured as a future flow, and hence a building block of structured finance.

According to the most recent World Bank *Migration and Remittances* brief, after two consecutive years of decline, worldwide remittance flows to all low- and middle-income countries rebounded to a record level in 2017, or an 8.5% increase to $466 billion. While the share for Sub-Saharan Africa was reported to stand at only $38 billion for 2017, this represents an 11.4% growth rate. Nigeria ranked fourth among the top remittance-receiving countries in dollar terms ($22 billion), and Liberia ranked sixth in terms of remittances as a share of GDP (at a whopping 27% of GDP). For Senegal, remittances made up 14% of GDP in 2017 (World Bank, 2018). The point for financial practitioners is that remittances are the continent's largest source of foreign currency inflows, after foreign direct investment (FDI) (Ratha and Mohapatra, 2011). In Nigeria, remittances are second only to oil exports as source of foreign exchange. But in all countries, these figures underestimate the total amounts received, since they depend on analyses of variable sources (e.g., local bank data versus World Bank Data). And of course most remittances to the African continent flow through undocumented channels, mostly due to the high cost of transfer through formal money transfer operators, such as Western Union. Ultimately, remittances to Sub-Saharan Africa are predicted to increase and they are more significant than institutional reporting suggests.

Typically, development economists and policymakers view remittances as an untapped source of economic growth because they fuel domestic consumption: funds sent to Somalia from the Gulf States are spent locally on goods and services. But international consultancies and the development economists they cite (Ketkar and Ratha, 2001, 2009) are not interested in recipients' use of remittances. They argue that remittances should feature in national accounting as a financial revenue stream. That is, they focus on the role of remittance transfers in asset-class formation: or the positing of remittances as a future-flow receivable (Ketkar and Ratha, 2004–2005, 2009; Ratha and Mohapatra, 2011; Bakker, 2015; Famoroti, 2018; IMF, 2018, 21). But what is the role of remittance transfers in asset-class formation? How are remittances a future-flow receivable? And how are remittances as future-flow receivables significant for mobilizing private financing of the public sector in Africa? Answers to these questions help us to see how international consultancy firms serve as intermediaries between African states, international private investors, and the African diaspora in the process of developing and extending financial products and their associated globally integrated markets.

Breaking the Sovereign Ceiling

The international private consultancies promote the accounting of remittances with an eye to investment-grade credit ratings and investment-grade financial products. In other words, if accounted for, remittance flows, as hard currency receivables, contribute to the level and stability of foreign exchange receipts. One can see how this accounting contributes to improved national accounts. But, most importantly, it is a way to improve a sovereign credit rating. The general rule is that when foreign debt is issued, it cannot be rated above the external foreign currency debt rating of the home country—this is known as the "sovereign ceiling" (Ketkar and Ratha, 2009). But the securitization of these future-flow receivables allows certain governments to break the sovereign credit ceiling and thus access financing on private international markets on improved terms, such as lower interest rates. The development economists, Suhas Ketkar and Dilip Ratha, are the main proponents of future-flow securitization, which they see as a means to "pierce the sovereign credit ceiling." Their work is the main reference for the international consultancies that promote innovations in development financing, such as McKinsey & Company (2013 and see McKinsey Global Institute, 2013, on international private capital and investment opportunities). Ketkar and Ratha maintain that, "In addition to providing lower cost funding, securitization also allows issuers to extend maturity of their debt, and improve risk management as well as balance sheet performance. Securitization also permits issuers from developing countries to tap a wider class of investors. For example, this asset class is attractive to insurance companies that face limitations on buying sub-investment grade" (2004–2005, 4; and cf. Ketkar and Ratha, 2009).

Remittances, traditionally defined as cross-border transfers between private parties, such as individuals or families, have thus been refigured by international consulting firms as a potential financial product, or a tradable financial asset. This practice of leveraging remittances is facilitated by their definition by both private and public financial agents—or redefinition—as a future-flow receivable, which allows them to be utilized *as collateral* in structured finance, or on international capital markets. This approach is based on the conviction that remittances can be leveraged for asset-class creation, which essentially means incorporating migrant financial flows into global financial markets. And this transpires through the securitization of future-flow hard currency receivables.

What is securitization? Securitization is a financing technique used for risk management, balance sheet management, and to obtain funding. This is a process by which a bank (or originator) converts stable and predictable cash flow streams in a segregated pool of somewhat illiquid financial assets (the asset pool) into debt instruments (securities) that are tradable in capital markets.

Simplifying significantly, the three main components are:

1. The pooling of risky but relatively homogeneous financial assets.
2. The trenching of cash flow and undifferentiated credit risk of the overall asset pool into multiple classes of securities with different payout and risk-return profiles, which allows investors (e.g. pension funds, private equity funds) to invest according to risk tolerance.
3. Typically, the asset pool is transferred to a special purpose vehicle (SPV) so as to protect investors, since it legally isolates the benefits of the assets (e.g., interest) from the potential insolvency of the originator.[6]

As we see, this process depends on stable and predictable cash flows. Often the underlying assets are existing receivables denominated in a foreign currency: residential mortgage loans, auto loans, credit card

[6] This is a very crude presentation of an extremely complex practice. And it should be noted that, in some cases, the diversified pool of loans that back the securities remain on the credit issuer's balance sheet to ensure that they have "skin in the game."

receivables. But in the case of future-flow receivables, the offshore SPV purchases from the originator the rights, title, and interest in all existing and future payment orders in USD and/or euro, which the originator is expected to receive from offshore correspondent banks between the closing of the securitization transaction and the final maturity of the notes. As a rule, underlying receivables for future-flow securitization must be denominated in a hard currency; they must be owed to the originator by investment-grade obligors located outside the originator's home country; and they must be payable outside of the originator's home country, as in the case of US dollar receivables owed to a bank by a credit card company. The credit rating agency rankings of future-flow receivables in terms of risk results in a hierarchy that places heavy crude oil receivables at the top, as the most secure, followed by diversified payment rights (DPRs), which includes airline ticket receivables, credit card receivables, and personal electronic remittances. It is noteworthy that tax revenue receivables are ranked at the bottom of the barrel. Part of the rationale for ranking personal electronic remittances so high as a form of collateral is their diversified source of origin—in the case of Africa, they originate in Europe, the Gulf States, and North America (for review, see Ketkar and Ratha, 2004–2005).

Ultimately, the significance of the securitization of future-flow hard currency receivables is that it allows national governments to leverage private remittances for public debt issuance. To recap, and to paraphrase Clive Rough, a legal expert on future-flow securitization: The attraction of future-flow securitizations is that it enables an originator located in an emerging market country with a foreign currency debt rating (i.e., the rating accorded to the external foreign currency debt of the home country) that is either below investment grade or low investment grade to improve its credit rating. The originator can structure a transaction so as to issue securities and obtain funding on international capital markets with a rating that is higher than the foreign currency debt rating of its home country (Rough, 2000).

This increased access to international capital markets ("breaking sovereign ceiling") is a means to "increase the supply of investment," or to devise investment-grade financial products for international investors, or the clients of the international consultancies. As noted above, and to remind ourselves of how structured finance in Africa emerged from the Africa Rising Narrative and the pursuits of transnational consultancies as intermediaries, these investors are not local African consumers; they are private equity funds, pension funds, endowments, etc.[7] In that sense, remittances, as a future flow, are part of the extension of globally integrated secondary financial markets that includes external private actors, such as transnational consultancy firms.

Conclusion

International consultancy firms have an obscure and yet effective role in the development and extension of financial markets on the African continent—a role that serves to further the integration of global financial markets. The consultancies serve as intermediaries between African states and their various agencies, international institutional investors, private equity firms, African consumers, and the African diaspora in this process of developing and extending financial products and their associated markets. And this role has intensified the propensity for African national governments and development banks to view remittances as a means to claim increased foreign exchange reserves as part of a strategy to improve sovereign credit ratings, the terms of dollar-denominated bond issuance, and access to capital markets. This is a growing trend. And yet it is not new.

In order to better understand the ways in which the forms of innovation for development finance that are endorsed and promoted by international consultancies result in new forms of global integration, it is worth considering their precedents. The first future-flow securitization transaction originated in 1987 when Mexico securitized Telmex telephone receivables (Ketkar and Ratha, 2009, 7). And both Israel and India have issued what are now known as Diaspora Bonds, which were seen as tools of development finance. In the case of Israel, private wealth located outside the country was leveraged for public financing, mostly involving infrastructure investment. These bonds, issued by the Development Corporation for Israel, were registered with the U.S. Securities Exchange Commission and could be exchanged like listed securities. In contrast, Indian Diaspora Bonds were issued specifically to support the balance of payments. They were not listed on a securities exchange; rather, they were issued by the State Bank of India and were only available

[7] For a view from financial analysts, see Chowdhury et al. (2009).

to investors of Indian origin. We could multiply the examples of Diaspora Bonds, which leverage remittances for national balance of payments accounting, debt reduction, or infrastructure financing (for example, Lebanese Diaspora Bonds issued in 1991).

African governments have not been unwise to this strategy of public financing, despite the reference to financial "innovation" in the recent international consultancy reports. Already in 1996, the African Export–Import Bank helped arrange the first future-flow securitization of remittances in Sub-Saharan Africa. This involved a $40 million medium-term loan for the Ghanaian development bank backed by Western Union remittance receivables. In 2001, the African Export–Import Bank arranged a $50 million remittance-backed note for a Nigerian entity using Moneygram receivables. And in 2004, the African Export–Import Bank helped arrange a remittance-backed term loan in the amount of $40 million in favor of an Ethiopian Bank using Western Union receivables (Afreximbank, 2005; and see Jidoud, 2015). Still, although future-flow securitization is not a novel innovation, until recently most African sovereigns did not have credit ratings. Since 2006, twenty-one sub-Saharan states have received sovereign credit ratings so as to issue foreign currency denominated bonds (Eurobonds), a movement that will grow (Guscina et al., 2014; Sy and Rakotondrazaka, 2015, 6–7), especially as strategies for improving these ratings, such as that described herein, are pursued in efforts to access private international capital markets and develop financial products for institutional investors. Indeed, in June 2019, Togo acquired a sovereign credit rating, which, as one financial reporter put it, "...open[s] up a new frontier for emerging market investors" (Aglionby, 2019).[8]

The international management consultancies portray these bond issuances, and the general trend of securitizing future-flow receivables, as "unlocking value from diaspora flows" (McKinsey & Company, 2013, 2). The authors of "Innovative Development Financing," a 2013 McKinsey report, note that, "Private capital is an enormous source of global wealth that has not historically played as significant a role in development as its scale would suggest. This is not for lack of interest. Private capital is constantly seeking investment opportunities" (3). This is what was referred to above as "developing the buy side," or creating a supply of

[8] The credit rating allows Togo to issue a Eurobond or seek a syndicated loan; and funds would be used to pay down the country's domestic debt.

investment-grade products in situations where the quality of collateral and both sovereign and foreign currency debt ratings would otherwise stymie international investment. In this sense, Africa is a new frontier for international finance—a horizon that is in part made visible by claims to Africa Rising, a call that has resounded over the last decade from popular reporting and the pages of international management consultancy reports. The creation of asset classes, such as remittances for structured finance, facilitates the sale of cash flow to third parties as a security, or a debt instrument that is tradable on capital markets. This financing practice is obviously unable to innovate away all risk.[9] But future-flow securitization allows governments to access foreign capital markets and to bypass long-standing channels of public credit, such as multilateral foreign aid. In this sense, while seemingly tangential to the emerging realm of finance, the international consultancy firms have a distinct role in the expansion of debt markets on the continent. In their role as intermediaries, the international consultancy firms are part of an emerging network of migrant workers, expatriate Africans, national development banks, and international private investors, generating new forms of private debt financing for public works.

References

Afreximbank (2005) Annual Report, http://www.afreximbank.com.

Aglionby, J. (2019) 'Togo vows to tap debt markets after "game changing" credit rating', *The Financial Times*, 7 June.

Bakker, M. (2015) *Migrating into Financial Markets: How Remittances Became a Development Tool*, Berkeley: University of California Press.

Bogdanich, W. and Forsythe, M. (2018a) 'How McKinsey lost its way in South Africa', *The New York Times*, 26 June.

Bogdanich, W. and Forsythe, M. (2018b) 'How McKinsey has helped raise the statue of authoritarian governments', *The New York Times*, 15 December.

Bogdanich, W. Forsythe, M. and Hickey, B. (2019) 'As McKinsey sells advice, its hedge fund may have a state in the outcome', *The New York Times*, 19 February.

[9] For African countries, there is the persistent threat of currency depreciation against the dollar or the euro, which makes debt servicing extremely difficult; and if the cost of debt increases rapidly, so does the risk of default. To be fair, these issues are noted in a 2019 Deloitte report, which focuses on rising government debt and the challenge of debt servicing.

Boston Consulting Group (2016) 'Why Africa remains ripe for private equity', September.
Chimhanzi, J. and Gounden, A. (2012) 'Deloitte on Africa: The rise and rise of the African middle class', *Deloitte on Africa Collection: Issue 1.* Deloitte and Touche, Johannesburg, South Africa.
Chitonge, H. (2015) *Economic Growth and Development in Africa: Understanding Trends and Prospects*, Routledge.
Chowdhury, A. Orr, R.J. and Settel, D. (2009) 'Multilaterals and infrastructure funds: *A New Era*', *The Journal of Structured Finance*, Winter: 68–74.
Deloitte (2015) 'Competitiveness: Catching the next wave Africa.' Deloitte and Touche, Johannesburg, South Africa.
Famoroti, M. (2018) 'Foresight Africa viewpoint—Debt by diaspora: Ties that bond', Brookings Institution. https://www.brookings.edu/blog/africa-in-focus/2018/01/24/foresight-africa-viewpoint-debt-by-diaspora-ties-that-bond/.
Gapper, J. (2017) 'McKinsey has closed its eyes in South Africa', *The Financial Times*, 20 September.
Groenewald, Y. (2017) 'McKinsey faces legal action over Gupta-linked Eskom Saga', *The Financial Times*, 18 September.
Guscina, A. et al. (2014) *First-Time International Bond Issuance—New Opportunities and Emerging Risks.* IMF Working Paper No. 14/127.
Hou, Z. Keane, J. Kennan, J. Massa, I. and Velde, D.W. (2013) *The Changing Nature of Private Capital Flows to Sub-Saharan Africa.* Shockwatch Bulletin, ODI Working Paper 376, March.
IMF (2018) *Regional Economic Outlook: World Economic and Financial Surveys: Sub-Saharan Africa: Domestic Revenue Mobilization and Private Investment*, Washington, DC: International Monetary Fund Publication Services.
Irving, J. (2017) 'Capital markets in East Africa: Developing the buy side', *This Is Africa: Financial Times*, 10 March.
Jidoud, A. (2015) *Remittances and Macroeconomic Volatility in African Countries.* IMF Working Paper, WP/15/49, Washington, DC: International Monetary Fund.
Johnston, D. and Abreu, A. (2016) 'The asset debates: How (not) to use asset indices to measure well-being and the middle class in Africa', *African Affairs* 115(460): 399–418.
Ketkar, S. and Ratha, D. (2001) *Development Financing During a Crisis: Securitization of Future Receivables.* Policy Research Working Paper No. 2582, World Bank, Washington, DC.
Ketkar, S. and Ratha, D. (2004–2005) 'Recent advances in future-flow securitization', *The Financier* 11/12: 1–14.

Ketkar, S. and Ratha, D. (2009) *Innovative Financing for Development*, Washington, DC: The International Bank for Reconstruction and Development/The World Bank.

Kiechel, W. (2010) *The Lords of Strategy: The Secret Intellectual History of the New Corporate World*, Cambridge, MA: Harvard Business Review Press.

Kinder, Tabby. (2019) 'KPMG Switches 820 UK Staff from Advisory to Audit', *Financial Times*, 26 September.

Kvangraven, I.H. (2016) 'The changing character of financial flows to Sub-Saharan Africa', in Gevorkyan and Canuto (eds). *Financial Deepening and Post-Crisis Development in Emerging Markets*, Palgrave Macmillan, pp. 223–245.

Lentz, C. (2016) 'African middle classes: Lessons from transnational studie and a research agenda', in H. Melber (eds). *The Rise of Africa's Middle Class: Myths, Realities and Critical Engagements*, Zed Books, pp. 17–53.

McGeary, J. and Michaels, M. (1998) 'Africa rising', *Time Magazine*, reprinted 2001.

McKenna, C. (2006) *The World's Newest Profession: Management Consulting in the Twentieth Century*, Cambridge: Cambridge University Press.

McKinsey & Company (2013) *Innovative Development Financing*, McKinsey Global Institute/McKinsey & Company, August.

McKinsey Global Institute (2010) *Lions on the Move: The Progress and Potential of African Economies*, McKinsey Global Institute/McKinsey & Company, June.

McKinsey Global Institute (2013) *Financial Globalization: Retreat or Reset?* McKinsey Global Institute/McKinsey & Company, March.

McKinsey Global Institute (2017) *Lions (Still) on the Move: Growth in Africa's Consumer Sector*, McKinsey Global Institute/McKinsey & Company, October.

Melber, H. (2016) *The Rise of Africa's Middle Class: Myths, Realities and Critical Engagements*, Zed Books.

Moules, J. (2019) 'How Columbia's new dean aims to redefine business education', *Financial Times*, 29 August.

Ncube, M. and Lufumpa, C.L. (2015) *The Emerging Middle Class in Africa*, Routledge.

Ncube, M. and Shimeles, A. (2013) *The making of middle class in Africa: Evidence from DHS data*, IZA Discussion Paper No. 7352, April, Institute for the Study of Labor.

Perry, A. (2012) 'Africa rising', *Time Magazine*, 3 December.

Ratha, D. and Mohapatra, S. (2011) 'Impact of migration on economic and social development', *A Review of Evidence and Emerging Issues WPS 5558*, World Bank.

Resnick, D. (2015) 'The political economy of Africa's emergent middle class: Retrospect and prospects', *Journal of International Development* 27: 573–587.

Rough, C. (2000) *The Asian Securitisation and Structured Finance Guide*, White Page, http://people.stern.nyu.edu/igiddy/ABS/future-flow.htm, accessed 14 October 2020.
Southall, R. (2016) *The New Black Middle Class in South Africa*, London: James Currey.
Stoffel, T. (2016) 'Human development and the construction of middle classes in the global South', in H. Melber (eds). *The Rise of Africa's Middle Class: Myths, Realities and Critical Engagements*, Zed Books, pp. 54–68.
Sy, A. and Rakotondrazaka, F. (2015) 'Private capital flows, official development assistance, and remittances to Africa: Who gets what?' *Policy Paper* No. 2015–02.
Taylor, I. (2014) 'Is Africa rising?' *Brown Journal of World Affairs* XXI(1, Fall/Winter).
The Economist (2011) 'Africa rising: The hopeful continent', 3 December.
White & Case (2017) *Africa focus: Unlocking international investment opportunities in Africa*, Autumn, White & Case LLP, https://www.whitecase.com/publications/insight/africa-focus-2017.
Wigglesworth, R. (2019) 'Wall Street banks look to sell more research to companies', *The Financial Times*, 18 September.
Wohlmuth, K. (2014) 'African Lions, African Tigers, and Emerging African Middle Classes—A Very Skeptical Note Extended', *Berichte, Oktober–Dezember 2014* 24, 205, Forschungsinstitut der IWVWW e V., Berlin: 4–32.
World Bank (2018) *Migration and remittances: Recent developments and outlook*, Migration and Development Brief 26, April.

"The DNA of Government": Consultants, Calculative Technologies, and the Politics of Municipal Benchmarking

Chris Hurl

Introduction

In a 2016 article entitled "Can you be a Smart City without a Smart Budget?" Alan Mitchell, the Executive Director of KPMG's Cities Global Center of Excellence, draws inspiration from the smart cities trend in speaking to the need to reform municipal accounts. Under traditional budgetary models, Mitchell argues, citizens do not know what is embedded in each line item—"you have no idea that buried in that budget for Public Works are seven (7) services, including: Water Supply, Roads, Sewers (Storm & Sanitary), Waste Collection & Disposal, Snow Clearing, etc. Furthermore, there is no indication how well or poorly the city is providing these seven services."[1] In the absence of such information, he argues that public officials often have to resort to unilateral budget cuts, indiscriminately slashing services across the board.

[1] http://smartcitybrand.com/articles-in-original-language/can-you-be-smart-city-without-smart-budget.

C. Hurl (✉)
Department of Sociology and Anthropology, Concordia University, Montreal, QC, Canada
e-mail: chris.hurl@concordia.ca

C. Hurl and A. Vogelpohl (eds.), *Professional Service Firms and Politics in a Global Era*, https://doi.org/10.1007/978-3-030-72128-2_8

Drawing connections with smart cities, Mitchell advances an alternative: Through the application of new reference models and benchmarking technologies, he argues, more information can be embedded in budgets, giving elected officials and citizens a better sense of where their money is being spent. The "smart budget" is "packed with information" that allows "management, elected officials and the public to wonder why one service costs more than another, why a service is rated so low/high in value, and foster discussion on whether the city should put its scarce financial resources into one service or another" (Mitchell, 2016). Adopting such methods, he argues that citizens and public officials will be able to make cuts "smarter."

This chapter explores how such classificatory systems and technologies, marketed as knowledge products by professional service firms (PSFs), have reformatted urban governance arrangements. As with other benchmarking technologies, smart budgets are presented as universally applicable, providing fine-grained and user-friendly accounts of municipal services. As advocates note, they set out to capture the "DNA" of government, providing a generic code that is applicable across jurisdictions (Wiseman and Amsden, 2012). However, while these technologies claim to better describe services, I argue, drawing from theories of performativity, that these systems have "more than a representational quality: they can also have an instrumental quality whereby they help create a world on which they reflect" (Christensen and Skaerbaek 2010, 525; see also Callon, 1998; Mackenzie and Millo, 2003). Following Mitchell's career trajectory back to Ontario, I explore how private firms and public agencies have been mutually transformed by these benchmarking technologies, which—while claiming to create a common language for municipalities—have played a performative role in creating the terrain that they set out to describe.

Beginning in the early 1990s, Mitchell, alongside other consultants, helped to introduce the Municipal Reference Model (MRM) through which they set out to extend a generic model for classifying services to municipalities across the province and, later, across the globe. Looking at the principles underpinning its application, I explore how the MRM has reshaped governance. As I will show, through practices of commensuration, such models have made services knowable in new ways, fostering a regime of competition through which municipalities target services deemed "discretionary" or "above standard" as areas for cutbacks, thus reinforcing austerity in urban governance.

However, beyond the impact of such measures on governments I am also interested in how such models have transformed the work of management consultants themselves. While these technologies have played a performative role in drawing municipalities into a regime of competition, I argue they have also enabled the entrenchment of professional services firms as "partners in government," engaged in continuous work of assessment and appraisal (Saint-Martin, 2013). As a schema requiring very little in-depth knowledge of local contexts, this model can be quickly mobilized by a small team of consultants across different institutional settings. Moreover, through the capacity to draw city services from all over the world into a single generic classificatory system, this model has facilitated the concentration of knowledge by large firms, which can take it up as an asset in extending their credibility across jurisdictions.

Benchmarking as Calculative Technology

A growing literature has explored the role and impact of benchmarking in public sector restructuring (Brown, 2015; Bruno, 2009; Davies, 2014). Widely taken up by governments over the past three decades, benchmarking involves the development of metrics for classifying and ranking business processes across jurisdictions in comparison with an industry "best practice" (see Möller in this volume). Along these lines, studies have looked at the role and influence of high profile benchmarking programs such as the World Economic Forum's *Global Competitiveness Report* (see Davies, 2014) and the European Union's Open Method of Coordination (see Bruno, 2009), as well as more mundane ranking exercises undertaken at the institutional level by universities (Sauder and Espeland, 2009), the civil service (Ilcan, 2009), and non-governmental organizations (Djama et al., 2011). In this chapter, I draw insights from this critical literature in two ways.

First, I highlight the performative role played by benchmarking technologies. While often framed as a descriptive device, showing public officials where they stand, critical scholars note that such calculative technologies have actively transformed governance arrangements, creating a novel regime of competition by which governments come to view each other as adversaries vying for top positions under an imagined hierarchy. As Kornberger and Carter (2010, 329) note, technologies such as the Municipal Reference Model,

> usher into existence a new form of competition that transforms the relationship between cities fundamentally: rankings create hierarchical relationships; they are not about singular relations between cities but generalizable characteristics that establish a homogeneous ordering framework.

Recently, critical studies have focused on how such technologies have modified the behavior of public agencies and their personnel (Espeland and Stevens, 1998; Bruno, 2009; Fougner, 2008). For instance, Sauder and Espeland (2009, 66) look at rankings as a form of disciplinary power operating through processes of surveillance and normalization. Conducting a case study of law school rankings, they look at "the evolving responses of an assortment of actors who struggle to reconcile their sense of themselves as professional educators with an imposed market-based logic of accountability." From this perspective, the introduction of rankings transforms both internal and external perceptions of organizations. On the one hand, organizations are opened up to scrutiny from external audiences. On the other hand, rankings facilitate processes of normalization by which actors are placed in a hierarchy through which they are subject to judgment. This can lead to a variety of responses by actors who are placed under the microscope, including anxiety, resistance, and allure (Sauder and Espeland, 2009, 74).

Second, the policy mobilities literature has explored how such technologies have transformed the movement of policy ideas across space and time (McCann, 2011, 2013; Larner and Le Heron, 2004; Broome and Quirk, 2015; Sum, 2009). By abstracting policy information from specific local contexts, it is argued that such technologies are capable of drawing previously distant jurisdictions into proximity, making them comparable in new ways. As Larner and Le Heron (2002, 417) note, "the global has become more knowable by placing the experiences and performances of others into quantitatively and qualitatively encoded proximity." This has involved both *disembedding* knowledges of specific activities from their local context and *translating* them into a "matrix of abstract measures and equivalences" (McCann, 2011). Such technologies have facilitated the quick movement of policy ideas across institutional settings, contributing to the generation of what Peck and Theodore (2015) describe as "fast policy," and empowering policy actors capable of acting as "transfer agents" (see McCann and Mahieus in this volume; Stone, 2004).

While there has been scholarship exploring how such models have been taken up in shaping the conduct of public actors, the relationships forged between professional service firms and governments in the establishment of such frameworks have seldom been examined. This is a significant gap considering just how prominent Professional Service Firms have become in advising governments. In 2018 alone, the revenue generated by management consultants in advising governments was estimated at over US $85 billion globally (IBISWorld, 2019). While this revenue comes from a range of different services, benchmarking has come to occupy a significant place in the products that such firms offer, particularly for large firms who are able to use their networks and scale advantages in establishing their benchmarks as the most reputable and recognized transnationally (Brooks, 2018). Large firms—like KPMG, PwC, EY, and Deloitte—have peddled products such as the Innovation Benchmark Report (PwC, 2017), the Industry Compliance Benchmark Report (Deloitte, 2018), and the Municipal Reference Model (KPMG, 2017) as a means of extending their credibility to a range of different areas and issues.

Drawing from consultancy reports, government records, and correspondence between public officials and consultants available on government and consultancy websites, as well as interviews with consultants and public officials, I explore how the use of such calculative technologies have enabled thickening relationships between PSFs and public actors over the past three decades. I begin by examining the professional discourses and modes of calculation underpinning benchmarking practices with a focus on the truth claims that they make and how they have fostered distinctive understandings of governance and new kinds of interventions by PSFs in government. I then look at how such technologies have facilitated the movement of policy ideas in new ways. On the one hand, I explore how such technologies have positioned PSFs as powerful intermediaries in drawing municipalities together under a common regime of competition. On the other hand, through tracing the career trajectory of consultants, I explore how such ideas have been taken up by PSFs in establishing global markets for benchmarking technologies. Charting the movement of the Municipal Reference Model as a benchmarking model and its associated personnel, classificatory models, and calculative technologies across contexts, over the course of thirty years, I explore how its distinctive format has facilitated the codification and commodification of policy ideas that have transformed both municipal policy networks and the market for advisory services, while entrenching PSFs as influential actors in brokering municipal policy ideas.

Enterprise Architectures and the Blueprinting of Urban Governance

In order to understand the reach and influence of benchmarking practices today, it is necessary to first locate their emergence in specific epistemological communities and at particular sites which have provided the breeding ground for such modes of calculation (Bockman and Eyal, 2002). While the logic of comparative assessment that underpins benchmarking has come to be taken for granted, it is premised on understandings of government with a specific history, arising from relationships forged between public and private actors in distinct institutional settings (Bruno, 2009; Larner and Le Heron, 2004).

In Ontario, the principles for municipal benchmarking were drawn from "enterprise architecture mapping," which was promoted by PSFs as a management tool in the late 1980s and early 1990s. During this time, a cadre of IT specialists drew inspiration from the discipline of architecture in setting out to reimagine organizations (Berman and Korsten, 2002; Tozer, 1986; Synnott, 1987; Kotusev, 2016). In a landmark article, "A Framework for Information Systems Architecture," published in the *IBM Systems Journal*, IBM consultant John A. Zachman (1987, 454) laid the groundwork, noting that the growing complexity of information systems demanded "the use of some 'logical construct'" in order to make sense of how the components of large organizations fit together. Just as architects assembled blueprints for a house in consultation with homeowners to assess their needs and purposes, he argued that IT analysts should work to translate the perceived needs of an organization into a sort of visual roadmap that made sense of its flow of activity as a unified system oriented to a particular goal, purpose, or output.

Such ideas were first promoted in the 1980s as a way of making sense of mergers and acquisitions taking place between multinational corporations (The Open Group, 2015). Often these firms were so large that it was difficult to determine exactly what activities they encompassed or where redundancies lay. Enterprise architecture was framed as a means of making business processes legible so that large organizations could be streamlined.

Building from their growing popularity in the private sector, such models also influenced a cadre of public officials and IT professionals seeking to "modernize" government. In many jurisdictions, IBM was the key player, effectively branding enterprise architecture mapping as a tool for government restructuring in order to extend their market in advisory services (Kotusev, 2016). However, these ideas were also widely popularized by IT professionals in government and smaller consultancies. Alan Mitchell promoted these concepts initially through his work with Chartwell Information Resource Management (IRM), a small Canadian firm that claimed experience in applying the "Zachman framework" to government. Established in 1984, Chartwell described itself as a "management consultant and technology portfolio investment adviser" that set out "to enhance the value and effectiveness" of an organization's information (Chartwell IRM, 2002). An appraisal of the organization's website from the early 2000s reveals the firm's connections to different levels of government—with several consultants being former public officials—as well as its track record in advising the Canadian public sector, with numerous federal, provincial, and municipal projects featured, as well as an ongoing lecture series pitched to public officials on "e-government" and "fundamentals of business architecture."

Beginning in the early 1990s, Chartwell worked with municipal IT professionals affiliated with the Ontario Municipal Information Systems Association (MISA) to promote enterprise architectures in government (Wiseman, 2015; Wiseman and Amsden, 2012). At the time, IT professionals were seeking to upgrade municipal information systems, which were often unique to specific municipalities (and even specific departments within municipalities) and could diverge considerably across jurisdictions. Chartwell was brought in to assist with developing a standard information system that could be taken up across municipalities. Drawing from enterprise architecture models, consultants took a expansive view of information, seeing it as central to the structure of government. As one municipal official recounts:

> [A]s that project unfolded, Chartwell said we would really like to help you with a data model but before you can have a data model you need to have a business model. You need to define what your lines of business are and how they relate and all of that kind of stuff ... Somehow or other, we got ourselves a business model but we never did get the data model. (Personal Interview, 2020)

Drawing from this perspective, Chartwell moved beyond advising on information systems to problematize existing budgetary models, which made spending legible at the departmental level but did not provide information on specific services and remained fragmented across jurisdictions. As a MISA newsletter noted: "just as each municipality …tended to develop its own technologies for delivering services, often regardless of whether other jurisdictions had similar solutions, each municipality also described its services and programs in different ways" (Moule, 2007, 37). Consultants argued that the lack of uniformity in municipal classifications inhibited comparisons across jurisdictions and contributed to inefficiencies as each municipality set out to develop their own classificatory systems from scratch.

Under the guidance of municipal information systems officers operating through MISA, municipal and provincial officials commissioned Chartwell IRM in the early 1990s to develop a Municipal Reference Model (MRM) that could be applied across municipalities in making sense of services. In the original proposal, it was described as a "a generic municipal model which could ultimately be used as foundation for a complete and integrated municipal information system" (cited in Wiseman, 2015, 110). The MRM framed government as a kind of "circuit board," broken down into a generic set of outputs (services) that could be measured and appraised against one another. Independent consultant, Melinda Munro (2008, 23), who played a central role in applying the MRM as the manager of the Service Delivery Transformation Program at the City of Windsor, compared it to a standard residential electrical box. "When I blow a fuse, I can go to the electrical box, look up the right switch, flick it, and the problem is solved. I neither can – nor want – to understand what happens behind the switch." The aim was not to understand the specific context in which services were carried out. Rather than looking at the nature of the work undertaken by a municipality, the focus was on the function. With the aim of providing an "overall picture of municipal data and functions," a "high level functional model" was designed by consultants, "defining what is done (not how it is done) in a generic municipality" (Wiseman, 2015, 111). By disaggregating costs at the level of services, rather than departmental jurisdictions, it was thought that budgets could be reoriented to calculate outcomes in a manner that would facilitate meaningful comparisons across jurisdictions.

The model presented municipal services through a hierarchically structured taxonomy according to programs, services, processes, and resources.

The aim was to unbundle information at the departmental level, in order to focus on the specific services provided. As Munro (N.D.) notes on her consulting blog:

> No one receives a 'unit' of Parks and Recreation, yet we often refer to Parks and Rec as a service. What does a unit of Parks and Rec look like? What is it worth? How do you generate it? The citizen, resident or visitor experiences a 'hectare of parkland' or a 'recreation class' or a 'rental space in a community centre'. These experiences are outputs of the services of Parks and Natural Areas, Recreation Programming or Recreational Space Rental/Lease.

By breaking down municipal programs into their component parts, it was then argued that citizens could measure outputs, getting a clearer sense of how their programs were organized.

Drawing from Star and Griesemer (1989), the MRM can be described as an "ideal type" classificatory system to the extent that it has a "hard outside," operating as a relatively immutable form, and a "plastic inside," that can be molded to suit different requirements. The MRM's "meta-model"—organized according to "programs," "services," and "subservices"—is unchanging across contexts, while its contents are adapted to different municipal settings and service areas. The meta-model is presented as simply a neutral form to be filled with a variety of contents. In this sense, it has been described by proponents as a genetic code or universal lexicon for understanding municipal services (Wiseman and Amsden, 2012; Moule, 2007; Munro, 2008). Such analogies speak to the apparent neutrality and purity of the model, which precedes all relationships, providing a sort of skeleton key for charting different municipal structures. Regardless of the politics of a city, its system of government, or its specific history, it is argued that this model can be applied in making sense of its services.

However, such technologies can also play a performative role in actively creating the field that they set out to describe. As I will show in the next section, the MRM has transformed the field of municipal services through rendering them commensurable, enabling the top-down analysis of how they measure up both within and across jurisdictions and the institution of a regime of competition by which municipalities feel pressure to perform according to specific criteria. In the process, it has provided a vehicle for generating enduring ties between government, private firms, and professional associations, while entrenching Chartwell, and later KPMG—which purchased Chartwell in 2008—as a key consultant for municipalities across the province.

Crafting a Regime of Competition: Understanding the Impact of the Municipal Reference Model on Urban Governance

While it is presented as a generic language for describing municipal services, the Municipal Reference Model has also established a normative framework through which services can be compared and ranked. Drawing previously distant regions and services together under a common framework, the MRM has fostered the formation of a competitive regime through which winners and losers can be identified. For this reason, it has been taken up by neoliberal reformers in Ontario, who have integrated it into their "citizen-centred" program that aims to make municipalities accountable to the "tax-payer" (Downey and Williams, 1998; Keil, 2002; Fanelli, 2016).

The implementation of MRMs changed the terrain through which actors operate. Such models, Söderström et al. (2014, 314) note, establish a "surface of equivalence," as cities are "no longer made of different—and to a large extent incommensurable—socio-technical worlds (education, business, safety and the like) but as data within systemic processes." The adoption of such a model creates the impression that such services can be known and compared from a distance, without a comprehensive knowledge of the context in which services are provided. Indeed, understanding these services does not seem "to require thematic experts familiar with the specifics of a 'field'" (Söderström et al., 2014, 314). Describing the implications, one consultant notes in a recent KPMG report promoting the MRM:

> Improved performance data will likely lead to some uncomfortable discussions as the opacity of 'gut feel' is replaced by the transparency of empirical evidence. New models and efficiency gains will require old models to be disrupted. City employees and politicians alike will need to learn to operate in a more evidence-based decision-making environment. (KPMG, 2017, 11)

Counterposing the "opacity" of professional discretion to the "transparency" of empirical evidence, the advancement of such a vantage point is premised on the idea that the city can be unproblematically translated into data and systems. As Söderström et al. (2014, 314) note: "the city seems to speak by itself, to be self-explanatory." This is reflected in the tendency by proponents to naturalize the model, treating it as a transparent lens for looking at municipal services. When the services are "mapped" in this way, one advocate notes, policymaking loses the "fog of uncertainty" (Munro, N.D.). Consequently, the performative aspects of the model tend to be effaced, as the numbers appear to speak by themselves, with consultants presenting themselves as simple rapporteurs (Davies, 2014).

Moreover, through rendering disparate services commensurable both within and across jurisdictions the MRM has also facilitated the normalization of municipal services, leading to the valorization of "standard" or "average" services at the expense of services framed as uncommon or anomalous. In this sense, the MRM is not just a descriptive model or vocabulary for classifying municipal services; it has been increasingly taken up as a means of *assessing* service levels—becoming what consultant Melissa Munro describes as a "a standard that imposes discipline" (Munro, 2008, 23). Through classifying municipal programs in a standard way, public officials are then able to make comparisons, seeing how they measure up to comparable jurisdictions. To the extent that they facilitate the standardization of policy knowledge across jurisdictions, the advancement of these sorts of assessment processes has facilitated the application of "soft power," by which municipalities are encouraged to self-police in order to ensure that they are not spending above comparable jurisdictions. In the context of Ontario, the provincial government has promoted such technologies as a means of exercising austerity at a distance, pressuring municipalities to refrain from going too far above "normal spending" without resorting to direct coercion.

Beginning in the mid-1990s, the Conservatives mounted a self-described "Common Sense" revolution across the province by which they set out to cut costs and rationalize services in the interests of the "taxpayer" (Conservative Party of Ontario, 1994). Drawing inspiration from the principles of New Public Management and the corresponding "audit explosion" taking root in other parts of the world (see Power, 1997), the provincial government pushed for performance metrics as a means of exercising soft power over public agencies, drawing them into a hierarchical regime by which they would be pressured to compete against one another for favorable ratings. This was reflected in the 1997 Ontario Budget, which committed to "open and accountable government," requiring public sector organizations "to identify opportunities to improve service delivery and involve the private sector in the design and delivery of those services," as well as developing and communicating "measurable performance indicators" in making services comparable across jurisdictions (Government of Ontario, 1997, 42). It was reinforced in 2001, when Ontario became the first state or province in North America to mandate a municipal performance measurement program for all municipalities, requiring municipalities to publicly disclose standardized information on nine service areas on an annual basis (Schatteman, 2010).

In this context, public officials at both the provincial and municipal levels took up the MRM as an instrument for benchmarking services. Beginning in the late 1990s, the MRM was periodically mobilized in reviews that set out to identify potential areas for cost savings. Working with city managers and senior staff, consultants compiled an inventory of programs provided by the municipality, which were then profiled according to their outputs. Once a relatively uniform set of outputs had been created, consultants could then subject services to a series of assessments. Two sorts of assessments have been developed.

First, consultants have developed a "Core Service Review," by which they set out to determine the extent in which services are necessary to the functioning of the municipality. Typically, consultants classify services in one of four categories, ranging from "mandatory" (statutorily required by government), to "essential" (necessary for the functioning of the city), "traditional" (customarily provided by municipalities), and "other." Positioning services along this continuum, they are able to identify services that are discretionary, and hence open to cutbacks. Along these lines, for instance, consultants have advanced arguments that community grants, subsidized dental care, accessibility programs in public transit, and fitness centers are more discretionary than long-term care or stormwater maintenance and therefore "opportunities" for cost savings (KPMG, 2020).

Second, consultants assess the "standard" of delivery, by benchmarking municipal accounts against comparable municipalities. Typically, consultants will draw on provincial financial data from three or four municipalities of similar size and composition in order to assess whether their services measure up. Along these lines, all those services that are "above standard" are deemed to be potential areas for cutbacks and restructuring. The logic is captured well by a KPMG report to the Township of Central Frontenac, which noted that "in some instances, the Township's service levels are higher than minimum standards and those adopted by comparator municipalities with similar populations and other characteristics, allowing the Township to reduce services to an acceptable level while reducing costs as well" (KPMG, 2013, 2). From this perspective, the "minimum" and "average" levels are deemed to be "acceptable," opening the door for municipalities running "above standard" services to cut costs.

Through the application of such metrics, the MRM has reformatted the field in which municipalities operate, cultivating a regime of competition between municipalities, which valorizes "average" and "mandatory" services, while rendering the "other" and "above standard" outliers legible as targets for policymakers. Such a classificatory model has generated a particular field of visibility, conditioning the public to adopt a zero-sum understanding of municipal management by positioning disparate services against one another in the effort to identify excess. In this context, the problem of urban governance is one of technological fine-tuning based on the identification and management of the "exceptional."

Crafting Knowledge Products: Understanding the Impact of the Municipal Reference Model on Management Consulting

The stabilization of the MRM as a model has empowered consultants, who have been able to package this model as a product that can be sold across jurisdictions. Given its generic format, the model can be easily circulated across institutional settings. Moreover, it facilitates the reformatting of municipal data in a manner that enables its codification and commodification, as "managerial knowledge is abstracted from context and reduced to a transparent and generic format that can be more easily leveraged within PSFs and sold in the marketplace" (Suddaby and Greenwood, 2001, 934).

In contrast to assessments involving lengthy, labor-intensive analysis of specific services, consultants applying the MRM do not need in-depth knowledge of specific services or the context in which they are delivered. Rather than compiling first-order data, they claim to render second-order data commensurable by drawing from existing provincial and municipal accounts. This makes the model portable. It can be easily mobilized from place to place by a small team of consultants working in consultation with senior public officials over a period of several weeks. As it renders services commensurable from a single vantage point, the MRM has also facilitated the concentration of knowledge, which can be banked, forming a database that consultants can draw from to deepen their influence.

Consequently, such technologies have transformed the market for advice. In the early 1990s, small information resource management firms like Chartwell, working with public officials, were able to carve out a niche for themselves. While the Municipal Information Systems Association retained ownership over the model, the firm was granted permission to market this model to other jurisdictions around the world. Building from their base in Ontario, they promoted the MRM to municipalities across Canada—including Calgary, Winnipeg, Surrey, and Coquitlam—later scaling it up as a reference model to both the provincial government under the Public Service Reference Model (PSRM) and the federal government under the Government of Canada Strategic Reference Model (GSRM) (Wiseman, 2015, 111).

They also promoted it on the global market, selling it to 40 municipalities in a number of countries, including Poland, Ethiopia, China, and the United States. In Phoenix Arizona, it was taken up in efforts to automate hazardous material purchasing, storage, distribution, and disposal. In Shanghai, it was introduced as a part of a World Bank assignment in monitoring the city's 21,000 construction projects and as a strategic planning information system (Municipal Reference Model Program, 1998). Over a two weeks period, a team of consultants including Chartwell drew from the MRM in developing a "straw model" of the Shanghai Construction Commission's programs and services. Alan Mitchell, the program consultant, noted the capacity of the MRM "to prepare a comprehensive model of the Shanghai Urban Construction Commission's business domain in relatively short order" while enabling the consulting team "to overcome barriers of language and culture" (Municipal Reference Model Program, 1998).

However, by the early 2000s, Chartwell was being outmatched by transnational professional service firms in the IT sector, such as IBM and Microsoft, as well as the "Big Four" auditing firms. Through instrumentalizing their expertise and accumulating expansive archives and databanks across jurisdictions, these large firms were able to achieve economies of scale in selling their advice to public officials (IBISWorld, 2019). From 2005 onwards, they undertook a wave of acquisitions, setting out to expand their capacity in advisory services, which included KPMG's purchase of Chartwell in 2008. Chartwell's experience with enterprise architecture and its networks with Canadian public officials were described as the chief motivating factors for the acquisition. As John Herhalt, a managing partner at KPMG noted at the time, "Chartwell's core skills in Enterprise Architecture are very much in demand by organizations in all industries. They complement KPMG's deep technical expertise in the IT space, and enrich our complete Advisory Services portfolio for our clients" (cited by Canada NewsWire, 2009).

Through appropriating Chartwell's enterprise architecture mapping models and expertise, KPMG set out to develop municipal benchmarking models as part of their global product line. Alan Mitchell was thus made the inaugural head of KPMG's Cities Global Center of Excellence in 2012, which promptly began promoting the MRM to other parts of the world. By 2014, a KPMG report features the MRM as "an integral tool to help a city meet new and innovative approaches to service delivery," taken up with over 40 cities worldwide (KPMG, 2014, 2). A 2017 project, integrating the MRM into a wider program of city benchmarking, was purported to be "the world's first attempt to comprehensively benchmark city service efficiency and effectiveness around the world" (KPMG, 2017, 14). Spearheaded by Mitchell, KPMG enlisted 35 cities around the world—including Barcelona, Brisbane, Cape Town, Philadelphia, Reykjavik, Sao Paulo, Kampala, and Moscow, alongside several Ontario municipalities that had initially developed the MRM.

At the same time, drawing from Chartwell's existing networks, KPMG further consolidated its influence in the Ontario market, selling municipal service delivery reviews to dozens of municipalities across the province. As there is no central database tracking these initiatives, it is difficult to determine the exact numbers. However, after contacting each of Ontario's 444 municipalities and searching municipal websites, I have identified at least 73 reviews undertaken by KPMG between 2005 and 2016, more than any other consultancy firm in the province. While Grant Thornton was also taken up by several municipalities, alongside individual consultants such as Melinda Munro (who championed the first Windsor MSDR), they do not provide services on the same scale.

Moreover, building from sunk costs in the MRM, KPMG has been able to market follow-up reviews to many municipalities across Ontario.

Once the MRM has been taken up in modeling a municipality, it provides a program to which consultants can return, providing a shorthand that enables them to quickly and comprehensively assess services in a manner that other firms might not be capable of matching. For instance, municipalities such as Sudbury have undertaken multiple reviews with KPMG, with each review framed as an "update" of the previous model. This has raised concerns from civic officials that auditing activities are being single-sourced to KPMG without competition from outside firms, speaking to the growing entrenchment of the firm in municipal politics (Della-Mattia, 2019).

Beyond an ad hoc program, taken up by municipal governments in times of need, the MRM has increasingly become embedded in government operations regionally and across political lines. By 2005, the Ministry of Municipal Affairs—working in collaboration with associations representing municipal managers and finance professionals[2]—had published a *Guide to Service Delivery Review for Municipal Managers* (republished in 2010), which encouraged municipalities to employ consultants in assessing the necessity of service delivery. Indeed, when I contacted the Ministry for more information on service reviews, I was referred to KPMG as the most experienced practitioner. The firm's consultants provide regular workshops to civic officials at events hosted by the Ministry, as well as through professional organizations, such as the Association of Municipal Clerks and Treasurers of Ontario (KPMG, 2016). Working through such networks, KPMG has achieved a considerable degree of influence in laying down assessment criteria at the provincial level.

Conclusion

At the time of writing, service reviews are being widely promoted by another provincial government. In responding to a perceived debt crisis, the right populist government of Doug Ford mandated service reviews for every municipality in Ontario with the aim of finding areas of "cost savings." This included a $200 million funding package for small and rural municipalities in March 2019, a $7.5 million package for larger urban

[2] The sponsors included the Association of Municipal Managers, Clerks and Treasurers of Ontario (AMCTO), the Municipal Finance Officers' Association of Ontario (MFOA), and the Ontario Municipal Administrators' Association (OMAA).

municipalities and school boards in May 2019, and an additional $143 million for reviews in October 2019 (Government of Ontario, 2019a, 2019b). While the outcome of these reviews is not clear, I have noted in my survey of service delivery reviews across the province, as well as in interviews, that KPMG remains the dominant firm being commissioned to undertake them, with many municipalities favoring the firm because of its previous experience with the Municipal Reference Model.

Through situating benchmarking in a broader history of managerial innovation, we can begin to understand the firm's influence. A return to the early history of this movement speaks to the way in which IT and auditing knowledge came to be hitched together in a discourse for reimagining government. Spearheaded by IT consultants in coalition with senior municipal information officers, the model was advanced through professional and institutional networks before being repackaged by KPMG as a vehicle for urban reform across municipalities. In many ways, this set the stage for the rise of new urban governance models, such as smart cities, which have built from these ideas, drawing from preexisting markets for advisory services, shaped by the institutional, professional, and culturally embedded relationships between civic officials and consultancies that emerged during the 1990s.

The fusion of IT and auditing knowledge under the MRM speaks to how a certain understanding of government, viewed as an information system composed of generic service outputs, came to be naturalized. Drawing from enduring imaginaries of government as a cybernetic model, there is a sense that consultants are providing a common lexicon for making sense of municipal services. The MRM is often framed as a descriptive model and nothing more. However, this belies the performative aspects of the model, which transform the field that it set out to describe. Through processes of commensuration and normalization, the MRM has fostered the establishment of a regime of competition, beginning in the late 1990s and becoming increasingly entrenched through the 2000s, by which municipal organizations are enticed to avoid providing services that are deemed to be discretionary or above standard.

This story is also interesting in speaking to the changing market for consultancy services. The firm that spearheaded this process in the 1990s was Canadian. Chartwell IRC was a firm of 30 people that built from long-standing relationships with different areas of government. However, more recently this technology has been appropriated by KPMG, which has set out to package it and promote it for an international market.

This has involved buying out Chartwell and integrating its staff into new transnational institutions for the diffusion of advisory services, most notably through the Cities Centre for Global Excellence. Ultimately, the adoption of such classificatory system has facilitated both the commodification of policy information, which can be transformed into a product that can be sold across jurisdictions, and the concentration of policy information, which can be expropriated by transnational professional service firms in a growing database that further entrenches their influence as knowledge brokers.

References

Berman, S.J. and Korsten, P.J. (2002) 'Corporate strategy for the new millennium', *IBM Institute for Business Value*, http://www-07.ibm.com/services/pdf/corp_strat.pdf, accessed 10 June 2020.

Bockman, J. and Eyal, G. (2002) 'Eastern Europe as a laboratory for economic knowledge: The transnational roots of neoliberalism', *American Journal of Sociology* 108(2): 310–352.

Brooks, R. (2018) *Bean Counters: The Triumph of the Accountants and how they Broke Capitalism*, London: Atlantic Books.

Broome, A. and Quirk, J. (2015) 'Governing the world at a distance: The practice of global benchmarking', *Review of International Studies* 41(5): 819–841.

Brown, W. (2015) *Undoing the Demos: Neoliberalism's Stealth Revolution*, New York: Zone Books.

Bruno, I. (2009) 'The "indefinite discipline" of competitiveness benchmarking as a neoliberal technology of government', *Minerva* 47: 261–280.

Callon, M. (1998) 'Introduction: The embeddedness of economic markets in economics', *The Sociological Review* 46(1): 1–57.

Canada NewsWire (2009) *KPMG to Acquire Consulting Firm Chartwell IRM Inc.* 2 March 2, http://news.top-consultant.com/uk/news_story.aspx?ID=5589, accessed 10 August 2020.

Chartwell IRM (2002) https://web.archive.org/web/20020408091855/http://chartwell-group.com/Home_nfl.htm, accessed 10 August 2020.

Christensen, M. and Skaerbaek, P. (2010) 'Consultancy outputs and the purification of accounting technologies', *Accounting, Organizations and Society* 35: 524–545.

Conservative Party of Ontario (1994) *The Common Sense Revolution*, Toronto: Party.

Davies, W. (2014) *The Limits of Neoliberalism: Authority, Sovereignty and the Logic of Competition*, London: Sage.

Della Mattia, E. (2019) 'City says no to single-sourcing city audit', *The Sault Star*, 18 June, https://www.saultstar.com/news/local-news/council-says-no-to-single-sourcing-city-audit, accessed 10 June 2020.

Deloitte (2018) *Benchmarking for the Corporate Sector: The Next Leap in Compliance*, https://www2.deloitte.com/content/dam/Deloitte/nl/Documents/risk/deloitte-nl-risk-compliance-psi-benchmark-report.pdf, accessed 23 September 2020.

Djama, M., Fouilleux, E. and Vagneron, I. (2011) 'Standard-setting, certifying and benchmarking: A governmentality approach to sustainability standards in the agro-food sector', in S. Ponte, P. Gibbon, and J. Vestergaard (eds). *Governing Through Standards: Origins, Drivers and Limitations*, New York: Palgrave Macmillan, pp. 184–209.

Downey, T.J. and Williams, R.J. (1998) 'Provincial agendas, local responses: The "common sense" restructuring of Ontario's municipal governments', *Canadian Public Administration* 41(2): 210–238.

Espeland, W.N. and Stevens, M.L. (1998) 'Commensuration as a social process', *Annual Review of Sociology* 24: 313–343.

Fanelli, C. (2016) *Megacity Malaise: Neoliberalism, Public Services and Labour in Toronto*, Halifax: Fernwood Publishing.

Fougner, T. (2008) 'Neoliberal governance of states: The role of competitiveness indexing and country benchmarking', *Millennium* 37(2): 303–326.

Government of Ontario (2019a) 'Ontario invests in small and rural municipalities to improve service delivery and efficiency', https://news.ontario.ca/mma/en/2019/03/ontario-invests-in-small-and-rural-municipalities-to-improve-service-delivery-and-efficiency.html, accessed 16 May 2019.

Government of Ontario (2019b) 'Premier ford asks partners to find four per cent savings and help front-line services', https://news.ontario.ca/opo/en/2019/05/premier-ford-asks-partners-to-find-four-per-cent-savings-and-help-protect-front-line-services.html, accessed 21 May 2019.

Government of Ontario (1997) *1997 Ontario Budget: Investing in the Future*, Toronto: Queen's Printer of Ontario.

IBISWorld (2019) *Global Management Consultants: L6712:GL*, IBISWorld Industry Report.

Ilcan, S. (2009) 'Privatizing responsibility: Public sector reform under neoliberal government', *Canadian Review of Sociology/Revue canadienne de sociologie* 46(3): 207–234.

Keil, R. (2002) '"Common–sense" neoliberalism: Progressive conservative urbanism in Toronto, Canada', *Antipode* 34(3): 578–601.

Kornberger, M. and Carter, C. (2010) 'Manufacturing competition: How accounting practices shape strategy making in cities', *Accounting, Auditing & Accountability Journal* 23(3): 325–349.

Kotusev, S. (2016) 'The history of enterprise architecture: An evidence-based review', *Journal of Enterprise Architecture* 12(1): 29–37.

KPMG (2013) *Corporation of the Township of Central Frontenac Service Delivery Review Final Report*, accessed 8 September 2019.

KPMG (2016) *Budget Policies, Multi-Year Budgeting and Best Practices*, https://www.amcto.com/getattachment/0826699b-b07b-4163-a981-81bcc1ed836d/.aspx, accessed 1 October 2020.

KPMG (2020) *The City of Greater Sudbury Core Service Review*, https://www.greatersudbury.ca/city-hall/pdfs/kpmg-final-report-of-core-service-review/, accessed 10 June 2020.

KPMG International (2014) *Services to Local Government*, https://home.kpmg.com/content/dam/kpmg/pdf/2015/03/ensuring-service-value-for-money.pdf, accessed 8 September 2019.

KPMG International (2017) *Benchmarking City Services: Finding the Courage to Improve*, https://home.kpmg/xx/en/home/insights/2017/09/finding-the-courage-to-improve-benchmarking-city-services.html, accessed 16 October 2019.

Larner, W. and Le Heron, R. (2004) 'Global benchmarking: Participating "at a distance" in the globalizing economy,' in W. Larner and W. Walters (eds). *Global Governmentality: Governing International Spaces*, New York, NY: Routledge, pp. 212–232.

Larner, W. and Le Heron, R. (2002) 'From economic globalization to globalizing economic processes: Towards post-structural political economies', *Geoforum* 33: 415–419.

MacKenzie, D. and Millo, Y. (2003) 'Constructing a market, performing theory: The historical sociology of a financial derivatives exchange', *American Journal of Sociology* 109(1): 107–145.

McCann, E. (2013) 'Policy boosterism, policy mobilities, and the extrospective city', *Urban Geography* 34(1): 5–29.

McCann, E. (2011) 'Urban policy mobilities and global circuits of knowledge: Toward a research agenda', *Annals of the Association of American Geographers* 101(1): 107–130.

Mitchell, A. (2016) 'Can you be a smart city without a smart budget?', http://smartcitybrand.com/articles-in-original-language/can-you-be-smart-city-without-smart-budget, accessed 7 June 2020.

Moule, L. (2007) 'The municipal reference model: Forging a common service language', *Municipal Interface* 14(3): 37–38.

Munro, M. (2008) 'City of windsor uses municipal reference model as foundation for service review', *Municipal Interface* 15(6): 23–24.

Munro, M. (N.D.) 'Your municipality needs a service model: No, you don't already have one', http://munrostrategy.com/your-municipality-needs-a-service-model-no-you-dont-already-have-one/, accessed 23 February 2020.

Municipal Reference Model Program (MRMP) (1998) 'Solutions—Shanghai, China', http://www.mrmp.com/subsol/solsnhai.html, accessed 10 August 2020.

The Open Group (2015) 'A historical look at enterprise architecture with John Zachman—An interview with The Open Group,' https://www.zachman.com/resource/ea-articles/182-a-historical-look-at-enterprise-architecture-with-john-zachman, accessed 23 August 2020.

Peck, J. and Theodore, N. (2015) *Fast Policy: Experimental Statecraft at the Thresholds of Neoliberalism*, Minneapolis: University of Minnesota Press.

Power, M. (1997) *The Audit Society: Rituals of Verification*, Oxford: Oxford University Press.

PwC. (2017) *Reinventing Innovation: Five Findings to Guide Strategy through Execution*, https://www.pwc.com/us/en/services/consulting/innovation-benchmark-findings.html, accessed 5 October 2020.

Saint-Martin, D. (2013) 'Making government more "business-like": Management consultants as agents of isomorphism in modern political economies', in J. Mikler (ed). *The Handbook of Global Companies*, West Sussex: Wiley-Blackwell, pp. 173–192.

Sauder, M. and Espeland, W.N. (2009) 'The discipline of rankings: Tight coupling and organizational change', *American Sociological Review* 74(1): 63–82.

Schatteman, A. (2010) 'The state of Ontario's municipal performance reports: A critical analysis', *Canadian Public Administration* 53(4): 531–550.

Söderström, O., Paasche, T. and Klauser, F. (2014) 'Smart cities as corporate storytelling', *City* 18(3): 307–320.

Star, S.L. and Griesemer, J.R. (1989) 'Institutional ecology, "translations" and boundary objects: Amateurs and professionals in Berkeley's Museum of Vertebrate Zoology, 1907–39', *Social Studies of Science* 19(3): 387–420.

Stone, D. (2004) 'Transfer agents and global networks in the "transnationalization" of policy', *Journal of European Public Policy* 11(3): 545–566.

Suddaby, R. & Greenwood, R. (2001). 'Colonizing knowledge: Commodification as a dynamic of jurisdiction expansion in professional service firms', *Human Relations* 54(7), 933–953.

Sum, N.L. (2009) 'The production of hegemonic policy discourses: "Competitiveness" as a knowledge brand and its (re-)contextualizations,' *Critical Policy Studies* 3(2): 184–203.

Synnott, W.R. (1987) *The Information Weapon: Winning Customers and Markets with Technology*, London: Wiley.

Tozer, E.E. (1986) 'Developing strategies for management information systems', *Long Range Planning* 19(4): 31–40.
Wiseman, R. (2015) 'Canadian governments reference models', in K. Kijima (ed). *Service Systems Science*, Tokyo: Springer, pp. 109–128.
Wiseman, R. and Amsden, J. (2012) 'The municipal reference model: Understanding the DNA of government', Webinar Organized for the Institute of Citizen-Centred Services. https://www.youtube.com/watch?v=PrPEEUJ_eo8, accessed 10 May 2020.
Zachman, J.A. (1987) 'A framework for information systems architecture', *IBM Systems Journal* 26(3): 276–292.

Connecting Local Government with Global Finance: Professional Service Firms as Agents of Financialization

Sebastian Möller

Introduction: Local Government Debt and Policy Consultants

The recent conjuncture of global capitalism is characterized by an unprecedented rise in the amount, pace, and transformative impact of transnational financial market activities (Harvey, 2011; Lapavitsas, 2013; Porter, 2005). Finance is constantly restructuring, reimagining, and reinventing economic, social, and political institutions and relations all over the globe. Why and how is this ongoing transformation evolving in so many different institutional contexts? This puzzle occupies scholars from different fields of study and various theoretical camps. The burgeoning literature on financialization, defined as "the increasing dominance of financial actors, markets, practices, measurements and narratives at various scales" (Aalbers, 2015, 214), has contributed much to our understanding of the diffusion of financial market rationalities within and beyond markets (Mader et al., 2020). In particular, a number of studies have

S. Möller (✉)
Cusanus Hochschule Für Gesellschaftsgestaltung, Koblenz, Germany
e-mail: sebastian.moeller@cusanus-hochschule.de

C. Hurl and A. Vogelpohl (eds.), *Professional Service Firms and Politics in a Global Era*, https://doi.org/10.1007/978-3-030-72128-2_9

called attention to the expertise required to generate and circulate financial models and modes of calculation across contexts (Besedovsky, 2018; Bousseba and Faulconbridge, 2019; Chiapello, 2015; Froud et al., 2017). The adoption of new practices, measurements, and ideas apparently not only requires the production and dissemination of technical knowledge but also a careful legitimation through financialized ideas and narratives. In this regard, professional service firms (PSFs) are playing a crucial role as agents of change. Their mundane technical, discursive, and strategic work therefore merits more academic and public attention in order to better understand and potentially contest processes of financialization.

This chapter focuses on new municipal borrowing practices as a specific manifestation of financialization that is particularly well suited to demonstrate the influence of private experts. While local governments have commissioned the advice of PSFs, consultants, and private sector experts for decades (Bowman et al., 2015; Froud et al., 2017; Harding et al., 2000; Hurl, 2017; see Hurl in this volume), the spread of financialized practices and rationalities to City Hall has often failed to garner scholarly and public attention. Starting in the late 1990s and thus prior to great financial crisis of 2008/09, many local authorities in the US and Western Europe have adopted so-called active debt or treasury management strategies that connected their debt portfolios with financial markets through the use of interest rate derivatives and the issuance of municipal bonds (Deruytter and Möller, 2020; Omstedt, 2020). This trend can be observed increasingly also in Africa (see Roitman in this volume). This was one of the various gateways for the infiltration of financial market rationalities to local government, with urban (re)development (Peck and Whiteside, 2016; Waldron, 2019; Weber, 2010), housing (Beswick and Penny, 2018; Botzem and Dobusch, 2017), and infrastructure (Ashton et al., 2016; Pike et al., 2019) being other prominent examples. This transformation has significant socioeconomic and political ramifications at the local level. Not only does it affect the balance of power between public and private actors and, thus, the scope of democratic policy autonomy. It also repurposes local government in line with the interests of investors and the financial system. Investors and other financial market actors emerge as a new constituency of the local state potentially exercising disciplinary power over the democratic process (Omstedt, 2020; Streeck, 2014).

In this chapter, I argue that the financialization of municipal borrowing, like other processes of state financialization, deeply relies on the technical, epistemological, and discursive work of policy consultants and other PSFs as well as on a complex network of public and private actors. Various private experts, financial institutions, and semi-private associations are involved in the careful construction and diffusion of a debt management narrative that paved the way for the successful marketing of financial instruments hitherto almost unknown among city treasurers and municipal finance officers. Treasury management advisors, brokers, and other PSFs create and diffuse new financialized rationalities and, thereby, connect global finance and local government. In a nutshell, I argue that local state financialization can be understood as a techno-political project actively spearheaded by a range of transnational and regional professional service firms (PSFs) acting as both disseminators of financial logics and narratives on the one hand and as intermediaries between global and local finance on the other hand. After all, private expertise should be conceived of as an integral part of the politics of financialization. Even in cases of financial turmoil caused by newly adopted supposedly low-risk and rational financial products, local governments often continue to rely on forms of private expertise for their immediate crisis management. This indicates a high degree of dependency of public policy on external experts and the self-reinforcing dynamic of financialization processes.

In what follows, I trace the role of private expertise in the diffusion of financialized municipal debt management by focusing on the emerging and consolidating German and British market for local government treasury management advice. Such a comparative case study approach is well suited to illustrating the different ways in which private expertise is embedded in municipal finance and to identify varieties of intermediation between global finance and local government. Germany and the UK are particularly interesting for such a comparison since they represent rather different varieties of capitalism with particular dynamics of financialization, Germany as the prototype of a Coordinated Market Economy (CME) and the UK as role model of a Liberal Market Economy (LME). Moreover, German and British local government is rather dissimilar legally, fiscally, and politically. Municipal debt management including the use of derivatives has, nonetheless, occurred in both countries which calls for an explanation. The chapter builds on extensive empirical research in both countries including expert interviews with public administrators, consultants, brokers, and representatives from banks as well as the analysis of official documents and media reports. Five stages of private expertise involved in the politics of local state financialization are identified and illustrated empirically: The crafting of a new debt management narrative targeting local council financial officers (stage 1), the provision of trial portfolio analyses (stage 2), the canvassing, brokering, and contracting of derivative deals (stage 3), the actual debt management operations within the municipal finance department (stage 4), and crisis management (stage 5). After some brief reflections on the politics of local state financialization, I will address each of these stages of consolidation separately. The chapter concludes by highlighting some cross-findings from the field of municipal borrowing for private expertise as a driver of financialization more broadly.

Theoretical Reflections: The Politics of Local State Financialization

The Precursor: New Public Management and the Marketization of the State

In order to understand the financialization of local government, it is necessary to first understand its precursors in New Public Management (NPM) reforms and the related marketization of local government. While often being represented by advocates and practitioners as mere modernization and rationalization of state bureaucracies, both NPM and financialization are deeply political processes as they change power relations and world views within the state and contribute to redrawing boundaries between states and markets (Jessop, 2008; Strange, 1996). As part of these changing power relations, the planning and fiscal capacities of local government have been undermined as a result of NPM reforms (Martin, 2002), state rescaling (Brenner, 2004), and austerity (Gray and Barford, 2018; Peck, 2012), while investors and other financial market actors have emerged as a new constituency of the state, exposing it to increasing disciplinary market powers (Livne and Yonay, 2016; Omstedt, 2020; Streeck, 2014). Consequentially, the influence of private expertise and corporate service provision has been on the rise for quite some time, rendering City Hall an easy target for financial experts with commercial interests.

Under the umbrella of NPM, private sector rationalities and tools have been introduced to public administrations on different levels of the state allegedly in order to increase the effectiveness of government.

NPM reforms have followed the rationale that if only the government was run in a corporate style with more effective internal procedures, money could be saved and invested into maintaining public services (Hood, 1991; Pollitt and Bouckaert, 2011; Sanderson, 2001). In the general market euphoria after the collapse of socialism in 1989/90, this narrative mirrored the widespread conception of state bureaucracies as too slow, too costly, and too ineffective. The transformation of the local state under the NPM narrative has significantly changed the workings and rationalities of local government in Northern America, Europe, and, through the vehicle of development cooperation conditional upon so-called good governance reforms in countries of the Global South. NPM reforms have included the adoption of private sector management principles and measurements to local government, the introduction of performance indicators and network governance, outsourcing, and privatization (Kjaer, 2009; Learmonth, 2005; Martin, 2002; Sanderson, 2001). In particular, NPM opened up spaces for municipal service provision by private companies and in cooperation with policy consultancy (Froud et al., 2017; Hurl, 2017; Wollmann, 2014). As a result, there have been fundamental transformations in the way that local government is organized, public policy is designed, and public services are provided. This transformation is often associated with a shrinking policy space, quality reductions in (formerly) public services, and uneven financial benefits enriching the public service industry (Bowman et al., 2015; Froud et al., 2017). It was driven by and further accelerated the influence of management theory and business consultancy in search of new markets for their advisory services (Saint-Martin, 2000). Such services were not only crucial for the process of restructuring local government but later also the municipal service provision itself.

The Next Level: Financializing the Local State

However big the NPM transformations were, in retrospect, they turned out to be only a pre-game for local state financialization gaining momentum in the early 2000s (Deruytter and Möller, 2020) with the state being not only its object but also a core driver and agent itself (Aalbers, 2020; Livne and Yonay, 2016; O'Brien et al., 2019). At the municipal level, the project of financialization has resulted in a new alignment of infrastructure, housing, and urban (re)development with financial market interests (Beswick and Penny, 2018; Pike et al., 2019; Waldron,

2019; Weber, 2010). It creates new bonds between local budgets and global finance through the use of new financial products (Hendrikse and Sidaway, 2014; Lagna, 2015; Mertens et al., 2019; Peck and Whiteside, 2016), the establishment of debt management policies (Deruytter and Möller, 2020), and the disciplinary power of rating agencies (Hackworth, 2002; Omstedt, 2020). Under financialization, entrepreneurial practices of local governments are increasingly separated from traditional strategies of local growth politics (Lauermann, 2018) and reshaped by financial market logics.

Viewed from a critical social science perspective, nothing is natural or inevitable about this remarkable transformation. As Livne and Yonay (2016: 340) note, "financialization is not an evolutionary phase in economic development, but a techno-political project, which (…) professional, political and economic actors promote." In other words, financialization has to be pushed for and maintained by someone. It is a project actively undertaken by actors with vested interests as much as a discursive shift. Therefore, financialization can be conceptualized as a process of producing and circulating specific financial ideas, cultures, techniques, and calculation methods (Chiapello, 2015) between and within organizations (Besedovsky, 2018; Davis and Walsh, 2017; Engelen et al., 2014; Faulconbridge, 2015). This is where private expertise comes in: While financial models and economic theories often have a performative effect on their own (Henriksen, 2013; MacKenzie, 2006; Merkus and Veenswijk, 2017), they are still put to work by people and organizations. As will be shown in the case of municipal debt management, the financialization of the state is essentially driven by policy consultants and other PSFs providing the necessary ideational, epistemological, legal, and technical framework, while at the same time generating a constant stream of revenue as management fees (Botzem and Dobusch, 2017). External advisors function both as intermediaries connecting local government and global finance, and disseminators of financial market logics. Without the significant influence of private expertise, for instance, the very concept of managing municipal debt (as opposed to administering debt) might not have become established within local government, since the very idea of managing debt with derivatives first had to be diffused and popularized among municipal finance officers, public administrators, and local councilors who previously had no or little experience with derivatives.

Similar to NPM reforms, state financialization has the tendency to evolve as self-reinforcing dynamic or, in the words of Ashton et al.

(2016, 1397), as "a recursive policy project – wherein each round of transactions creates powers, orientations, and constraints that pattern a tendency towards more financialization." There are different mechanisms for diffusing ideas and practices at play here, ranging from personal networks among finance officers and regular conferences and workshops organized by local government associations to broader political and administrative discourses.

Besides this diffusion of ideas, there is also material pressure towards financialization created through both demand and supply-side dynamics. On the one hand, austerity and, in some cases, increasing levels of sovereign debt have made local governments much more susceptible to financial innovation that has been praised as an effective tool to reduce financing costs and even as a profit center by PSFs, regulators, and the finance press. Accordingly, previous research has highlighted financial and socioeconomic stress as a core driver for local government's use of interest rate derivatives (Mertens et al., 2019; Singla and Luby, 2020). On the other hand, finance itself and banking in particular have increasingly become financialized through technological advancements, the adoption of new calculation methods, and increasing competitive pressures reinforced by the liberation and deregulation of European financial markets. As a result, the supply of new financial products and services has intensified significantly.

These general tendencies towards financialization are mediated through specific political and socioeconomic contexts. Accordingly, financialization has been rolled out differently in the UK and Germany. While the British economy was reoriented towards finance from the 1980s onwards, financialization gathered momentum in the early 2000s and was often introduced through established institutions and organizations. Therefore while PSFs played a crucial role in the diffusion of financialization in both jurisdictions, they are embedded rather differently in their respective organizational culture.

The Culmination: The Financialization of Municipal Borrowing

NPM and local state financialization culminated in the establishment and consolidation of financialized municipal debt management which concerns a key capacity of the local state, namely the provision of financial resources. Prior to local state financialization, municipal borrowing used to be a rather boring and risk-averse activity within local government. In the UK, local councils traditionally borrowed from an institution called the Public Works Loan Board (PWLB). In this case, the central state provided cheap credit with minimal administrative costs. In fact, a simple phone call was enough to take on an investment loan. For decades, the very existence of this option effectively prevented both banks and consultants to enter municipal finance. In Germany, by comparison, local governments traditionally take on long term, fixed interest rate loans from their house banks which are often local savings banks (Sparkassen) or regional state banks (Landesbanken). While this resembles much more a market transaction, social networks, and local proximity are key to this business and, except for the bank, private expertise is usually not involved.

However, with the growing liberalization of European financial markets and banking from the late 1990 onwards, private expertise became a core driver for change. At this time, international banks and PSFs entered the municipal finance scene, playing a key role in the diffusion of new financial models to local governments. For this to happen, PSFs and banks had to first generate interest in and demand for new financial products. This seemed to be a rather challenging task given the established systems of credit provision and the well-known prudence and traditional training of local council financial officers. NPM reforms, austerity, financial innovation, and increasing competitive pressures within the banking sector, however, gradually generated much more conducive conditions for the financialization of municipal borrowing.

From the late 1990s until the last great financial crisis of 2008/09, many local authorities across Europe were turned into customers of new and often risky financial products including interest rate derivatives by treasury management advisors and brokers. As a core instrument of contemporary capitalism (Bryan and Rafferty, 2006), derivatives introduced corporate style debt management practices and rationalities to local government and created new bonds with global financial markets. Previous research (Deruytter and Möller, 2020; Hendrikse and Sidaway, 2014; Lagna, 2015; Mertens et al., 2019; Petzold, 2014; Singla and Luby, 2020; Tickell, 1998; Trampusch and Spies, 2015) and empirical evidence from municipalities of varying size, socioeconomic situation, and political affiliation suggest the occurrence of a structural change rather than individual cases of policy experimentation, overambitious banking, misconduct or even bribery (all of which might be part of the story but cannot account for its systematic diffusion). While the introduction of debt management approaches to the municipal government was often associated with the prospect of increasing fiscal and political leeway for highly indebted local councils, market volatilities during the financial crisis turned many of these derivatives toxic and, in some cases, caused additional fiscal and political stress for already cash-strapped local governments. Thus, the desire to increase the room for maneuver by adopting debt management strategies often remained unfulfilled.

Besides these fiscal effects of municipal debt management, PSFs, and other actors involved in local state financialization, actively transform the self and market perception of municipal finance departments, for instance in line with portfolio theory. In an interview, a German municipal finance officer with a professional background in banking repeatedly referred to the importance of portfolio theory as guiding principle for his mundane debt management activities. In accordance with this model, he firstly perceived municipal debt as a debt portfolio to be managed as a whole rather than as a multitude of individual liabilities to different creditors. This portfolio approach allowed him to measure different characteristics of the overall debt, such as the ratio between fixed and floating rate loans and the related risks and to compare them with textbook targets. In fact, this approach has been taught in countless commercial municipal finance workshops all over the UK and Germany from the late 1990s onward gradually changing the rationalities and market perceptions of local finance officers.

Private Expertise in Local State Financialization: Five Stages of Consolidation

The involvement of PSFs in municipal finance varies significantly over time and across cases. It includes everything from giving informal nonbinding advice on distinct loans and derivatives to taking over the complete financial management operations of the council. In any case, PSFs accumulate relevant market knowledge and rise to powerful actors in their own right (Bowman et al., 2015; Hurl, 2017). Their influence can be traced within five stages from crafting a debt management narrative to crisis management. These analytical stages emerge from my own empirical fieldwork in England and Germany. Through interviews, official documents, and media accounts, I reconstructed the integration of British and German municipalities, into derivative markets. These stages partly overlap and not all of them are equally relevant in each empirical case.

Still, they represent an escalating dynamic of private expertise involvement in public policy at the municipal level. While they are rather specific to the case of municipal debt management with derivatives, lessons can be learned as well for other policy fields and activities of PSFs targeting the public sector.

Stage 1: Crafting and Disseminating a Debt Management Narrative

Before local governments experience a demand for new financial products to manage their debt portfolio (and, in fact, conceive of their accumulated liabilities as a debt portfolio), the very concept of active debt and treasury management has to be established and promoted. Thus, PSFs play a crucial role way in advance of any actual service provision. Financialization generally relies on a new conception of risk as calculable opportunity (Besedovsky, 2018). For city treasurers to embrace new financial instruments and strategies, their understanding of fiscal prudence has to be changed. In the brave new world of derivative capitalism, not using derivatives is increasingly branded by consults and perceived by financial officers as risky and irresponsible strategy, turning traditional conceptions of prudence upside down. This discursive shift first occurred within banking and corporate finance and, in the late 1990s and early 2000s, gradually also emerged within British and German public finance. In Germany, the introduction of new accounting rules in municipal finance and the quickly increasing costs of servicing municipal debt accelerated this process while in the UK earlier failures of local authorities to generate income through financial speculation (Tickell, 1998) slowed it down. In both cases, PSF staff played a key role in disseminating these ideas as authors or experts in local government periodicals, especially those published by local government and professional associations such as "*Room 151*" or "*Der Neue Kämmerer*" (see also Petzold, 2014, 44). These journals are broadly and frequently read within the public finance profession and serve as a medium to spread best practice examples and to discuss new trends. Besides city treasurers and legal experts, policy consultants, and representatives from the financial sector are among the regular contributors to such periodicals which also frequently advertise debt management workshops and trainings.

Commercial workshops and presentations form bank representatives and treasury management advisors at regular conventions of municipal finance officers and other local government actors were crucial for the dissemination of this new way of doing public finance. Moreover, some city treasurers with a professional background in finance performed the role of policy entrepreneurs.

In this stage, three types of private actors were dominant within the field: Public sector consultancies such as Capita, Tullet Prebon, Butlers, finance active, brokers like ICAP, and banks including Barclays, RBS, Deutsche Bank, WestLB, and Sparkassen on the other hand. Regarding the market for policy advise, we can witness a significant concentration of an originally rather segmented marketplace with many smaller, highly specialized, and regional actors. More recently, fintech firms such as Loanbox and Commnex have entered the market for public sector advise and could contribute to a break of its rather oligopolistic structure. Interestingly, PSFs have often collaborated with both renowned academics and research institutes in the field of public administration and professional and local government associations. This made the fabrication and diffusion of the new debt management narrative even more successful since it provided epistemic and organizational legitimacy.

Stage 2: Trial Portfolio Analysis

Similar to the promotion of a new debt management narrative, some banks provided individual local governments with analyses of their debt portfolios, often free of charge or at low cost. In doing so, they also accustomed municipal finance departments to conceive of their liabilities as a debt portfolio which is a precondition of debt management. Such trial analyses were offered among others by Barclays, RBS, Dexia, and German public banks including West.LB, NRW.Bank, and local savings banks. Deutsche Bank offered a more comprehensive Risk Coaching. Through the analyses, banks gained access to valuable information on the municipalities' finances and contracts with their respective competitors. The main goal, however, was to identify and present potentials for interest rate optimization or hedging. Results were usually communicated in elaborate presentations for the finance department or the city council's finance or budget committee including information brochures with new measurements and "pictorial representations" (Hurl, 2017, 59) of the debt portfolio. Together with the emerging narrative of prudent but active debt management, such tailored information increased the willingness of local governments to adopt new instruments. Often, the respective documents are not disclosed due to business secret provisions. However, some of the presentations have been given in front of finance committee and have been entered in the minutes. In other cases, trial portfolio analyses could be reconstructed through interviews.

Stage 3: Canvassing, Brokering, and Contracting

Canvassing and contracting are constant and integral elements of the politics of local state financialization. The contract itself has recently received more academic attention as a policy device (Froud et al., 2017; Raco in this volume). As with the previous stages, this stage is concerned with market creation but much more on the level of individual transactions. Municipal derivatives have been aggressively promoted by both financial institutions and consultancy firms for quite some time. As Geisst (1997, 363) notes, "The corporate world was not the only place that derivatives packages were being sold. Many municipalities and their treasurers became targets of aggressive Wall Street selling of the hard-to-understand fixed-income portfolios. Bond and derivative salesmen became so aggressive that 'they were like camels, trying to put their nose in our tent', remarked one Idaho municipal investment manager (…)." In many cases, interest rate swaps came or LOBO (Lender Option Borrower Option) loans were sold with teaser rate, a special discount for the first years of a usually rather long contractual period. In the UK, PSFs and banks did face a huge challenge in their efforts of market-making namely the public provision of municipal debt through the PWLB. In contrast to Germany, British PSFs had to firstly popularize the idea of a market for municipal debt including the brokerage of inter-municipal lending and municipal bonds. In Germany, on the other hand, local councils were used to borrowing from banks which created another problem for PSFs, namely competition from the advisory services provided by the local government's principal banks (often Sparkassen, Landesbanken or Deutsche Bank).

Stage 4: Performing Municipal Debt Management

For the actual performance of debt management, another type of PSF enters the scene, namely treasury management advisors (TMA) like CAPITA, Butlers, Arlingclose, or Sector. Such firms provide daily support and regular training for the finance department, monitor both the debt portfolio and the ongoing transactions, and provide market analyses and product updates. The degree of TMA involvement varies from selective support to a fully outsourced debt management. Usually, debt management is conceived of as a continuous task including some degree of market observation and client relations between the finance departments, their advisors, brokers, and bank officers. Related procedures and reporting have undergone a process of standardization both in the UK and Germany as a result of individual scandals, the financial crisis, and related legal uncertainties. For this standardization, local government and professional associations played a key role. In some cases, municipal finance officers use tailored debt management software provided by banks or TMAs and financial market information systems like Reuters. A crucial feature of this stage is the persistent asymmetry of information between different actors. While brokers, TMAs, and banks professionally monitor the markets and collect all sorts of information, local governments have little capacities to do so and, thus, deeply rely on information and interpretation provided by TMA. In fact, this is the very business model of public sector advise.

Stage 5: Crisis Management

Particularly illuminating for our understanding of private expertise as a driver of the financialization of municipal borrowing are cases of failure. The inverse interest curve during the last great financial crisis has turned many municipal interest rate swaps and LOBO loans toxic and causes huge financial losses. While this development certainly caused reputational damage for the debt management narrative, it did not reverse the trend of local state financialization nor constrain private expertise influence over local government. On the contrary, the political, legal, and financial uncertainty caused by toxic financial products served as an additional entry point for external advice. Banks and consultancy firms were called for help regarding the restructuring of derivatives and loans, reputational management, and legal advice. Here, big international consultancies like Deloitte and PwC and smaller highly specialized advisors were commissioned to support local authorities hit by financial and political stress. Apart from some regulatory responses by the central states and a further push toward standardization, financialized municipal borrowing was not effectively contested.

Conclusion: Private Experts as Drivers of Financialization

Private expertise is one of the core driving forces of local state financialization in general and the establishment of municipal debt management with derivatives in particular. Professional service firms are providing the ideational, epistemological, legal, and technical framework for municipal debt management with derivatives. By fabricating and diffusing the narrative of active debt and treasury management as modern, responsible, and prudent alternatives to traditional ways of doing public finance in City Hall, PSFs paved the way for the financialization of municipal borrowing. They are indeed engaged in multilayered processes of "reducing the normative to the normal" (Hurl, 2017, 64) in the sense that active debt and treasury management is presented as a purely technical and rational value for money solution.

This view, however, which is shared in much of the administration literature, veils the political nature and redistributive character of local state financialization: While it is not possible to assess the costs and benefits of derivatives for the local governments given the absence of reliable and complete data, it is fair to assume that consultants and brokers have significantly benefitted from this newly created market both in financial and organizational terms. In fact, the more complex debt management operations become and the more the local state is deprived of own expertise by staff reductions due to austerity policies, the more dependent local government will become (and stay) on private expertise. This integration of new customers to global derivative markets further deepens, stabilizes, and reproduces financialized capitalism.

The great financial crisis rendered many of the municipal derivatives toxic and thereby generated an intensified political contestation. Nevertheless, local state financialization did not come to an end—not then and not now. Quite to the contrary, joint efforts by local government associations, banks, and consultancy firms to standardize (and legally safeguard) municipal derivatives and the established infrastructures within City Hall secured the continuity of debt management policies as the new normal of doing public finance. Since financial literacy has the remarkable tendency of producing overconfident investors (Wolf, 2018), municipal finance departments with some degree of experience in and knowledge of debt management strategies are likely to further engage in financial market transactions of some sort. Moreover, scandalized cases of huge losses for either the city budget or the bank's balance sheet (such as in Pforzheim, Hagen, Newham, Hammersmith, and Fulham) could paradoxically even serve as contrast and legitimation for due process and, indeed, as additional selling-point for the use of private expertise. PSFs as intermediaries between the local state and the banking industry had actually the greatest interest in the continuation of municipal debt management with derivatives. Ironically enough, it is the current low/zero interest rate environment that puts this continuity at risk since it makes it much more challenging to convince local finance officers of the need to actively manage their debt.

I would like to draw three cross-cutting conclusions. While we can, firstly, observe similar transformations of municipal debt management in many different jurisdictions, the process of intermediation between administrative practices and financial market know-how varies considerably among cases. Differences consider the number and type of intermediaries and the depth of consultancy, the scope of regulatory interventions by the state apparatus, and the degree to which civil servants and local policymakers have normalized and internalized financial market cultures. Such differences stem from established institutional patterns and organizational features of both local government and the public sector consultancy within different political systems and, at least partly, account for the observable variety of state financialization. Thus, private expertise has proven to be rather flexible and adaptable both in organizational and strategic terms. Evidence from this research suggests that this is not only the case for smaller policy consultancies originating from their own target jurisdiction but also for transnational consultancies and financial service firms that seem to operate highly specialized and attuned to different legal and political conditions.

Secondly, the example of municipal debt management also sheds light on the type of intermediaries that is often overlooked, namely public or professional associations. Local government associations, such as LGA and DStGB, and professional associations of municipal finance officers and public administrators, such as CIPFA, have played a crucial role in the dissemination, standardization, and legitimation of financialized practices. They provide a platform for the presentation of new concepts, strategies, and products by consultancy firms and banks in the form of workshops or best practice reports in the association's periodicals. Moreover, not only the flow of information is crucial here but also the fabrication of a certain social pressure of adapting to presumed innovations. The desire of not being perceived as old-fashioned public administrator or as a local government that refuses progress and does not seize new opportunities has occurred as core theme in many interviews conducted for this research. Accordingly, associations served as a catalyst for the influence of private expertise over public policy and they merit more attention also in other areas of state transformation.

Finally, and probably most importantly, private expertise often contributes to a depoliticization not only of particular public policies but also of state activity in general. By presenting debt management with derivatives as a rational and normal thing to do, consultancy firms, financial institutions, and city associations veil both the political foundations of the expertise itself and its political implications for the state. This renders political contestation more difficult. This dynamic is crucial in understanding the sprawling character of private expertise influence. The policy space does not only shrink due to new financial dependencies created through financialization but also as a consequence of the very dependence on external expertise in the setting up and daily implementation of policies. Thus, a meaningful and transformative critique of financialization and other forms of state transformations must not only confront changing policies and practices but also their ideational and epistemological foundations.

References

Aalbers, M.B. (2015) 'The potential for financialization', *Dialogues in Human Geography* 5(2): 214–219.

Aalbers, M.B. (2020) 'Financial geography III: The financialization of the city', *Progress in Human Geography* 44(3): 595–607.

Ashton, P., Doussard, M. and Weber, R. (2016) 'Reconstituting the state: City powers and exposures in Chicago's infrastructure leases', *Urban Studies* 53(7): 1384–1400.

Besedovsky, N. (2018) 'Financialization as calculative practice: The rise of structured finance and the cultural and calculative transformation of credit rating agencies', *Socio-Economic Review* 16(1): 61–84.

Beswick, J. and Penny, J. (2018) 'Demolishing the present to sell off the future? The emergence of financialized municipal entrepreneurialism', *International Journal of Urban and Regional Research* 42(4): 612–632.

Botzem, S. and Dobusch, L. (2017) 'Financialization as strategy: Accounting for inter-organizational value creation in the European real estate industry', *Accounting, Organizations and Society* 59: 31–43.

Bousseba, M. and Faulconbridge, J. (2019) 'Professional service firms as agents of economic globalization: A political perspective', *Journal of Professions and Organization* 6(1): 72–90.

Bowman, A., Ertürk, I., Folkman, P., Froud, J., Haslam, C., Johal, S., Leaver, A., Moran, M., Tsitsianis, N. and Williams, K. (2015) *What a Waste: Outsourcing and How It Goes Wrong*, Manchester: Manchester University Press.

Brenner, N. (2004) 'Urban governance and the production of new state spaces in Western Europe 1960–2000', *Review of International Political Economy* 11(3): 447–488.

Bryan, D. and Rafferty, M. (2006) *Capitalism with Derivatives: A Political Economy of Financial Derivatives, Capital and Class*, Basingstoke: Palgrave Macmillan.

Chiapello, E. (2015) 'Financialization of valuation', *Human Studies* 38(1): 13–35.

Davis, A. and Walsh, C. (2017) 'Distinguishing Financialization from Neoliberalism, *Theory, Culture & Society* 34(5–7): 27–51.

Deruytter, L. and Möller, S. (2020) 'Cultures of debt management enter city hall', in P. Mader, D. Mertens and N. van der Zwan (eds). *The Routledge International Handbook of Financialization*, London: Routledge, pp. 400–410.

Engelen, E., Fernandez, R. and Hendrikse, R. (2014) 'How finance penetrates its other: A cautionary tale on the financialization of a Dutch University', *Antipode* 46(4): 1072–1091.

Faulconbridge, J. (2015) 'Knowledge and learning in professional service firms', in L. Empson, D. Muzio, J. Broschak and B. Hinings (eds). *The Oxford Handbook of Professional Service Firms*, Oxford: Oxford University Press, pp. 425–451.

Froud, J., Johal, S., Moran, M. and Williams, K. (2017) 'Outsourcing the state: New sources of elite power', *Theory, Culture & Society* 34(5–7): 77–101.

Geisst, C.R. (1997) *Wall Street: A history*, New York: Oxford University Press.

Gray, M. and Barford, A. (2018) 'The depths of the cuts: The uneven geography of local government austerity', *Cambridge Journal of Regions, Economy and Society* 11(3): 541–563.

Hackworth, J. (2002) 'Local autonomy, bond-rating agencies and neoliberal urbanism in the United States', *International Journal of Urban and Regional Research* 26(4): 707–725.

Harding, A., Wilks-Heeg, S. and Hutchins, M. (2000) 'Business, government and the business of urban governance', *Urban Studies* 37(5–6): 975–994.

Harvey, D. (2011) *The Enigma of Capital and the Crises of Capitalism*, London: Profile Books.

Hendrikse, R.P. and Sidaway, J.D. (2014) 'Financial wizardry and the Golden City: Tracking the financial crisis through Pforzheim, Germany', *Transactions of the Institute of British Geographers* 39(2): 195–208.

Henriksen, L.F. (2013) 'Economic models as devices of policy change: Policy paradigms, paradigm shift, and performativity', *Regulation & Governance* 7: 481–495.

Hood, C. (1991) 'A public management for all seasons?', *Public Administration* 69(1): 3–19.

Hurl, C. (2017) 'Operationalizing austerity: The role of transnational professional service firms in local government restructuring', *The European Journal of Social Science Research* 31(1): 55–67.

Jessop, B. (2008) *State Power*, Boston: Polity Press.

Kjaer, A.M. (2009) 'Governance and the urban bureaucracy', in J.S. Davies and D.L. Imbroscio (eds). *Theories of Urban Politics*, 2nd edition, London: Sage, pp. 137–152.

Lagna, A. (2015) 'Italian municipalities and the politics of financial derivatives: Rethinking the Foucauldian perspective', *Competition & Change* 19(4): 283–300.

Lapavitsas, C. (2013) *Profiting Without Producing: How Finance Exploits Us All*, London: Verso.

Lauermann, J. (2018) 'Municipal statecraft: Revisiting the geographies of the entrepreneurial city', *Progress in Human Geography* 42(2): 205–224.

Learmonth, M. (2005) 'Doing things with words: The case of "management" and "administration"', *Public Administration* 83(3): 617–637.

Livne, R. and Yonay, Y.P. (2016) 'Performing neoliberal governmentality: An ethnography of financialized sovereign debt management practices', *Socio-Economic Review* 14(2): 339–362.

MacKenzie, D. (2006) *An Engine, Not a Camera: How Financial Models Shape Markets*, Cambridge: MIT Press.

Mader, P., Mertens, D. and van der Zwan, N. (2020) 'Financialization: An introduction', in P. Mader, D. Mertens and N. van der Zwan (eds). *The Routledge International Handbook of Financialization*, London: Routledge, pp. 1–16.

Martin, S. (2002) 'The modernization of UK local government: Markets, managers, monitors and mixed fortunes', *Public Management Review* 4(3): 291–307.

Merkus, S. and Veenswijk, M. (2017) 'Turning New Public Management theory into reality: Performative struggle during a large scale planning process', *Environment and Planning C: Politics and Space* 35(7): 1264–284.

Mertens, A., Trampusch, C., Fastenrath, F. and Wangemann, R. (2019) 'The political economy of local government financialization and the role of policy diffusion', *Regulation & Governance* advance online publication October 10. https://doi.org/10.1111/rego.12285.

O'Brien, P., O'Neill, P. and Pike, A. (2019) 'Funding, financing and governing urban infrastructures', *Urban Studies* 56(7): 1291–1303.

Omstedt, M. (2020) 'Reading risk: The practices, limits and politics of municipal bond ratings', *Environment and Planning A: Economy and Space* 52(3): 611–631.

Peck, J. (2012) 'Austerity urbanism: American cities under extreme economy', *City* 16(6): 626–655.

Peck, J. and Whiteside, H. (2016) 'Financializing Detroit', *Economic Geography* 92(3): 235–268.

Petzold, C. (2014) *Kommunale Finanzgeschäfte: Die Auswirkungen der Finanzialisierung auf die lokale Demokratie*. Frankfurt am Main: Goethe Universität. Forum Humangeografie no. 11.

Pike, A., O'Brien, P., Strickland, T. and Tomaney, J. (2019) *Financialising City Statecraft and Infrastructure*, Cheltenham: Edward Elgar.

Pollitt, C. and Bouckaert, G. (2011) *Public Management Reform: A Comparative Analysis. New Public Management, Governance, and the Neo-Weberian State*, 3rd edition, New York: Oxford University Press.

Porter, T. (2005) *Globalization and Finance*, Cambridge: Polity Press.

Saint-Martin, D. (2000) *Building the New Managerialist State: Consultants and the Politics of Public Sector Reform in Comparative Perspective*, Oxford: Oxford University Press.

Sanderson, I. (2001) 'Performance management, evaluation and learning in 'modern' local government', *Public Administration* 79(2): 297–313.

Singla, A. and Luby, M.J. (2020) 'Financial engineering by city governments: Factors associated with the use of debt-related derivatives', *Urban Affairs Review* 56(3): 857–887.

Strange, S. (1996) *The Retreat of the State: The Diffusion of Power in the World Economy*, Cambridge: Cambridge University Press.

Streeck, W. (2014) *Buying time: The delayed crisis of democratic capitalism*, London: Verso.

Tickell, A. (1998) 'Creative finance and the local state: The Hammersmith and Fulham swaps affair', *Political Geography* 17(7): 865–881.

Trampusch, C. and Spies, D.C. (2015) 'Was treibt Kommunen zu Spekulationsgeschäften? Eine Analyse der Swap-Geschäfte von Kommunen in Nordrhein-Westfalen', *Politische Vierteljahresschrift* 56(1): 104–129.

Waldron, R. (2019) 'Financialization, urban governance and the planning system: Utilizing development viability as a policy narrative for the liberalization of Ireland's Post-Crash Planning System', *International Journal of Urban and Regional Research* 43(4): 685–704.

Weber, R. (2010) 'Selling city futures: The financialization of urban redevelopment policy', *Economic Geography* 86(3): 251–274.
Wolf, M. (2018) 'Ain't misbehaving: Behavioural economics and the making of financial literacy', *Economic Sociology: The European Electronic Newsletter* 19(2): 10–18.
Wollmann, H. (2014) 'Public services in European countries: Between public/municipal and private sector provision—And reverse?', in C. Nunes Silva and J. Bucek (eds). *Fiscal Austerity and Innovation in Local Governance in Europe*, Farnham: Ashgate, pp. 49–73.

Privatization and Public Private Partnerships

"Infrastructure" and the Big 4: Public–Private Partnerships, Corridors, and the Expansion of Capital

Nicholas Hildyard

Introduction

In 1985, I reached the age of 30, considered by some (my family included) to be a milestone birthday. Many of the gifts I received, though treasured at the time, have long since been lost, fallen out of use, or been discarded. By the end of the decade, Dire Straits' *Brothers in Arms*, a vinyl LP, was too scratched to play and had been replaced by a cassette. A wallet lasted longer but eventually came apart at the seams. But one present remains: a two-volume edition of the *Shorter Oxford English Dictionary* (OED). I still regularly reach for it when I want to learn more about the etymology of a word.

Such verbal archaeology offers many insights: none more so, perhaps, than when a word that is widely used today does not appear in my not-so-dated dictionary. "Infrastructure" is one such word. This is not to say that the word did not exist in the English language in the mid-1980s

N. Hildyard (✉)
Corner House Research, Plumber Cottage, Fifehead
Neville, Dorset, UK
e-mail: nickhildyard@gn.apc.org

C. Hurl and A. Vogelpohl (eds.), *Professional Service Firms and Politics in a Global Era*, https://doi.org/10.1007/978-3-030-72128-2_10

(Batt, 1984; Carse, 2017) or that it did not feature in specialist dictionaries (Lewis, 2008; Prud'homme, 2004): just that it was not considered by the OED's compilers to be in regular literary or colloquial use. As an analysis of articles in the *New York Times* by Alex Marshall (2015) reveals, even in the 1990s and 2000s the word was hardly common parlance: but, by 2014, it had taken hold, reaching "a whopping 5,357" mentions. Significantly the phrase "public works"—used for decades to describe roads, housing, and the like—gradually declined as "infrastructure" rose. By 2000, concludes Marshall (2015), "Infrastructure had shoved 'public works' almost out of the arena of public discourse."

"So what?" one might ask: words replace each other—that is the nature of language. But words are never just words: they are loaded with social, political, economic, and other meanings that are an endless source of contestation; and changes in vocabulary rarely happen by accident—they reflect the outcomes of broader conflicts within society as different forces vie with each other to resist or subvert the everyday social and cultural practices that manufacture consent for dominant political and economic power structures. In this "war of position" (to use the terminology of Italian Marxist Antonio Gramsci [1971, 323]), language is a key battleground. It would be unwise, therefore, to view the shift from "public works" to "infrastructure" as just a matter of one phrase going out of fashion and its replacement by another whose meaning is essentially similar. "Public works" are *not* the same as "infrastructure": most obviously, "public works" contains the word "public" while "infrastructure" does not. That alone should alert us to the possibility that the consent that the two expressions are intended to manufacture is different—in effect, that they embody entirely different political projects.

This chapter explores the role of the "Big Four" consultancy firms—Deloitte, PricewaterhouseCoopers (PwC), Ernst & Young (EY), and KPMG—as shock troops in various skirmishes where infrastructure has been capital's weapon of choice in a war of position over the role of the state in containing or furthering capital accumulation. In the spirit of an archaeological dig, the chapter starts by sifting through the loose soils of "infrastructure" to excavate its origins in "big push" theories of economic development and its honing into a tool for capitalist expansion. It then explores how, in response to a growing crisis of capital accumulation in the 1980s, "infrastructure" has been deployed by the Big Four to create new rents that might otherwise have been unavailable to capital, notably through the privatization of public services (see also Valentukeviciute in this volume), and, more latterly, to further the expansion of capital through mega corridors and logistics.

Unearthing "Infrastructure"

All archaeological digs require turf to be cut somewhere: and the middens around 1818 H Street, Washington, DC—the headquarters of the World Bank group—offer a promising starting point for our excavation. For it was here in the 1950s and 1960s that a ragtag collection of what to many would have seemed entirely unconnected projects, policies, and programs—from roads to schools, electricity grids, hospitals, airwaves, public subsidies, regulations, and legal systems—were bundled together to create "infrastructure."

The starting point was a concept known as "social overhead capital." Pioneered by economists such Paul Rosenstein-Rodan, who served as Assistant Director in the Bank's Economic Department from 1947 to 1953, social overhead capital was said to comprise all those "basic industries" (Rosenstein-Rodan, 1957, 6)—from transportation to the generation of thermodynamic energy—that make industrialized forms of capitalist production possible. Because the use of these services is not exclusive to any one productive entity but common to all, Rosenstein-Rodan argued, their costs should be viewed as "the 'overhead costs' as it were of the economy as a whole" (Rosenstein-Rodan, 1957, 6). In common with many other modernization theorists of the time, such as Walt Rostow, Rosenstein-Rodan (1957, 7) was adamant that industrialization in "under-developed countries" (his very contemporary phrase) would simply not happen unless the necessary social overhead capital was in place. Relying on single firms to provide such shared services would not work: the investments were too "lumpy" (Rosenstein-Rodan, 1957, 7),[1] too expensive, and required too much coordination. Instead, the necessary investments should be financed through internationally funded but nationally planned programs.

For the World Bank, which in the 1950s was still carving out an institutional niche for itself, social overhead capital quickly became, in the

[1] An expression used to convey unusually long periods of gestation and of pay off.

words of historian William Rankin (2009, 65), a "heuristic for justifying how Bank funds were being used." The term was not employed only to describe large engineering projects: the Bank's 1953 development plans for Mexico also included "education" as a necessary social overhead capital, while "mapping" and "geological surveys" were listed for Formosa (Rankin, 2009). Indeed, social overhead capital soon embraced just about everything that capital then needed to have in place for the profitable production of commodities and the managed social reproduction of the global labor force. For Walt Rostow, whose influential book *The Stages of Economic Growth* (Rostow, 1960) was tellingly subtitled "A Non-Communist Manifesto," the project also included developing "a new elite – a new leadership" willing "to uproot traditional societies" in the cause of "modernization" (Rostow, 1960, 26). To achieve economic growth, Rostow wrote, required governments that were capable of organizing "the nation so that unified commercial markets develop" and of leading the way "through the whole spectrum of national policy – from tariffs to education and public health - towards the modernisation of the economy and the society of which it is a part" (Rostow, 1960, 30). Capital's Great Leap Forward would be achieved through countries being managed as corporations with the Bank (and national governments) deciding what social overhead capital was most needed at any given time, enabling individual private sector enterprises to provide the entrepreneurial thrust that would power the lift-off of "backward economies" through their profit-making operations (Rankin, 2009).

By the mid-1950s, the bundle of perceived "prerequisites" (Rankin, 2009, 68) for capitalist production was increasingly being referred to as "infrastructure"—and by the early 1960s, World Bank country reports regularly reported on progress in such "infrastructure" implementation. But the power of "infrastructure" as a pioneer for capital did not lie only in the programs and projects it initiated and imposed. Embedded in infrastructure was a theory of the state, which strictly circumscribed the extent of state intervention—and this is as much a part of "infrastructure" as its individual social overhead projects for capitalist expansion. Although Walt Rostow, whose influence on the Bank was considerable, insisted that "it was the inescapable responsibility of the state to make sure the stock of social overhead capital required for take-off is built" (Rostow, 1960, 30), that responsibility extended only to the take-off period: once the plane, to use Rostow's metaphor, was in the air, the private sector should run the show. Moreover, intervention was to be restricted to overhead capital formation: intervention in production was to be strictly off-limits (Rankin, 2009). The role of the interventionist "infrastructure" state, as envisaged by the Bank, was thus as servant, not controller, let alone container, of capitalist production.

Here then was the "infrastructure" that the Bank forged at 1818 H Street during the 1950s and 1960s: a tool intended to secure the policies and built environment that would provide capital with the markets and labor it needed worldwide. To ensure its implementation, the Bank relied on more than just the provision of funds: it also set about constructing its own political "infrastructure"—creating niches within Southern governments through which it could cultivate factions and interests sympathetic to capital and its expansion. By providing funds for "institution building," it fashioned autonomous agencies—national energy authorities, for example—responsive to the demands not of national governments but of the Bank (Broad, 1988, 26). Staff for such agencies were often selected by the Bank, who trained them in its own Economic Development Institute.

Infrastructure 2.0—Enter the Big 4

As the Prussian Field Marshall Helmuth von Moltke the Elder wryly observed, "No plan survives first contact with the enemy" (Ratcliffe, 2016): and the Bank's "infrastructure" was no exception. The Bank's vision was, inevitably, both resisted and reshaped as different interests picked up on "infrastructure" and used it for their own political ends.

Keynesian economists and politicians, for example, embraced "infrastructure" but used it to "steer the state into taxation and planning regimes historically resisted by private capital" (O'Neill, 2016, 3), while at the same time promoting infrastructure expenditure as "the counter-cyclical tool of governments to refit capitalism with bigger markets, and more complex divisions of labor, while delivering legitimacy and reproduction outcomes though jobs creation and enduring urban betterments" (O'Neill, 2016, 3–4).

Others seized on infrastructure's embedded notion of social overhead capital to justify state control of the "commanding heights" of the economy (Krueger, 1990)—not at all what the Bank had in mind. Indeed, far from state ownership of key national "infrastructure" being a temporary measure, in many countries it became the norm.

Meanwhile, grassroots resistance to "infrastructure" was growing: by the late 1980s, dams and agricultural schemes, in particular, had spawned social movements that were (at least in the South) increasingly questioning not just individual projects but the whole thrust of infrastructure's promised "development." More critical still, infrastructure had not led to Rostow's promised "economic lift-off."

In 1994, the Bank pushed the reset button. Presaging the direction of the Bank's counterattack, a 1990 article by Anne Krueger, who had served as the Bank's chief economist from 1982 to 1986, opined that "governments in most developing countries were mired down in economic policies that were manifestly unworkable" and that "in many countries, there could be little question but that government failure significantly outweighed market failure" (Krueger, 1990, 9–10). The theme was taken up with gusto in the Bank's 1994 World Development Report (World Bank, 1994)—a propaganda tool widely distributed to university libraries, think tanks, and government departments throughout the world. Entitled *Infrastructure for Development*, the Bank's report deployed "infrastructure-as-a-theory-of the-state" to press for a fire sale of state-owned infrastructure to the private sector. The issue was not whether the state should continue to fund infrastructure for capital's benefit—the Bank remained firmly committed to infrastructure as social overhead capital, defining it as such—but whether the state should manage it. The failure of infrastructure to achieve "development," argued the Bank, lay in the incentives facing providers, which could only be addressed through "commercial management, competition, and stakeholder involvement" (World Bank, 1994, 2). Infrastructure, argued the Bank (echoing Rostow), must be run "like a business, not a bureaucracy" (World Bank, 1994, 2). The Bank's solution lay in opening up state-run services to private sector management and developing new "Public–Private Partnerships" (PPPs) in order to bring private sector know-how and (claimed) efficiency to infrastructure construction and operation. In effect, the state was to be disciplined back into the role that "social overhead capital" had originally carved out for it.

Critically, the reboot responded directly to the growing crisis of accumulation within capital (too much money sloshing around in search of too few investment opportunities) by creating new profit-making opportunities through "infrastructure," not least through selling off state-owned public works at knock-down prices.

The Bank and other development agencies, both multilateral and bilateral, also used infrastructure to open up new markets for private sector consultancy firms who were contracted to advise governments on drafting the legislation needed to enable infrastructure privatization and to establish PPPs.

The Big 4 consultancy firms were among the first to seize this opportunity. KPMG, PricewaterhouseCoopers (PwC), and Deloitte Touche Tohmatsu (as they then were named) were soon earning vast sums, often paid for out of government aid budgets, to direct the privatization of water, rail, electricity, and other services in developing countries. By 1999, PricewaterhouseCoopers held a total of 193 such privatization mandates worldwide, while KPMG held 153 (Hilary, 2004, 9). Often the employment of one of the Big 4 consultants was a condition of World Bank loans (Hilary, 2004).

Although advising governments still forms a core element of the Big 4's infrastructure portfolios (all four companies have been specifically recommended by the World Bank as the "go to" advisors for PPP programs) (World Bank, 2007, 202), the Big 4's infrastructure clientele now also includes investors, infrastructure operators, private sector contractors, logistics companies and a range of other private sector entities. The name of the Big 4's infrastructure game is to enable such clients to capitalize on the opportunities of infrastructure and to "drive value" (KPMG, 2014a, 59). To that end, the Big 4's infrastructure operations now encompass everything from project design to project finance, contract structuring, and organizing seminars to promote infrastructure.

The potential for conflicts of interest are clear (Barker, 2009): with the Big 4 batting for both sides—government on the one hand and the private sector of the other—the likelihood that government contracts on which they advise will be carried out by one of their private sector clients is built into the Big 4's business model. In 2000, for example, KPMG acted as financial adviser to the UK highways agency for the £146 m A13 Thames Gateway widening project (Mondaq, 2000), while reportedly auditing and acting as a consultant for Amec, which headed the winning consortium (Vasagar and Evans, 2002).

Today, the Big 4 form a central plank of the political infrastructure that has been constructed since the mid-1990s to push "infrastructure." Their reach is global—KPMG boasts of operating "in every corner of the world, across all sectors and stages of the infrastructure lifecycle"

(KPMG, 2020a)—and their influence on policy and practice is considerable. Timothy Stone, who was chairman of KPMG's Global Infrastructure and Projects Group from 1995 to 2011, is widely recognized as "one of the masterminds behind the Private Finance Initiative in the UK" (Liebe and Howarth, 2019, 26) and a key influence in encouraging the European Investment Bank, on which he served as an external advisor, to embrace Public–Private Partnerships.

The Big 4's individual influence is amplified by various industry forums—the PPP Forum in the UK being an example (Hilary, 2004)—whose role is to "engage" (lobby in plain English) government departments to press for greater private sector involvement in infrastructure (PPP Forum, 2020). Such "engagement" is greased by contacts made possible by the revolving doors between government and the infrastructure industry: indeed KPMG specifically stresses the "senior infrastructure roles in government" previously held by many in its Global Infrastructure team as a reason why KPMG should be the infrastructure advisor of choice (KPMG, 2014a, 59) for private sector clients. The resulting web of contacts has placed the Big 4 at the heart of decision-making on "infrastructure"—influencing standards nationally and internationally (PSI, 2018) and using "infrastructure" to engineer new profit-making opportunities for capital.

New Rents Through "Infrastructure"

For capital, infrastructure has never been about mere bricks and mortar. What historian Joel Tarr (2005, 97) termed "the physical sinews of society" have only ever been of interest where they provide the wherewithal to create profits through production or through the generation of rents.

The general public may view a railway line or a road or sewage pipe or hospital as "public works" and even (now that the word has entered common parlance) as "infrastructure": but private sector investors take a very different view. A "road" does not mean a "road," but a "toll road"—an altogether different entity. Financial yield, not physical characteristics, is the determinant of what is or is not an "infrastructure" asset. As Jean Perarnaud, Managing Director of the Private Infrastructure team at Partners Group, a Swiss investment management firm, explains: "For us, infrastructure is stable, contracted cash flow for the long term … You could have a pipeline that you don't want to touch because there are no contractual rights on it and it is completely market-exposed to price.

These are the sort of things we don't consider infrastructure" (Kranc, 2014, 5, emphasis added).

Many investors flocked to the privatizations of the late 1980s and early 1990s, believing (then as now) that divested state-owned power plants, roads, oil companies, and other "infrastructure" assets would provide such stable, guaranteed cash flows. Opportunistic fortunes have certainly been made, but those who sought to reap a financial killing by running newly sold public service infrastructure in the global South have often come a cropper. They simply have not been able to make the profits they sought through relying on user fees from the pesky poor.

Many investors have found themselves nursing loss-making investments and facing increasing public hostility over rising user fees and declining services. One study of privatized utilities in 31 developing countries found that 80% "experienced negative changes in profitability" (Cook and Uchida, 2004, 9). As a result, by 2002, all the major multinational companies with water supply contracts in developing companies were looking for an exit. Indeed, by 2005, even the World Bank was describing infrastructure privatization as "oversold and misunderstood" (Kessides, 2004, 6), although this did not stop the Bank from continuing to impose privatization programs as part of its loan conditions.

PPPs (known in the UK as PFIs—Private Finance Initiatives; see Shaoul in this volume) provided the way forward: instead of directly buying public utilities, the private sector would gain access to public service income streams through contracts in the form of leases, concessions, and management agreements.[2] The Big 4 provided both the intellectual laboratories in which these contracts were constructed and the boiler room sales teams to spread their uptake. In the mid-1990s, for example, KPMG's corporate finance team was advertising its skills in the "creation of sophisticated models to assess the financial and risk implications of private finance initiative projects" and in "managing all aspects of the new PFI business, including PR, lobbying, human resource issues etc." (KPMG, 1997).

A key feature of the new contracts, pioneered by the Big 4, is "risk sharing"—the idea being that the private sector takes the risk of building

[2] Such PPP contracts take various forms: some involve the construction and operation of new infrastructure, others the provision of services from existing facilities; in some, the ownership of the underlying asset is ultimately transferred to the private sector operator, in others it remains with the state.

and operating facilities in exchange for the state offering guarantees on the projected income streams. Although Big 4 firms are careful to caveat their endorsement of such guarantees by stressing the need for them to be "balanced" and "appropriate" (PwC, 2005), the reality, repeated time and again, is that it is the private sector that has dictated the terms: the public has taken on the risks while the private sector has reaped profits through new rents. Heavily lawyered-up, investors have succeeded in securing inter alia:

- *Minimum guaranteed income streams* which bind governments to pay the difference if a concession's revenues are lower than those that have been pre-defined in a PPP contract. In the case of Colombia's El Dorado airport PPP, for which KPMG provided financial, legal, and technical advice on the structuring of the concession process (CAF, 2015), the Colombian authorities provided guarantees worth up to $225 million (World Bank Institute, 2012).
- *Availability payments*, where the government undertakes to pay the concessionaire a fee based on the availability of the infrastructure asset once it has been constructed. These payments must be made, even if the asset is not actually being used.
- *Non-compete clauses* (specifically recommended by the World Bank for PPPs in developing countries [World Bank, 2015]) that oblige governments to compensate PPP investors where "similar infrastructure" is constructed that undermines the PPP's financial viability. So a government would be forbidden from building a non-toll road on the same route as a privately operated toll road.
- *Guarantees on loan repayments* that require governments to service project loans if the private sector partner fails to keep up its payments. The UK Government, for example, was forced to bail out Transport for London, a public body, which had guaranteed 95% of the debt for a contract with Metronet to upgrade the London Underground under Britain's Private Finance Initiative (PFI). The final bill is estimated to have been between £170 million and £410 million (NAO, 2009, 25). KPMG earned £2.4 m from auditing services on the Metronet PPP deal: Ernst & Young earned approximately £1 m for advice to both Transport for London and the Department for Transport (Neveling, 2007) and a further £30 million in administration fees when the deal went south (NAO, 2009, 26).

- *Financial and economic equilibrium clauses*, also known as "stabilisation clauses," which entitle PPP concessionaires to compensation for changes in laws or regulations that adversely affect a project's revenues or its market value. Specifically recommended by the World Bank for inclusion in PPP contracts, such clauses not only lock in profits but also lock out democracy, giving private parties a disproportionate influence (enforceable via the courts) over which laws get passed and which do not (Dannin, 2011).

The above list of guarantees is by no means exhaustive; others exist, and new ones are being developed all the time, not least by the Big 4. The financial value to the private sector has been estimated at $100 billion (Hall, 2015), adding to the burgeoning off-balance sheet liabilities that countries have incurred through PPPs. But, from finance's point of view, the guarantees are a crock of gold, providing legally enforceable liens on future public flows of money that are irrevocable for the length of the contract. Once signed, they cannot be withdrawn, unlike tax breaks and other subsidies which remain at a government's discretion. And because the underlying contracts enjoy the full backing of a sovereign guarantee, they provide building blocks for financial engineering—for example by bundling together government-backed PPP loans and selling their income streams to investors, a process known as "securitization." A range of new investment vehicles has also sprung up to service private sector infrastructure investors—from dedicated private equity funds to specialist venture capital firms (Hildyard, 2016).

The implications go beyond potential financial instability: with infrastructure investors typically seeking 20–25% rates of return a year on investments in the global south, facilities (such as community, off-grid solar) that might most benefit the poor do not get financed—they simply cannot provide the yields that investors seek. The trajectory is thus profoundly undemocratic and elitist. Undemocratic because a handful of private sector companies and fund managers increasingly determine what gets funded and what does not. Elitist because it is the rich who primarily benefit.

Capital's Corridors

The Big 4 have sought to justify PPPs as necessary because of the huge sums of money required to build the infrastructure that society is said to need. KPMG (2020b), for example, argues that worldwide investment in infrastructure, currently running at $3 trillion a year, will need to double or treble over the next 10 years to deliver the UN Sustainable Development Goals. Bringing in private sector investors is critical (says KPMG) because "government finance alone is not sufficient and public institutions generally lack the critical capacity of qualified people required" (KPMG, 2014b).

In fact, there is more than enough public funding available to ensure heating, lighting, healthcare, clean water, and other amenities for ordinary people, the more so were governments to replenish their depleted coffers by abandoning the low-tax regimes imposed through neoliberal structural adjustment programs, or (the Big 4, please take note) by clamping down on tax avoidance and capital flight. No, the "deficit" lies elsewhere: in the finance for the massive infrastructure schemes that capital currently needs to expand. And, as in the past, capital has had few options but to attempt to expand the pool of finance on which it can draw: hence the push for Public–Private Partnerships to provide both an enticement to private investors and the foundation stone on which other extractive forms of finance can be built.

Central to capital's "infrastructure" project today is the need to bridge what financiers call the "production-consumption disconnect" (Antropov and Perarnaud, 2013). While fifty years ago, production was still concentrated in single factories, production has since become more fragmented. The components for a computer—perhaps as many as 4000—typically come from 250 different suppliers in multiple countries. A prime reason for this fragmentation of production has been to undermine the power of labor. By breaking up the old Fordist factory, and offshoring production to numerous different locations, capital was able to break unions; and by shifting production to wherever labor was cheapest, capital has been able to increase its profits.

But offshoring creates problems for capital too. The distances between points of resource extraction, points of production, and points of consumption are now huge, involving multiple journeys and multiple forms of transport. Distance matters because time matters; and time matters because the faster commodities can be produced and exchanged, the greater the profits for individual firms.

The problem is not new. Almost 150 years ago, Karl Marx revealed how the more that capital expands, the more it needs to improve infrastructure to "annihilate space by time" (Marx, 1858). One solution is to speed up delivery through constructing new roads, railways, ports, and airports. Some of the plans are national in scale, others regional and still others continent-wide or near-global. In Africa, over 30 such mega infrastructure corridors have been initiated (Laurance et al., 2015); in Latin America, some 581 projects are in the pipeline or under construction (IIRSA, undated); and, globally, there is China's Belt and Road Initiative (BRI), stretching from the Pacific to the Baltic Sea. Billions of people will be impacted (the Delhi–Mumbai corridor in India will alone affect 180 million) (Guttal, 2014) and the environmental impacts are likely to be devastating as forests are destroyed, rivers canalized, mountains bored through, and agricultural land tarmacked over.

But corridors are about more than speedy transportation. Using management techniques developed through the logistics industry, they are being turned into the factories of the new just-in-time economy (Cowan, 2014). The labor force is no longer conceived as confined to the places where parts are manufactured: it now includes everyone who works along the supply chain—whether assembling goods or transporting or working on the algorithms that control inventory management systems. Even consumers are now viewed as producers, the data harvested on their spending patterns being widely traded. The name of the game is the extraction of surplus labor (Danyluk, 2017): the old capital con of paying you less than the value of what you produce; or, in the case of logistics consumers, not paying you at all. Indeed, the logistics corridor-as-factory is built on busting unions; just-in-time work; constant, intrusive monitoring; and automation as a means of keeping wages low (Hildyard, 2020).

Corridors and logistics (now a $4.7 trillion industry and said to be the world's largest employer) increasingly frame the world of infrastructure today—they are the "social overheads" that capital needs society at large to pay for in order to expand. Unsurprisingly corridors and logistics also a growing focus of the Big 4. One of the five "pillars" that Ernst and Young use to rank African countries for their "attractiveness" to investors is "investment in infrastructure and logistics" (EY, 2017), while KPMG (2018) advertises its "significant role in facilitating the development of [China's] Belt and Road Initiative," offering its clients a "deep knowledge of the strategic objectives of Chinese infrastructure players, as well as a wide network of contacts in the mainland market." For KPMG, the opportunities to capitalize on the BRI project include PPP contracts, real estate openings (as land values rise along corridors), and "knock-on opportunities across supply chains" (including "professional services work for lawyers, architects and engineering consultancies") (KPMG, 2018).

The Big 4 have also been at the forefront of what KPMG (2019a) calls "thought leadership" on logistics. One focus is on the increased digitalization of the supply chain—in the words of EY, information is now "the new 'blood' within the lifelines of the world, carrying within it the nutrients for future success" (EY, 2016). Increasingly "infrastructure" is about data collection and its monetization into new income streams. Data is also promoted by KPMG (2019b) as key to addressing "business challenges relating to the workforce," including identifying workers at "risk from attrition," "differentiating behaviors between high versus low performers," or "tracking data beyond the traditional HR system to understand patterns of behavior via email, chat, calendar, social media."

For KPMG (2019c), such data mining and analysis is central to ensuring that businesses can manage increasingly hybrid workforces, consisting of "all worker types, including permanent, gig, contingent, and machine"—or in the jargon, "who to buy, build, borrow, bot"? EY also underlines the value of data when it can be monetized and sold (EY, 2018). For workers, past experience suggests that this can only lead to more monitoring, more disciplining, and a downward pressure on wages as labor is increasingly squeezed through surveillance techniques (Hildyard, 2020).

Conclusion

Today if one turns to the Oxford English Dictionary, "infrastructure" is benignly defined as "The basic physical and organizational structures and facilities (e.g. buildings, roads, power supplies) needed for the operation of a society or enterprise" (Lexico, 2020). No mention of "social overhead capital" or of "infrastructure" being what capital needs to expand or of disciplining and squeezing labor or of new rents for capital.

Indeed, it is a testament to the hegemonic power of "infrastructure" that the dams, roads, logistics centers, corridors, outsourced supply chains, data mining, and digital surveillance technologies that have been put in place over the past 75 years are now commonly viewed just as "structures" and "facilities." Unsurprisingly, many may find the Big 4's intimate relationship with "infrastructure" problematic only in so far as PPPs are promoted or conflicts of interest arise from legalized forms of corruption such as resolving doors.

These are indeed problems—and must be challenged wherever and wherever they arise. But if "infrastructure" itself remains untouched, it will continue to constitute terrain on which capitalism seeks to shape relationships with the state that serve its interests and which subsidize, facilitate and promote its expansion. You can be sure that the Big 4 will be there to assist. Activism informed by the capital's previous deployments of "infrastructure" may be better placed to resist.

References

Antropov, D. and Perarnaud, J. (2013) *Emerging Markets Infrastructure: Risk, Returns and Current Opportunities*, https://web.archive.org/web/20150601180516/https://www.partnersgroup.com/fileadmin/user_upload/Content_PDFs/documents/Research_Flashes_PDF/201310_INFRA_Emerging_markets_infrastructure_-_risk__returns_and_current_opportunities.pdf, accessed 18 April 2020.

Barker, J. (2009) 'Sticky fingers: KPMG and the accountancy oligopoly', *Variant* 36: 25–29.

Batt, W.H. (1984) 'Infrastructure: Etymology and import', *Journal of Professional Issues in Engineering* 110(1).

Broad, R. (1988) *Unequal Alliance, 1979–1986: The World Bank, the International Monetary Fund and the Philippines*, Quezon City: Ateneo de Manilla University Press.

CAF—Corporación Andina de Fomento (2015) *APP, Public Private Partnerships in Latin America: Learning from Experience*, Bogota: Corporación Andina de Fomento.

Carse, A. (2017) 'Keyword: Infrastructure: How a humble French engineering term shaped the modern world', in P. Harvey, C. Bruun Jensen and A. Morita (eds). *Infrastructures and Social Complexity: A Companion*, London: Routledge, pp. 27–39.

Cook, P. and Uchida, Y. (2004) *An Appraisal of the Performance of Privatized Enterprises in Developing Countries*. Manchester: Centre on Regulation and Competition, University of Manchester, September 2004. Working Paper Series Paper No. 105. Available at: http://r4d.dfid.gov.uk/PDF/Outputs/RegComp/CRCwp105.pdf.

Cowan, D. (2014) *The Deadly Life of Logistics: Mapping Violence in Global Trade*, Minneapolis: University of Minnesota Press.

Dannin, E. (2011) 'Crumbling infrastructure, crumbling democracy: Infrastructure privatization contracts and their effects on state and local governance', *Northwestern Journal of Law and Social Policy* 6(1), 47–105.

Danyluk, M. (2017) 'Capital's logistical fix: Accumulation, globalization, and the survival of capitalism', *Environment and Planning D Society and Space* 36(2), 630–647.

EY—Ernst & Young (2016) *Supply Chain Innovation in a Digital World*, https://web.archive.org/web/20190712044957/https://consulting.ey.com/supply-chain-innovation-in-a-digital-world/, accessed 14 October 2020.

EY—Ernst & Young (2017) *Connectivity Redefined: EY's Attractiveness Program Africa*, https://web.archive.org/web/20181020092218/https://www.ey.com/Publication/vwLUAssets/ey-africa-attractiveness-report/%24FILE/ey-africa-attractiveness-report.pdf, accessed 18 April 2020.

EY—Ernst & Young (2018) *How to Make Big Data Even Bigger for Your Business*, https://www.ey.com/en_gl/advisory/how-to-make-big-data-even-bigger-for-your-business, accessed 14 October 2020.

Gramsci, A. (1971) *Selections from the Prison Notebooks*, London: Lawrence and Wishart Ltd.

Guttal, S. (2014) *Pursuing Privatization: The ADB's Unchanging Vision of Development*, https://web.archive.org/web/20180422171215/http://focusweb.org/content/pursuing-privatization-adbs-unchanging-vision-development, accessed 14 October 2020.

Hall, D. (2015) *Why Public–Private Partnerships Don't Work*. Public Services International Research Unit (PSIRU) report, 18 March, http://www.psiru.org/sites/default/files/2015-03-PPP-WhyPPPsdontworkEng.pdf, accessed 18 April 2020.

Hilary, J. (2004) *Profiting from Poverty: Privatisation Consultants, DfID and Public Services*, https://web.archive.org/web/20070704103348/https://www.waronwant.org/download.php?id=254, accessed 14 October 2020.

Hildyard, N. (2016) *Licensed Larceny: Infrastructure, Financial Extraction and the Global South*, Manchester: Manchester University Press.

Hildyard, N. (2020) *Corridors as Factories: Supply Chains, Logistics and Labour*. Corner House-Counterbalance Report, February, http://www.thecornerhouse.org.uk/resource/corridors-factories, accessed 18 April 2020.

IIRSA (undated) 'Project Portfolio', IIRSA article, http://iirsa.org/en/Page/Detail?menuItemId=32, accessed 14 October 2020.

Kessides, I.N. (2004) *Reforming Infrastructure: Privatization, Regulation, and Competition*. World Bank Policy Research Report, Washington, DC: World Bank.

KPMG (1997) *Corporate Finance—Private Finance Initiative*, https://web.archive.org/web/19970608014942/http://www.kpmg.co.uk/uk/direct/corpfin/privatef/index.html, accessed 14 October 2020.

KPMG (2014a) *Infrastructure 100*, KPMG report, https://www.lampadia.com/assets/uploads_documentos/08db1-infra-100-world-markets-report_web-ready.pdf, accessed 14 October 2020.

KPMG (2014b) *Public Private Partnerships to Drive Infrastructure Projects in China*, KPMG Press Release, 26 November, https://home.kpmg/cn/en/home/news-media/press-releases/2014/11/public-private-partnerships-drive-infrastructure-projects.html, accessed 18 April 2020.

KPMG (2018) *Collaborating Along the Belt and Road*, https://home.kpmg/cn/en/home/insights/2018/03/collaborating-along-the-belt-and-road/infrastructure-development.html, accessed 14 October 2020.

KPMG (2019a) *Our Deal Advisory Thought Leadership Library*, https://home.kpmg/uk/en/home/insights/2019/11/our-deal-advisory-thought-leadership-library.html, accessed 14 October 2020.

KPMG (2019b) *Shaping Workforce Insights Through Data*, https://home.kpmg/xx/en/home/insights/2019/11/shaping-decisions-about-the-workforce-by-using-insights-from-data.html, accessed 14 October 2020.

KPMG (2019c) *Future of HR 2020: Which Path Are You Taking?* KPMG report, https://assets.kpmg/content/dam/kpmg/xx/pdf/2019/11/future-of-hr-2020.pdf, accessed 14 October 2020.

KPMG (2020a) *Infrastructure*, https://home.kpmg/si/en/home/industries/infrastructure.html, accessed 14 October 2020.

KPMG (2020b) *Achieving sustainable infrastructure*, https://home.kpmg/xx/en/home/insights/2020/01/enabling-sustainable-infrastructure.html, accessed 14 October 2020.

Kranc, J. (2014) 'Separating the wheat from the chaff', in *Infrastructure investor: Emerging markets handbook*, June 2014, p. 5, https://www.infrastructureinvestor.com/Emerging_Markets_Handbook.

Krueger, A.O. (1990) 'Government failures in development', *Journal of Economic Perspectives* 4(3): 9–23.

Laurance, W.F., Sloan, S., Weng, L. and Sayer, J.A. (2015) 'Estimating the environmental costs of Africa's massive "development corridors"', *Current Biology* 25: 3202–3208.

Lewis, S. (2008) 'The etymology of infrastructure and the infrastructure of the internet'. *Hak Pak Sak*, 22 September, https://hakpaksak.wordpress.com/2008/09/22/the-etymology-of-infrastructure-and-the-infrastructure-of-the-internet/.

Lexico (2020) *Online Oxford dictionary*, https://www.lexico.com/definition/infrastructure.

Liebe, M. and Howarth, D. (2019) 'The European Investment Bank as Policy Entrepreneur and the Promotion of Public–Private Partnerships', *New Political Economy, Early View*, https://doi.org/10.1080/13563467.2019.1586862.

Marshall, A. (2015) *Why the Word 'Infrastructure' Replaced 'Public Works'*, https://www.governing.com/columns/transportation-and-infrastructure/gov-the-word-infrastructure.html, accessed 18 April 2020.

Marx, K. (1858) *Grundrisse*, https://www.marxists.org/archive/marx/works/1857/grundrisse/ch10.htm, accessed 18 April 2020.

Mondaq (2000) 'KPMG corporate finance advises highways agency on £201 m financing', *KPMG* online publication, 17 April, https://www.mondaq.com/uk/corporate-finance/8569/kpmg-corporate-finance-advises-highways-agency-on-201m-financing.

NAO—National Audit Office (2009) *The Failure of Metronet*, London: NAO.

Neveling, N. (2007) 'MPs question firms' £25 m Metronet bill', *Accountancy Age*, 25 July.

O'Neill, P. (2016) *How Infrastructure Became an Investment Sector: A Theoretical Approach to the Penetration of Private Capital Into the Operation of Cities*, SSRN, 28 March, https://papers.ssrn.com/sol3/Delivery.cfm/SSRN_ID2755179_code1661181.pdf?abstractid=2755179&mirid=1, accessed 18 April 2020.

PPP Forum (2020), https://www.pppforum.com/, accessed 18 April 2020.

PwC—PriceWaterhouseCoopers (2005) *Delivering the PPP Promise: A Review of PPP Issues and Activity*. PwC report, https://www.webssa.net/files/pwc05.pdf, accessed 18 April 2020.

Prud'homme, R. (2004) *Infrastructure and Development*. Paper prepared for World Bank Annual Bank Conference on Development Economics: 3–5 May, Washington, DC, USA.

PSI—Public Services International (2018) *Conflict of Interest: How Corporations That Profit from Privatisation Are Helping Write UN Standards on PPPs*. PSI briefing to UNECE Working Party on PPPs, November, https://www.world-psi.org/sites/default/files/attachment/news/briefing_note_-_conflict_of_interest_-_corporations_writing_un_ppp_standards.pdf, accessed 18 April 2020.

Rankin, W.J. (2009) 'Infrastructure and the international governance of economic development, 1950–1965', in J.-F. Auger, J.J. Bouma and R. Künneke (eds). *Internationalization of Infrastructures*, Proceedings of the 12th Annual International Conference on the Economics of Infrastructures; Delft: Delft University of Technology.

Ratcliffe, S. (ed) (2016) *Oxford Essential Quotations*, https://www.oxfordreference.com/view/10.1093/acref/9780191826719.001.0001/q-oro-ed4-00007547, accessed 18 April 2020.

Rosenstein-Rodan, P. (1957) 'Notes on the Theory of the Big Push', unpublished memorandum for the Center for International Studies, Cambridge.

Rostow, W.W. (1960) *The Stages of Economic Growth*, Cambridge: Cambridge University Press.

Tarr, J. (2005) 'The city and technology', in Pursell, C. (ed). *A Companion to American Technology*, Oxford: Blackwell.

Vasagar, J. and Evans, R. (2002) 'KPMG: The government's friend -Investigation into accountancy firm reveals alarming conflict of interest', *Guardian*, 30 June.

World Bank (1994) *World Development Report: Infrastructure for Development*, Washington, DC: World Bank.

World Bank (2007) *Caribbean Public–Private Partnership (PPP) Toolkit: Developing Infrastructure and Improving Service Delivery*, Washington, DC: World Bank.

World Bank Institute (2012) *Best Practices in Public–Private Partnerships Financing in Latin America: The Role of Guarantees*, Washington, DC: World Bank.

World Bank/PPIAF (2015) *Report on Recommended PPP Contractual Provisions*, Washington, DC: World Bank.

The Corporate Takeover of Public Policy: The Case of Public–Private Partnerships in Britain

Jean Shaoul

Introduction

It has become an almost universally recognized phenomenon that governments around the world are today dependent upon and advised by the global financial services industry in the development of public policy. What is less well-known is the process by which this dependency was achieved. This chapter describes and analyzes the role that Public–Private Partnerships (PPP), a policy now nearly 30 years old, played in the process of transferring the control of public policy to the financial services and broader corporate sectors.

In 1993, the UK government, under the Conservatives, introduced the Private Finance Initiative (PFI) as a means of procuring investment in public infrastructure and associated services for public bodies. A private sector company would raise private or commercial finance to build the hospitals, schools, roads, or prisons and run the "non-core" services for thirty years, often after considerable restructuring to make them attractive to the private sector, in return for an annual fee to cover the cost of finance and service provision.

J. Shaoul (✉)
University of Manchester, Manchester, UK

C. Hurl and A. Vogelpohl (eds.), *Professional Service Firms and Politics in a Global Era*, https://doi.org/10.1007/978-3-030-72128-2_11

In 1997, the incoming Labor government gave the policy, controversial from the start and slow to get off the ground, new life under the umbrella term of Public–Private Partnerships (PPP). By 2018, when the policy was officially terminated, some 700 such deals were signed and/or operating, with a capital value of £60 billion and an estimated cost to the taxpayer of £199 billion, although this figure excludes at least £35 billion worth of contracts that collapsed or were renegotiated or terminated early.

Although academics, public watchdogs, and the public authorities themselves have criticized both the policy and individual projects as expensive, poor value for money (VFM) and financially destabilizing for public entities and service delivery, successive governments continued to sign new deals, until October 2018, when the government terminated the policy, implicitly conceding the case. By then, its central purpose had been achieved.

While the official rhetoric focused on VFM and private sector efficiency, PPP/PFI was bound up with the broader policy of privatization. By the early 1990s, the Conservative government had privatized all the state's commercial activities that could be made commercially viable, leaving only public services that could not be sold for financial or political reasons. PPP/PFI provided a means of transferring both the provision of infrastructure and services to the private sector in politically sensitive areas such as health and education. More than half of the public expenditure is spent outside the public sector, in contrast to just 25% in 1977 (Shaoul, 2011).

But crucially the policy also provided a mechanism for the integration of the major accountancy firms—including the Big Four (PWC, KPMG, Deloitte, EY), other large auditing firms and their consulting arms—into the administration of government, particularly the Treasury, and the design of the policy from which they benefited. It is this less well-known and understood aspect of the policy that is the subject of this chapter.

These firms were not only involved in the design, appraisal, and implementation of both the policy and individual projects for the Treasury and public entity; they also acted—on different projects—as advisors to the bidders (Unison, 2002). This was justified in part at least because the public sector did not have the financial expertise to either devise policies, develop the procedures, or appraise individual projects. Their consulting arms became major players in the emerging PPP market as partners in or major subcontractors to PFI consortia, both at home and abroad, as the government promoted the policy on their behalf internationally.

Thus, they were able to consolidate their grip on a policy they had a commercial interest in expanding via their presence and positions of influence in the corridors of power and their social networks. At the same time, they played an important part in the broader restructuring of public services, not just in Britain, but internationally. This took place at the expense of both the quantity and quality of tax-funded services, thereby effecting a redistribution of wealth, not just from the rich to the poor, but from the broad mass of the population to a privileged few. It therefore raises important questions surrounding accountability and democracy in the provision of public services.

While the chapter charts the British experience in the 1990s and 2000s, this has global significance because Britain actively championed its PPP expertise, using it to promote both the City of London and the policy internationally (see Hildyard in this volume). As a result, the policy was widely adopted elsewhere, albeit in many hybrid forms, with similar outcomes, including the corporate control of public policy (see Raco in this volume).

In the absence of a broader and comprehensive evaluation of the accountancy industry's role in PPP and with an abundance of shade surrounding the activities of the financial and corporate sectors that plead "commercial sensitivity," the evidence is necessarily fragmentary. This evidence includes academic, official and business reports, media disclosures, often the result of freedom of information (FoI) requests, and transient sources no longer readily available, largely derived during the policy's heyday in the 2000s.

This chapter starts by explaining the policy, its mode of operation, and the de facto privatization of the procurement and appraisal process, before describing the financial advisors' role in: (i) developing methodologies for controlling policy choices; (ii) providing self-interested financial "advice" to the public procurers and its financial impact on the various parties to the transaction; and (iii) writing self-interested evaluations of the policy. The final section considers some of the broader implications of the corporate control of such a major policy initiative.

Background to the Policy and Its Modus Operandi

The introduction of the Private Finance Initiative (PFI) by the Conservative government in 1993, later subsumed under the general rubric of

Public–Private Partnerships (PPP)—the terms are used interchangeably—was neither the result of a widespread movement among the public at large, nor was it popular. It was driven by the requirements of big business, particularly the construction and financial sectors, and was to a large degree devised and implemented by the international financial and business services sector, particularly the accountancy firms.

By the early 1990s, the then Conservative government had privatized all the former state-owned commercial enterprises, such as the utilities and transport, that could be restructured to enable their new owners to make a profit, in the short to medium term at least. But public services, such as transport, health, education, social services, and administrative functions, could not so easily be sold for either political reasons—such as the threat of public opposition or risks to state security—or financial reasons, such as the lack of a revenue stream or enough income to generate a profit. This therefore necessitated the development of other policies to open up public services to private profit, under conditions where public expenditure still accounted for around 42% of GDP, which included changes in the financial management, structure, and organization of the public sector itself. Starting in the late 1980s, individual publicly funded service providers such as schools and hospitals were reorganized as business units, each with its own devolved budget, drawing upon advice from the financial sector.

"Partnerships" is an umbrella term that includes a range of hybrid forms of funding and financing public services. Its most frequent form in Britain is the contractual relationship under PFI whereby the public sector procures new assets, and/or refurbishes old ones, and their associated services from the private sector in return for a two-part annual fee to cover the cost of finance for the construction of the underlying asset and the cost of service provision. Thus, PFI functions as both a finance and an operating lease, typically for a thirty-year period, after which the asset reverts to the public authority.

The public entity contracts with a consortium of several companies, including typically a bank and construction, property management and facilities management firms, structured as a legal entity known as a special purpose vehicle (SPV), whose sole business is this one project. The SPV raises about 10% of the capital cost of the project in the form of equity from its parent companies and the remaining 90% via debt, often from its banking parent. Typically, no more than a shell company with no employees, often located in an offshore tax haven, the SPV operates by subcontracting service provision to its consortium members' subsidiaries (PAC, 2018).

The legal format serves to separate the SPV from its parent companies, thereby limiting their risk to their initial, small equity stake. Thus, the SPV can hand back the keys—and the debt—to the public entity should the contract prove unprofitable, at minimal cost to the parent companies. As private sector companies, they are exempt from FoI legislation, even though they operate as de facto public authorities, dependent upon taxpayers' monies and are able to sell additional services to captive users directly, such as car parking and telephones in hospitals, and room hire at the end of the school day.

The organizational and legal complexity of a PFI project played an important part in making the public sector dependent upon the financial services sector for designing PFI deals and drawing up the contracts. It created a huge bureaucratic structure for managing the service element of the contract. It enabled the subcontractors to pass responsibility for inadequate performance to other subcontractors. And it ensured that the ultimate responsibility for the private sector's debt that carries a higher interest rate than sovereign debt lay with the public authority.

Despite introducing the policy in 1993, the Conservative government was unable to sign more than a handful of deals. It was the incoming Labor government in 1997 that got the policy up and running, particularly in the politically high-profile sectors such as health, education, and public transport. This vastly accelerated the number of staff brought into the civil service from the global accounting firms to implement the policy, as described in the next section.

De-Facto Privatization of the Procurement and Appraisal Process

In 1997, the Labor government brought in Sir Malcolm Bates, director of a global consultancy firm and chairman of a major UK financial services company, to chair a review of the PFI policy. He recommended the creation of a high-level Treasury Task Force (TTF), staffed by former private sector personnel and secondees from the accountancy firms—some provided free of charge (Craig, 2006)—that would train civil servants, and champion and manage the process, providing a focal point for PFI. The TTF's policy arm would direct and streamline the policy, developing rules and best practice guidelines to standardize procurement, while its projects arm would manage the PFI process for individual projects, and ensure that the projects were suitable for private finance.

On Bates' advice, the TTF's Projects Division was reconstituted as a PPP in 2003 becoming Partnerships UK (PUK), whose mission was to help the public sector deliver fast and efficient development and procurement of PPPs and better value for money. Private sector institutions, including financial services companies involved in the financing of PPP projects and/or holding PPP contracts, held 51% of the shares. Thus, the government transferred the management of the PFI/PPP procurement process—a task formerly carried out by civil servants, albeit on secondment from the private sector—to a company owned by the very corporations closely involved as owners, financiers, and subcontractors in such projects (Shaoul et al., 2007) and legislation was amended to give PUK the authority to do so.

In addition, the PFI project, and the development of its business case, were managed and/or vetted by the Treasury, the Departmental Private Finance Units, PUK, in the case of central government, or 4Ps, in the case of local authorities, all of whom were largely staffed by private sector secondees from firms with a vested interest in the policy. This meant that the control process was dominated by parties with a vested interest in the policy's expansion (Gosling, 2003; Craig, 2006). Under such circumstances, conflicts of interest abounded.

Following the Bates Review, there was a constant flow of personnel passing between the higher echelons of the civil service and the Treasury on the one hand, and the financial sector, particularly the Big Four accountancy firms on the other, mirroring the "revolving doors" between defense contractors and the Ministry of Defence (one of the first was Lord Levene from United Scientific Holdings) in the 1980s. The Big Four and other large accountancy firms that dominate the accountancy industry, whose growth was bound up with its monopoly of the statutory annual external audit, occupy an important position within the financial services sector. They offer a wide range of financial services along with overlapping management consultancy and the legal services that they cross-sell to their audit clients and others. Such cross-selling of services has long been recognized as jeopardizing auditor independence and representing a dangerous conflict of interest (Mitchell et al., 1994). Despite being forced to sever their consultancy arms some years ago, financial services have once again grown to more than half of the Big Four's revenues.

The big firms also cross-sell their audit and advisory services to the public sector. They audit public bodies such as the hospital trusts, carry out audit work on behalf of the public sector auditor, the National Audit Office (NAO), and sell their management consultancy services to government departments, local authorities, and other public agencies. In its report on the government's use of management consultants' services (NAO, 2006), the NAO, which also serves as the parliamentary watchdog, warned that many of the consultancy firms' reports did not represent value for money and recommended that public bodies should start with the presumption that their own staff were best suited to do the work.

The NAO was unable to ascertain the full extent of the government's use of such services. It found that central government's spend on consulting had fallen from around £2.8 billion in 2005–2006 to £1.7 billion in 2009–2010 and to around £600 million in 2014–2015. But it warned that this figure was incomplete, since it excluded, for example, consultancy firms which managed outsourced services, provided legal and financial advice and carried out research at a cost of £4.65 billion in 2014–2015, a reduction of £430 million (8%) since 2009–2010 (NAO, 2016).

The Big Four not only entered the civil service and the Treasury and provided consultancy services to government departments and public bodies, their consulting or IT divisions also took equity stakes in some PFI consortia and/or were major subcontractors to the consortia. This was particularly the case with IT projects, many of which became a byword for catastrophic failure, most notably the Department of Social Security's National Insurance Recording System 2 (NIRS2) that led to billions lost in overpayments, incorrect tax assessments and rectifying the system (Edwards and Shaoul, 2003).

Members of the Big Four accountancy firms involved in PFI actively championed PPPs in Britain and on the global arena. For example, Tim Stone, who headed KPMG's PFI unit, chaired a government PFI advisory group and advised the Ministry of Defence on its then largest PFI project, also led a PPP working group at International Financial Services London, a private sector lobby group marketing its close links with government departments. The firms also actively promoted PPPs via a raft of British and international lobby groups with close links to government departments, acting as advisors on many overseas projects to one or other of the parties involved in the deals. They thereby used their UK experience to expand their business and control of public policy overseas.

It was only in 2001 that the government agreed to publish the names of all 112 personnel on secondment from private firms and publish a register every year, starting in 2002. This showed that in 2002, 37% of the Treasury's new entrants were seconded or on loan from private firms (Treasury, 2005, 34). This was important because the Treasury became by far the paramount government department under New Labor and was responsible for approving all PFI/PPP projects. PwC provided its technical director for local government to the Strategic Partnership Task Force to encourage greater use of PFI by local government, while parliamentary questions revealed a string of other secondments by the firms into a range of government departments (Gosling, 2003), with others reporting a constant merry go round (Craig, 2006; Oborne, 2007).

By opening up the Treasury to the Big Four, bypassing the long-standing conventions relating to the recruitment of civil servants in central government departments, the government was able to sideline officials skeptical of PPPs, push through policies and sign deals with the private sector. Secondees and senior civil servants would, in turn, leave to take up lucrative posts in the private sector—after the required six months interregnum—where they could put their knowledge of and contacts in government to good use (Craig, 2006; Oborne, 2007).

The Financial Advisors' Role in PPPs

Devising Financial Methodologies to Secure Private Sector Objectives

One of the tasks of the government's financial advisors and seconded staff in the Treasury was to establish detailed financial appraisal procedures for controlling PFI deals that would disguise the enormous extra cost of using the private sector to finance, build, and operate public infrastructure, including the higher cost of private finance, the SPV and subcontractors' profit margins, and the transaction costs of all the financial advisors (to the public entity, the private sector corporations, the parent Department, and the Treasury). These additional costs would necessarily create affordability problems, adversely affect workers' jobs, wages, and conditions and reduce both the quantity and quality of services.

The Treasury—staffed by personnel from the accounting industry, financial advisors, and seconded staff—responded to this dilemma by arguing that PFI would provide greater VFM than an equivalent public sector option that bears all the risks when things go wrong and devising a procedure purporting to measure this (Treasury, 2003).

This involved identifying and discounting the whole life costs of a hypothetical project financed under conventional procurement methods and compared against the discounted costs of the PFI option. The comparison would include the cost of some of the risks associated with the construction and management of the asset and delivery of services to be transferred to the private sector in the (hypothetical) public option. The scheme with the lower cost would offer the greater VFM. In effect, the Treasury was saying that the higher cost of private sector borrowing constituted the "risk premium," the price the public sector would pay for greater efficiency, expertise and innovation plus the cost of risk transfer.

However, this highly technical VFM appraisal methodology is seriously flawed. Firstly, it rests upon the options appraisal technique, originally developed to evaluate the cash flows to be derived from different oil exploration options, which is of questionable value in the private sector because it assumes mutually exclusive options, reliable cost estimates and relatively short-term projects. This is even more questionable in the context of public services (Tribe, 1972; King, 1975; Ross, 1995). Secondly, the VFM methodology uses a high discount rate to compare the public and private sector options (Greenaway et al., 2004; Shaoul, 2005), chosen, according to a senior Treasury Economist, to "prevent any bias in favour of public sector financing" (Treasury, 1991, § 49). The Treasury retained the 6% discount rate when it updated its Green Book in 1997, because it was closer to the prevailing cost of capital in the private sector. Thirdly, these techniques are also value-laden as others have noted (Tribe, 1972). In the context of the choice between public and private finance, it is not simply the selection of particular projects but also the allocation of resources between the public and private sectors of the economy that is at stake (Brown and Jackson, 1990), and the important distributional consequences that flow from that choice.

Gaffney et al. (1999a, 1999b, 1999c) and Pollock et al. (1999) demonstrated the conceptually and methodologically flawed nature of the VFM valuations in hospital business cases. These studies showed that the VFM, resting upon uncertain projections of costs far into the future, relies overwhelmingly upon *estimates* of the cost of "risk transfer" to the private sector, which is at best difficult to measure (Froud and Shaoul, 2001), while the difference between the publicly and privately financed options was marginal even after factoring in risk transfer (Pollock et al., 2002).

While the crucial element in VFM is the risk transfer, it is indisputable that the public sector retains the ultimate responsibility for essential and often statutory services for which there is usually no alternative, limiting the ability to transfer risk in practice. This, in turn, makes it questionable whether private finance can deliver VFM in practice, as the NAO (2000) acknowledged in the context of the three London Underground PPPs, by far the largest, with a capital value of £30 billion. All three PPPs either failed or were terminated within a few years.

Crucially, the Treasury and its advisors privileged the dubious VFM methodology over affordability, a vague term whose assessment does not demonstrate what is displaced to make it "affordable." Studies of early PFI hospitals showed that affordability was indeed a problem (Gaffney et al., 1999a, 1999b, 1999c; Pollock et al., 1999; Froud and Shaoul, 2001). This led to the first wave of PFI hospitals being 30% smaller than the ones they replaced, subsidies from the Department of Health, land sales, a shift of resources within the local healthcare economy to the PFI hospitals, and "challenging performance targets" for the Trusts' reduced workforce. The emphasis on VFM thus served to disguise the high cost of PFI and its impact on service provision, which in turn raises questions about VFM.

Fully aware that the business cases demonstrating that the privately financed option was better VFM than conventional procurement would not withstand public scrutiny, the government refused to release the business cases either before or after financial close. The only exception has been the hospital trusts which do publish their business cases, but only after the deals have been agreed due to "commercial confidentiality." This lack of publicly available information, plus the complexity of the schemes, raises concerns about not only the objective nature of the VFM assessment but also about political accountability.

To conclude, the new VFM techniques devised by the Treasury and its advisors were crucial in justifying both the policy and individual projects. Crucially, the Treasury made it clear that should the public finance option prove better VFM, no public money would be forthcoming, in effect forcing the public authorities and their financial advisors to collude in this deceit, cook the books, and produce a business case that favored the private option. Finally, the business cases that might reveal this chicanery were shielded from public oversight.

Self-Interested and Unsound Project Advice

The same auditing firms and their consultancy arms also provided advice to the government and public bodies on how to structure deals to make them attractive to the private sector. To cite but a few examples, PWC, the government's financial advisors for the use of private finance in roads, devised a system of shadow tolls for design, build, finance, and operate (DBFO) contracts, because it believed that direct tolls would be unpopular and jeopardize the development of a private road operating industry (Glaister et al., 1997). In the case of hospitals, the consultants advised against refurbishment in favor of new builds and in the case of Glasgow schools, proposed the bundling together of 20 or more schools, after merging and closing several, in order to create larger and more profitable projects.

Despite their much-vaunted financial skills, the financial advisors approved deals that turned out to be expensive. For example, one study (Shaoul et al., 2008) found that 20% of the hospital trusts' annual payments and between 20 and 40% of the various transport authorities' annual payments were attributable to the *additional* annual cost of private over public finance because of the higher cost of private over public debt and the profit margins. This provides financial institutions with a state-backed income at commercial rates of interest and the construction and facilities management companies with a guaranteed income, courtesy of the taxpayer, while destabilizing public entities that have never been cash-rich. With PFI fees being obligatory, this means diverting funds from elsewhere and/or cutting back on "core" services to ensure payment. Furthermore, there is no evidence that the service element in PFI contracts is any cheaper than public sector provision, with the Treasury's own review saying, "PFI has not led to a step-change in soft service delivery" and acknowledging that VFM was reduced in PFI contracts with a large service element (Treasury, 2006).

These findings were echoed in numerous NAO reports and most recently in the Public Accounts Committee's extremely critical report of the PFI (PAC, 2018). In an analysis of costs for building one group of schools, it "found costs are around 40 percent higher than the costs of a project financed by government borrowing." It said, "Some private investors had made large returns from PFI deals, suggesting that departments are overpaying for transferring risk to the private sector, one of the Treasury's stated benefits of PFI" and called for the government to calculate and publish the investors' returns. Furthermore, since offshore infrastructure funds owned around half the equity in PFI and its post-financial credit squeeze successor PF2 projects, the five largest funds paid less than 1% in tax on their PFI profits. It also expressed concern about the high cost of PFI on public authorities' budgets and that the government had done little to alleviate or even monitor this.

Not only were the deals costly, but more than a few were financially unsound. A significant number of transport projects, the largest sector by value, resulted in project collapse, early termination, and/or renegotiation. To cite but a few examples of the most well-known scandals, Britain's Channel Tunnel Rail Link had to be renegotiated within months of signing. Two of the three flagship London Underground PPPs collapsed with £2bn of debts guaranteed by Transport *for* London, while the third was terminated at a breakpoint in the contract because the private partner demanded a price far higher than originally estimated and considered reasonable by the Rail Arbiter. The Skye Bridge toll project was terminated due to the public opposition to the exorbitant tolls, at a cost far greater than the original construction cost it had sought to avoid.

Some of these deals were so manifestly unviable, even ex ante, that this author's students (in their end of course assignments) were able to predict the failure of the National Air Traffic Services (NATS) PPP, which collapsed within three months of financial close. The Civil Aviation Authority (CAA), NATS' parent body, dismissed this author's spreadsheet and questions in an interview—before financial close—saying, "Our advisors have gone through the figures." But this in turn means that the advisors to NATS/CAA, the bidders, and the bidders' bankers had all passed the business case that even students questioned (Shaoul, 2003).

While there are no publicly available figures on the number of such failures, the capital value of just the failed/renegotiated transport projects in the UK was more than £35bn or more than one-third of the value of all the £91billion signed projects across all sectors. Such a high failure rate is hardly a ringing endorsement of the financial advisors' ability to ensure a robust project specification and implementation.

Since the consultants also advised the private sector companies bidding for PFI contracts, albeit not on the same projects where they were advising the public bodies, every PFI contract generated fee income from the procurer, each of the several bidders as well as the lead government department and the Treasury, amounting to a hefty fee income for all the different advisors and thus high transaction costs for the projects. While there is no publicly available breakdown of the fees earned on policy and project advice to government, procurers, and bidders, the first 15 PFI hospitals generated £45 million in fees for all the advisors, 4% of the capital value of the deals (NAO, 2007). Extrapolated across all signed deals, then the advisors may have earned £3 billion, of which the Big Four took a major share, with Unison stating "£2.8bn to £4bn has been spent on consultants and lawyers" (Unison, 2013).

In short, the "advice" the global accounting firms gave the government and public bodies was not characterized by either the public interest, objectivity, or rigor. They approved deals that were loaded in favor of private sector interests, without ensuring that the deals were robust or beneficial to the public, while generating a healthy revenue stream for themselves.

Self-Interested Evaluations of the PFI Policy

The government also turned to the same global consulting firms—which had helped devise the policy and had advised the public authorities and the private sector bidders on individual projects—to carry out evaluations of PFI projects, evaluations that would once have been carried out by independent researchers, institutions, and academia. Their reports were characterized by flawed methodologies and/or conclusions inconsistent with their evidence base, as the following analysis shows.

The first of three reports purporting to show the benefits of PFI, came from Arthur Andersen (2000). Based on a sample of 29 projects out of a possible 400 projects, it claimed that PFI had "saved" 17% on the cost of conventionally procured projects. These savings, derived from the expected "risk transfer" in the business cases used to justify the PFI project to the Treasury, came from a handful of schemes, with 80% coming from just one project NIRS2 (described earlier) that, in the end, became a byword for failure. In other words, the study was based upon *anticipated* savings that were not achieved in practice. Despite this, the government never repudiated the report. The second, from PwC (2001), did not explain its methodology and based its results on the views of senior managers responsible for commissioning 27 PFI schemes, without any objective evidence on service or volume levels. A third report, also purporting to show the befits of PFI, albeit with reservations about its use in health and education, came from the Institute of Public Policy

Research (2001), a think tank close to the government and sponsored by KPMG.

Following criticisms of its VFM methodology, the government commissioned two reports from consultants, who had frequently provided advice to both the government and the private sector on PFI deals (KPMG, 2002; Mott Macdonald, 2002), to revise the PFI appraisal methodology. Both recommended methodologies that retained the built-in bias in favor of PFI. The first declared that PFI would yield a 22% tax return to the Treasury, even though many PFI consortia pay very little tax (Edwards et al., 2004). The second reported that VFM should include an assumption of an "optimism bias" in project estimates of both cost and time to build and therefore increase the cost of the hypothetical public sector option by 28%. This was based on flaws in the design and methodology that made evidence uninterpretable (ACCA, 2002; Pollock et al., 2005).

In summary, the government commissioned the same consultancy firms that had played a major role in the design and implementation of the policy and individual projects to evaluate some of the early projects, resulting in self-serving reports that would be used to further justify the policy and thereby the advisors' role.

In contrast, the government commissioned no overall assessment of the policy, the costs of PFI, or the financial impact on public services. Any honest assessment would have revealed the exact opposite of the government's case, confirmed the widespread popular understanding that it was a waste of money and above all discredited the very advisors who had devised and approved the policies. Neither did the government make any attempt to rebut the evidence-based criticisms of the policy and projects. It simply ignored them. The government maintained this position until the Public Accounts Committee's condemnatory report (2018), when it announced the end of PFI, saying the deals no longer represented VFM—although not renouncing the PPP policy itself—thereby conceding its critics' case.

Conclusion

While this study relates to PPPs in the 1990s and 2000s, the findings are important because they reveal some of the processes and mechanisms by which the corporate takeover of public policy has been achieved not just in Britain but elsewhere. The financial consultants played a key role in directing and implementing PFI/PPP, a policy which they had a commercial interest in expanding, via their presence and positions of influence in Whitehall and PUK, and their social networks. The partnerships policy served to increase both the wealth and power of the global accountancy industry, itself part of the broader financial sector that became increasingly dominant following the turn to neoliberal policies/financialization in the 1980s. This gave them a direct and commanding role in the economic decision-making and administration of the British state, enabling them to control the future direction of public policy and service provision.

It is part of a wider trend that has accelerated over the last 40 years throughout the increasingly integrated world economy, reaching its apotheosis in the bailout of the banks following the 2008 global financial crisis, when the Treasury in Britain—and central banks elsewhere—took measures to shore up the banks, creating liabilities of more than £1 trillion (NAO, 2009, 2010) and more recently in the bailout of the corporate and financial sectors during COVID-19 pandemic.

The involvement of the financial consultants in so many aspects of the policy produced conflicts of interest/partisanship that led to decisions detrimental to the interests of the broad mass of the population. To cite but one example, the NAO (2002) reported that the advisors in the case of the NATS PPP sought to gain valuable experience of PPPs in order to win future contracts in this new and expanding market, meaning that they ignored evidence that did not fit with their—and the government's—own preferred outcome.

At the same time, their activities are semi-submerged and opaque. At both the policy, decision-making, and post-implementation levels, FoI rules enable government to avoid disclosure where it relates to policy formation and commercially sensitive information, thereby preventing the public, its representatives and the media from scrutinizing these new arenas of decision-making outside the established structures.

The opacity is exacerbated by the financial reporting rules and practices of the private sector partners, which the accountancy industry determines through its professional bodies, making it difficult if not impossible to track, control and scrutinize ex post facto public expenditure. This in turn renders the traditional, if limited, mechanisms of accountability for public expenditure and control of the executive ineffective. The net result was to give the accountancy industry—and the broader financial sector—via its control of the PPP policy and process, a gateway into the Treasury and access to taxpayers' money with little or no accountability.

It was not just union leaders such as Unison's general secretary who termed the relationship between the government and its financial advisors "a web of deceit bordering on corruption" (Unison, 2002). Sampson (2005) found that senior accountants "were also shocked that the government could allow such an obvious conflict of interest." He believed that the Big Four were becoming a serious threat to democracy as their networks penetrated Whitehall. This is particularly important when the government excludes oppositional voices. While large corporations have always been able to exert power and influence, the last 30 years have seen a huge intensification of this process in which PFI/PPP has played a major role.

Taken together, their integration into the civil service, their private sector status, the opaque nature of the PFI corporate structure, with its limited financial disclosure requirements relating to "related parties," and the Freedom of Information Commissioner's refusal to extend their operations to FoI legislation, despite operating as de facto public authorities, mean that the traditional norms and conventions of bourgeois democracy, never very strong, have become ever weaker.

Under conditions where the corporate and financial sectors have taken control of public policy with little if any transparency and accountability, we are on the road to state secrecy and censorship, and ultimately tyranny, because uncontrolled power corrupts. This is because in the final analysis economic policies that create a plutocracy along with ever-increasing social inequality are incompatible with democratic norms. In short, the financial elite has to resort to anti-democratic methods because it is impossible to reconcile the economic welfare of the majority with the ever-increasing wealth and power of the privileged few *and* preserve democratic norms. It poses the question: is all economic life to be run in the interests of the financial elite? To ask the question is to answer it.

References

Arthur Andersen and Enterprise LSE (2000) *Value for Money Drivers in the Private Finance Initiative*, London, UK: Report commissioned by the Treasury Taskforce.

Association of Chartered Certified Accountants (2002) *Appraisal and Evaluation in Central Government: A Consultation Response*, London, UK: Association of Chartered Certified Accountants.

Brown, C.V. and Jackson, P.M. (1990) *Public Sector Economics*, 4th Edition, Oxford, UK: Basil Blackford.

Craig, D. (2006) *Plundering the Public Sector*, London, UK: Constable.

Edwards, P. and Shaoul, J. (2003) 'Partnerships: For better for worse?', *Accounting, Auditing and Accountability Journal* 16(3): 397–421.

Edwards, P., Shaoul, J., Stafford, A. and Arblaster, L. (2004) *Evaluating the Operation of PFI in Roads and Hospitals*, London, UK: Association of Chartered Certified Accountants, Research Report no 84.

Froud, J. and Shaoul, J. (2001) 'Appraising and evaluating PFI for NHS hospitals', *Financial Accountability and Management* 17(3): 247–270.

Gaffney, D., Pollock, A., Price, D. and Shaoul, J. (1999a) 'NHS capital expenditure and the private finance initiative-expansion or contraction?' *British Medical Journal* 319: 48–50.

Gaffney, D., Pollock, A., Price, D. and Shaoul, J. (1999b) 'PFI in the NHS-is there an economic case?' *British Medical Journal* 319: 116–199.

Gaffney, D., Pollock, A., Price, D. and Shaoul, J. (1999c) 'The politics of PFI and the "New" NHS', *British Medical Journal* 319: 249–253.

Glaister, S., Burnham, J., Stevens, H. and Travers, T. (1997) *Transport Policy in Britain*, London: Macmillan Press Ltd.

Gosling, P. (2003) *Stitched Up: How the Big Four Accountancy Firms Have PFI Under Their Thumbs*, London, UK: Unison.

Greenaway, J., Salter, B. and Hart, S. (2004) 'The evolution of a meta-policy: The case of a private finance initiative and the health sector', *British Journal of Politics and International Relations* 6(4): 507–526.

Institute of Public Policy Research (2001) *Building Better Partnership*, London, UK: Institute of Public Policy Research, The final report of the Commission on Public Private Partnerships.

King, P. (1975) 'Is the emphasis of capital budgeting theory misplaced?' *Journal of Business, Finance and Accounting* 2(1): 69–82.

KPMG (2002) *PFI and Tax*, London, UK: KPMG.

Mitchell, A., Puxty, T., Sikka, P. and Willmott, H. (1994) 'Ethical statements as smokescreens for sectional interests: The case of the UK accountancy profession', *Journal of Business Ethics* 13(1): 39–51.

Mott Macdonald (2002) *Review of Large Public Procurement in the UK*, London, UK: The Treasury.

National Audit Office (2000) *The Financial Analysis for the London Underground Public Private Partnership*, London, UK: The Stationery Office, House of Commons Paper 54, Session 2000–01.

National Audit Office (2002) *The Public Private Partnership for National Air Traffic Services Ltd*, London, UK: The Stationery Office, Report by the Comptroller and Auditor General, HC 1096 Session 2001–02.

National Audit Office (2006) *Central Government's Use of Consultants*, London, UK: The Stationary Office, Report by the Comptroller and Auditor General, HC 128 Session 2006–07.

National Audit Office (2007) *Improving the Tendering Process*, London, UK: Report by Comptroller and Auditor General, HC 149, Session 2006–07.

National Audit Office (2009) *Maintaining Financial Stability Across the United Kingdom's Banking System*, London, UK: The Stationary Office, Report by Comptroller and Auditor General, HC 91, Session 2009–10.

National Audit Office (2010) *The Asset Protection Scheme*, London, UK: Report by Comptroller and Auditor General, HC 567, Session 2010–11.

National Audit Office (2016) *The Use of Consultants and Temporary Staff*, London, UK: The Stationary Office, Report of the Comptroller and Auditor General, HC 603, Session 2015–16.

Oborne, P. (2007) *The Triumph of the Political Class*, London, UK: Simon and Schuster.

Pollock, A., Price, D. and Player, S. (2005) *The Private Finance Initiative: A Policy Built on Sand*, London, UK: Unison.

Pollock, A., Shaoul, J. and Vickers, N. (2002) 'Private finance and "Value for Money" in NHS hospitals: A policy in search of a rationale?' *British Medical Journal* 324: 1205–1208.

Pollock, A.M., Dunnigan, M., Gaffney, D., Price, D. and Shaoul, J. (1999) 'Planning the "New" NHS: Downsizing for the 21st century', *British Medical Journal* 319: 179–184.

Public Accounts Committee (2018) *46th Report: Private Finance Initiatives*, House of Commons, HC 894, London.

PwC (2001) *Public Private Partnerships: A Clearer View*, London, UK: PwC.

Ross, S.A. (1995) 'Uses, abuses and alternatives to the net present value rule', *Financial Management* 24(3): 96–102.

Sampson, A. (2005) *Who Rules This Place? The Anatomy of Britain in the 21st Century*, London, UK: John Murray (Publishers).

Shaoul, J. (2003) 'Financial analysis of the National Air Traffic Services Public Private Partnership', *Public Money and Management* 23(3): 185–194.

Shaoul, J. (2005) 'A critical financial appraisal of the private finance initiative: Selecting a financing method or reallocating wealth?', *Critical Perspectives on Accounting* 16: 441–471.

Shaoul, J. (2011) 'The economic and financial context: Paying for the banks', in S. Corby et al. (eds). *Working for the State*, London: Macmillan, pp. 43–65.

Shaoul, J., Stafford, A. and Stapleton, P. (2007) 'Private control over public policy: Financial advisors and the private finance initiative', *Policy and Politics* 35(3): 479–496.

Shaoul, J., Stafford, A. and Stapleton, P. (2008) 'The cost of using private finance to build, finance and operate the first 12 NHS hospitals in England', *Public Money and Management* 28(2): 101–108.
Treasury (1991) *Economic Appraisal in Central Government: A Technical Guide for Government Departments*, London, UK: HM Treasury.
Treasury (2003) *PFI Meeting the Investment Challenge*, London, UK: HM Treasury.
Treasury (2005) *Treasury Departmental Report 2005*, London, UK: HM Treasury.
Treasury (2006) *Value for Money Assessment Guidance*, London, UK: HM Treasury.
Tribe, L.H. (1972) 'Policy science: Analysis or ideology?' *Philosophy and Public Affairs* 2(1): 66–110.
Unison (2002) *A Web of Private Interest: How the Big Five Accountancy Firms Influence and Profit from Privatisation Policy*, London, UK, Unison Report.
Unison (2013) *The costs of privatisation Factsheet #36*, https://www.unison.org.uk/content/uploads/2013/06/On-line-Catalogue206333.pdf, accessed 27 October 2020.

Camouflaged Privatization: The Influence of the Fratzscher Commission and PricewaterhouseCoopers on Berlin's Schools

Laura Valentukeviciute

Introduction

Berlin's present coalition government—consisting of the Social Democrats, the Greens, and the Left Party (Die Linke)—is currently planning an extensive school renovation and construction program, the so-called "School Construction Offensive" (*Berliner Schulbauoffensive*—BSO). This case provides important insights into how private firms such as PricewaterhouseCoopers (PwC) and expert commissions such as the Fratzscher Commission[1] pave the way for new privatization models—models that do not immediately appear as privatization at first glance as they are hidden within a public company. That is why I call this

[1] The commission is named after Professor Marcel Fratzscher, Head of the German Institute for Economic Research, DIW, convened in 2014 by the then Minister of Economic Affairs Sigmar Gabriel, officially: Commission of experts to strengthen investments in Germany, see Expertenkommission 2016.

L. Valentukeviciute (✉)
Gemeingut in BürgerInnenhand (GiB) e.V, Berlin, Germany
e-mail: laura.valentukeviciute@gemeingut.org

C. Hurl and A. Vogelpohl (eds.), *Professional Service Firms and Politics in a Global Era*, https://doi.org/10.1007/978-3-030-72128-2_12

process “camouflaged privatization.” In this article, I critically investigate this trend as a board member and coordinator of the NGO “Gemeingut in BürgerInnenhand—GiB” (“Public Goods in Citizens’ Hand”), an organization which has opposed privatization schemes in Germany, and specifically Public–Private Partnerships (Fig. 1).

Camouflaged privatization is conceived by PwC. The firm elaborated on complicated financial and institutional models that complicate, partly obscure actual ownership and responsibilities. In case of the schools in Berlin, the terms of the BSO mandate stipulate that the construction and renovation of schools should be partly executed by two state-owned companies. However, these companies—HOWOGE Ltd. (HOWOGE Wohnungsbaugesellschaft mbH) and BIM Ltd. (Berliner Immobilienmanagement GmbH)—operate under private law and the school property to be constructed or renovated will be transferred to these companies under a lease for 37 years. The result is that the schools will become the property of the companies and the investments will be written off by them, while the districts will be forced to rent the schools back.

Fig. 1 Our logo for the “Our Schools”-ballot measure (Copyright: GiB)

Surprisingly, even the Left Party, as part of the governing coalition in Berlin, supports the decision due to austerity constraints, defending this project in articles such as "Make Future Investment Possible – How to use the leeway of the debt brake in the Federal States!"[2] (Dullien et al., 2018). The debt brake is established by the German constitution and enjoins the federal states from contracting new debts. Through taking the costs of borrowing off of the books of local government, they argue that pursing HOWOGE and BIM will help the city evade the conditions of the debt break: "In contrast to the State of Berlin, HOWOGE will be able to continue to take out loans from 2020 onwards" (Senate Department of Finance, 2019).

The Left's proposals bear striking similarities to a report by the consulting firm PricewaterhouseCoopers Legal (PwC, 2016). In 2016, the firm was commissioned by the Federal Ministry of Economic Affairs to provide advice on how to bundle, centralize, and standardize several school-construction projects. Their report is called an "advisory opinion" on "legal and institutional prerequisites for introducing new forms of private financing for public infrastructure projects involving a state-owned infrastructure company." Their proposal argues: "The company [the public infrastructure company yet to be established, L.V.] can act as intermediaries for investors, who, on the basis of standardised solutions, are available as financing and management partners for a large number of similar projects. By bundling a large number of projects, economies of scale can be generated" (PwC, 2016, 7). The Left Party employs the same justification. The Left Party paper states: "The Berlin Senate's argument is also convincing on the grounds of the necessity of centralizing school construction and involving general contractors to enable economies of scale and to accelerate construction procedures through modular system construction and standardisation" (Dullien et al., 2018, 7).

The Berlin Senate's current plan to privatize school property, both land and real estate, did not come about by chance. It is the product of many years of reflection on how private players—in particular banks, pension funds, but also smaller investors, consulting firms, and the construction industry—can directly benefit from investments in public service provision. The latest relevant guidelines were produced by, among

[2] All German quotes are translated into English by the author.

others, the Fratzscher Commission and PwC: The Fratzscher Commission was commissioned by the Ministry of Economic Affairs in 2014 and laid the foundation for the abovementioned PwC report. The Fratzscher Commission recommended to explore new funding models that could mobilize additional private infrastructure financing. Because of this recommendation, PwC was commissioned to suggest feasible implementation possibilities in their advisory report in late 2016.

In the following sections, I analyze the PwC report and describe the concrete steps they developed to implement the proposals of the Fratzscher Commission. While some journalists and NGOs have already analyzed the Fratzscher Commission report, PwC's report has received little attention so far. Analyzing the PwC report, published in 2016, is worthwhile because it provides an insight into both the wishful thinking and political influence of privatization players.

Centralization

The PwC report points the way to more private borrowing with a growing array of private investors and lenders. Further, it envisions an enormous expansion of Public–Private Partnerships (PPPs), with the PPP structures to be nested in such a way that they can only be identified through in-depth analysis that compares the report's recommendations with the eventual structure of the BSO. This comes as no surprise, because, based on past experience with PPPs, opinion polls show increased public reservations toward PPPs (Fricke, 2019). This form of privatization has faced challenges like the successful referendum in 2011, which required the disclosure of Berlin water contracts, and eventually led to the remunicipalization of the Berlin waterworks. The enormous cost increase for many projects under PPPs (highways, schools, administration buildings, etc.) has also led to strong criticism by the Federal Audit Office. In response, PPP proponents have attempted to counteract growing political resistance to privatization by refraining from more localized, individual projects—whether building schools or building motorway sections—to argue that projects should be bundled and centralized, thus taken out of the hands of local decision-makers, and then implemented as PPPs (see Raco in this volume).

Such an approach was already proposed for motorways by the Fratzscher Commission. With the changes to the German Constitution at the beginning of June 2017, the members of the German parliament "Bundestag" decided to centralize and transfer the construction, renovation, and operation of the motorways into a federal infrastructure company that, while owned by the federal government, operates under private law. Under the revised paragraphs regarding Article 90 and 143e of the German Constitution, the federal states (Länder), which were previously responsible for constructing and operating motorways on behalf of the federal government, are no longer able to stop or reject planned PPP motorway projects.

In their report, PwC justifies centralization through cost reduction: "Project financing [...] regularly requires a complex structuring process and thus carries high transaction costs [...]. This problem can be solved by setting up a central institution that largely standardises the structuring process, bundles the projects, and acts as an intermediary between the municipality and investors" (PwC, 2016, 7).

Furthermore, "In order to make smaller projects attractive for infrastructure funds or for the typical investors of such funds, it will be necessary to bundle many standardised similar projects" (PwC, 2016, 31).

Regarding funding arrangements, according to the PwC report, investors in such an infrastructure fund could, for example, be pension funds. The only thing missing to enable pension fund participation, they state, is the legal framework (PwC, 2016, 39). With this statement, PwC fails to mention that blending pension funds and PPP projects potentially extort taxpayers. Numerous prior examples, including highway construction and bank bailouts, show that if a PPP project is in trouble, taxpayers have to pay for it as a motorway cannot simply remain closed for long periods of time. With pension funds involved, politicians in addition would employ the argument: "should pensioners be dropped?" Under this type of pressure, is likely that the public sector will not withdraw from the PPP contract and rescue the pension fund contributions. The private lenders involved continue to benefit.

Management

The PwC report also provides proposals for how projects should be managed. According to PwC, investors should thus not only provide financial capital, but should also be responsible for managing the projects. Justified by the fact that the municipalities are relieved of both financial and personnel burdens, PwC emphasizes private management skills and asserts: “If institutional investors provide management skills to take over typical municipal infrastructure projects such as the construction of schools and kindergartens, the refurbishment of municipal road bridges or refugee accommodation and simple flats for a large number of municipalities, economic potential can be realised and the municipalities can be relieved both financially and administratively” (PwC, 2016, 6).

According to PwC, however, not everyone is capable of assuming a management: “The provision of management competences and the assumption of control functions are only possible and meaningful for appropriately specialised institutionalised investors” (PwC, 2016, 7). This means particularly the large funds. Although PwC recommends that management be selected by tender, this is little consolation to local actors. After all, whose interests will a manager from, for example, Deutsche Bank or Allianz insurance serve?

Cluttered Structures and Conflicts of Interests

PwC proposes a nested PPP structure of first-degree project companies (financing and project management) and second-degree project companies (implementation of projects or commissioning of executing companies such as for construction). Participating actors from the public and private sectors are to act jointly in both project companies. The project company of the first degree, according to PwC (2016, 7), should proceed as follows: “In order to ensure that the interests of the project commissioners [i.e. e.g. municipalities, L.V.] are adequately taken into account, it is advisable to provide for the participation of the public sector. This participation should be carried out by an institution that enjoys the trust of the investors at the same time, so that it can actually perform the function of a supervisory authority and a corrective of interests on the investor side. One possible option would be a participation of the Kreditanstalt für Wiederaufbau (KfW).” The KfW is a large state-owned German bank, the Reconstruction Loan Corporation. It is, however not clear which interests KfW should represent: those of the public sector or those of private investors.

A further conflict of interest arises from the next level of the nested PPP structure. The second-degree company is responsible for actually implementing the projects (“a concrete project of a particular project-commissioner”) and “is provided with (equity) capital by the superordinate project company [the first-degree company, L.V.] and is controlled by this company" (PwC, 2016, 8). In addition, both the public sector and the executing company can participate in this company: "Optionally, the project commissioner or the executing company [e.g., general contractor, L.V.] can participate in the subordinate project company as a minority shareholder" (PwC, 2016, 8f.). The complicated and opaque structure makes conflicts of interest more likely as the roles of owning, managing, and controlling are blended.

New Name, Old Habits

The third actor in the cluttered model is the state-owned infrastructure company, which works closely with the first-degree project company and "provides standardised financing structures, tender documents and contracts, taking into account a fair balance of interests, and enjoys the trust of all parties involved" (PwC, 2016, 7). It is also intended to create a framework for the involvement of the fourth actor—the public–private infrastructure fund.

Advisory services play an important role in the choice between a PPP and a public sector project. The risk of consultants who do not recommend PPPs being called in via calls for tender must be eliminated. This happens inconspicuously through in-house procurement: By involving the Federal Government, the Länder, and the municipalities as owners of the infrastructure company, public tenders for the advisory services can be circumvented if the service is commissioned to another public company. An important player in the consultancy process is "PD Berater der öffentlichen Hand GmbH" ("PD Consultant of the public sector ltd.," previous company names were "ÖPP Deutschland AG" and "Partnerschaften Deutschland AG"). This company is organized to provide advice on PPPs to government agencies in Germany. It has been in public hands since January 2017. However, prior to this time, it involved state and private sector players, with Bernward Kulle, a former manager of the German construction giant Hochtief at the top. The experience from the past is that PD was regularly recommending PPP. The infrastructure company now proposed by PwC bears great similarities to PD.

Gateway: Equity Capital

In its report, the Fratzscher Commission demanded that participating companies contribute more equity capital to projects in order to achieve a "real transfer of risk" (Expertenkommission, 2016, 43) because too often the financing of projects worth millions and billions of Euros stands on shaky legs with little equity capital. One example is the A1 Mobil project company. The shareholders Bilfinger, John Laing, and Johann Bunte invested only 36,000 Euros of equity capital in a company that is to build and operate a motorway project that costs a good one billion euros (Waßmuth, 2017/2018). When the planned revenues were not achieved, the project company was threatened by insolvency and took the government to court to acquire additional funding for allegedly escaped profits.

Against this background, the proposal for more equity sounds reasonable. On closer inspection, however, it turns out to be another way in which financialization instruments redirect public funds to private benefactors. Because equity is expensive, i.e., higher interest rates are demanded, such projects become particularly interesting for investors. According to the PwC report, "Such an infrastructure fund typically invests in equity, and even a credit fund usually does not have sufficient incentive to invest in claims that are subject to interest rates similar to those of municipal loans" (PwC, 2016, 19).

Municipal-bond-like conditions mean that only very low-interest rates can be charged on loans taken out because the public sector is a secure debtor and Germany in particular (the Federal Government, the Länder, and the municipalities) pays back its loans reliably. Thus, there is no credit default risk and therefore no reason to demand higher interest rates. In order, however, for the financial industry to receive higher returns for the same secure loans that the public sector regularly and reliably serves, a euphemism was created: more equity. The result is that investors increase their share of equity and receive higher interest for this share. Increasing equity, however, does not alter the creditworthiness of the public sector. It will continue to pay back the loans and interest, which will, however, become more expensive as a result of the trick, as returns on equity of 30 percent per year are usual for PPP projects (Waßmuth, 2017/2018, 5).

Nevertheless, "more equity" in the language of the financial industry also means "more risk," and according to the PwC report: "Alternative forms of financing in this area, involving the contribution of equity, are basically suitable for meeting the Fratzscher Commission's demand for a genuine transfer of risk to the private partner" (PwC, 2016, 20). The PwC report thus describes what the Fratzscher report still concealed: If the private sector allegedly assumes more risk, the public sector will pay a dear price for it.

Furthermore, the larger context reveals that a risk transfer does not actually take place. As touched on above, the private sector is, after all, in charge of managing and controlling the projects: "This new form of municipal infrastructure provision is based on the provision of equity paired with control and monitoring options for private investors and therefore enables a genuine transfer of risk" (PwC, 2016, 6). If a private company takes over management and control, it will certainly ensure that all risks are not borne by itself, but are left to the public sector.

Conclusion: Understanding and Resisting Camouflaged Privatization

Analyzing the Fratzscher Report from 2015 and the PwC report from 2016 shows that the new model does not move away from privatization, but instead camouflages it more effectively. The risks and the maintenance of public infrastructure are still financed by taxpayers (see Hildyard in this volume). As this case shows, new ways are constantly being devised for ensuring that the private sector gets as much of the cake as possible from the large investment volume required by public sector projects.

The aim is to create structures that are particularly complex and non-transparent. This creates a confusion of financing and decision-making, in that the interests of the private sector can be concealed or even confused with the interests of the public sector. The allegedly necessarily complex structures are to be taken over by particularly capable managers, and these are the managers of the large funds; this also reduces the decision-making power of the public sector. In the Fratzscher commission's proposal, the further leverage to get more taxpayers' money is called "real risk transfer." This means that more equity will flow into the projects. The consequence is that the equity capital contributions will be paid back to the investors by the taxpayers at a higher interest rate. The structure proposed by Fratzscher Commission and PwC allows for various forms of privatization, e.g., formal privatization or PPPs, and thus the outflow of taxpayers' money to private actors. In order to further conceal the privatization character of this structure to be created and so that "especially the representatives of the municipal side can be convinced of the advantages," PwC suggests "finding a concise name for the new type of financing" (PwC, 2016, 102).

Growing public mistrust of privatization and PPPs, however, is putting privatization profiteers under pressure. The first and most important way to counter this is to create publicity about such projects. This is what I and the NGO GiB are doing[3]: Immediately after the Fratzscher Commission was convened, GiB gathered information about the members of the Commission and their project and brought it to the public. This was taken up by journalists and brought to a wider audience. With our analyzes, street protests, collection of signatures, and even a successful disruption of the press conference of the then Minister of Economics Sigmar Gabriel on the results of the Fratzscher Commission, we successfully disrupted the privatization process (Fig. 2).

We also highlighted the PPP-like nature of the school-construction initiative, even though it was officially labelled differently. We made all these information public through many channels (such as explanatory videos, our website, or public events) and we discussed alternatives during 36 open round-table discussions. We were officially invited to a public hearing in order to present our concerns. Even though we couldn't stop the privatization process, some changes have eventually been made to the agreement between the city of Berlin and HOWOGE due to our critique.

So at least, the proposed reforms in the school-construction sector could not be pushed through as originally planned. We achieved similar changes in highway-infrastructure politics. But a wider change of mind is needed to generally protect the common goods sustainably and comprehensively from privatization. In 1968, Garrett Hardin created a narrative for privatization with his essay "Tragedy of the commons." He later withdrew his theses because he realized that they were flawed. But they were already widely disseminated. Today, people all over the world are experiencing how damaging privatization is, many reject it, massive resistance is stirring up. But a narrative is missing—establishing this is a task for future-oriented, sustainably thinking scientists.

[3] For an overview in German see: https://www.gemeingut.org/unser-einsatz-gegen-schulprivatisierung-was-haben-wir-erreicht/.

Fig. 2 GiB handing over the signatures supporting the "Our Schools"-ballot measure in the entrance hall of the Berlin House of Representatives (Copyright: GiB)

References

Dullien, S., Hirschel, D., Priewe, J., Reiner, S., Trochowski, D., Troost, A., Truger, A. and Wolf, H. (2018) *Zukunftsinvestitionen ermöglichen—Spielräume der Schuldenbremse in den Bundesländern nutzen!* Rosa-Luxemburg-Stiftung, https://www.rosalux.de/fileadmin/rls_uploads/pdfs/sonst_publikationen/Zukunftsinvestitionen_erm%C3%B6glichen_-_Spielr%C3%A4ume_der_Schuldenbremse_in_den_Bundesl%C3%A4ndern_nutzen.pdf, accessed 8 October 2019.

Expertenkommission „Stärkung von Investitionen in Deutschland" (2015) *Bericht der Expertenkommission im Auftrag des Bundesministers für Wirtschaft und Energie, Sigmar Gabriel*, https://www.bmwi.de/Redaktion/DE/Downloads/I/investitionskongress-report-gesamtbericht-deutsch-barrierefrei.pdf?__blob=publicationFile&v=1, accessed 20 Dezember 2019.

Fricke, T. (2019) 'Angst im Aufschwung. Repräsentative Umfrage zu ökonomischen Ansichten der Deutschen', *Wirtschaftsdienst* 99(12): 849–854.

PwC—PricewaterhouseCoopers Legal (2016) *Gutachterliche Stellungnahme für das Bundesministerium für Wirtschaft und Energie. Rechtliche und institutionelle Voraussetzungen zur Einführung neuer Formen zur privaten Finanzierung öffentlicher Infrastrukturvorhaben unter Einbindung einer staatlichen Infrastrukturgesellschaft. Schlussbericht*, https://www.gemeingut.org/wp-content/uploads/2018/10/2016-10-27_PwC-gutachten.pdf, accessed 8 October 2019.

Senate Department of Finance (2019) *Die Schulbauoffensive des Berliner Senats*, https://www.berlin.de/sen/finanzen/haushalt/schulbauoffensive/artikel.613867.php, accessed 8 October 2019.

Waßmuth, C. (2017/2018) 'ÖPP-Pleite mit Ansage—der exemplarische Fall A1 mobil', *Lunapark21* Extra No. 16/17: 5. https://www.lunapark21.net/oepp-pleite-mit-ansage-der-exemplarische-fall-a1-mobil/, accessed 21 January 2020.

Professional Service Firms and Administration: Entrenching Private Expertise

Hegemonic Privatization and Its Discontents: Reflections on the Rise and Limitations of the Parastate and Local Governance Reform in England

Mike Raco

Introduction

One of the defining features of governance reform in England since the mid-1980s has been the growth of private sector involvement in the management of the welfare state and the delivery of public services. The scale of what this chapter terms *the parastate* is growing rapidly with approximately 30% of *all* public spending in 2018 (or approximately £250billion) going to contracted-out professional service firms (House of Commons, 2018a).[1] The expansion of the parastate has arisen surreptitiously under the neoliberal reforms of successive governments, whose core objectives have been to depoliticize debates over public service provision (Bevir and Trentmann, 2007). Underpinning reform has been a reforging of relationships between the public and private sectors, in which

[1] In 2018 total UK government spending was £840billion (Office of Budget Responsibility, https://obr.uk/forecasts-in-depth/brief-guides-and-explainers/public-finances/). Figures given for total spending are collected as UK totals.

M. Raco (✉)
University College London, London, England
e-mail: m.raco@ucl.ac.uk

C. Hurl and A. Vogelpohl (eds.), *Professional Service Firms and Politics in a Global Era*, https://doi.org/10.1007/978-3-030-72128-2_13

a new generation of professional firms have emerged to deliver welfare services at a "distance" from the political process. It is a model of governance that sees political oversight and intensive scrutiny of public services as an impediment to effective forms of expert-led, private delivery.

The traditional notions of hierarchy and formal bureaucratic rules that underpinned the rise of welfare systems in the postwar era are dismissed as being outdated "repressive, authoritarian, favoring a management perspective, [and] lacking spontaneity" (Du Gay and Lopdrup-Hjorth, 2016, 33).

While much academic and policy focus has been on state reform and processes of privatization, much less emphasis has been given to two elements, examined in this chapter: the mutually constitutive interrelationships between parastate reforms and professional service firms; and the growing politicization of the parastate in the wake of its relentless expansion and increasing public failures and limitations. The discussion draws on the example of state reform in England, a country in which privatization experiments have gone further and deeper than those found in most European countries (Meek, 2013). It begins by defining and characterizing the rise of the parastate and outlines how it differs from traditional state or market-led systems of governance. It then explores how and under what conditions governance failures have emerged in the deployment of the model before looking at recent policy reforms that are seeking to promote further rounds of contracting out. The discussion draws specifically on an analysis of the *Annual Reports and Accounts* of some of the largest and powerful firms, Capita, Kier, Serco, and Veolia, to assess their conceptions of governance, politics, risk, and return. A final section looks at examples of parastate firms and broader changes taking place among civil society groups to explore the limits of reform and the form and character of politicization that has taken place.

The chapter will establish the following lines of argument. First, the process of contracting out is creating growing tensions for private companies who face a structural challenge in acting simultaneously as both profit-seeking economic actors *and* political actors who have to manage complex types of political risk. The analysis shows that firms are increasingly aware that their actions are subject to growing public scrutiny and they are re-aligning their practices and structures to improve and legitimate their reputations and contracts. However, as will also be discussed, attempts to limit political risks are fraught with difficulty, owing to their reliance on traditional system-led management models used in the private sector. They are finding that the delivery of welfare services, in diverse social, economic, and political environments, is presenting significant new challenges even for the biggest, globally oriented parastate firms.

Second, the chapter also shows that attempts by pro-privatization governments to use outsourcing as a way of creating "arms-length" forms of accountability and state practice are also increasingly subject to failure and growing political tensions. Recent high-profile cases, such as the collapse of the multinational company Carillion, that relied on public contracts and outsourcing, have generated a new level of critical scrutiny and debate over the limits of parastate models. As a critical Parliamentary Report argued:

> Carillion's rise and spectacular fall was a story of recklessness, hubris and greed. Its business model was a relentless dash for cash, driven by acquisitions, rising debt, expansion into new markets and exploitation of suppliers. It presented accounts that misrepresented the reality of the business, and increased its dividend every year, come what may. Long term obligations, such as adequately funding its pension schemes, were treated with contempt. Even as the company very publicly began to unravel, the board was concerned with increasing and protecting generous executive bonuses. Carillion was unsustainable. The mystery is not that it collapsed, but that it lasted so long. (House of Commons, 2018b, 3)

Such examples show that the inter-twinning of private sector activities and state practices is generating intense forms of *politicization* along three principle axes: (i) the structural difficulties parastate firms face in adapting to political demands; (ii) the perceived inefficiencies of private practice; and (iii) the delegitimization of private sector engagement. The discussion concludes by setting out some broader directions for research and highlighting the lack of sufficient recognition given in academic writing to parastate structures and private firms.

The Rise of the Parastate and Its Discontents

In a direct echo of neoliberal public choice theories of the 1970s, political deliberations, and processes were seen as being aligned to populist agendas and electoral cycles, rather than the common good of publics and businesses (Blythe, 2013). The solution was a shrunken state and new forms of leaner, reflexive, and entrepreneurial governance. The parastate was designed to separate out the processes of policymaking and implementation so that the latter could be freed from the restrictive influences of the political sphere on efficient service provision (Newman and Clarke, 2009; Murphy, 2011). In short, reforms aimed to depoliticize policymaking and hand power over to professional service firms, such as Capita or G4S, who are presented as being best able to deliver programs free of political interference (Newman and Clarke, 2018). It is a process within which the state itself has become a *market-state*, giving out contracts to private companies who are "best able" to deliver welfare programs.

Despite the optimism of public management theories, the reality has been that private firms have found it increasingly difficult to accommodate the complex and competing demands that public service delivery involves. There has been a growing mismatch between the systems-based management models used within the private sector and the accumulation of new responsibilities taken on by outsourced firms. These models were principally developed during the 1950s in the fields of organizational studies and management sciences (Mirowski, 2002). They were founded on simplified representations that attempt to break down organizational problems and challenges and arrange them into logical and effective compartmentalizations that can be ordered and met. Effective private sector management requires the identification of system components, boundaries, hierarchies, goals, and equifinality or the belief that there are multiple pathways that could be followed to achieve the same outcome (Akoff, 1990; Thrift, 2008). They are modes of thinking and organization that are designed for vertically integrated, bounded private corporations working in competitive, product-based markets.

Applying such models to the messy complexities of politicized public service provision has proved to be extremely challenging. As Jessop (1999) argues, all systems of governance and management are prone to failures given the complexity of socioeconomic processes and the restless dynamism intrinsic to politicized forms of representation. What is of significance over time is how failures are understood and (re)politicized in order to justify reforms and the introduction of new policy measures. It has become common for neoliberal writers and policymakers to argue for more deregulation as a way of tackling market failures—as though it is regulation that is to blame for limiting market action across the economy and society (Pennington, 2002). This approach, Jessop argues, is itself flawed as "much of what passes as market failure is actually an expression of the underlying contradictions of capitalism" (14). In other words, calls for more market are likely to entrench, rather than solve such failures. Similarly, where state-led approaches to governance problems have met limitations, political actors, usually on the Left, call for more state intervention as a cure even though this may also exacerbate causes for failure (see Sami and Anand in this volume).

As will be discussed later in the chapter, despite their seemingly "non-political," "delivery-focused" emphasis, parastate arrangements, and agents, have faced similar challenges and tensions to those that characterized traditional postwar market or state-led political systems. In order to develop a broader understanding of this phenomenon, a starting point is to draw on Crouch's (2011) analysis of what "pure" market principles and practices consist of and how these can be compared to the markets established under parastate conditions (see Fig. 1). For a pure market to function conditions need to be created in which: (i) all prices are made comparable; (ii) market entry is without barriers and there is a churn of buyers and sellers; (iii) there is a high volume of transactions; (iv)

Conditions for Pure Markets	**Conditions for Parastate Arrangements**
All prices are comparable, everything is traded	Public assets and services are converted into tradeable prices under contractual agreements
Market entry is without barriers, with multiple providers and purchasers	Market entry highly limited to those with the capacities to deliver state contracts and meet regulatory requirements.
Maintenance of a high volume of transactions	Increasingly complex contractual rigidities implemented that
Market participants are perfectly informed	Market participants draw on knowledge of political and regulatory opportunities to take on State contracts
Economy and polity are separated	Economy and polity are inter-twinned

Fig. 1 Conditions for pure and parastate markets

participants have perfect knowledge; and (v) the economy and polity are conceptualized as representing separate spheres of action. These, Crouch claims, are conditions that cannot be met in a regular economy owing to systematic inequalities throughout the market that lead to monopolization and uneven access to information, resources, and opportunities on the part of firms.

As set out in Fig. 1, these core features also provide insights into the conditions that characterize parastate arrangements and politics, given that they are ostensibly being introduced to marketize public services and welfare states. They also indicate where and how parastate arrangements are generating new governance failures.

- First, in the same way that under market conditions, everything is traded, under parastate conditions a process of commensuration is implemented in which complex welfare demands are converted into quantifiable, calculable, and numerical forms of ordering, such as through the introduction of contractual targets and Performance Service Agreements (Espeland and Stevens, 1998). However, the process of conversion is intensely politicized and fraught with difficulties, inconsistencies, and contradictory trends. Not all qualitative values can be converted into quantitative values and contract negotiations "generally require more and more complex calculations…that try to bridge the gap between quantitative elements and qualitative assessments" (Miller, 2002, 231). The presence of these gaps opens up opportunities for political challenges and increases the likelihood of governance failures.
- Second, one of the core characteristics of parastate arrangements is the high barriers to entry that exist and the limited pool of firms that possess the capacities to deliver and manage complex government contracts. Arrangements tend to be long-lasting, bidding processes are costly and time-consuming, and there is relatively little turnover across the sector. As writers such as Loewenstein (2015, 10) show the actions of big corporations "entrench a crisis" of state legitimacy and inaction "and then sell themselves as the only ones who can resolve it" on the part of governments and citizens. The costs associated with slow processes of contracting can only be met by bigger firms, with significant financial capacities. Moreover, specialist firms have emerged in fields such as transport provision and healthcare,

that increasingly dominate the "market" and make it difficult for smaller actors to bid for new contracts.

- Third, a functioning market requires a high and ongoing volume of transactions to ensure a churn of activities and companies. Under parastate conditions contractual relationships act as a form of rigidity that limits the churn of transactions. It can be difficult to establish contracts that are both flexible enough to shift risk onto private corporations, with the possibility of firm failure (as in open markets), while also encouraging private interests to invest in welfare projects by pushing the risk of failure back on to the state. For authors such as Braithwaite (2008), this lack of churn has created new modes of "regulatory capitalism" under which private interests become locked into complex systems of government and regulation in ways that not only generate significant profits, but also create new forms of market lock-in, rather than fluidity (see Linovski in this volume).
- Fourth, market models assume that participants are perfectly informed and that knowledge and information over market conditions are widely shared to enable competition to function. Under parastate conditions successful participants and firms have to have a stronger grasp of policy regulations and privatization opportunities, than they do of open markets and trading conditions. This means that lobbying and political networking take on a new degree of significance in ways that benefit larger corporations with the power and resources to invest in such activities and who tend to possess stronger existing networks. All markets are characterized by systematic information asymmetries in which diverse actors possess unequal access to knowledge. Within parastate markets these inequalities are amplified as market opportunities are created through political action and embedded understandings of governance reforms and regulatory changes.
- And fifth, the neoliberal notion that the economy (market) and polity (state) are separate spheres of action (Crouch, 2011; Vogl, 2017) effectively collapses under parastate arrangements in which the two become so inter-twinned that it can become increasingly difficult to identify which type of actor has responsibility for what service. Recent examples in England in which transport ministers claim that they are no longer "directly responsible" or accountable for the delivery of public transport services, or in which justice ministers argue that the performance of the prison service is now a

matter of delivery management, rather than public scrutiny, reflect this wider trend (see Financial Times, 2019). The paradox within such claims is that they reflect a simultaneous narrative of separation between public and private actors, at the same time as they also establish new forms of structural interdependence.

The tendency of parastate systems to generate governance failures creates political problems for governments intent on sustaining or expanding existing models. The next section outlines recent policy initiatives that demonstrate how and in what ways policy instruments are being used to try to resolve some of the broader tensions with parastate models outlined above.

Maintaining and Entrenching the Parastate—Recent Government Reforms in England

Post financial crisis governments in countries such as England have opted for programs of welfare austerity and a deepening of parastate models of governance (Penny, 2017). However, as noted above there are strong tendencies toward governance failures inherent in such models. Programs of austerity are reducing the size and scope of welfare contracts that are available to private companies, thereby threatening their longer-term financial viability. At the same time, high-profile outsourcing failures are also becoming more visible and subject to challenge by political groups and citizens. Governments are, therefore, faced with new dilemmas. On the one hand, they may opt for a *shallow politicization and reformist* approach in which efforts are made to make existing models work "better" through more intelligent forms of contracting and/or the identification of effective private sector partners. Alternatively, policymakers may opt for the rolling out of *deeper forms of politicization* under which models of private provision are rejected and (re)placed by powerful state-managed bureaucratic systems, funded through new modes of taxation and/or borrowing.

In England, the dominant response from Central Government during the 2010s has been one of shallow reform and a rebooting of the model, rather than a deeper rejection. For instance, in February 2019 an *Outsourcing Playbook* was published by the Treasury in order to provide guidance on outsourcing decisions and contracting for both public and private actors. In its Foreword the document states that owing to recent high-profile failures, processes of outsourcing are "under intense scrutiny...firmly under the microscope." It outlines a set of rules and managerial procedures through which contracting-out processes can be "embedded" into the government's ways of working. It is designed to "provide commercial, finance, and project delivery professionals with guidelines, rules and principles that will help them to avoid the most common errors observed in outsourcing projects" (Cabinet Office, 2019, 7). Eleven key changes are being introduced, as set out in Fig. 2.

The introduction of these Guidelines represents the evolution of the parastate model in two important ways. First, they highlight ever-closer working relationships between the state and companies, as evidenced by the recognition that "the outsourcing companies themselves have contributed fully and wholeheartedly with this work" (3). The *Playbook* is supported by an associated *Supplier Code of Conduct* that sets out "joint

1. Publication of Commercial Pipelines
2. Market health and capability assessments
3. Project Validation Reviews
4. Make Versus Buy assessments
5. Should cost modelling
6. Requirement for pilots
7. Key Performance Indicators
8. Risk allocation
9. Pricing and payment mechanisms
10. Assessing the economic and financial standing of suppliers
11. Resolution planning

Source: Cabinet Office (2019)

Fig. 2 Key new policies for contracting-out in the civil service

commitments" from public and private sectors to develop more integrated models of working—a clear recognition of the failures of existing models. The interconnections between polity and market are exemplified by the attention given to so-called critical service contracts "where significant disruption would occur should services be interrupted" (7)—indicating the scale of mutual interdependence.

Second, the new rules indicate that despite the failures of policy, efforts are being made to resuscitate parastate models and use them to drive forward new managerial modes. In its associated publication, *Market Management—Guidance Note* (Government Commercial Function, 2019), public actors are required to "understand the markets we source from, recognizing our influence on these markets, and designing commercial strategies and contracts that promote healthy markets over the short, medium and long term" (3). Despite the structural barriers to market entry that accompany the parastate model, there is still an ideological framing that views market principles and a promotion of more competition in the contract sector, as the basis to improved value for money and better forms of governance: "healthy competitive markets matter because they support our ability to achieve value for money for taxpayers" (5). A series of steps are set out that are designed to promote market health by reducing barriers to entry and switching between different players. There is an explicit recognition that "government is a market-maker and/or accounts for a large part of the market." It is therefore incumbent on government, it is argued, to create additional certainty and security by ensuring that risks are "shared" between public and private sectors. Rather than rejecting the parastate model, the proposals call for further entrenchment and outline a future in which deeper relationships between public and private sectors are forged.

While much academic and policy writing has focused on state regulations and political agendas, less attention has been paid to the ways in which professional service firms are changing and how their growth and expansion makes them *more* prone both to delivery failures (through over-expansion) and political oversight. The next section, draws on a critical discourse analysis of the Accounts and Annual Reports of four of the biggest parastate firms Capita, Kier, Serco, and Veolia to examine the broader governmental transformations taking place in England and the evolving roles and responsibilities of professional service firms. The analysis looked for evidence of shifts in company strategies and tactics, forms of networking, and definitions of political risk. The case study firms have received growing and increasingly hostile public criticism of their activities in recent years, with the construction firm Kier, for instance, reporting that was close to going out of business in 2018. The firms are representative of a broader crisis within the service firm sector with other high-profile failures include the company Carillion that went bankrupt in 2018 and whose contracts were nationalized by state bodies. Other examples that have attracted political attention include the privatization of part of the criminal justice system, local-government outsourcing, Ministry of Defence contracts, and the delivery of social housing projects (National Audit Office, 2017, 2018). The discussion examines their size and scope of activities and how they are seeking to "manage" the process of policy delivery but are struggling to simultaneously meet changing political and economic demands.

The Politicization of Parastate Firms

Parastate companies face a structural challenge: they are both profit-seeking *economic* actors; and simultaneously *political actors* whose activities face growing scrutiny and challenges at a variety of scales. As this section will show, they are compelled to respond to ever-changing political demands but this, in turn, requires embedded understandings and practices in ways that (over)stretch their managerial capacities. Most firms are geared up to lobbying functions, rather than those of engagement, negotiation, and legitimacy-building that are increasingly required to manage the politics of welfare delivery. As the parastate has grown, so regulators, civil society groups, and critics have become increasingly active in shedding light on its workings in ways that were not envisaged during the heyday of mass-privatization in the 1990s and 2000s (see Valentukeviciute in this volume).

At the same time, all of the case study firms are undergoing a process of constant reform in their *corporate structures* in an attempt to navigate the increasingly complex political and economic environments in which they are working. This has required a combination of expansion and reorganization. Keir's (2019) *Annual Report and Accounts 2018*, for instance, makes much of acquisitions during 2017 of firms in the power generation and road infrastructure sectors. Other, more established parastate actors such as the Veolia Group, are organized through a subsidiary structure and emerged with the gradual privatization and outsourcing of the water treatment and distribution, transport, energy management, waste management, and technical and communal services sectors.[2] The company's growth since the mid-1990s has been remarkable, with 102 registered subsidiaries and entities acting as contractors to state organizations directly or indirectly. Its structure is reminiscent of a governmental bureaucracy requiring management, coordination, financing, contracting/further outsourcing, evaluation, and monitoring. The advantages of acting as a giant parastate organization are set out in its *Directors' Report 2017* in which is it noted that the company "largely trade[s] with large well-established and local authority clients" meaning that the risk of losing market share "is considered low" (Keir, 2019, 2). As a provider of welfare services, it still uses the market discourse of "trade," even though the company presents itself as a co-producer of state policy and those that it is trading with:

> the UK Group has an open relationship with all UK regulatory bodies, including the various Environment Agency bodies across the UK. The UK Group is committed to a sustainable future by protecting and conserving the natural environment, helping customers to gain value through the circular economy, and closed loop thinking. (ibid., 2)

What is also clear is that firms are especially focused on *political activities*. Identified risks lie in political and regulatory reform as opposed to market fluctuations. Keir, for example, note how their continued profitability is dependent on what they term a "political consensus for continuing investment" (7) in public services and infrastructure but also highlight vulnerabilities and impact of events such as Brexit uncertainties or the Grenfell fire and its impacts on social housing budgets and priorities. Its Directors admit that its "operations are subject to increased scrutiny, regulation and oversight due to external factors" and that owing to widespread perceived failures in private provision it has "recently experienced a significant increasing the level of public focus…we expect that scrutiny to increase, particularly for major suppliers to the public sector" (8). This is to be mitigated through "regular engagement" with government and government agencies in an attempt to reduce the risk that contracts may be removed now or in the future.

[2] With a Head Quarters in Paris and the presence of an organizing firm, Veolia UK Ltd, that co-ordinates its UK activities and firms. Veolia was formerly known as Vivendi UK and changed its name is 2003.

The growth in complexity of these companies has paradoxically enhanced their vulnerability to shifts in government policy and welfare reforms. Serco (2011), for instance, exists to "deliver essential services mainly in the public sector by managing people, processes, technology and assets" (2). As with Veolia (2018, 5), it has broadened out into a remarkable range of sectors and has taken on the role of wishing to be "a trusted partner of government," rather than just a provider of contractual services. However, in the wake of government austerity cutbacks since 2010, the firm has faced significant new "risks" to its business model as the state it depends on for its core business has been faced with budget cuts and multiple new demands. By 2011 the firm was already reporting revenue declines in dealing with local and regional government, "driven by the impact of government spending reductions in a number of areas" (3).[3] In an explicit admission of the politicized nature of Serco's business, the Directors noted that:

> as a major proportion of Serco's customers are governments and governmental agencies, a substantial part of the business is dependent on government policies, budgets priorities and regulatory or political constraints...susceptible to changes in government, government policy, budget allocations and the political environment. (ibid., 4)

By 2018 the company was even more open about the complex and interconnected nature of the risks it faced and noted that:

> our business is linked to changes in the economy, fiscal and monetary policy, political stability and leadership, budget priorities, and the perception and attitude of governments and the wider public to outsourcing, which could result in decisions not to outsource services or lead to delays in placing work. (ibid., 6)

Under such pressures it was admitted that "market conditions continue to be challenging" in which there is a fear of losing contracts if company performance is seen to be failing.

The company has responded to these potential threats by establishing elaborate management oversight structures and appointing Subject

[3] The closure of the Regional Development Agencies and associated agencies, such as the Business Link program, reduced the size and scale of the market for contracts that Serco had managed to acquire.

Matter Experts, Heat Maps of Risks, Key Risk Indicator Dashboards of action. They are drawing on the techniques and processes found within the private sector and applying them to understandings of governance and regulation. The Directors point out that in the UK there exists "established legal systems providing protection to change in contract terms" (4), or a degree of insulation from political demands and changes in policies and regulations. However, there is also concern that the length and complexity of government contracts can make it especially difficult to provide accurate assessments of financial risk over the long term. As providers of public services, parastate firms also have to cope with regulatory changes relating to inherited financial costs and liabilities. Most notably there is an ongoing concern with the inflation of public sector pensions for workers and the negative impacts of any attempt to curtail pensions on industrial relations.

Other giant corporations such as Capita (2018, 20) have an order book with government departments of £2.1billion, and possess a "market share of 13%" of being "a provider to government." The combined value of their Central and Local Government services is valued at £6.7billion/year and is growing at 3% per annum. However, this reliance on state funds has made the firm vulnerable to political pressure. In response, it has sought to re-orient activities and focus more on "creating better outcomes" and establishing a reputation for being "a trusted strategic partner to central government" (28). The firm has been under growing pressure over perceived failures and is reframing its activities in line with shifting political pressures and priorities. Its Directors highlight the dangers that it is facing: "the local government market for large outsourced contracts is declining with a significant drop-off in the number and size of opportunities coming to market and existing clients choosing to end contracts early and take services in-house" (28). But they also note that the emergence of new contracting out policies and the outsourcing reforms discussed above, are very much welcomed and they use these to promote their firms as potential sites for financial investment.

This section has highlighted that even in their own terms, private companies have found it increasingly difficult to make financial profits from the parastate and are facing structural challenges to their longer term competitiveness (see Froud et al., 2017). The conversion of complex and highly politicized service provision into manageable contracts and financial profits has proved to be extremely challenging and many private firms, particularly in the construction, housing, and infrastructure sectors have found it increasingly difficult to maintain profitability. Larger firms are acquiring contracts on the basis of their intensive political lobbying but this is overstretching their capacities. Private firms are also facing new pressures from civil society actors as will be discussed below. In the longer term a combination of these factors may undermine the attractiveness of parastate models to the private sector and their investors, thus further undermining the rationale for future privatization and contracting out models of reform.

The Parastate and Civil Society

The rise of parastate organizations has generated growing political resistance among *local* government actors, welfare providers, and citizens as well as creating new alliances between unions, public actors, and civil society groups. Privatization is acting as a lightning rod for broader discontents over workers' rights, statutory pay and pensions, the quality of service provision and much bigger challenges such as environmental breakdown and aging populations. It has triggered trade union activism and increasingly mainstream leftist politics. Moreover, there is a new, place-based politics emerging in which the focus of political activism is increasingly targeted at private companies and the neoliberal political actors whose projects sustain their power.

There is evidence that local governments, with multiple political allegiances, are acting as one particularly significant focus for resistance to centralized parastate models. In England and beyond they are increasingly re-municipalizing services that had previously been contracted-out owing to inflated costs and public criticism. Cumbers and Becker (2018) define remunicipalization as "the transfer of previously privatized services back into forms of local public ownership and control...and diverse and hybrid forms of non-private collective ownership that have emerged at the local level" (505). The importance of "taking back local control," the authors contend, has emerged internationally as a response to the failures of privatization and a perceived lack of accountability to service users, citizens, and state authorities. They draw on German examples in which grassroots campaigns have emerged in policy fields such as local energy utilities to challenge national and regional policies. But similar processes have been happening in England where local governments are asserting control over parastate bodies who are seen to have failed.

The limits of parastate models are increasingly evident in high-profile cases where reformist local authorities have tried to adopt mass-congratulation models. In London, Barnet Council sought to adopt a so-called EasyCouncil set of reforms in the 2010s that were designed to mimic corporate practices and convert the authority principally into a manager of contractual relations. The implementation has, however, been subject to a series of very public failures and difficulties owing to their cost and complexity. By 2018 the authority finally proposed to bring some services back "in-house" owing to the costs and failures of private provision, particularly by the company Capita that had taken on the majority of professional service contracts on the Council's behalf (Chakarabortty, 2018). Other international examples have highlighted similar difficulties. The city of Maywood in California, for instance, sacked all of its municipal workers in 2010 and contracted-out all government posts (Loewenstein, 2015). However, by 2018 the city authority had launched lawsuits against some of its contractors alleging fraud, once again underlining the difficulties that local governments face is contracting out services (PR Newswire, 2018).

Privatization has also invigorated political activism at a variety of scales. Organizations such as *The People's Assembly* have been particularly active in launching protests and support marches for those campaigning to end or reduce privatization processes. Trade Unions, such as UNISON, have become front-line critics of privatization processes, with its Head of Local Government recently claiming that, "when services are privatised everyone suffers, service quality declines, workforce conditions are eroded and equality considerations take a back seat" (Wakefield, 2018, 1). UNISON has also engaged in rounds of local action, seeing the local context as space through which challenges can be launched. Despite its lack of success in the UK General Election of December 2019, the British Labor Party brought the issue of what it termed "radical insourcing" back into mainstream political debates. This take-up of local activism at the national scale also reflects a wider critical politics emerging internationally. Groups such as *Fearless Cities* (2019) have established global campaigns that seek to coordinate municipal action and empower urban authorities to take control of private-owned and managed infrastructure and services.

At the same time civil society groups have launched fierce campaigns against local welfare managers and privatization programs across England, in part because of a lack of traditional political options through representative systems of democracy. An instructive example is that of challenges made in South East London against private finance-led changes to local hospital services. The Justice for Lewisham Hospital Campaign (2013) challenged the decisions principally by taking the local Health Trust and the UK Government to court to claim that they did not have the technical powers to reconfigure local services in ways that were detrimental to local communities. In some hospitals in England workers subject to private contracts have started to organize strikes with the explicit aim of changing the legislation that enables enhanced private provision (Halliday, 2018). Such examples further reflect the ways in which local welfare services have become the focus for political activism and the repoliticization of neoliberal managerialism that was designed to be beyond politics and focus on efficient forms of delivery.

Conclusions

The chapter has argued that the form and character of the English state has undergone profound changes since the 1980s. New parastate arrangements have emerged under which private companies are directly involved in the development, delivery, and implementation of welfare programs. The first part outlined some of the core characteristics of the parastate and compared and contrasted them to what Crouch (2011) identifies as "pure" market-led systems. It showed that despite claims from reformists that privatization programs represent a marketization of public policy, the rise of the parastate is characterized by new forms of co-constituted policy reform and delivery between public and private actors. It combines many of the weaknesses of market models, (such as a lack of competition and a growing concentration of power in the hands of relatively few firms) with those of traditional state bureaucracies (including the difficulties that state actors have in establishing effective contract procurement systems). Rather than acting as a positive supplement to state capacities, the rise of parastate organizations is therefore having a damaging effect on the ability of the state, particularly local government, to meet growing and rapidly changing demands.

The chapter has also argued that the objective of creating greater "distance" between policymaking and policy delivery, enshrined in the stated objectives of contracting out models since their emergence in the 1980s, has not been met and that there has, in contrast, been a strong politicization along three principle axes: the structural difficulties parastate firms face in adapting to political demands; the perceived inefficiencies of private practice; and the delegitimization of private sector engagement. The reliance of parastate companies on state budgets and procurement practices makes them especially vulnerable to future regulation and reform and the largest parastate firms, including Veolia, Keir, Capita and Serco are seeking to refocus and strengthen their political activities in an effort to prevent "damaging" reforms. Such firms have found that acting on behalf of the state, exposes them to a degree of political scrutiny, at multiple scales, that their delivery and contract-focused managerial systems are ill-equipped to manage.

The longer term implications for welfare states in England and beyond are profound. The accepted social contract under which citizens paid for and received state-led welfare services has been undermined to such an extent that new forms of distance now exist between providers and recipients. Lines of accountability have dissolved, even though it is commonly assumed that governments and state bodies still have responsibility for policies and the implementation of programs. However, recent examples of systematic failures in the parastate model have demonstrated that private companies cannot stay immune from the political pressures that state actors have traditionally faced. The growing *mismatch* between the capacities of private sector managerial models and the complexities of regulated and highly politicized market-states have been increasingly exposed. And while it is relatively easy to initiate privatization programs and reduce number of state employees, the process of re-establishing capacities to make up for private sector failings is a costly and long-term exercise that will require significant inputs of resources. It may take a generation to rebuild state infrastructures that have been systematically undermined by parastate reforms. The chapter has also shown that forms of resistance are emerging at multiple scales and that the parastate is acting as a focus for broader political projects and discontents. These, in the longer run, may bring about deeper changes in the organization of state practices and a return to state-led forms of governance.

And finally, given the increasing role of parastate firms in welfare systems in multiple contexts, it is surprising how little attention they receive in much academic writing on neoliberalism and contemporary reforms. The focus of much work continues to be statist and driven by policy analysis and the interrogation of formal frameworks. The chapter has argued that there should be a stronger focus on private firms themselves—how they are organized, managed, act (in diverse contexts), and are becoming governance agents. This in turn draws attention to private sector codes, laws, ethics, and judgments and how these can be better understood and regulated.

Acknowledgements The author would like to express thanks to Chris Hurl and Anne Vogelpohl for their constructive and supportive thoughts and comments on an earlier draft. The work was supported by the Economic and Social Research Council UK [Grant Number: ES/S015078] under the project "WHIG What is Governed in Cities: Residential investment landscapes and the governance and regulation of housing production."

References

Akoff, R. (1990) 'Redesigning the future', *Systems Practice* 3(6): 521–524.

Bevir, M. and Trentmann, R. (2007) *Governance, Consumers, Citizens*, London: Palgrave.

Braithwaite, J. (2008) *Regulatory Capitalism*, London: Edward Elgar.

Blythe, M. (2013) *Austerity: The History of a Dangerous Idea*, Oxford: Oxford University Press.

Cabinet Office. (2019) *Outsourcing Playbook*, London: HMSO.

Capita. (2018) *Annual Reports and Accounts*, London: Companies House.

Chakarabortty, A. (2018) 'Some call it outsourcing I call it spivvery', *The Guardian*, 23 April, https://www.theguardian.com/commentisfree/2018/apr/23/capita-carillion-outsourcing-local-elections-aditya-chakrabortty, accessed 1 August 2019.

Crouch, C. (2011) *The Strange Non-Death of Neo-liberalism*, Cambridge: Polity Press.

Cumbers, A. and Becker, S. (2018) 'Making sense of re-municiapalisation: Theoretical reflections on and political possibilities from Germany's *Rekommumalisierung* process', *Cambridge Journal of Regions, Economy and Society* 11(3): 503–517.

Du Gay, P. and Lopdrup-Hjorth, T. (2016) 'Fear of the formal', *European Journal of Cultural and Political Sociology* 3(1): 6–40.

Espeland, W. and Stevens, M. (1998) 'Commensuration as a social process', *Annual Review of Sociology* 24: 313–343.

Fearless Cities. (2019) *A Guide to the Global Municipalist Movement,* London: New Internationalist.

Financial Times. (2019) 'Probation services renationalised after chaotic privatisation', 6 May.

Froud, J., Johal, S., Moran, M. and Williams, K. (2017) 'Outsourcing the state: New sources of elite power,' *Theory, Culture and Society* 34(2): 77–101.

Government Commercial Function. (2019) *Market Management—Guidance Note*, London: HMSO.

Halliday, J. (2018) 'NHS hospital staff to strike over 'back door privatisation' in Bradford', *The Guardian*, 8 July, https://www.theguardian.com/society/2019/jul/08/nhs-hospital-staff-bradford-strike-backdoor-privatisation?CMP=Share_AndroidApp_Gmail, accessed 12 July 2019.

House of Commons. (2018a) *After Carillion: Public Sector Outsourcing and Contracting*, London: HMSO.

House of Commons. (2018b) *Carillion*, London: HMSO.

Jessop, B. (1999) 'The Dynamics of Partnership and Governance Failure', in G. Stoker (ed.) *The New Politics of Local Governance in Britain*, Basingstoke: Macmillan, pp. 11–32.

Justice for Lewisham Hospital Campaign. (2013) *High Court quashes decision by Jeremy Hunt to close Lewisham Hospital*, 31 July, http://www.savelewishamhospital.com/latest-news/victory-for-lewisham-hospital-as-high-court-quashes-jeremy-hunts-decision, accessed 12 July 2019.

Keir Ltd. (2019) *Annual Report and Accounts 2018–2019*, London: Keir Group.

Loewenstein, A. (2015) *Disaster Capitalism: Making a Killing Out of Catastrophe*, London: Verso.

Meek, J. (2013) *Private Island: Why Britain Now Belongs to Someone Else*, London: Verso.

Miller, D. (2002) 'Turning Callon the right way up', *Economy and Society* 31, 218–233.

Mirowski, P. (2002) *Machine Dreams; Economics Becomes a Cyborg Science*, Cambridge: Cambridge University Press.

Murphy, R. (2011) *The Courageous State—Rethinking Economics, Society and the Role of Government*, London: Searching Finance Publications.

National Audit Office. (2017) *Housing in England: An Overview*, London: HMSO.

National Audit Office. (2018) *PFI and PFI2*, London: HMSO.

Newman, J. and Clarke, J. (2009) *Publics, Politics, and Power*, London: Sage.

Newman, J. and Clarke, J. (2018) 'The instabilities of expertise: Remaking knowledge, power and politics in unsettled times', *Innovation: The European Journal of Social Science Research* 31(1): 40–54.

Pennington, M. (2002) *Liberating the Land: The Case for Private Land-use Planning*, London: Institute of Economic Affairs.

Penny, J. (2017) 'Between coercion and consent: The politics of cooperative governance at a time of austerity localism in London', *Urban Geography* 38(9), 1352–1373.

PR Newswire. (2018) 'The City of Maywood files lawsuit against its contracted waste Hauler Consolidated Disposal Service, LLC and Republic Services, Inc', *PR Newswire*, 26 March, https://www.prnewswire.com/news-rel

eases/the-city-of-maywood-files-lawsuit-against-its-contracted-waste-hauler-consolidated-disposal-service-llc-and-republic-services-inc-300619009.html, accessed 1 August 2019.

Serco Ltd. (2011) *Annual Report and Accounts 2010–2011*, London: Serco.

Thrift, N. (2008) *Knowing Capitalism*, London: Sage.

Veolia Ltd. (2018) *Annual Report and Accounts 2017–2018*, London: Veolia Ltd.

Vogl, J. (2017) *The Ascendancy of Finance*, Cambridge: Polity Press.

Wakefield, H. (2018) *Privatisation*, Unison, https://www.unison.org.uk/at-work/local-government/key-issues/privatisation/, accessed 12 July 2019.

Expert Advice? Assessing the Role of the State in Promoting Privatized Planning

Neha Sami and Shriya Anand

Introduction

Over the last two decades, non-state actors, especially corporate players like consultants, have emerged as much more central to and visible in contemporary urban and regional planning processes. Often, as Weinstein (2010) notes, they help to legitimize developmental agendas and policies that the state feels both obliged and constrained to pursue. The failure of the state to "control the city" has led to demands for increased private involvement and control of city building and infrastructure from middle and upper-middle-class urban residents (Shatkin, 2011).

There has also been a shift globally toward an increasing and active presence of hybrid actors, and private or quasi-private authorities that are often enabled by, but are also increasingly taking the place of, local and regional state agencies in erstwhile state-managed planning and governing processes (Balakrishnan, 2019; Anand and Sami, 2016; Sami, 2013, 2017; Shatkin, 2017; Kundu, 2011; Vogelpohl and Klemp, 2018). There is a

N. Sami (✉) · S. Anand
Indian Institute for Human Settlements, Bangalore, India
e-mail: nsami@iihs.ac.in

S. Anand
e-mail: sanand@iihs.ac.in

C. Hurl and A. Vogelpohl (eds.), *Professional Service Firms and Politics in a Global Era*, https://doi.org/10.1007/978-3-030-72128-2_14

need to understand the implications that this has for urban governance for existing as well as emerging urban settlements.

Our broader research question addresses the role of the state as a facilitator in enabling the increasing prominence of consultants in formerly state-run and managed planning processes; the policies and processes that have enabled this; and the implications this has for governance processes and equitable urbanization. We demonstrate this through two different types of planning processes: first, the development of master plans at the urban/regional scale, and second, the planning of large-scale industrial infrastructure projects such as infrastructure corridors and industrial areas.

Drawing on primary research across four states—Delhi, Karnataka (focusing on the greater Bangalore region), Rajasthan, and Gujarat—as well as analyses of government reports, plans, and policy documents, we make two key arguments. First, we argue that it is important to analyze the *process* by which consultants are gaining prominence in planning processes and not only the *outcomes* of their involvement. Secondly, we show how there have been multiple policies, programs, and legislative shifts within the state that have actively created the opportunities for consultants to take over former public functions. Finally, using the case of Infrastructure Leasing & Financial Services (IL&FS), a prominent Indian private infrastructure firm, we demonstrate the ways in which the state has enabled the outsourcing of certain public functions and the consequences.

The enhanced involvement of private consultants in public planning is a concern for multiple reasons that other researchers have also pointed out, including the erosion of local capacity within government, the disregard for existing knowledge within public administration, neglecting demands for broader participation, and the insertion of private players and resources into government processes (Sadoway et al., 2018; Vogelpohl and Klemp, 2018). Consultants involved in contemporary planning processes rarely embed themselves in local practice and culture, which continues to result in master plans and infrastructure projects that often fail to address the needs and requirements of existing and emerging urban settlements (Sami, 2017).

We begin this paper by placing our research in the context of other work that has been done on the role of consultants in planning and development processes in India and elsewhere. We use the processes of master planning and planning of mega infrastructure projects to demonstrate how the role of the state as the facilitator has encouraged the involvement of consultants in former state-run and managed activities. We find that the locus of the state's functions have shifted in the Indian context, from making the plans themselves to hiring and managing consultants through increasingly complex contracting arrangements. We emphasize that this is not merely a question of a lack of capacity: the state also exercises agency and control in determining the modalities through which consultants engage, thereby shaping the processes and outcomes of plans. We conclude by arguing for a better and more nuanced understanding of the relationship between the government and corporate actors, and pointing to future directions for research.

Contextualizing the Role of Consultants in Planning

Globally, there has been a set of trends in the past few decades such as the increasing use of new technologies such as GIS and increasingly complex planning processes that has enabled the outsourcing of former public functions, such as planning, to private consultants (Loh and Norton, 2013, 2015; Shatkin, 2017; Sami, 2017). At the same time, there has been a growing application of the new public management paradigm in the Asian context in the form of an increased emphasis on efficiency, and bringing private management practices into the public sector (Cheung, 2005). Over time, this, along with budgetary cuts or fiscal austerity measures at local levels, has led to a reduction in permanent staff within government and planning agencies, which constrain the ability of local governments to retain skilled staff that can carry out these specialized tasks (Sadoway et al., 2018; Personal interview with faculty at Chulalongkorn University, Bangkok).

At the same time, there remains a shortage of trained professionals that are able to deal with urban challenges in the global South, leading to a crippling scarcity of expertise in Southern cities (Banerjee, 2009; Sami, 2017). The emergence of consultants as key actors is also therefore a way of bringing in "external input ... to counter limited local capacity and confidence," leading to "international development discourse and national policy imperatives fram(ing) local strategy formation" (Sami, 2017; Parnell and Robinson, 2012, 337).

Partnerships between regional and local governments and international experts like consultants also enable governments to keep pace with and participate in contemporary global policy ideas and debates around issues such as sustainability, economic development, and good governance. Southern cities often leverage these partnerships with experts to learn from other contexts and to attract global investments (Bunnell and Das, 2010). For example, in the field of resilience planning, recent work has highlighted the desire of some local governments to align with new international commitments and a shifting global discourse around sustainability, and to demonstrate their commitment to addressing climate change through the formulation of high profile plans (Weinstein et al., 2019).

Networks of consultants—including both global and domestic, large and small firms—have enabled the transfer of so-called transnational "fast policy learning" that has emphasized rapid analyses, technocratic modelling, and the promise of effective strategies to deal with crises (Peck and Theodore, 2010; Vogelpohl and Klemp, 2018; Bunnell and Das, 2010). Datta (2015, 6), writing about plans for emerging urban settlements along industrial corridors in India, reflects on "how the 'global intelligence corps' (Olds, 2011, cited in Datta, 2015) as vested in companies like McKinsey, Halcrow, and Cisco contribute to 'policy mobility'" (Peck, 2002, cited in Datta, 2015). Vogelpohl and Klemp (2018) highlight the means by which consulting firms like McKinsey influence city plans by stabilizing and establishing a consensus around economic growth as key for development, but also leveraging connections within city governments. This highlights how consultants build coalitions with key government agencies or individual powerful actors to gain traction in policymaking.

Consultants, and large multinational/global firms in particular, have also enabled the movement of particular ideas around urban development, promoting urban fantasies and specific forms of urban imaginaries (Watson, 2014; Bunnell and Das, 2010; Bombay First and McKinsey & Company, 2003). Research on the role of consultants in planning has also focused on their influence on the master plan relative to state agencies, and their role in the privatization of community participation (Loh and Norton, 2015; Raco et al., 2016). Several of these studies emphasize the outcomes of the growing involvement of consultants in public planning processes as well as their entrepreneurial nature.

The Role of External Experts in the Indian Context

There has been extensive writing on the role of foreign and private expertise in planning Indian cities in the post-Independence era, particularly during the 1950s and 1960s. Because of a lack of local capacity in India, foreign architects, planners, sociologists, as well as Western design and engineering firms were centrally involved in urban planning for a set of cities including Delhi, Kolkata, Gandhinagar, Chandigarh, Bhubaneswar, and Jamshedpur (Kalia, 1994, 1999, 2004; Sinha and Singh, 2011; Sundaram, 2015). Writing about urban planning in India and the role of international experts, Banerjee (2005, 147) highlights three distinct phases of modern urban planning for Indian cities: "the British town planning tradition during the colonial era, followed by the post-colonial Ford Foundation paradigm, and finally the current era of economic liberalization and globalisation." He argues that with the involvement of institutions like the Ford Foundation, a shift began in Indian urban planning that was not embedded in local planning culture and to which the local public remained outsiders (Banerjee, 2005).

Even though Indian urban planning practice relied extensively on foreign experts and knowledge during the Nehruvian era (1947–1964), these experts were considered necessary "to acquire the capabilities for a self-directed, import-substituting industrialisation and the realization of a national economic space" (Levien, 2013, 386).[1] The use of foreign experts also provided a way of addressing the lack of planning programs and institutions to train domestic architects and planners who could cope with the task of building new cities for a newly independent country (Kalia, 1999).

Planning in the Economic Liberalization era (post-1991) represents a disconnect from those earlier models of foreign reliance (see Purandare in this volume).[2] Not only has the type and nature of the work changed, but also the kind of experts that are appointed and the processes by which

[1] The Nehruvian Era was a period of approximately 18 years following independence from British colonial rule in 1947 when Jawaharlal Nehru was Prime Minister of India. His tenure was characterized by an emphasis on state-led planning and state-promoted industrialisation coupled with economic policies such as import substitution.

[2] India faced a severe Balance of Payments crisis in 1991, and had to be bailed out by international institutions like the IMF. In response to conditionalities imposed by lenders, India implemented sweeping economic reforms which included opening up of its economy

they are identified and hired (Sami, 2017). For instance, Datta's (2015) work on Dholera points to the distinction between the kind of planning pursued currently and the earlier plans put forward by visionary architects and planners. As Kalia (2006) writes, a newly independent India was faced with the challenge of housing resettled refugees, providing new capitals for newly formed states, and signifying a departure from its colonial history while indicating the potential for an independent future. The purpose of inviting visionary architects and planners to plan cities in post-independence India at that time was to build cities "unfettered by tradition," while simultaneously providing training grounds for emerging, home-grown planners and architects (Kalia, 2006, 134). In contrast, the plans for Dholera and other settlements like it along the proposed Industrial Corridors in India represent a form of "entrepreneurial urbanism," involving increased emphasis on corporate values within government processes, as well the growing influence of consultants, who see urban development as a form of product development, leveraging their networks to expand to multiple locations and projects to gain clients and projects (Datta, 2015, 19).[3]

The State as Facilitator

National and regional governments in the Indian context have been instrumental in opening up opportunities for non-state actors. This has emerged, in part, from a need to retain power over urban regions, but also partly from India's fragmented governance structure. There are also pressures to compete economically at the international level as well as

to international capital. The period post-1991 following these reforms is referred to as the Economic Liberalisation era.

[3] There is a wide body of work on the increasing entrepreneurial nature of governments, beginning with David Harvey's (1989) seminal work Harvey, D. (1989) 'From managerialism to entrepreneurialism: The transformation in urban governance in late capitalism', *Geografiska Annaler: Series B, Human Geography* 71(1): 3–17. More has been written lately focusing particularly on urban governments and processes of planning Peck, J. (2014) 'Entrepreneurial urbanism: Between uncommon sense and dull compulsion', *Geografiska Annaler: Series B, Human Geography* 96(4): 396–401, Datta, A. (2015a) 'New urban utopias of postcolonial India "Entrepreneurial urbanization" in Dholera smart city, Gujarat', *Dialogues in Human Geography* 5(1): 3–22, Ward, K. (2003) 'Entrepreneurial urbanism, state restructuring and civilizing "New" East Manchester', *Area* 35(2): 116–127.

inter-regional economic competition that are playing out increasingly in urban regions (Bunnell and Das, 2010; Mitra, 2015).

Over the past three decades since economic liberalization, national and regional governments in India have created new institutions and processes across scales to deal with the challenges that come with rapid urbanization. This proliferation of actors and institutions across different levels of government often leads to even more administrative, managerial, and political difficulties, transforming the nature of urban politics in India (Milbert, 2008; Sami, 2012; Weinstein, 2010). This has manifested itself in different ways in the case of master plans and infrastructure development. Focusing on two different types of planning processes has enabled us to examine the different mechanisms that the state has used to enable the greater involvement of consultants in planning (see Raco in this volume).

Here we highlight three sets of processes through which this has taken place, each of which we explain in detail in the sub-sections below. The first set includes policy & legislative shifts that have led to an increasing reliance on consultants for the development of urban master plans and city development plans. The second set focuses on how the increasing scale and complexity of infrastructure projects and conditionalities imposed by donors have led to an increasing involvement of consultants and other corporate actors in planning and governing processes. Finally, the third set of processes examines the use of institutional mechanisms such as Special Purpose Vehicles (SPVs) and Public–Private Partnerships (PPPs) to embed private actors in public processes, using improvements in efficiency as a rationale.

Policy and Legislative Shifts

With economic liberalization in the early 1990s, urban regions in India emerged as key drivers of economic growth and targets for domestic and international investment. Regional and local governments have simultaneously been competing to attract domestic and international investment while struggling to provide basic services and infrastructure to an ever-increasing urban population. However, these governments did not have (and continue to lack) the capacity to deal with the demands that came from global capital and competing economic interests while keeping pace with rapidly transforming urban environments. Urban renewal and reform therefore emerged as a key component of the national government's policy agenda.

The national government's response to these challenges has been twofold. The first was to create urban development agendas through large government-sponsored urban reform programs like the Jawaharlal Nehru National Urban Renewal Mission (JNNURM) and the Atal Mission for Rejuvenation and Urban Transformation (AMRUT).[4] Through these programs, the national government made funds available to selected cities for infrastructure projects, conditional on them introducing a specified set of reforms. The second response was to invite non-state actors especially private sector companies and multilateral agencies like the Asian Development Bank (ADB), and the World Bank to participate in the planning and development of infrastructure as well as urban planning processes (Ministry of Finance, 2007; Kundu, 2011; Kamath, 2006; Ghosh, 2005; Balakrishnan, 2019; Shatkin, 2017; Sami, 2013).

One of the key requirements for cities to access funding under JNNURM was the formulation of City Development Plans (CDPs) that indicated "policies, programmes and strategies, and financing, followed by Detailed Project Reports (DPRs) for identified projects" (Mahadevia, 2006, 3400). However, given the specificity of the requirements, many of the cities, irrespective of their size, included under JNNURM lacked in-house capacity to do so (Mahadevia, 2006; Ministry of Urban Development, 2006; Ministry of Urban Development, 2005; Sami, 2017). The aim was to make Indian cities attractive to investors, while also building

[4] The Jawaharlal Nehru National Urban Renewal Mission (JNNURM) was India's first large, post-independence urban reform sponsored by the national government. Launched in December 2005, it provided support to about 65 Indian cities of different sizes, estimated at approximately USD 20 billion, to implement reforms structured by two sub-missions: Urban Infrastructure and Governance and Basis Services to the Urban Poor. Sivaramakrishnan, K.C. (2011) *Re-visioning Indian Cities: The Urban Renewal Mission*. New Delhi, India: Sage Publications India Pvt, Ltd, Mukhopadhyay, P. (2006) 'Whither urban renewal?', *Economic and Political Weekly* 41(10): 879–884, Ministry of Urban Development (2006) *Jawaharlal Nehru National Urban Renewal Mission*: Ministry of Urban Development. Available at: http://jnnurm.nic.in/, accessed 22 February 2011.

The Atal Mission for Rejuvenation and Urban Transformation (AMRUT) is the successor to the JNNURM with an explicit focus on water supply, sewerage and sanitation; urban transport; and the creation of green spaces in cities. Ministry of Housing and Urban Affairs (2020) *Atal Mission for Rejuvenation and Urban Transformation*. New Delhi, India: Ministry of Housing and Urban Affairs. Available at: http://amrut.gov.in/content/, accessed 13 August 2020.

capacity within local governments (Sadoway et al., 2018). However, instead of strengthening local capacity, the program structure did quite the opposite: by imposing short turnaround times and stringent timelines for the development, and by pushing city governments to turn to an empanelled list of consultants, the JNNURM opened the door to direct private sector involvement in urban planning processes in Indian cities (Sadoway et al., 2018; Mahadevia, 2006).

Further, as Sadoway et al. (2018) demonstrate, the template that JNNURM created for the engagement and involvement of consultants in urban planning has been replicated in current government programs such as AMRUT and the Smart Cities Mission (SCM). While there were similar visions in other parts of Asia, and indeed globally, India's SCM that aims to create and push 100 Smart Cities stands out for a few reasons: the scale and scope of the undertaking, the investment required, and its departure from earlier forms of planning (Datta, 2015; Bunnell, 2015). As Bunnell (2015, 46) writes, "India's smart plans... appear to diagnose a context in which the technical services and expertise of high-tech companies have become integral to the very envisioning of (smarter) futures." The SCM, in fact, mandated that, in order to be selected for the mission, cities would have to consult with Bloomberg Philanthropies, work with empanelled consultants, and employ multinational companies such as IBM and CISCO to implement these plans (Reddy, 2016; Sadoway et al., 2018). The increasing role of corporate actors in the SCM as well as other infrastructure projects tend to limit the possibility of citizen involvement in reimagining our cities (Datta, 2015; Kummitha, 2019).

Although JNNURM was instrumental in facilitating the initial transition to using private sector consultants, local planning agencies (like the parastatals) were also eager to bring in external experts. In some of the larger cities like Bangalore, the shift toward contracting private consultants to make the Master Plans had taken place a few years earlier. For example, the new Karnataka state government elected in 1999 emphasized urban development and reform focusing on upgrading infrastructure and implementing policies that would enable Bangalore to face stiff competition from other cities like Hyderabad and Pune.[5] Recognizing that the Bangalore Development Authority (BDA), the chief planning

[5] The Karnataka state government implemented a range of policies including generous financial incentives and access to land to attract information technology companies specifically to locate in Bangalore away from other cities like Hyderabad and Pune that were

agency for Bangalore, lacked the capacity to deliver such a plan, the state government and its pool of advisors recommended bringing in external consultants. It was the first time since its inception that the BDA did not make the master plan for the city, and this practice has continued since then (Sundaresan, 2013; Sami, 2017).

The preparation of plans by consultants has also had important implications for the outcomes of planned development. As our work in the case of Bangalore has shown, for example, three successive plans were drawn up by international consulting firms with little familiarity or local knowledge of the particular challenges and constraints the city faced (Sami, 2017; Sundaresan, 2013). These plans had minimal public participation and have been stalled due to litigation that contests the validity of the plans, as well as the process undertaken to develop them. As a result, the city has effectively been without a legally sanctioned Master Plan for the past two and a half decades, leading to uncontrolled development, and unsustainable growth trajectories for Bangalore.

While the above case illustrates the planning process for the Bangalore Metro Region, smaller towns and cities in India are facing similar situations. The requirement to prepare CDPs has led them to also try to find expertise in order to help them prepare these plans (Mahadevia, 2006). In addition to public programs such as the JNNURM, AMRUT, and the Smart Cities Mission, there have also been legislative shifts that have encouraged the involvement of private actors in urban development. For instance, the Special Economic Zones Act passed in 2005 actively facilitated the development of industrial townships by private actors, encouraging the private provision of infrastructure and services, and leading to the creating of urban enclaves and "clubs," promoting what the authors term as "corporate urbanisation" (Sood, 2015; Jenkins et al., 2014).

The shifts in legislation and policy governing master planning have also, as we shall see below, paralleled an increase in the scale and complexity of infrastructure projects that planners need to contend with.

also aiming to become destinations for technology companies. Benjamin, S. (2006) *Inclusive or Contested? Conceptualising a Globalized Bangalore* via *a closer look at territories of the IT dominated territories in East and South Bangalore*: IDPAD (1), Benjamin, S., Bhuvaneswari, R., Rajan, P. and Manjunath ibid. *'Fractured' Terrain, Spaces left over, or Contested? A closer look at territories of the IT dominated territories in East and South Bangalore* (2).

Scale, Complexity, and Conditionalities

With the renewed emphasis on urban infrastructure investment, the national government has also pushed specific types of industrial and economic development policies that have led to the emergence of different kinds of settlements, including the development of industrial corridors between major Indian cities (Anand and Sami, 2016). Here, we use the case of one of these: the Delhi-Mumbai Industrial Corridor (DMIC), which is planned as a mega-region for industrial development along a Dedicated Freight Corridor (DFC) linking Delhi and Mumbai. The project passes through 6 states, and involves the development of multiple industrial cities and nodes in the buffer region of the freight corridor, which will act as the spine. This has been described as a project of an unprecedented scale in the Indian context (Kumar, 2015), and the project itself was conceived by the Indian national government in partnership with the Government of Japan, and modelled on the Tokyo-Osaka Corridor. The project was originally proposed in 2005, but implementation has been delayed with various sub-projects currently at different stages of planning and development.

In the case of infrastructure mega-projects of increasing ambition and scale such as the DMIC, the projects themselves require increasingly complex financial instruments and arrangements, bringing in layers of intermediaries and special institutions to manage the flow of funds (Cantarelli and Flyvbjerg, 2013; Flyvbjerg, 2009). To illustrate, consider the case of Infrastructure Leasing & Financial Services (IL&FS), which was the Project Master Consultant for the DMIC. IL&FS is a private Indian financial and consulting firm (see below). The overall project plan for the DMIC was prepared by IL&FS, in partnership with Scott Wilson, a private consulting firm. The role of IL&FS was not restricted to preparing the overall project plan alone. They were also responsible for planning multiple smaller projects within the DMIC, but significantly, they also worked with state governments to select consultants for planning the individual nodes and projects within their jurisdictions (Anand and Sami, 2016).

The role of IL&FS as Project Master Consultant, and in selecting other consultants for the other sub-projects of the DMIC highlights how the government relied on specialized agencies to bring in the knowledge required to plan a project at this scale. Our interviews also highlight that the rationale for bringing in consultants might be a fundamental incompatibility of the governmental setup with the requirements of implementing a mega-project of a certain scale and timeline. Quoting a respondent who was speaking about the DFC, which forms the spine of the DMIC, "This is probably the largest project in the transport sector in the world. The Railway ministry is essentially an Operations & Maintenance organization. They cannot deal with large project implementation – bureaucrats are only around to serve time. This scale of project development needs a specific skill set/problem solving ability – needs to be mega-scale for a mega-project. The Railway ministry is typically focused on problem solving at the micro-scale" (Personal interview with a former senior official at the DFC, 2017). This shows the limits on the capacity of the existing administrative machinery to take on the planning of a large, greenfield project of this nature, and therefore, explaining the rationale for the reliance on external expertise.

Often, our fieldwork also revealed situations where the government did not choose to hire consultants for a particular role, but was forced to do so by multilateral agencies or other partners. For example, in the DFC case, the use of consultants at the overall project scale was imposed by the funders (in this case, it was the ADB), and was not a choice of the government itself. The complexities of these projects as well as the conditionalities imposed by lending institutions reveal that there are multiple reasons and processes by which the government engaged with private firms for planning and implementation. Further, new modalities such as Special Purpose Vehicles (SPVs) are needed to be created in order to manage these projects, as we discuss in the next section.

Institutional Mechanisms

There has been a shift within the national government, and consequently at sub-national levels, in how the process of master planning as well as the implementation of urban infrastructure improvement projects are structured. There is a growing acceptance among public officials and politicians that government agencies alone cannot cope with the demands made from rapid urbanization and the infrastructure and development needs that come with it. Several national government documents have indicated that Public–Private Partnerships (PPPs) are not only desirable but also essential to fulfill the needs of an urbanizing India. A Ministry of Finance report from 2007 lays out in detail the process for engaging in PPPs specifically for large urban infrastructure projects (Ministry of Finance, 2007). This also lays out the structure and architecture of Special Purpose Vehicles (SPVs) that have now become critical to the routing of funds, and the planning, management and governing of large infrastructure at the urban and regional scale.

This has led to a proliferation of SPVs across urban regions with changes in the structure of agencies tasked with the building of urban infrastructure: for example, the Bangalore Metro Rail Corporation Limited (BMRCL) is structured as a SPV with a Managing Director and the ability to raise funds independently through a range of financial instruments including bonds (Bangalore Metro Rail Corporation Limited [BMRCL], 2020). This is true also of various agencies across the city that have been created for the development of "Smart City" projects (Ministry of Housing and Urban Affairs, 2016), as well as for the various projects emerging along the proposed Industrial Corridors. There is a transition therefore, beginning in 2007 (Ministry of Finance, 2007), that has pushed more corporate-type structures and processes in urban planning and development.

This is a concern, not only because officials in these agencies are appointed and not elected, but also because they often comprise of private players from consulting firms who are seconded to these agencies. As interviews with key informants involved in the planning of the DMIC have shown, the SPVs that have been created to deal with complex project management and planning processes are gradually transitioning into critical regional governance roles as well, in the absence of locally elected governments in these emerging settlements. This limits the possibilities for elected governments to emerge in these new industrial cities as power becomes increasingly entrenched within these existing structures. The following section uses the case of a private Indian financial and consulting firm to show how these state mechanisms allowed a corporate actor to gain power and the consequences thereof.

The Case of IL&FS

IL&FS is a private Indian infrastructure development and finance company, comprising of over 200 subsidiary companies, that "houses the expertise to provide the complete array of services necessary for successful project completion — from visioning, documentation, development and finance, to management, technology and execution" (Infrastructure

Leasing & Financial Services Limited, 2017). IL&FS was originally established in the late 1980s to fill a gap that existed in the market for a financing institution that could provide loans for long-gestation infrastructure projects. It was originally formed with equity from public banks and financial institutions with the purpose of financing infrastructure projects. Over the years, IL&FS expanded its shareholding pattern to also include some overseas institutional investors as well as private financing companies, and became the holding company for a large group of companies that played numerous roles including infrastructure planning and financing.

Since its inception, IL&FS has been involved in infrastructure projects across multiple sectors and for both public and private clients, in some cases as a financing institution and in others, performing an advisory role. For the DMIC, it acted as the Project Management Consultant, as well as an equity partner in an SPV that was setup to coordinate the implementation of the project across multiple jurisdictions. It also advised regional governments on the selection of consultants for the planning of their respective industrial areas.

However, in 2018, IL&FS underwent a serious crisis, which ultimately led to it defaulting on its loan obligations, triggering a crisis in the Non-Banking Financial Companies (NBFCs, or shadow banks) in India. Widely termed in Indian media as India's "Lehman moment," IL&FS, as a financial institution that was "too big to fail," was bailed out by the Indian government, who constituted a new board of directors for the company and set up a series of inquiries into its dealings. The IL&FS crisis subsequently had serious implications for both the banking and the urban real estate sector, as well as for the infrastructure projects that IL&FS companies were managing and funding.

One reason for the state bailout of IL&FS was the fact that critical public sector financial institutions (Life Insurance Corporation of India, and the State Bank of India) were shareholders of the company.[6] Other reasons included the extent and nature of IL&FS' involvement in the financial sector, and the repercussions its default would have had on credit markets. The report of the Serious Fraud Investigation Office that

[6] The Life Insurance Corporation of India (LIC) an Indian insurance group and investment corporation owned by the Government of India.

The State Bank of India is an Indian multinational, public sector banking and financial services statutory body.

followed from a 9-month investigation into IL&FS' dealings revealed collusion between the management of IL&FS and the auditors (the Indian arms of Deloitte, and KPMG), which led to falsification of the books of accounts and financial statements in the 5 years leading up to the loan defaults in 2018.

The impacts of a corporate governance failure in this case had wide-ranging repercussions for a large portfolio of public infrastructure projects, several of which were stalled or seriously delayed. Not much work has attempted to estimate the public costs or losses imposed by the IL&FS default, partly because of the opacity of the financial data involved. However, an interview with a former director of Gujarat International Finance Tec (GIFT) City reveals the various mechanisms through which the loss to the exchequer might have occurred (Srivas, 2018).

GIFT City was considered Prime Minister Narendra Modi's pet project to build an international finance tech-city in his home state of Gujarat. IL&FS was the private partner in developing GIFT City, and held a 50% stake in GIFT. In 2015, its first independent director, and former head of the board's audit committee, filed a Public Interest Litigation (PIL) against GIFT City, particularly focused on the role of IL&FS. In the PIL, he raised several issues about the public nature of the project, and about undue benefits to IL&FS. On the former, he noted that despite being a public project, GIFT City is not subject to requests under the Right to Information Act, and does not undergo audits by the Comptroller and Auditor General of India.[7] Regarding the question of undue benefits to IL&FS, the PIL highlights the following reasons that cause a loss to the public exchequer: charging of management fees despite being an equity partner, being granted effective control over the land and not paying fees to the state government of Gujarat in violation of agreements, as well as awarding service contracts to the subsidiaries of IL&FS, constituting a conflict of interest (Srivas, 2018). However, IL&FS has refuted these charges, and the matter remains sub-judice since hearings have been delayed and are now temporarily halted in the light of the COVID-19 pandemic (ibid.).

[7] The Comptroller and Auditor General (CAG) of India is is empowered to audit all expenses from the combined fund of the union or state governments.

The Right to Information Act (2005) is an Act of the Parliament of India that lays out the rules, regulations, and processes by which citizens of India may request information under the control of public authorities.

The case of IL&FS demonstrates how the state, because of its investments in IL&FS through publicly owned financial institutions, allowed a private firm to participate in and benefit from public planning projects, with little to no accountability, and was not subject to public scrutiny. In addition to the costs to the exchequer, which are still emerging, this case also demonstrates the implications of private participation on critical public infrastructure projects as well as cascading effects on land markets, communities, and livelihoods.

Conclusion

In this paper, we have attempted to highlight the different policy, legislative and institutional mechanisms that the state has employed to facilitate the growing involvement of consultants in planning and governing urban regions in India. In doing so, we attempt to highlight that the state in the Indian context has not been a passive recipient of global trends toward a privatization of planning (Shatkin, 2008, 2011), but rather has actively participated in creating the conditions for these shifts and also in shaping the terms on which these engagements take place. Emphasizing the process by which the state has enabled these engagements and transitions has allowed us to point to ways in which the state has facilitated the growing corporatization of public planning processes and its potential outcomes for transparency and accountability in the planning process.

We have also used the case of a private Indian financial and consulting firm to highlight how the state has allowed private entities to profit from public projects with little accountability. While urban studies researchers have often focused on the role of financialization in land markets and its implications for urban development (Shatkin, 2017; Mitra, 2015), there is not enough research that investigates the fallout of these kinds of lending practices and corporate governance on urban areas and infrastructure projects. We need to assess the consequences of these trends for public participation, costs to the public exchequer, and eventually to understand the cities that are being built or improved through these processes.

Our work also raises questions about the challenges that come with entrusting private, corporate players alone with the responsibility of public functions such as these—leading to financial irregularities, lack of accountability, and a violation of democratic reforms that mandate public participation and decentralized representative governance. All of these are important to investigate in future research.

Acknowledgment This article was completed with support from the PEAK Urban programme, funded by UKRI's Global Challenge Research Fund, Grant Ref: ES/P011055/1.

References

Anand, S. and Sami, N. (2016) 'Scaling up, scaling down: State rescaling along the Delhi–Mumbai industrial corridor', *Review of Urban Affairs, Economic & Political Weekly* 51(17): 51.

Balakrishnan, S. (2019) *Shareholder Cities: Land Transformations Along Urban Corridors in India*, Philadelphia, PA: University of Pennsylvania Press.

Banerjee, T. (2005) 'Understanding planning cultures: The Kolkata paradox', in B. Sanyal (ed). *Comparative Planning Cultures*, New York: Routledge, pp. 145–164.

Banerjee, T. (2009) 'US planning expeditions to postcolonial India: From ideology to innovation in technical assistance', *Journal of the American Planning Association* 75(2): 193–208.

Bangalore Metro Rail Corporation Limited (BMRCL) (2020) *Namma Metro*, Bangalore, Karnataka: Bangalore Metro Rail Corporation Limited (BMRCL), https://english.bmrc.co.in/AboutUs, accessed 3 September 2020.

Bombay First and McKinsey & Company (2003) *Vision Mumbai*, Mumbai: Bombay First.

Bunnell, T. (2015) 'Smart city returns', *Dialogues in Human Geography* 5(1): 45–48.

Bunnell, T. and Das, D. (2010) 'Urban pulse—A geography of serial seduction: Urban policy transfer from Kuala Lumpur to Hyderabad', *Urban Geography* 31(3): 277–284.

Cantarelli, C.C. and Flyvbjerg, B. (2013) '15. Mega-projects' cost performance and lock-in: Problems and solutions', *International Handbook on Mega-Projects*, 333.

Cheung, A.B. (2005) 'The politics of administrative reforms in Asia: Paradigms and legacies, paths and diversities', *Governance* 18(2): 257–282.

Datta, A. (2015) 'New urban utopias of postcolonial India "Entrepreneurial urbanization" in Dholera smart city, Gujarat', *Dialogues in Human Geography* 5(1): 3–22.

Flyvbjerg, B. (2009) 'Survival of the unfittest: Why the worst infrastructure gets built—And what we can do about it', *Oxford Review of Economic Policy* 25(3): 344–367.

Ghosh, A. (2005) 'Public-private or a private public: Promised partnership of the Bangalore Agenda Task Force', *Economic and Political Weekly* [Special article].

Harvey, D. (1989) 'From managerialism to entrepreneurialism: The transformation in urban governance in late capitalism', *Geografiska Annaler: Series B, Human Geography* 71(1): 3–17.

Infrastructure Leasing & Financial Services Limited (2017) *IL&FS*: Infrastructure Leasing & Financial Services Limited, https://www.ilfsindia.com/, accessed 16 September 2020.

Jenkins, R. Kennedy, L. and Mukhopadhyay, P. (2014) *Power, Policy, and Protest: The Politics of India's Special Economic Zones*, Oxford University Press.

Kalia, R. (1994) *Bhubaneswar: From a Temple Town to a Capital City*, SIU Press.

Kalia, R. (1999) *Chandigarh: The Making of an Indian City*, New Delhi: Oxford University Press.

Kalia, R. (2004) *Gandhinagar: Building National Identity in Postcolonial India*, University of South Carolina Press.

Kalia, R. (2006) 'Modernism, modernization and post colonial India: A reflective essay', *Planning Perspectives* 21(2): 133–156.

Kamath, L. (2006) *Achieving global competitiveness and local poverty reduction? Examining the public-private partnering model of governance in Bangalore, India*. Doctor of Philosophy, Rutgers, New Jersey: The State University of New Jersey, New Brunswick.

Kumar, R. (2015) 'The world's largest infrastructure project is being built in India—Stretching from Delhi to Mumbai', *Scroll*, www.scroll.in. Available: Scroll, http://scroll.in/article/746736/the-worlds-largest-infrastructure-project-is-being-built-in-india-stretching-from-delhi-to-mumbai, accessed 19 February 2016.

Kummitha, R.K.R. (2019) What do our cities need to become inclusive smart cities? *EPW Engage* 54(13), https://www.epw.in/engage/article/what-do-our-cities-need-become-inclusive-smart-cities, accessed 3 September 2020.

Kundu, D. (2011) 'Elite capture in participatory urban governance', *Economic & Political Weekly* 46(10): 23–25.

Levien, M. (2013) 'Regimes of dispossession: From steel towns to special economic zones', *Development and Change* 44(2): 381–407.

Loh, C.G. and Norton, R.K. (2013) 'Planning consultants and local planning: Roles and values', *Journal of the American Planning Association* 79(2): 138–147.

Loh, C.G. and Norton, R.K. (2015) 'Planning consultants' influence on local comprehensive plans', *Journal of Planning Education and Research* 35(2): 199–208.

Mahadevia, D. (2006) 'NURM and the poor in globalising mega cities', *Economic and Political Weekly* 41(31): 3399–3403.

Milbert, I. (2008) 'Law, urban policies and the role of intermediaries in Delhi', in I.S.A. Baud and J. de Wit (eds). *New Forms of Urban Governance in India: Shifts, Models, Networks & Governance*. First ed. New Delhi, Thousand Oaks, CA, London, Singapore: Sage, pp. 176–212.

Ministry of Finance (2007) *Meeting India's Infrastructure Needs with Public Private Partnerships: The International Experience and Perspective*, New Delhi: Ministry of Finance, Government of India.

Ministry of Housing and Urban Affairs (2016) *Smart Cities Mission*, Government of India, http://smartcities.gov.in/upload/uploadfiles/files/SPV_ContactDetails.pdf, accessed 3 September 2020.

Ministry of Urban Development (2006) *Jawaharlal Nehru National Urban Renewal Mission*, Ministry of Urban Development, http://jnnurm.nic.in/, accessed 22 February 2011.

Ministry of Urban Development, G. o. I., Urban Development Division (2005) *Jawaharlal Nehru National Urban Renewal Mission Guidelines*.

Mitra, S. (2015) 'Anchoring transnational flows: Hypermodern spaces in the global south', in F. Miraftab and N. Kudva (eds). *Cities of the Global South Reader*, London and New York: Routledge, pp. 106–113.

Parnell, S. and Robinson, J. (2012) '(Re)theorizing Cities from the Global South: Looking Beyond Neoliberalism', *Urban Geography* 33(4): 593–617.

Peck, J. (2002) 'Political economies of scale: Fast policy, interscalar relations, and neoliberal workfare', *Economic Geography* 78(3): 331–360.

Peck, J. and Theodore, N. (2010) 'Recombinant workfare, across the Americas: Transnationalizing "fast" social policy', *Geoforum* 41(2): 195–208.

Raco, M. Street, E. and Freire-Trigo, S. (2016) 'The new localism, anti-political development machines, and the role of planning consultants: Lessons from London's South Bank', *Territory, Politics, Governance* 4(2): 216–240.

Reddy, C.R. (2016) 'To locate the scam, use GPS', *Outlook India*, https://www.outlookindia.com/magazine/story/to-locate-the-scam-use-gps/297693, accessed 20 August 2020.

Sadoway, D. Gopakumar, G. Baindur, V. and Badami, M.G. (2018) 'JNNURM as a window on urban governance', *Economic & Political Weekly* 53(2): 71.

Sami, N. (2012) *Building Alliances: Power and Politics in Urban India*. Doctor of Philosophy, University of Michigan, Ann Arbor, MI.

Sami, N. (2013) 'Power to the people? A study of Bangalore's urban task forces', in G. Shatkin (ed). *Contesting the Indian City: Global Visions and the Politics of the Local Wiley Blackwell Series in Urban and Social Change*, West Sussex, UK: Wiley Blackwell, pp. 121–144.

Sami, N. (2017) 'Learning by doing: Urban planning in Bangalore', in S. Vidyarthi, S. Mathur and S. Agrawal (eds). *Understanding India's New Approach to Spatial Planning and Development: A Salient Shift?* Delhi, India: Oxford University Press, pp. 90–113.

Shatkin, G. (2008) 'The city and the bottom line: Urban megaprojects and the privatization of planning in Southeast Asia', *Environment and Planning A* 40(2): 383–401.

Shatkin, G. (2011) 'Planning privatopolis: Representation and contestation in the development of urban integrated mega-projects', in A. Roy and A. Ong (eds). *Worlding Cities: Asian Experiments and the Art of Being Global Studies in Urban and Social Change*, Oxford, UK: John Wiley & Sons, pp. 77–97.

Shatkin, G. (2017) *Cities for Profit: The Real Estate Turn in Asia's Urban Politics*, Ithaca, NY: Cornell University Press.

Sinha, A. and Singh, J. (2011) 'Jamshedpur: Planning an ideal steel city in India', *Journal of Planning History* 10(4): 263–281.

Sood, A. (2015) 'Industrial townships and the policy facilitation of corporate urbanisation in India', *Urban Studies* 52(8): 1359–1378.

Srivas, A. (2018) 'Modi's "Gift City" Project Helped IL&FS Walk Away With Rs 2,000 Crore: Ex-Director', *The Wire*, https://thewire.in/political-economy/gujarats-gift-city-project-helped-ilfs-walk-away-with-over-rs-2000-crore-ex-independent-director, accessed 31 August 2018.

Sundaram, R. (2015) 'Post-postcolonial sensory infrastructure', *e-Flux Journal* 64: 1–10.

Sundaresan, J. (2013) *Urban Planning in Vernacular Governance: Land Use Planning and Violations in Bangalore*. Doctor of Philosophy, London: The London School of Economics.

Vogelpohl, A. and Klemp, F. (2018) 'The creeping influence of consultants on cities: McKinsey's involvement in Berlin's urban economic and social policies', *Geoforum* 91: 39–46.

Watson, V. (2014) 'African urban fantasies: Dreams or nightmares?', *Environment and Urbanization* 26(1): 215–231.

Weinstein, L. (2010) 'The Entreprenurial Bureaucrat: Locating State Power in Mumbai's Dharavi Redevelopment Project', *Workshop on 'Contesting the Indian City: State, Space and Citizenship in the Global Era'*, Kolkata, India.

Weinstein, L. Rumbach, A. and Sinha, S. (2019) 'Resilient growth: Fantasy plans and unplanned developments in India's flood prone coastal cities', *International Journal of Urban and Regional Research* 43(2): 273–291.

Regulating Relationships

Conflicting Interests: Professional Planning Practice in Publicly Traded Firms

Orly Linovski

Introduction

Traditionally, urban planning practice has included two aspects of "public," both of which are increasingly contested: planning as devoted to serving the public interest (Campbell and Marshall, 2002), and planning as an activity largely undertaken by the public sector (Howe, 1980). Yet, in many jurisdictions, private-sector firms are now involved in every aspect of the planning process, including developing long-range plans, transportation and infrastructure planning, public engagement, and development review. The increasing scale and scope of their influence have re-shaped notions of the public interest and the broader purpose of planning (e.g. Wargent et al., 2020; Raco, 2018; Steele, 2009; Slade et al., 2021).

This outsourcing of planning is also situated in the context of significant changes *within* the private sector. Over the past 30 years, there has been substantial consolidation by publicly traded planning and engineering firms (such as AECOM, SNC-Lavlin, and WSP), creating global companies with thousands of employees, operating on every continent,

O. Linovski (✉)
University of Manitoba, Winnipeg, MB, Canada
e-mail: orly.linovski@umanitoba.ca

C. Hurl and A. Vogelpohl (eds.), *Professional Service Firms and Politics in a Global Era*, https://doi.org/10.1007/978-3-030-72128-2_15

and followed closely by financial analysts (Linovski, 2019). Financialization—a process marked by the growing influence of financial actors and financial metrics in corporate governance—also arguably impacts professionals working within firms, shaping their values and practices (Cushen, 2013; Faulconbridge and Muzio, 2009; Alvehus and Spicer, 2012).

There has been little consideration of how such substantial changes may impact professional conduct and ethics for planners. Norms of ethical practice are set by professional bodies through codes of conduct, and can be critical in establishing professional values (Thomas, 2019). As in other fields, conflicts of interest—where the potential for financial or personal gain can influence professional expertise—are a concern, with the expectation that planners would seek to mitigate these types of conflicts. Yet codes of conduct from professional organizations tend to focus on planners as individuals, and often do not account for how the financial interests of an organization, or its senior leadership, may influence—or appear to influence—the decision-making of employees (Lo and Field, 2009). While conflict of interest policies assume that an individual will gain from their actions, for institutional conflicts of interest, the question of who benefits is much more difficult to both determine and mitigate.

This chapter explores conflicts of interest for planners working in publicly traded firms, and how these differ from professional understandings of ethical practice. The increasing concentration and consolidation in these types of firms, combined with the pressures from financialization, make it critical to examine how institutional changes within professional service firms may impact professional practices. I begin by contrasting professional and corporate codes of conduct, and assessing their attention to both individual and institutional conflicts of interest. As I will show, institutional conflicts of interest are largely unaddressed by existing professional codes, and at odds with corporate policies that often stress loyalty to the firm, rather than social responsibility. The chapter then examines the areas of potential risk and conflict that are introduced through management strategies and tactics in publicly traded firms. With corporate strategies that promote cross-selling between service lines (Linovski, 2019), firms may be involved in inter-linked processes: advising agencies or involved in policy development, and bidding on projects that result from that advice. I argue that these are conflicts of interest that exist at the institutional level, as a result of explicit corporate strategies designed to increase shareholder value, and are exacerbated by the significant consolidation in the field, with a reduction in the number of firms that are able to take on large-scale projects. Lastly, I reflect on the implications of these types of conflicts of interest in the broader context of the financialization of professional services firms.

Ethical Conduct for Planners

There has been a long-standing interest in the meaning of ethical practice for planners, both in an academic context (Wachs, 1985; Marcuse, 1976; Johnson, 2014), and through regulation by professional bodies. While public interest is a contested concept (Campbell and Marshall, 2002), it is still seen as integral to the profession (Johnson, 2010), and forms the basis of professional conduct for planners in many jurisdictions. Despite this foundational responsibility, professional ethics are largely rooted in the relationship between professional and client, or employer-employee, which can lead to conflicts with the broader public interest, as financial or other interests may influence decision-making (Marcuse, 1976). Some have criticized the orientation of professional codes, arguing that ethical behavior "may be shown merely by planners acting competently," a much lower standard than protection of the public interest (Marcuse, 1976, 270; Thomas, 2019). For planners and other professionals, codes of conduct are intended to mitigate the influence of external factors, such as potential for financial gain, on the decision-making process. While there has been considerable debate in the field about ethical conduct, there has been less investigation on types of conflict of interest or how they are enacted.

In contrast, other fields have explored the roots of bias and limitations of these understandings for professional practice. Professionals may believe that conflicts of interest arise from intentional corruption, or that their professionalism or scientific training make them immune from these types of bias (Cain and Detsky, 2008). In reality, it is more often a case of *unintentional* bias (Cain and Detsky, 2008) or a strategic ignorance of harm (Dana, 2005). Although professionals may believe that unbiased professional expertise can be maintained irrespective of relationships, there is substantial evidence that bias is both unconscious and unintentional, and is compounded by over-optimism in the ability to be objective (Dana, 2009).

Despite the long-standing interest in ethical conduct for planning professionals, there has been relatively less work on how institutional contexts—such as public or private sector—may shape these professional practices. More recently, work has begun to address potential differences for those working in the private sector, noting the varying constraints, attitudes, and approaches compared with public sector professionals (Read and Leland, 2011; Steele, 2009). For planners in private practice, client demands often present different dilemmas than for those working for public agencies, such as issues of market competition or fair business practices (Loh and Arroyo, 2017).[1] In a broad survey of American planners, it was found that many private-sector planners, unlike those employed by public agencies, do not believe that the professional code of conduct reflects the ethical dilemmas they experience in practice (Lauria and Long, 2019). Issues that go beyond the scope of individual professional practices or overlap with businesses development goals, such as offering pro-bono services to public agencies, have often not been addressed, nor has there been much consideration of differences between types of private-sector employer (Linovski, 2019, 2017).

Institutional-Level Ethics

While conflicts of interest are an established element of professional ethics, the focus has been primarily, if not exclusively, on the actions of the individual (Davis and Craft, 2000), such as whether professionals can accept gifts, have a financial or familial relationship with a client, or speak publicly on professional issues (Davis and Johnston, 2009). However, some professions have addressed conflict of interest at the institutional level, where an "institution's own financial interests or those of its senior officials pose risks of undue influence on decisions" (Lo and Field, 2009, 218). The medical profession has perhaps grappled with this type of conflict to the greatest extent, such as in cases where hospitals have a financial interest in the outcome of clinical trials, though this too has been limited (Lo and Field, 2009).

The difference between individual and institutional conflicts of interest can be seen as related to the motivating goals of actors, either as individuals or institutions. The foundation of professional practice is based on a

[1] These issues are addressed by professional codes of conduct, though arguably they deal with protecting the professions' own interest, as Marcuse (1976, 267) notes—"an ethical obligation to fellow professionals, and to the profession as a corporate body"—rather than a broader public service commitment.

> We have advanced one step – and only one – in approaching the notion of populism. We know, so far, that populism requires the dichotomic division of society into two camps – one presenting itself as a part which claims to be the whole; that this dichotomy involves the antagonistic division of the social field; and that the popular camp presupposes, as a condition of its constitution, the construction of a global identity out of the equivalence of a plurality of social demands.

This notion of social demands draws from Lacan's idea that when someone makes a request for an object, what they are often really demanding is recognition, love, and understanding.[9] This principle of subjectivity and transference is then applied to the political realm through the idea that when people are protesting, they are always making demands addressed to an authority, and these demands can be joined together through the rhetorical process of hegemony.[10] Moreover, the political demand itself is predicated on a separation between the demanding class and the class that has the power to respond to the demand.

Like Lacan, Laclau insists that demands can never be fully met, and this lack of fulfillment drives the desire to make more demands.[11] The next stage in this process is to collect together diverse demands so that they can be organized under the heading of a single populist identity: "What is involved in this identification? I have already described how the transition from individual to popular demands operates – through the construction of equivalential links. Now I have to explain how this plurality of links becomes a singularity through its condensation around a popular identity" (94). Just as a dream image can represent several different associations through the process of condensation, distinct political demands are able to be unified through the use of an empty signifier, and like a dream, there is an underlying impossible desire that the demands seek to satisfy: "But in an equivalential relation, demands share nothing positive, just the fact that they all remain unfulfilled. So there is a specific negativity which is inherent to the equivalential link" (96). Coalitions are therefore built on empty phrases and unfulfilled demands, and it is this negativity that is often missed by political scientists. Also, as I pointed out above, while Baudrillard equates the spread of meaningless signifiers to the liberation of representations from their traditional meanings in a form of viral contingency, Laclau emphasizes how the emptying of signifiers actually makes political formations possible.[12]

To further define this rhetorical construction of political coalitions, Laclau provides the following examples:

> It would be a waste of time trying to give a positive definition of 'order' or 'justice' – that is, to ascribe to them a conceptual content, however minimal it might be. The semantic role of these terms is not to express any positive content but, as we have seen, to function as the names of a fullness which is constitutively absent. It is because there is no human situation in which injustice of some kind or another does not exist that 'justice', as a term, makes sense. Since it names an undifferentiated fullness, it has no conceptual content whatsoever: it is not an abstract term but, in the strictest sense, empty. (97)

The political signifiers of justice and freedom, thus, must be seen as necessary but impossible ideals since they point to demands that can never be fulfilled. It is in fact, their lack of content and fulfillment that enables them to be the drivers and organizers of political ideology.[13] Furthermore, he relates this rhetorical structure to the primary processes in the unconscious: "like the process of condensation in dreams: an image does not express its own particularity, but a plurality of quite dissimilar currents of unconscious thought which find their expression in that single image" (97). In this return to Freud, we see that the manifest dream content represents latent dream thoughts that have been condensed around a single representation.[14] What then prevents us from falling back into a biological model of viral infection is the understanding that our own minds function on an automatic, unintentional figurative level.

We are therefore prone to be influenced by external ideas not because we are infected by some mysterious germ but because our minds do not always function through intentionality. By using psychoanalysis and rhetoric, Laclau is thus better able to escape Neo-Animism and the search for biological determinism. In fact, we can use his model of political signification to understand why so many thinkers today want to base mental and social processes on natural selection.[15] Just as a political group seeks to unify itself by organizing around an empty signifier, the return to natural order provides a way to unify diverse ideas under the banner of a universal, but empty theory. According to the logic of evolutionary theory, anything that is universal, automatic, and unconscious must be derived from natural selection.[16] Moreover, calling something "natural," not only implies that it is produced by nature but also that it is inevitable.

Therefore, if we claim that computer viruses are a natural thing, then we are affirming that there is really nothing we can do about them.[17] The same logic applies to political ideas and conspiracy theories; once we say that the spread of memes is a natural process, we also declare that any resistance is futile.

As a way of de-naturalizing these viral metaphors, Laclau describes how the unconscious structure of language functions to unite diverse people and ideas under a single name through a process of performative designation: "the popular symbol or identity, being a surface of inscription, does not passively express what is inscribed in it, but actually constitutes what it expresses through the very process of its expression. In other words: the popular subject position does not simply express a unity of demands constituted outside and before itself, but is the decisive moment in establishing that unity" (98). Since Laclau does not believe that there is an inherent connection between words, meanings, and referents, he is able to show how certain groups are unified around their shared identification with the same open sign; in fact, the group has no meaning or unity until they all recognize themselves by the same signifier. This process can only work if the signifiers are open enough to designate several attributes.

Just as the Republican party is a name that serves to unite different policies and demands together, any proper name can be read as an arbitrary marker of a particular person: "According to Kripke, words refer to things not through their shared descriptive features, but through a 'primal baptism' which does away with description entirely. Names would, in this sense, be rigid designators" (102). From this perspective, the act of naming something brings it into being, and so the speech act constructs the reality it designates.[18] For instance, if I call a media representation "viral," the act of giving it a label creates the entity I am discussing. However, what Laclau's formalistic approach often leaves out is the actual content of the structures he is describing. In fact, while the term "justice" may appear to be an empty signifier void of any meaning, it still does have a particular set of associations it connotes. It is therefore counterproductive to use the term "empty signifier" since every signifier relates to other signifiers, and these signifiers also produce meanings.

It is important to realize that Baudrillard's work showed the destructive effect of separating signifiers from their signifieds, and so Laclau's focus on empty signifiers could be seen as merely repeating the nihilistic aspects of contemporary society. In fact, I would argue that one reason why he is able to use the same rhetorical model to explain the populism of the Left and the Right is that his overly formalistic approach separates signifiers from their signifieds.[19] What is then missing from many of his formulations is the way that meaning is generated through a process of gathering together related signifying associations.

Stopping the Flow of Signifiers

In pointing to the work of Slavoj Zizek, Laclau adds that there must be some way of stopping the endless association of different signifiers, and this something is the role played by punctuation as a form of present absence:

> According to Žižek, the quilting point (the point de capiton) whose name brings about the unity of a discursive formation – Lacan's objet petit a – has no positive identity of its own: 'we search in vain for it in positive reality because it has no positive consistency – because it is just an objectification of a void, of a discontinuity open in reality by the emergency of the signifier'. It is not through a wealth of signifieds but, on the contrary, through the presence of a pure signifier that this quilting function is fulfilled. 'If we maintain that the point de capiton is a 'nodal point', a kind of knot of meanings, this does not imply that it is simply the 'richest' word, the word in which is condensed all the richness of meaning of the field it 'quilts': the point de capiton is rather the word which, as a word, on the level of the signifier itself, unifies a given field, constitutes its identity: it is, so to speak, the word to which 'things' themselves refer to recognise themselves in their unity'. (103–104)

The idea here is that the empty signifier is able to bring together different demands and representations by unifying them through an act of quilting.[20] However, the problem with Zizek's interpretation of Lacan here is that he does not distinguish between the signifier and the object. After all, Lacan stresses that signifiers always relate to other signifiers, so the notion of the empty signifier is itself problematic.[21] It would be better to say that the name has been turned into an object, and as Lacan posits, an object can be equal to itself (a = a), but a signifier can never signify itself.[22]

Political identity is then derived from the process of turning signifiers into objects, but these objects represent the presence of desire and the failure to fulfill the demands for a just society. Laclau describes this political unification of unfulfilled demands in the following way:

> Moreover, my earlier analysis of popular identities as empty signifiers allows me to show that the exclusive fullness/emptiness alternative is a spurious one: as we have seen, the popular identity expresses/constitutes – through the equivalence of a plurality of unfulfilled demands – the fullness of the community as that which is denied and, as such, remains unachieved – an empty fullness, if you like. If we were not dealing with the signifier of emptiness as a particular location, but with one that is not attached to any signified while nevertheless remaining within signification, that could only mean that it is the name of a fully achieved totality which, as such, would have no structural fails. (109–110)

What Lacan calls the object *a* can be interpreted as the presence of empty fullness in politics and subjectivity, but this object has no real existence since it is just a necessary but impossible ideal.[23] What then drives political desire is the quest for an object that can never be attained, and in this way, the drive for justice will never be complete.

The Contagion of Pleasure

A problem with Laclau's whole presentation is that he does not differentiate between the desire caused by unfulfilled demands and the pleasure generated by drives. On the most basic level, the catharsis generated through the pleasure principle is founded on the release of feelings and the escape from conflict, tension, and responsibility.[24] Although Aristotle does not consider catharsis as one of the main modes of rhetoric, his work on theater reveals that he sees the goal of cultural productions to be the purging of pity and fear.[25] When we compare this use of catharsis with Freud's original cathartic method, we find that humans are often driven to rid themselves of all mental and physical energy, and this law of inertia structures our drives and relation to objects.[26]

What then in part differentiates the unfulfilled demands of the Left from the reactionary populism of the Right is the way the latter relies on a defensive reaction to the former, and this reaction itself brings a high level of pleasure and catharsis. Moreover, when Freud posits that in the state of hypnosis, the ego ideal is replaced by the object, he is indicating that part of the hypnotic cathartic effect is derived from the removal of feelings of guilt and shame. In the context of the uncontrollable spread of conspiracy theories, it is therefore important to see how pleasure and catharsis drive the process: what people on the libertarian Right want is to be liberated from responsibility and their own conscience.[27]

Of course, the Right often borrows the tactics and structure of the Left, but what is usually missed by commentators is the Right-wing addition of pleasure to Leftist organizing processes. Laclau repeats this problem by confusing the use of empty signifiers with the enjoyment gained by reactionary movements. Without a consideration of catharsis, it is easy to focus on the uncontrollable spread of ideas through the power of empty signifiers to unite a group; however, if we want to fully make a break with biology, evolution, and viral rhetoric, it is necessary to see how the pleasure principle represents a break with nature since the humans not only have the ability to turn everything into an object of enjoyment, but they also are able to use enjoyment to escape from reality. If human drives are always partial, it is because they are only partially shaped by natural instincts, and when we repress this partiality, we end up equating nature with human subjectivity.[28]

Laclau's misunderstanding of drives and the pleasure principle is evident in the following passage:

> If this fullness is a mythical one, the actual search for it could lead only to destruction, except for two facts that Copjec stresses: '(1) that there is no single, complete drive, only partial drives and thus no realisable will to destruction; and (2) the second paradox of the drive, which states that the drive inhibits, as part of its activity, the achievement of its aim. So some inherent obstacle – the object of the drive – simultaneously brakes the drive and breaks it up, curbs it, thus preventing it from reaching its aim, and divides it up into partial drives' (p. 34). So the drives content themselves with these partial objects which Lacan calls objet petit a. (112)

The first problem with this theory coming from Joan Copjec is that it does not see that all drives must be partial because they are no longer guided by the goal of biological reproduction.[29] This theoretical misconception is then coupled with a second misunderstanding of psychoanalysis: while Copjec and Laclau want to present the object as an obstacle to the drive, what we learn from Lacan is that the drive always meets its object, and this object allows one to efface the ideals of the ego by replacing the conscience with enjoyment.[30]

In terms of political organization, Laclau simply equates the desire of the Left with the enjoyment of the Right, and therefore he is unable to differentiate between these two fundamental forms of populism. We encounter this problem in the following passage:

> The aspiration to that fullness or wholeness does not, however, simply disappear; it is transferred to partial objects which are the objects of the drives. In political terms, that is exactly what I have called a hegemonic relation: a certain particularity which assumes the role of an impossible universality. Because the partial character of these objects does not result from a particular story but is inherent in the very structure of signification, Lacan's objet petit a is the key element in a social ontology. The whole is always going to be embodied by a part. In terms of our analysis: there is no universality which is not a hegemonic one. (115)

If on the Left, the demand for better wages or criminal justice reform can never be fully attained, it creates a desire to seek more progress; however, what we find on the Right is that the backlash against the Left's demands produces cathartic enjoyment. The populism of the Left is then structured by desire, while the populism of the Right is driven by the enjoyment, and yet Laclau continues to apply desire as the central hegemonic mechanism.

When Laclau does discuss the role played by enjoyment in these structures, he misunderstands the meaning of drives and the pleasure principle:

> The object of the investment can be contingent, but it is most certainly not indifferent – it cannot be changed at will. With this we reach a full explanation of what radical investment means: making an object the embodiment of a mythical fullness. Affect (that is, enjoyment) is the very essence of investment, while its contingent character accounts for the 'radical' component of the formula. (115)

For Laclau, the object of enjoyment is equated with the desire for total fulfillment, but as I have been arguing, enjoyment is centered on escape and the negation of desire caused by unfulfilled demands. Like so many other theorists, Lacalau fails to understand contemporary politics because he simply confuses the desire of the Left with the reactionary enjoyment of the Right:

> No social fullness is achievable except through hegemony; and hegemony is nothing more than the investment, in a partial object, of a fullness which will always evade us because it is purely mythical (in our terms: it is merely the positive reverse of a situation experienced as 'deficient being'). The logic of the objet petit a and the hegemonic logic are not just similar: they are simply identical. (125)

In equating the process of political hegemony with the investment in objects of enjoyment, Laclau is simply replacing psychoanalysis with rhetoric as he blocks us from seeing the true driving force behind the "viral" spread of libertarian ideology.

At one point, Laclau does seem to differentiate desire and enjoyment, but his distinction only replicates his inability to separate the populism of the Left from its counter-part on the Right:

> In psychoanalytic terms: while desire knows no satisfaction, and lives only by reproducing itself through a succession of objects, the drive can find satisfaction, but this is achievable only by 'sublimating' an object, raising it to the dignity of the Thing. Let us translate this into political language: a certain demand, which was perhaps at the beginning only one among many, acquires at some point an unexpected centrality, and becomes the name of something exceeding it, of something which it cannot control by itself but which, however, becomes a 'destiny' from which it cannot escape. When a democratic demand has gone through this process, it becomes a 'popular' one. But this is not achievable in terms of its own initial, material particularity. It has to become a nodal point of sublimation; it has to acquire a 'breast value'. It is only then that the 'name' becomes detached from the 'concept', the signifier from the signified. Without this detachment, there would be no populism. (120)

At first glance, this discussion of sublimating the object appears to be derived from Freud's theory of idealization, but what Laclau misses is the fact that the object of fascination and enjoyment is not representing a central political demand; rather, the object represents the effacement of the subject's morality and reality testing. We are therefore prone to the uncontrollable spread of Right-wing conspiracy theories that take on the appearance of being biological viruses because we trade our psychological and cultural filtering systems for the pure pleasure of escape.

In terms of the fight against racism and the COVID-19 virus, we find the same conflict between the Left's desire to impose a social desire for justice and health that is opposed by the Right's drive to pursue their own pleasure, even if it means destroying themselves. While both groups can be shown to be prone to the submission of a collective idea or leader, in the case of the Left, subjection is tied to impossible demands, while with the Right, it is dedicated to activating the drives in the id by externalizing the super-ego. In this structure, the Left is seen as embodying the censoring super-ego that seeks to castrate the free speech and libertarian enjoyment of the Right.

Notes

1. Laclau, Ernesto. *On populist reason*. Verso, 2005.
2. Laclau, Ernesto. *The rhetorical foundations of society*. Verso Trade, 2014.
3. Samuels, Robert. "Catharsis: The politics of enjoyment." *Zizek and the rhetorical unconscious*. Palgrave Macmillan, Cham, 2020. 7–31.
4. Baudrillard, Jean. "The ecstasy of communication." *New York* (1983).
5. Kaplan, Michael. "The rhetoric of hegemony: Laclau, radical democracy, and the rule of tropes." *Philosophy & Rhetoric* 43.3 (2010): 253–283.
6. Torgovnick, Marianna. *Gone primitive: Savage intellects, modern lives*. University of Chicago Press, 1991.
7. Gras, Vernon W. "Myth and the reconciliation of opposites: Jung and Levi-Strauss." *Journal of the History of Ideas* (1981): 471–488.
8. Samuels, Robert. "The unconscious and the primary processes." *Freud for the twenty-first century*. Palgrave Pivot, Cham, 2019. 27–42.
9. Lacan, Jacques. "The ethics of psychoanalysis: The seminar of Jacques Lacan: Book VII" (2015).
10. Laclau, Ernesto, and Chantal Mouffe. *Hegemony and socialist strategy: Towards a radical democratic politics*. Verso Trade, 2014.
11. Lacan, Jacques. "The subversion of the subject and the dialectic of desire in the Freudian unconscious." *Hegel and Contemporary Continental Philosophy* 19.6 (1960): 205–235.
12. Baudrillard, Jean. "'What are you doing after the orgy'." *Artforum* 22.2 (1983): 42–46.
13. Samuels, Robert. "Logos, global justice, and the reality principle." *Zizek and the rhetorical unconscious*. Palgrave Macmillan, Cham, 2020. 65–86.
14. Freud, Sigmund, and A. J. Cronin. *The interpretation of dreams*. Read Books Ltd., 2013.
15. Samuels, Robert. *Psychoanalyzing the politics of the new brain sciences*. Springer, 2017.
16. Petersen, Michael Bang, et al. "Who deserves help? Evolutionary psychology, social emotions, and public opinion about welfare." *Political Psychology* 33.3 (2012): 395–418.
17. Rose, Steven, Richard Charles Lewontin, and L. Kamin. "Not in our genes: Biology, ideology and human nature." *The Wilson Quarterly* 152 (1984).
18. Stanley, Jason. "Names and rigid designation." *Hale, Wright and Miller (eds.)(2017)* (2017): 920–947.
19. Flisfeder, Matthew. "Reading emancipation backwards: Laclau, Žižek and the critique of ideology in emancipatory politics" (2008).
20. Lacan, Jacques. "The quilting point." *The Psychoses: The Seminar of Jacques Lacan Book*. Vol. 3, 1956.

21. Miller, Jacques-Alain, Paul Verhaeghe, and Ellie Ragland. *Jacques Lacan and the other side of psychoanalysis: Reflections on seminar XVII, sic vi*. Vol. 6. Duke University Press, 2006.
22. Stavrakakis, Yannis. *Jacques Lacan*. No. IKEEBOOKCH-2020-408. Aristotle University of Thessaloniki, 2017.
23. Žižek, Slavoj. "Against the populist temptation." *Critical Inquiry* 32.3 (2006): 551–574.
24. Samuels, Robert. "Catharsis: The politics of enjoyment." *Zizek and the rhetorical unconscious*. Palgrave Macmillan, Cham, 2020. 7–31.
25. Schaper, Eva. "Aristotle's catharsis and aesthetic pleasure." *The Philosophical Quarterly (1950–)* 18.71 (1968): 131–143.
26. Freud, Sigmund. "Project for a scientific psychology (1950 [1895])." *The standard edition of the complete psychological works of Sigmund Freud, Volume I (1886–1899): Pre-psycho-analytic publications and unpublished drafts*, 1966. 281–391.
27. Flanagan, Scott C., and Aie-Rie Lee. "The new politics, culture wars, and the authoritarian-libertarian value change in advanced industrial democracies." *Comparative Political Studies* 36.3 (2003): 235–270.
28. Flanagan, Scott C., and Aie-Rie Lee. "The new politics, culture wars, and the authoritarian-libertarian value change in advanced industrial democracies." *Comparative Political Studies* 36.3 (2003): 235–270.
29. Copjec, Joan. *Read my desire: Lacan against the historicists*. Verso Books, 2015.
30. Lacan, Jacques. "The seminar of Jacques Lacan: Book XX: Encore: 1972–1973" (2011).

CHAPTER 7

Zizek's Pandemic

Abstract At times, Slavoj Zizek's book *Pandemic* helps to clarify these differences by separating the spread of the coronavirus from the viral spread of culture and the endless replications of computer viruses. On a basic level, employing Lacan's fundamental three-part theory, we can say that biological viruses belong to the Real, mental virus belong to the Imaginary, and computer viruses belong to the Symbolic. As we shall see in reading Zizek's text, while it is hard to keep these different viral forms separate, it is necessary to maintain these distinctions. Moreover, as Zizek insists, if we want to have an effective global response to this pandemic and other pressing issues, then we have to affirm a mode of understanding that is universal and scientific, which could be seen as representing the fourth dimension in Lacan's structure.

Keywords Zizek · Pandemics · Lacan · Viral media · COVID-19 · Real

I have argued throughout this book that we have to be careful to distinguish among four levels of human life: the biological, the technological, the cultural, and the psychological. At times, Slavoj Zizek's book *Pandemic* helps to clarify these differences by separating the spread of the coronavirus from the viral spread of culture and the endless replications of computer viruses.[1] On a basic level, employing Lacan's fundamental

R. Samuels, *Viral Rhetoric*,
https://doi.org/10.1007/978-3-030-73895-2_7

three-part theory, we can say that biological viruses belong to the Real, mental virus belong to the Imaginary, and computer viruses belong to the Symbolic.[2] As we shall see in reading Zizek's text, while it is hard to keep these different viral forms separate, it is necessary to maintain these distinctions. Moreover, as Zizek insists, if we want to have an effective global response to this pandemic and other pressing issues, then we have to affirm a mode of understanding that is universal and scientific, which could be seen as representing the fourth dimension in Lacan's structure.[3]

The Meaningless Real of the Coronavirus

Zizek's first important intervention into how we think about the novel coronavirus is to stress that we should not seek to project signification onto this natural entity:

> we should resist the temptation to treat the ongoing epidemic as something that has a deeper meaning: the cruel but just punishment of humanity for the ruthless exploitation of other forms of life on earth. If we search for such a hidden message, we remain premodern: we treat our universe as a partner in communication. Even if our very survival is threatened, there is something reassuring in the fact that we are punished, the universe (or even Somebody-out-there) is engaging with us. We matter in some profound way. The really difficult thing to accept is the fact that the ongoing epidemic is a result of natural contingency at its purest, that it just happened and hides no deeper meaning. In the larger order of things, we are just a species with no special importance. (14)

This call for humility in the face of a natural contingency can be related to Freud's claim that modern science only really begins when we give up our belief in the omnipotence of our thinking and realize that we will never be able to completely control or understand the natural Real.[4] In fact, the desire to see the virus as some type of lesson or communication from nature is based on the way we project our own thoughts onto nature itself.

The difficulty in resisting the temptation to read nature as a book is displayed in Zizek's own work because, at times, he falls back into viral rhetoric and uses the term "virus" to define both natural and cultural processes:

> The ongoing spread of the coronavirus epidemic has also triggered a vast epidemic of ideological viruses which were lying dormant in our societies: fake news, paranoiac conspiracy theories, explosions of racism. The well-grounded medical need for quarantines found an echo in the ideological pressure to establish clear borders and to quarantine enemies who pose a threat to our identity. (39)

As I have argued throughout this book, the danger of calling ideologies viruses is that by projecting a natural entity onto culture, we make ideology appear to be inevitable. Here, we lose our ability to distinguish nature from culture as we repress the separation of language from material reality. There is also the problem of not clearly differentiating between the virus itself and our social precautions against the spread of this natural force.

Zizek's use of viral rhetoric to talk about political influence is perhaps the most extreme in the following passage: "But maybe another and much more beneficent ideological virus will spread and hopefully infect us: the virus of thinking of an alternate society, a society beyond nation-state, a society that actualizes itself in the forms of global solidarity and cooperation" (45). As I have been arguing, the problem with using the metaphor of the virus to explain the spread of ideas is that it confuses different orders of being and can have the unintended effect of removing human will and purpose from our own social constructions.

As Zizek indicates, one reason why people may turn to natural entities in order to promote social change is that they think that only a natural catastrophe can motivate people to do things differently[5]:

> Years ago, Fredric Jameson drew attention to the utopian potential in movies about a cosmic catastrophe such as an asteroid threatening life on earth, or a virus wiping out humanity. Such a universal threat gives birth to global solidarity, our petty differences become insignificant, we all work together to find a solution—and here we are today, in real life. This is not a call to sadistically enjoy widespread suffering insofar as it helps our Cause—on the contrary, the point is to reflect upon the sad fact that we need a catastrophe to be able to rethink the very basic features of the society in which we live. (41)

This desire to encounter a natural catastrophe so that people will unite together and fight for a common cause often provides a false hope for Left-wing thinkers.[6] Although it is true that people do sometimes affirm a greater sense of solidarity when they are facing a shared crisis, the question remains of how long this solidarity lasts if it is based on nothing but a perceived present threat.

It turns out that politicians on the Left and the Right often rely on natural or unnatural disasters in order to motivate people to seek a radical change:

> While US presidential candidate Bernie Sanders is mocked by skeptics for his advocacy of universal healthcare in the US, isn't the lesson of the coronavirus epidemic that even more is needed, that we should start to put together some kind of global healthcare network? (41)

While I would not argue against the need for a global healthcare system, it is still risky to pin our hopes for positive social change on the risks posed by natural forces, like viruses.[7]

It is interesting that Zizek begins his book by declaring that we should not try to project meaning onto the virus, but he cannot help himself as he continues to use the virus as way of promoting political ideas:

> The day after Iran's deputy health minister, Iraj Harirchi, appeared at a press conference in order to downplay the coronavirus spread and to assert that mass quarantines are not necessary, he made a short statement admitting that he has contracted the coronavirus and placed himself in isolation (even during his TV appearance, he had displayed signs of fever and weakness). Harirchi added: 'This virus is democratic, and it doesn't distinguish between poor and rich or between the statesman and an ordinary citizen.' In this, he was deeply right—we are all in the same boat. (42)

By seeing the virus as being democratic, it is clear that political ideology is being projected onto a natural entity, and so we once again encounter the mixing of discourses and the animistic desire to perceive our thoughts circulating in natural processes. As the above passage reveals, one reason why we might desire to turn to the naturalization of culture is that we do not believe that people will accept universal principles on their own.

It is very ironic that Zizek himself points to the danger of using natural catastrophes to motivate social and political transformation: "And we are not only dealing with viral threats—other catastrophes are looming on the horizon or already taking place: droughts, heatwaves, killer storms, the list is long. In all these cases, the answer is not panic but the hard and urgent work to establish some kind of efficient global coordination"

(42). The problem with using catastrophes to initiate social change is that as Freud discovered, panic often makes people regress so that they employ unconscious associative thinking instead of logical analysis.[8] In other words, the hard work to produce global coordination will not come about through unconscious irrational responses.

From the Viral to the Virtual

Zizek not only often confuses biological viruses with the spread of cultural ideas, but he also combines natural viruses with a consideration of computer "infections":

> But even here, at the level of virtual reality and the internet, we should remind ourselves that, in the last decades, the terms "virus" and "viral" were mostly used to designate digital viruses that infected our web-space and of which we were not aware, at least not until their destructive power (say, of destroying our data or our hard drive) was unleashed. What we see now is a massive return to the original literal meaning of the term: viral infections work hand in hand in both dimensions, real and virtual. (44)

What is interesting about this passage is that the projection of nature onto technology is coupled with a projection back onto nature itself. At first, through the use of metaphor, computer viruses are equated with biological viruses, and then we are told that one of the results of this metaphor is that it becomes literalized in the Real.[9] Here we see the reversible aspect of rhetorical figures: just as technology is being substituted for nature, nature itself takes on technological features.[10]

What is surprising is that at times, Zizek shows himself to be prone to animistic thinking, but at other times, he directly critiques this way of thinking:

> Another weird phenomenon that we can observe is the triumphant return of capitalist animism, of treating social phenomena such as markets or financial capital as living entities. If one reads our big media, the impression one gets is that what we should really worry about are not the thousands who have already died and the many more who will, but the fact that "markets are panicking"—coronavirus is ever more disturbing the smooth functioning of the world market. Does all this not clearly signal the urgent need for a reorganization of global economy which will no longer be at the mercy of market mechanisms? (44)

Once again, the virus is used to motivate people to change their political ideology, but we are also told that ideology functions by projecting human intention onto nonhuman systems.[11]

Since Zizek is quick to move between different ideas, he often does not bother with making sure that his arguments are not in contradiction with themselves.[12] Thus, after spending pages trying to interpret the social meaning of the virus, he returns to the idea that this natural thing is without signification:

> What we should accept and reconcile ourselves to, is that there is a sub-layer of life, the undead, stupidly repetitive, pre-sexual life of viruses, which has always been there and which will always be with us as a dark shadow, posing a threat to our very survival, exploding when we least expect it. And at an even more general level, viral epidemics remind us of the ultimate contingency and meaninglessness of our lives: no matter how magnificent the spiritual edifices we, humanity, construct, a stupid natural contingency like a virus or an asteroid can end it all. ... (52)

The paradox here is that the only way we can affirm the meaning of life is if we recognize the meaninglessness of contingent accidents, like viruses and natural disasters. Although the meaning may be that we are prone to meaningless natural events, it should be clear that there is a world of difference between the event itself and our responses to the event. However, if we do not separate the Real from the Symbolic, we will be left in the type of apathetic indifference that Baudrillard highlights.[13]

A Global Subject

The spread of the virus throughout the world forces us to acknowledge that we need a global response to a global problem.[14] We also are pushed to realize that we cannot just think of our own health since we are prone to be infected by others. As Zizek posits, this confrontation with the pandemic may help to create a different political order: "One thing is sure: isolation alone, building new walls and further quarantines, will not do the job. Full unconditional solidarity and a globally coordinated response are needed, a new form of what was once called Communism" (69). It is strange that Zizek returns to communism as the solution to global issues since the history of actual communist countries reveals a deep commitment to nationalist ideologies, which counter the need for international cooperation.[15] Zizek might just be trying to be provocative here, but his insistence on the term communism blocks his ability to provide a more realistic approach.[16]

Since we still think of politics mostly on the level of the nation-state, we need to realize that due to the interconnectedness of our current world, we have to start thinking in terms of global institutions.[17] Unfortunately, people fear a new global order because they have been influenced by conspiracy theories easily spread on the Web.[18] Many of these anti-global discourses are derived from a libertarian rejection of big government, but as Zizek insists, big government is exactly what we need to confront global issues like pandemics and climate change: "The coronavirus epidemic does not signal just the limit of the market globalization, it also signals the even more fatal limit of nationalist populism which insists on full state sovereignty" (68). As we saw in the previous chapter, the promotion of nationalistic populism is itself derived from the combination of identification and idealization, which motivates individuals to replace their own moral conscience and reality testing with an ideal coming from a glorified leader or ideology. As Zizek insists, we need to oppose nationalism with a new spirit of global cooperation: "it's over with "America (or whoever) first!" since America can be saved only through global coordination and collaboration" (68).

Zizek also posits that his call for global solidarity in the face of the pandemic is not based on a form of utopian thinking or idealization: "I am not a utopian here, I don't appeal to an idealized solidarity between people—on the contrary, the present crisis demonstrates clearly how global solidarity and cooperation is in the interest of the survival of all and each of us, how it is the only rational egotist thing to do" (68). Like Freud's theory that our desire for social equality is derived from our envy and jealousy, Zizek seeks to base a new form of global social consciousness on rational self-interest.[19] However, isn't the very definition of social equality based on suspending the self?[20]

While our confrontation with the virus should make us more socially aware and concerned for others, we are seeing on both the political Left and Right, responses blocking universal justice.[21] As Zizek indicates, one reaction on the Left is to see all social responses to the pandemic as an excuse for increased political control over our lives: Agamben's reaction is just the extreme form of a widespread Leftist stance of reading the "exaggerated panic" caused by the virus spread as a mixture of an exercise of social control combined with elements of outright racism, as when

Trump refers to "the Chinese virus" (75). Thus, some people on the Left resist wearing masks or social distancing because they think the government is using the pandemic as an excuse to impose some form of martial law.[22] On the other hand, libertarians tend to reject both global thinking and social precautions because they do not want to give up their cherished individual liberty. Likewise, the Right often responds with racism as a way of blaming all problems on an invading foreign force.[23]

Even after Zizek has himself argued that we need to use the virus as a way to motivate people to accept the communist alternative, he returns to his argument that the real problem is the way different political ideologies project their own agendas onto the virus itself:

> Both Alt-Right and fake Left refuse to accept the full reality of the epidemic, each watering it down in an exercise of social-constructivist reduction, i.e., denouncing it on behalf of its social meaning. Trump and his partisans repeatedly insist that the epidemic is a plot by Democrats and China to make him lose the election, while some on the Left denounce the measures proposed by the state and health apparatuses as tainted by xenophobia and therefore insist on continuing social interaction, symbolized by still shaking hands. Such a stance misses the paradox: not to shake hands and isolate when needed IS today's form of solidarity. (77)

As I have shown throughout this book, this desire to politicize natural entities and to naturalize political ideologies is hard to resist. In fact, we must consider Zizek's own discourse to be ironic and contradictory because he keeps jumping between separating nature and culture and then collapsing their differences.[24]

This self-contradictory perspective is evident in the way he seeks to use the virus in order to illustrate Freud's theory of the death drive: "A virus is alive in its drive to replicate, but it is a kind of zero-level life, a biological caricature not so much of death-drive as of life at its most stupid level of repetition and multiplication" (79). In highlighting the repetitive and meaningless nature of viruses, Zizek seeks to project meaning onto them by relating them to Freud's concept of the death drive: here the drive to escape all tension and conflict is confused with the meaningless nature of biological processes.[25]

One of the problems with Freud's notion of the death drive is that at times he sees it as a purely biological force and other times as purely psychological process. In fact, he will call all drives a borderline concept because they are placed between the mental and the physical, which can help us to understand the essence of the borderline personality disorder.[26] On a fundamental level, the death drive embodies the pleasure principle and the law of mental and physical inertia. Since humans seek to use as little mental and physical energy as possible, they desire to avoid all tension and conflict.[27] The pleasure principle in the form of the death drive is therefore positioned by an anti-natural natural force: on one level, human drives are unnatural because they are not determined by animal instincts, but this break with nature can also be seen as a natural force.

It is therefore misleading to equate a virus with the death drive since in reality, the pleasure principle separates us from evolution and biological determinism, and yet Zizek continues to return to the metaphor of the virus to define human thought itself: "Human spirit is a kind of virus that parasitizes on the human animal, exploits it for its own self-reproduction, and sometimes threatens to destroy it. And, insofar as the medium of spirit is language, we should not forget that, at its most elementary level, language is also something mechanical, a matter of rules we have to learn and follow" (79). Here we see that a key aspect of viral rhetoric is the conflation of language with nature; since language is also an external entity prone to uncontrollable repetition, it is easily equated with the blind repetitive structure of viral infections.[28]

Zizek's misinterpretation of the death drive as a virus leads him to affirm the evolutionary psychology equation of memes with genes: "Richard Dawkins has claimed that memes are "viruses of the mind," parasitic entities which "colonize" human might, using it as a means to multiply themselves" (80). Here both nature and subjectivity are mystified as a new form of animism is promoted:

> "A person is a hominid with an infected brain, host to millions of cultural symbionts, and the chief enablers of these are the symbiont systems known as languages"—is this passage from Dennett not pure Tolstoy? The basic category of Tolstoy's anthropology is infection: a human subject is a passive empty medium infected by affect-laden cultural elements which, like contagious bacilli, spread from one to another individual. And Tolstoy goes here to the end: he does not oppose a true spiritual autonomy to this spreading of affective infections; he does not propose a heroic vision of educating oneself into a mature autonomous ethical subject by way of getting rid of the infectious bacilli. The only struggle is the struggle between good and bad infections: Christianity itself is an infection, although—for Tolstoy—a good one. (80)

I understand this description of mental viruses as a regression away from Freud's effort to base the spread of mental ideas on consciousness, identification, and idealization. In seeing our minds as a struggle between different infections, Zizek once again naturalizes human constructs.

For Zizek, the ultimate message of viruses is that nature is punishing us for how we have treated it: "Maybe this is the most disturbing thing we can learn from the ongoing viral epidemic: when nature is attacking us with viruses, it is in a way returning us our own message. The message is: what you did to me, I am now doing to you" (81). Here nature takes on the role of the pathological super-ego: we are being punished for our past transgressions through the destructive threats of the virus. The foreclosed super-ego thus returns in the Real, as the Real itself becomes the sources of our projections.[29]

As an ultimate irony, Zizek insists that the coronavirus helps us to fight against ideological mystification by forcing us to take an ideological position in relation to nature: "The struggle against coronavirus can only be fought together with the struggle against ideological mystification, and as part of a general ecological struggle" (89). It is hard to see how we can use rational science to combat natural threats if we continue to politicize nature itself. In fact, one reason why people may not respond to the coronavirus in an effective and rational manner is that they see the virus itself as political in nature.[30]

The difficulty of understanding Zizek's potion in relation to viral rhetoric is that he keeps switching between seeing viruses as meaningless natural phenomenon and representing them as evidence of culture and politics. Ironically, at times, he does draw attention to the need to distinguish between nature and culture:

> Some Leftists evoke another parallel: is capital also not a virus acting as a parasite on us humans, is it also not a blind mechanism bent on expanded self-reproduction with total indifference to our suffering? There is, however, a key difference at work here: capital is a virtual entity which doesn't exist in reality independently of us; it exists only insofar as we, humans, participate in the capitalist process. As such, capital is a spectral entity: if we stop acting as if we believe in it (or, say, if a state power nationalizes all productive forces and abolishes money), capital ceases to exist, while a virus is a part of reality that can be dealt with only through science. (100)

At the end of this passage, he makes the important argument that we need to realize that the real virus can only be dealt with through science, but since we see capitalism itself as embodying a blind mechanism, some people on the Left want to see this cultural structure as viral and natural.

This need to firmly differentiate among natural, cultural, and technological viruses is complicated by the way that these different systems interact with each other:

> This does not mean that there is no link between the different levels of viral entities: biological viruses, digital viruses, capital as a viral entity. The coronavirus epidemic itself is clearly not just a biological phenomenon which affects humans: to understand its spread, one has to consider human cultural choices (such as our food habits), economy and global trade, the thick network of international relations, ideological mechanisms of fear and panic. To properly grasp this link, a new approach is needed. The path was shown by Bruno Latour, who was right to emphasize that the coronavirus crisis is a "dress rehearsal" for the forthcoming climate change which is "the next crisis, the one in which the reorientation of living conditions is going to be posed as a challenge to all of us, as will all the details of daily existence that we will have to learn to sort out carefully." (111)

Like climate change, our relation to the coronavirus forces us to change how we interact with other people, but we still need to realize that there is an important distinction between the way our societies help to enable the spread of infections and the infection itself.

In what is often called New Materialism or Object-Oriented Philosophy, there is often a tendency to stress the interactions among culture, nature, and technology to the extent that the difference between these realms is denied. Through the concept of "assemblages," these theorists try to place the human on the same level as other animals and different technological systems:

> The ethical implication of such a stance is that we should recognize our entanglement within larger assemblages: we should become more sensitive to the demands of these publics and the reformulated sense of self-interest calls upon us to respond to their plight. Materiality, usually conceived as inert substance, should be rethought as a plethora of things that form assemblages of human and nonhuman actors (actants)—humans are but one force in a potentially unbounded network of forces. (112)

Once again, the problem with this focus on the interaction between different realms is that it tends to naturalize culture and anthropomorphize nature. Not only does this unconscious process of projection distort our view of the truth, but it also participates in the confusing mixing of discourses.

In a key passage, Zizek seeks to politicize the virus by making it a cause for a better response to climate change; however, this need to tie culture to nature forces him to take the ironic position of both separating nature from culture and collapsing them together:

> To confront the forthcoming ecological crisis, a radical philosophical change is thus needed, much more radical than the usual platitude of emphasizing how we, humans, are part of nature, just one of the natural species on Earth, i.e., of how our productive processes (our metabolism with nature, as Marx put it) is part of the metabolism within nature itself. The challenge is to describe this complex interaction in its detailed texture: coronavirus is not an exception or a disturbing intrusion, it is a particular version of a virus that was operative beneath the threshold of our perception for decades. Viruses and bacteria are ever present, sometimes even with a crucial positive function (our digestion works only through the bacteria in our stomach). It is not enough to introduce here the notion of different ontological strata (as bodies, we are organisms which act as hosts for bacteria and viruses; as producers, we collectively change the nature around us; as political beings, we organize our social life and engage in struggles in it; as spiritual beings, we find fulfilment in science, art and religion; etc.) "Assemblage" means that one has to make a step further here towards a kind of flat ontology and recognize how these different levels can interact at the same level: viruses as actants are mediated by our productive activities, by our cultural tastes, by our social commerce. (115)

On one level, I believe we should follow Zizek in first separating the natural virus from culture, and then tracing how culture interacts with this natural process. The problem is that in his move to the concept of assemblages, he opens the door to effacing the distinction between nature and culture.[31]

On the most basic level, we can affirm that we need to turn to science in order to understand as much as we can about how viruses function. Then in response to scientific findings, we should develop a political reaction to our best understanding of what is happening. This collective response, itself, needs to be protected against the distorting effects of conspiracy theories and ideological manipulations, which is not an easy thing to do.[32] Finally, as individuals, we have to understand the science and the collective response, so that we can make the right decisions in our own lives. All of these stages of this process are undermined when we fail to recognize the distinctions among nature, culture, and technology: "The coronavirus epidemic can be seen as an assemblage of a (potentially) pathogenic viral mechanism, industrialized agriculture, fast global economic development, cultural habits, exploding international communication, and so on. The epidemic is a mixture in which natural, economic and cultural processes are inextricably bound together" (117). Of course it is true that nature, culture, and technology affect each other, but if we do not distinguish these different realms, we will be unable to stop the destructive rhetoric I have been describing.

Notes

1. Zizek, Slavoj. *PANDEMIC!: Covid-19 Shakes the World*. Wiley, 2020.
2. Julien, Philippe. *Jacques Lacan's return to Freud: The real, the symbolic, and the imaginary*. Vol. 2. NYU Press, 1995.
3. Samuels, Robert. "Global solidarity and global government: The universal subject of psychoanalysis and democracy." *Psychoanalyzing the left and right after Donald Trump*. Palgrave Macmillan, Cham, 2016. 77–101.
4. Eyers, Tom. *Lacan and the concept of the 'Real'*. Springer, 2012.
5. Klein, Naomi. *This changes everything: Capitalism vs. the climate*. Simon and Schuster, 2015.
6. Spence, Des. "Bad medicine: Catastrophe thinking." *British Journal of General Practice* 67.658 (2017): 221.
7. Séror, Ann. "The Internet, global healthcare management systems, and sustainable development: Future scenarios." *The Electronic Journal of Information Systems in Developing Countries* 5.1 (2001): 1–18.
8. Freud, Sigmund. "A note on the unconscious in psycho-analysis." *The standard edition of the complete psychological works of Sigmund Freud, Volume XII (1911–1913): The case of Schreber, Papers on technique and other works*, 1958. 255–266.
9. Maggioli, Gabriel H. Díaz. "Of metaphors and literalization: Reconceptualizing scaffolding in Language Teaching." *Encounters in Theory and History of Education* 14 (2013): 133–150.

10. Weingarden, Lauren S. "Naturalized nationalism: A Ruskinian discourse on the search for an American style of architecture." *Winterthur Portfolio* 24.1 (1989): 43–68.
11. Žižek, Slavoj. *The sublime object of ideology*. Verso, 1989.
12. Samuels, Robert. "Žižek's rhetorical matrix: The symptomatic enjoyment of postmodern academic writing." *JAC* (2002): 327–354.
13. Rojek, Chris. "Baudrillard and politics." *Forget Baudrillard* (1993): 107–123.
14. McNabb, Scott JN, et al. "Triumphs, trials, and tribulations of the global response to MERS coronavirus." *The Lancet Respiratory Medicine* 2.6 (2014): 436–437.
15. Smith, Anthony D. *Nationalism in the twentieth century*. Australian National University Press, 1979.
16. Samuels, Robert. "Conclusion: Communism or commonism?" *Zizek and the rhetorical unconscious*. Palgrave Macmillan, Cham, 2020. 87–92.
17. Stiglitz, Joseph, and Robert M. Pike. "Globalization and its discontents." *Canadian Journal of Sociology* 29.2 (2004): 321.
18. Spark, Alasdair. "Conjuring order: The new world order and conspiracy theories of globalization." *The Sociological Review* 48.2_suppl (2000): 46–62.
19. Freud, Sigmund. *Group psychology and the analysis of the ego*. WW Norton & Company, 1975.
20. Samuels, Robert. "Global solidarity and global government: The universal subject of psychoanalysis and democracy." *Psychoanalyzing the left and right after Donald Trump*. Palgrave Macmillan, Cham, 2016. 77–101.
21. Pastor, Lubos, and Pietro Veronesi. *Inequality aversion, populism, and the backlash against globalization*. No. w24900. National Bureau of Economic Research, 2018.
22. Manson, Joseph H. "Right-wing authoritarianism, left-wing authoritarianism, and pandemic-mitigation authoritarianism." *Personality and Individual Differences* 167 (2020): 110251.
23. Wodak, Ruth. *The politics of fear: What right-wing populist discourses mean*. Sage, 2015.
24. Samuels, Robert. "Catharsis: The politics of enjoyment." *Zizek and the rhetorical unconscious*. Palgrave Macmillan, Cham, 2020. 7–31.
25. Samuels, Robert. "The pleasure principle and the death drive." *Freud for the twenty-first century*. Palgrave Pivot, Cham, 2019. 17–25.
26. Freud, Sigmund. "Instincts and their vicissitudes." *The standard edition of the complete psychological works of Sigmund Freud, Volume XIV (1914–1916): On the history of the psycho-analytic movement, Papers on metapsychology and other works*, 1957. 109–140.
27. Freud, Sigmund. "Project for a scientific psychology (1950 [1895])." *The standard edition of the complete psychological works of Sigmund Freud,*

Volume I (1886–1899): Pre-psycho-analytic publications and unpublished drafts, 1966. 281–391.

28. Hook, Derek. "Of symbolic mortification and 'undead life': Slavoj Žižek on the death drive." *Psychoanalysis and History* 18.2 (2016): 221–256.
29. Seckin, Banu Kevser. *"Absence" as desire and "presence" as foreclosure: A psychoanalytic exploration of clinical phenomena, contemporary culture, and science fiction films*. Diss. City University of New York, 2007.
30. Abbas, Ali Haif. "Politicizing the pandemic: A schemata analysis of COVID-19 news in two selected newspapers." *International Journal for the Semiotics of Law-Revue internationale de Sémiotique juridique* (2020): 1–20.
31. Fox, Nick J., and Pam Alldred. "New materialism." *The SAGE encyclopaedia of research methods*. Sage, London, 2018. 1–16.
32. Swami, Viren, and David Barron. "Analytic thinking, rejection of coronavirus (COVID-19) conspiracy theories, and compliance with mandated social-distancing: Direct and indirect relationships in a nationally representative sample of adults in the United Kingdom" (2020).

CHAPTER 8

Conclusion: Science, Politics, Media, and the Virus

Abstract People tend to project their politics onto natural entities, like viruses, and these projections can distort our perceptions of reality and our views of science. For instance, if people think that science has a direct view of nature, they will dismiss scientific findings when there is a dispute among scientists. Instead of seeing science as a process of discovery that makes predictions based on probability and consensus, the ideology of scientism presents a false understanding of how science actually works. Since some people will reject all of science when they see a dispute over a single issue, the totalizing view of this discourse helps to fuel reactionary conspiracy theories.

Keywords Science · Reason · COVID-19 · Scientism · Politics · Viral rhetoric

As we have seen throughout this book, people tend to project their politics onto natural entities, like viruses, and these projections can distort our perceptions of reality and our views of science. For instance, if people think that science has a direct view of nature, they will dismiss scientific findings when there is a dispute among scientists. Instead of seeing science as a process of discovery that makes predictions based on probability and consensus, the ideology of scientism presents a false understanding of how

R. Samuels, *Viral Rhetoric*,
https://doi.org/10.1007/978-3-030-73895-2_8

science actually works.[1] Since some people will reject all of science when they see a dispute over a single issue, the totalizing view of this discourse helps to fuel reactionary conspiracy theories.[2] The first step of breaking this cycle is to recognize that science will never be able to completely know the Real.

By maintaining a more realistic view of how science actually works, we can affirm the separation between nature and culture so that we stop seeing cultural and psychological forces as the direct result of natural laws. A key lesson of viral rhetoric is that due to the power of culture to shape our perceptions, we need to be constantly aware of how language mediates our experiences. For example, with the spread of conspiracy theories concerning the coronavirus on the Web, it is necessary to comprehend why people are prone to re-circulating false and misleading information. On one level, people desire to make the incomprehensible virus understandable by projecting ideologies onto the virus itself.[3] Thus, when Trump called the virus the "Kung FU Virus," it is clear that he was using a wordplay to blame the problem on China.[4] In using this natural phenomenon as a symbol of a cultural conflict, he was able to combine nature and culture for political gain. Likewise, on another level, the Web enables the spread of ideas all over the world, but this does not mean that this structure is the same thing as a viral infection. When we fail to distinguish between nature and culture, we distort our views of reality by treating things as if they were alive and live things as if they are just dead objects to manipulate.

While it is important to understand why and how bad ideas spread, we should not equate this cultural circulation with biological infection. It is therefore necessary to educate people about the differences among the realms of nature, culture, psychology, and technology. If we do not understand these different realms, we will all be prone to the confusing mixing of discourses, which Baudrillard has shown results in a general indifference and apathy.[5]

It is also important to understand how evolution and viruses actually work. Since these processes do not rely on purpose or intentionality, they cannot be compared to human thinking or culture. Unfortunately, many of the new brain sciences provide the illusion that our minds and social institutions are determined by evolution, and this form of scientism not only prevents us from understanding natural processes, like viruses, but it also gives us a false view of culture and science itself.[6] Since our minds and social systems are not determined only by nature, they can be changed, and so the current focus on biological determinism should be seen as a reactionary political ideology. Likewise, when we think that our minds are open systems prone to mental infections, we distort our own self-understanding of the unconscious process of projection, identification, and idealization that are misunderstood as natural forces.

Psychoanalysis also tells us that since pleasure is derived from escaping all tension and conflict, we run the risk of not dealing with real problems such as pandemics and climate change.[7] Moreover, politicians like Trump and many of his followers who seek to deny the need for social distancing and mask wearing reveal the close connection between the pleasure principle and the death drive: people are willing to risk their lives and the lives of others so that they can reject any limitations to their individual freedom.[8] Since these people also equate liberty with the free market and free speech, they are willing to defend their freedom to enjoy at all costs. Moreover, due to the fact that they are not focused on the suffering of others or the long-term effects of their actions, they see the world as a battle between isolated individuals all fighting over the same scarce resources. Unfortunately, Darwin's theory of natural selection has been often employed to shape this libertarian worldview, and so it is important to once again separate culture from nature.[9] Although some of the new brain sciences want us to believe that we are preprogrammed by natural selection to be competitive individualists, psychoanalysis tells us that what makes us human is our break with nature, evolution, and biology. Since we have language and mental autonomy, we are able to design social structures that transcend the worlds of other natural beings.

One piece of evidence of our social transcendence is our ability to use reason and law to make a more just and understandable world. As we have seen in response to the coronavirus, our encounters with natural catastrophes can motivate us to see how we are all connected and reliant on each other since our actions can affect everyone else. However, we have also seen that this type of global consciousness can be blocked by many ideological distortions.

A psychoanalytic mode of rhetorical analysis is so important now because we have to fight against Neo-Animism and other modes of projection. This need to critique scientism is challenged by the fact that so many students have bought into the idea that the only things worth studying are the STEM disciplines and business.[10] As people reject the Humanities, they lose access to rhetorical and psychoanalytic thinking, if it exists at all at the contemporary university. One of the goals of this book has been to argue for the use of rhetoric and psychoanalysis to closely read society and subjectivity.

Notes

1. Kuhn, Thomas S. *The structure of scientific revolutions*. University of Chicago Press, 2012.
2. Grant, John. *Denying science: Conspiracy theories, media distortions, and the war against reality*. Prometheus Books, 2011.
3. Mason, Fran. "A poor person's cognitive mapping." *Conspiracy nation: The politics of paranoia in postwar America* (2002): 40–56.
4. Gao, Grace, and Linna Sai. "Opposing the toxic apartheid: The painted veil of COVID-19 pandemic, race and racism." *Gender, Work & Organization* (2020).
5. Baudrillard, Jean. *The transparency of evil: Essays on extreme phenomena*. Verso, 1993.
6. Samuels, Robert. *Psychoanalyzing the politics of the new brain sciences*. Springer, 2017.
7. Samuels, Robert. "Catharsis: The politics of enjoyment." *Zizek and the rhetorical unconscious*. Palgrave Macmillan, Cham, 2020. 7–31.
8. Tarnopolsky, Christina. "Melancholia and Mania on the Trump Campaign Trail." *Theory & Event* 20.1 (2017): 100–128.
9. Frank, Robert H. *The Darwin economy: Liberty, competition, and the common good*. Princeton University Press, 2012.
10. Samuels, Robert. *Educating inequality: Beyond the political myths of higher education and the job market*. Taylor & Francis, 2017.

Index

R. Samuels, *Viral Rhetoric*,
https://doi.org/10.1007/978-3-030-73895-2

The manufacturer's authorised representative in the EU is Springer Nature Customer Service Centre GmbH, Europaplatz 3, 69115 Heidelberg, Germany. If you have any concerns regarding our products, please contact ProductSafety@springernature.com

Printed and bound by CPI Group (UK) Ltd, Croydon, CR0 4YY
30/09/2026
02225666-0003